THE
FIRST FIFTY YEARS

of the
British Mountaineering Council

FRANK SOLARI I.S.O.
Acting President 1969-1970, Vice-President 1968-1969
Equipment Sub-Committee 1946-1974, Honorary Member 1975-1996

The publication of this history of the BMC was assisted by a donation from the
Alpine Club Library in memory of Frank Solari and in recognition of his numerous
services to mountaineering.

THE
FIRST FIFTY YEARS

of the
British Mountaineering Council

Edited by Geoff Milburn
with Derek Walker and Ken Wilson

Preface by
THE LORD HUNT OF LLANFAIR WATERDINE
K.G. C.B.E. D.S.O.

Foreword by
SIR CHRISTIAN BONINGTON C.B.E.

THE BRITISH MOUNTAINEERING COUNCIL
Manchester

First published in 1997 by the British Mountaineering Council
© The British Mountaineering Council

ISBN 0 903908 07 7
A CIP catalogue record for this book is available
from the British Library.

Produced in Great Britain by The Ernest Press
Typeset by Askvik Språktjenester, Norway

Frontispiece: Charles Evans, photographed by Tom Bourdillon, on the South
Peak of Everest at 1 pm on 26 May, 1953. Three days later Hillary and Tensing
completed the remaining 300ft of ascent to the main summit to bring success to
John Hunt's historic expedition. This success was all the more notable as all the
climbers returned unscathed, a record maintained on Evans's subsequent
Kangchenjunga expedition.

The Everest climb had far-reaching consequences in Britain. Not only did it
serve as a leitmotif for the new Elizabethan age, but it also had a major political
and social impact – at a stroke making a risky activity seem highly respectable
in official eyes (in marked contrast to the official disapproval throughout the
Victorian era following the Matterhorn tragedy of 1865 and other high profile
alpine accidents in 1882). John Hunt was knighted, and for the next decade
filled the role of roving advisor on adventure to the nation – he was the first
Director of The Duke of Edinburgh's Award Scheme and the inspiration behind
the establishment of Plas y Brenin. The Everest ascent also spawned an eager
new generation of climbers and a series of youth adventure programmes. The
success of the Duke of Edinburgh's Award, the Outward Bound and the
blossoming of Local Authority, Youth and Scout training programmes as well
as the impact on Mountaineering Association course patronage and the
proliferation of ordinary climbers can all, arguably, be traced back to the impact
of the Everest climb. There appeared to be a widespread view that mountain
adventure – though hazardous – was, in some indefinable way, a good thing.

Over the following years Everest '53 veterans Hunt, Band, Westmacott and
Evans all served the BMC and they, and other expedition members, took other
mountaineering and mountain training posts. The subsequent highly-publicised
expedition successes on Kangchenjunga (1955), Annapurna (1970) and the
South-West Face of Everest (1975) together with (in the mid-Sixties) a series of
televised climbs built around the master rock-climber Joe Brown, were to have
similar rejuvenating effects on climbing and its positive public image.

Contents

Photographs in the text

Foreword

by THE LORD HUNT OF LLANFAIR WATERDINE

K.G.   C.B.E.   D.S.O.

In the summer of 1942 I organised a so-called 'toughening course', based on Helyg, for members of an armoured brigade in which I was serving at the time. It was, I have to admit, partly a pretext to return to Snowdonia under cover of a title which my superiors would approve of. The result of that experience was so positive that I wrote a memorandum on the value of such a mode and setting for the training of leaders in the armed forces. I sent a copy of that paper to the President of the Alpine Club.

Of course, this kind of training was not unique at that time. Geoffrey Young may have foreseen its significance in the wider context of education. However that might be, he sent my paper on to Dr Kurt Hahn, Headmaster of Gordonstoun who later founded the Outward Bound schools.

I mention this personal episode simply in order to make the point that war-time training, the experience of many thousands of young men while on active service, as well as the examples set by Gordonstoun and Abbotsholme private schools, and the initiative of leading personalities in the public sector of education such as Clegg, Hogan, Newsom and Longland, added impetus to the sense of adventure in our young people at the end of the war. Their influence played a part in the profound social changes which were taking place when peace was restored.

G.W. Young's initiative in calling a meeting of the climbing clubs in February 1944, which Mike Holton has referred to in this book, doubtless derived from Young's awareness, as an educationalist, that outlets for that adventurous spirit would be sought in the mountains of Britain, and farther afield. It would be an urge which, notwithstanding the bureaucratic implications, would call for a body to manage and steer its course; a body which would spread the knowledge and skills of mountain-craft, limit the risks, and keep the environmental impact of this outpouring of humanity into the hills within acceptable bounds. The British Mountaineering Council was born of that necessity.

Alas for those of us, the fortunate few, who had known Snowdonia, the Lake District and the Scottish Highlands before the war, and who had perceived those mountains as our privileged preserve! There was understandable reluctance to accept the dynamic change in circumstance. But there was no turning back. And who, today, would grudge or gainsay the benefits and delights of our mountains for everyone to enjoy?

I applaud the part which the BMC has played in opening up those opportunities for all climbers and hill-lovers; for setting high standards of skill and conduct, and for helping to protect the hills and crags for present and future generations.

JOHN HUNT
Henley on Thames, Oxon

Preface

by SIR CHRISTIAN BONINGTON C.B.E.

I'm quite sure that neither Geoffrey Winthrop Young, nor any climber in 1944, could possibly have foreseen how the activity was going to develop but that small group of climbers, members of the few senior clubs, laid the foundations for the BMC. In doing so they gave birth to an organisation that is truly representative of the body of climbers and which has grown and developed with the sport itself, reacting to changing attitudes and circumstance. Climbing has always encompassed a broad range of interests which at times seem to have been in conflict and yet these differences have usually been reconciled, admittedly on occasion with passionate, and even acrimonious, debate. It is perhaps the nature of climbing and the climber, filled as they are with an intriguing mix of contradictions, which form part of the fascination of our activity, one incidentally that has perhaps spawned the richest and certainly the most extensive literature of any sport, and indeed has made climbing so much more than a sport. It means so many different things to such a diversity of people – a lifestyle, a means of spiritual discovery, a game of risk, exploration of the self or of new places, be they an obscure crag at the back of Borrowdale, a mountain range in Antarctica or a new route up Everest, pure sporting athleticism, or competition, formal or overt.

There are other possible contradictions. Climbing, as John Hunt has described, was seen as a useful educative process, as indeed it was, but this inevitably means that it must also be made as safe as possible, something that is in direct conflict with one of the prime attractions of climbing, the exploration of risk, of pushing the limits to extreme levels.

The British climbing scene has always been strongly influenced by our love of clubs. It started with The Alpine Club, the first of many, and then developed into more regional clubs, particularly as rock-climbing within the confines of this country became a sport in its own right. Many of the main ones, such as the Climbers' Club, Fell and Rock, Rucksack Club, Wayfarers, Scottish Mountaineering Club and Yorkshire Ramblers, came into existence at the end of the last century or the beginning of this one. Then the Second World War triggered the explosion, not just of climbing, but of clubbing as well. Today there are over 300 clubs in the BMC, most of them with around 25 members – the small informal group which meets at the pub, has local evening meets and goes to the mountain areas at weekends.

It is on this club structure that the BMC is based and from which its democratic process works. It is argued that the modern climber is less clubbable. This might well be true, particularly with the development of climbing walls and sport climbing, but the individual membership of the BMC is an important effort to represent the non-club member. We owe a great deal to so many climbers who have given their time and ideas to the BMC over the years but one name I believe must be mentioned – that of Alan Blackshaw – who in the early 1970s masterminded the move of the BMC from London to Manchester and gave it the committee structure which has enabled it to cope with the challenges and changes of the last few years. The BMC had its first professional officer in 1972, with the appointment of Dennis Gray as National Officer. He became General Secretary and helped steer the BMC through the next decade. Derek Walker, who retired in June 1995, was only the second General Secretary, bringing a relaxed diplomacy to the role. The BMC has also been fortunate in its National Officers, combining outstanding climbing ability with immense enthusiasm and character. The names of Mark Hutchinson, Peter Boardman, Alex MacIntyre and Andy Fanshawe will long be remembered. The fact that three died in the mountains is an indication of their high level of commitment and the dangers of the extreme climbing game.

Climbing as an activity today is perhaps in the greatest process of change that it has encountered in the hundred and fifty years of its existence. Development of Sport Climbing with its pre-set bolts challenges more than just the risk-playing game – it calls into question the exploratory side of the activity and affects the way we look at the environment. All too easily it can become a struggle for territory, as sport climbers seek to open up new areas of rock for bolted climbs.

It is an arena where the BMC becomes all the more important as a body, helping to find a consensus between groups with different aspirations, representing this very wide church and at the same time acting as custodian to the rich traditions of climbing without becoming authoritarian or dogmatic. It's a challenge, and yet one that I believe the BMC can meet through the strength of its structures and because it has an effective democratic process.

The BMC no doubt will continue to change and develop as it has done in the last fifty years. It is this flexibility that will help it respond to change in the future at the same time as building upon the firm foundations of the past.

CHRIS BONINGTON
Hesket Newmarket, Cumbria

Introduction

'It [the BMC] exists to further the interests of mountaineering as a whole, and it will succeed in this only in so far as it receives the full support of each and every mountaineer ...

The benefits it has already gained are substantial, but they are not of the tangible kind that are computable in terms of pounds, shillings and pence ...

This year the BMC has been asked to run three meets for the Central Council [C.C.P.R.] and there seems every prospect of their becoming a permanent factor in our mountaineering life. As far as possible we are trying to build up in them a tradition akin to that of a university mountaineering club, in which men trained on their first meet in the elements of mountain-craft become the instructors of the next generation with a leavening of guidance from more senior men. The meets will be held in club huts or youth hostels, and for the sake of informality and to avoid any taint of the conducted tour will be small and limited in numbers. It should be needless to add that there will be no attempt to introduce anything so foolish as a qualification scheme for 'mountain leaders'.'

G. A. Dummett
Pembroke College, Cambridge, 1946

In many respects the mere thought of a national body to represent our sport (another controversial word) is anathema to rock-climbers and mountaineers. Doing our own thing in the mountains is what it is all about. At the simplest level we merely want to pack a rucksack, sling a rope over our shoulder (or hide it in the sack) and head off up the hill with free access to whichever mountain or cliff that takes our fancy. We certainly don't want a guidebook to lay down limits for our adventure. Our friends and companions will show us what to do and we will help each other to get out of trouble if things go wrong in any way. Sadly that might have been largely true a hundred years ago, but things have now changed as thousands of other people now want to share our ideals, while others wish to control us politically.

The large number of climbers dictates that we must conserve our mountain landscape, and continued access must be negotiated by 'someone'. To protect the masses there is now a need for safety measures including a check on technical aspects of equipment (ropes, slings, karabiners, harnesses, footwear etc). Although some would say otherwise, there is also a great demand for organised mountain-training in some form or other – other than by just joining the various clubs. And then of course, being very territorial, we need to protect and have some say in what happens on our own patch.

We may be jealously protective of our own club but we also want to criticise and apportion blame when things go wrong. How often do we hear such jibes as ... "You'd have thought that the BMC would have sorted it out by now" ... or ... "That's just blooming typical of the BMC." But we must at some point accept that we can't detach ourselves from environmental problems for we *are* the BMC whether or not we like it – and as such we have both an individual as well as a corporate responsibility. Some public-spirited (or gullible) individuals have sometimes very reluctantly accepted that responsibility and set their shoulders to the wheel. To the critics on the sidelines one might simply enquire as to what has been their contribution.

Although the BMC has gradually evolved into what appears to be a one-party state, it is nonetheless our representative body in Britain and through an ever-growing professional staff it exists to 'oversee' and administer a wide range of services and issues such as: access, conservation, insurance, training, technical problems, guidebooks, publicity, international exchanges, standards, grants for expeditions, etc. Despite frequent accusations that it is somewhat nebulous in nature, the BMC is constantly involved in finding widely acceptable solutions to very real issues which affect the climbing world in general. Through dedicated amateur representation on the Area Committees and then up to Management and Executive levels, controversial issues are thrashed out by strong debate and with a peripheral wide range of lobbying, bullying tactics, sought opinion, cabals and downright skulduggery worthy of any political arena. Although the BMC as a body is far from being whiter than the driven snow, any incompetence, malpractice or slide towards a corporate malaise has so far been kept to a minimum owing to a hard core of ever-vigilant and often strident individuals.

During the development of the BMC much time and effort has been made towards embracing new initiatives or fighting current battles. There has been relatively little time for evaluating events and recording history, apart from the usual thankless minute-taking, bland annual reports, and John Neill's listing of all known Officers and Officials. Certainly there are very few people about who have a sufficient feel for all areas of BMC activity to be able to write authoritatively.

The First 50 Years of the British Mountaineering Council was first conceived by Derek Walker as the 50th anniversary approached. He became aware that unless the history was recorded as accurately as possible now, perhaps it never would be. Some people expressed an interest when the idea of a publication was first mooted, while others were 'persuaded' to make a contribution. Mike Holton and Dennis Gray wrote major sections before a hiatus which was overcome when Ken Wilson volunteered to step in and research the missing decade. At some stage the idea of a book was taken up by an independent publishing company which came up with the idea of a sumptuous A4 magazine-style format in full colour, to be given free to all and sundry. It was eventually thought best to opt for a publication which could take its place alongside the *Alpine Journal* as part of our historical annals. This is only fitting as the BMC owes its origin to the Alpine Club.

While the script was being written several people urged us to publish the full unexpurgated BMC story (warts and all) – and certainly there have been a few highly controversial issues over the years. But that's typical of politics, religion and sport – and yes there are a few skeletons in the cupboard. Would, or should we publish the facts of 'Brazilgate' or the full political machinations of the Mountain Leadership tussle for control? Certain issues have caused suspicion, accusations, heated exchanges and even resignations. Certainly a stand was made over the issue of payments for work, when there was breach of the hallowed principle of guidebook production – that work is done voluntarily. Another issue was the (mis)use of guidebook funds to help fund the Sheffield Poly Climbing Wall and even to help a worthy charitable trust. One skeleton might be dismissed as inefficient paperwork; another as an enthusiastic search for power; while a third might be put down to an eccentric memory lapse leading to a highly unorthodox one-way use of financial resources. And then there are the laws of libel to consider, especially in our litigiously aware society ... No, let us remember that mountaineering is full of colourful individuals who, despite their many faults, do care passionately about their freedom on the hills. Even the controversial events leading up to the formation of the BMC have so far been enshrouded in a cloud of mystery and intrigue. Certainly, Geoffrey Winthrop Young proposed the setting up of a National Body for Mountaineering as early as 1920, but the Inaugural Meeting of the BMC should be accepted as 2 December 1944. The constitution of the BMC however was not adopted until its first AGM on 15 December 1945. The date of our 50th anniversary thus seems open to debate, although the stated Inaugural date in December 1944 appears to clinch the issue.

Looking ahead to the future it is appropriate to note that we are once more embroiled in various conflicts such as: how are we to check the spread of bolts in Britain?; have the days of voluntarily produced guidebooks gone – and should British guidebooks be left to commercial bodies, or even to be produced centrally by the BMC?; and even, can the BMC continue to exist in its current form or will there be a schism? Are we about to see a national reorganisation to cater for traditional climbers in one camp, while the young sport climbers and competition climbers join forces to reshape the climbing world? Much has taken place in the past fifty years but the history of the BMC has only just begun.

GEOFF MILBURN

A Note on Photography

Of the 300 photos in this book two-thirds are portraits of climbing politicians and other luminaries of the climbing world. All Presidents, Vice-Presidents, Patrons, Honorary Members, Treasurers, General Secretaries and other officers are depicted. The many activists are represented by Area and Sub-Committee Chairmen and Chairwomen – a bit unfair to long-serving Area Secretaries and many other keen supporters, but a limit had to be defined somewhere. Among those whose portraits could not be found are Peter Pirie, a prolific Editor of Mountaineering, and Miss Corby, the BMC's original secretarial assistant (1945–1962). Others submitted their own photos and a large number of pictures were selected from the files of the General Secretaries or well-known photographers – John Cleare, Ian Smith, Terry Tullis, Dennis Gray, Roger Payne, Derek Walker, Tom Weir, John Jackson, David Jones, Bernard Newman, myself, and the late Frank Solari. Smith, Newman and Solari also contributed valuable additional darkroom work. Others who made important contributions were Cordelia Newsome who did much of the early photo research and Geoff Birtles who loaned pictures from the High picture archive. Introductory illustrations (in colour) of the Everest, Kangchenjunga (a rare unpublished picture) and Frêney Pillar successes, were chosen as a reminder of the political as well as sporting importance of those ascents. They also involved climbers who have since given notable service to the climbing world, including George Band, the current President, who has signed, with others, all pledged copies of the book.

With luck, the appearance of this book might trigger a spate of late picture discoveries, both portraits of the missing editors and early secretaries, and other photos of interest of important early BMC events. Anyone who has pictures of interest should send them to me c/o the BMC and at a suitable juncture those selected can be published (in addendum format) in Summit plus a definitive list of picture credits.

KEN WILSON

PRESIDENT		VICE-PRESIDENT	
1945–47	G W Young	1947–53	Dr J M Wordie
1947–50	A S Pigott	1953–55	P A Fletcher
1950–53	Lord Chorley	1955–59	C C Gorrie
1953–56	Sir James Wordie	1959–63	R G Folkard
1956–59	B R Goodfellow	1963–68	I H Ogilvie
1959–62	Dr G G MacPhee	1968–70	F Solari
1962–65	J L Longland	1968–71	W H Murray
1965–68	Sir John Hunt	1970–73	J L Longland
1968–69	B R Goodfellow (second term)	1971–72	M H Westmacott
1969–70	Hiatus due to illness of B R Goodfellow; F Solari (Vice–President) acted as President	1972–73	A Blackshaw
		1973–76	D Whillans
		1973–76	Dr J Wilkinson
1970–73	A J J Moulam	1975–78	J E Byrom
1973–76	A Blackshaw	1976–79	C J S Bonington
1976–79	R G Pettigrew	1976–79	J Cunningham
1979–82	J Walmsley	1978–81	I MacCallum
1982–85	T Price	1979–81	Dr W Butler
1985–88	J Neill	1979–82	P D Boardman
1988–91	C J S Bonington	1982–83	J Walmsley
1991–94	I G McNaught–Davis	1982–85	W Peascod
1994–95	P J Nunn	1982–85	Dr D Roberts
1996-	G C Band	1984–87	G C Band
		1985–86	A Rouse

HONORARY MEMBERS

1971–80	H D Greenwood	1985–88	C J S Bonington (2nd term)
1972–79	A S Pigott	1986–90	P J Nunn
1973–77	Sir J Longland	1987–90	I G McNaught–Davis
1983–93	Sir J Longland	1988–89	D W Walker
1974–	J Llewellyn–Jones	1989–93	J Porter
1975–96	F Solari	1990–93	Angela Soper
1975–	Dr W H Ward	1990–93	S Venables
1976–	J Neill	1993–94	P J Nunn (second term)
1983–96	A B Hargreaves	1993–96	Jancis Allison
1986–	R G Pettigrew	1993–96	M Rosser
1986–	Lord Hunt	1994–	D Scott
		1996–	L N Griffin
		1996–	A D Petkins

HONORARY MEMBERS (cont.)		**PATRONS**	
1986–96	W H Murray	1968–77	Lord Hunt
1987–	V Machin	1984–	Lord Hunt
1991	M Bennett (posthumous)	1979–	A Blackshaw
1991	P Wild (posthumous)	1984–95	Prof. Sir Robert Grieve
1992–	G Steele	1984–87	W V Thomas
1996	H Spilsbury (posthumous)	1988–95	Sir Charles Evans, FRCS
1996–	D Gregory	1991–	Sir Christian Bonington
1996–	G Milburn	1996–	Lord Chorley
1996–	K Wilson		

N.B. In the beginning the Vice-President was chosen from the representatives of Scottish clubs until in 1957 when the ASCC hived off from the BMC. From then until 1970 (when the MCofS was formed) the Vice-President was an SMC member, except in 1968–70 when there were two Vice-Presidents, one from the SMC.

The Early Years (1944–1960)

Introduction

On 2nd October 1946, just after my 19th birthday, I picked up a slim paperback at Euston to read on the train to Warrington where I had to report for military service with the RAF. Just published by Penguin Books, price one shilling (5p) it was called *Climbing in Britain*, the BMC's first beginner's handbook for the post-war generation of young people who aspired to walk and climb our hills. Skilfully drafted in simple English there could not have been a more comprehensive and better written introduction. The editor was J.E.Q. Barford, the Climbers' Club representative on the BMC who had become the Council's first Honorary Secretary in 1944. No mean climber and alpinist, he had a wide knowledge of the sport and of where it was practised in Britain and the Alps. When not climbing or instructing he devoted the rest of his 'spare' time to the structure and development of the sport which was then at a crucial stage in its development. With vision, perception and the practical application of an engineer, he laid the foundations of the Council, built the machinery, got it working and had already achieved results before his untimely death in the Dauphiné in 1947.

In the RAF I began to climb, joined the RAF Mountaineering Association and in due course its Committee, later representing the Association on the BMC. After becoming an elected member of the BMC Committee in 1954, I was invited by the Alpine Club to become the BMC's fourth Honorary Secretary, retiring with some relief at the end of 1959. Thus I came to write up the early years, soon to find that the story began long before 1944.

How did it come about? As John Barford explained: in this country the popularity of rock-climbing and hill-walking had been a comparatively recent phenomenon. Early in the nineteenth century relatively few people, mostly drawn from the professional or prosperous classes, walked for pleasure in the mountainous districts of Britain. However, during the second half of the same century mountain climbing was discovered as a sport, the credit being largely due to British pioneers from the same groups who went to the Alps to climb. They formed The Alpine Club in 1857.

As the result of the progress made in Alpine mountaineering, men began to look for opportunities to practise a part at least of their technique in Britain; and during the 1880s the sport of rock-climbing, as such, in this country, was born. In each decade either side of 1900, climbers, both men and women, found that they could pursue their sport more readily and sociably if they associated, usually in single-sex clubs. Most were regional in character, but the first, the Scottish Mountaineering Club in 1889, was national. These clubs formed nurseries for the development of climbing and mountain craft. Among their members, experience, good traditions and past achievements were passed on by word of mouth as well as in the club journals which had a relatively limited circulation.

In the next period, between the two world wars, there was a marked increase in popular interest in the hills. In a foreword to Alan Blackshaw's *Mountaineering* (published in 1965 by Penguin as the official successor to *Climbing in Britain*), John Hunt wrote that since his introduction to mountaineering in 1924 'a great social revolution has taken place and among its benefits are the far wider opportunities now open to almost everybody to enjoy such adventurous, stimulating and challenging activities as hill-walking and mountain climbing which were obvious, but open to few people in my youth'. This explosion of interest was fostered by such groups as the Youth Hostels Associations, Boy Scouts, and camping movement in the 1930s, but it was due as much to the growing realisation by people from every walk of life, including the unemployed, that open-air activities were enjoyable for their own sake. A few local clubs emerged, most with minimal resources, but the vast majority of those people on the hill, although anxious to climb safely, had little knowledge of the techniques or traditions of the sport, or where to look for information or advice. Even if they had known how to find them, the now long-established senior clubs generally set relatively high entry standards.

However, there were signs of change. In 1935 The Central Council of Physical Recreation was formed to promote the development of all forms of physical recreation among those who had left school. The Council was eventually to arrange residential courses and there was even legislation in the form of the Physical Training and Recreation Act 1937, but the 1939-45 war intervened. One of the few advantages that a war presents is a chance to think about how to order the future in a better way, not only as regards political, economic and social terms, but also recreation and leisure – important for both enjoyment and health. So, in the 1940s, and not waiting for the end of the war, statutory planning or legislation was in hand for free universal education, social welfare, town and country planning, and the introduction of national parks in England and Wales, all of which were to have some relevance to walking and climbing on the British hills.

The Contribution by Geoffrey Winthrop Young

The voluntary sector was similarly engaged to some extent in forward thinking, and against this background it is not surprising to find the foundation of the BMC emerging in 1944, though the precise timing was mainly due to the culmination of a campaign by Geoffrey Winthrop Young to set up such a body. His role and contribution were by far the most important individual factors in this development. Young and Barford foresaw that once the war was over (no-one in Britain doubted the result) the pre-war boom of enthusiasm for the hills would be resumed with added strength, but this time there would be a new generation, new materials and types of equipment with the development of new techniques to match.

Young (1876–1958) was one of the leading rock-climbers, mountaineers and alpinists of his age. He was a distinguished educationalist, writer and communicator, with vision, and thus understood the significance of the mass movement towards the hills. Unlike some of his contemporaries he accepted change and sympathised with the ambitions of the young. He was also the first to see the value of mountain craft as an educational medium, and became the principal driving force in achieving the adoption of this principle. Young first raised the idea of a single organisation to represent all mountaineers in Britain as long ago as 1907. He was more successful in 1919 when an advisory council of British clubs was formed, but no permanent, central body emerged. Perhaps due to the strength and interests at that time of the main and by then well-established 'regional' clubs in England and Wales, the need for a national body had yet to be established. The Scottish Mountaineering Club had been founded 30 years earlier. Various other suggestions were put forward in vain, and not until Young became President of the Alpine Club (1941-43) and thus generated even more respect and influence, did he finally succeed. In his last year of office he organised a conference attended by 23 representatives of all the main British clubs which met at the AC on 5th February 1944. Addressing the meeting, Young made four points. First, individual British clubs had been able to give relatively little advice and help to the armed forces throughout the war. Secondly, a central organisation was needed to act as a clearing house for advice and also to speak in the name of all mountaineers in Britain on matters affecting the appearance and use of mountain country, e.g. for electric power schemes, deforestation and the location of industry. Thirdly, a way was needed to make the collective experience of the clubs as a whole available to the large number of young people then starting to climb. Finally, industrial and educational authorities, as well as the Services, were asking for advice on mountain training which could be better given through a central authority.

Young quoted the success and effectiveness of the First-Aid Committee of the mountaineering clubs set up in 1934 (and to become the Mountain Rescue Committee in 1946) as an example of practical co-operation which had been a complete success, even during the difficult years of wartime. Those present affirmed the value of such collective action and agreed on a body to be called The Standing Advisory Committee on Mountaineering (SACOM) of representatives of the clubs present to pursue these matters during 1944 and make proposals for the setting up of a national body to be called the British Mountaineering Council. Meanwhile at the Alpine Club itself there had been a few mutterings. Some disliked change and did not relate to the explosion of interest before the war, let alone the expected repetition once it was over. However, the great majority of members, many influenced by the strength of Young's valedictory address as he demitted the office of President in December 1943, accepted that the AC, while performing a modest role to date in representing British mountaineering interests as a whole, was not really an appropriate body for this purpose. Furthermore, other clubs of many types and ages often had a much closer interest and detailed knowledge of the issues in Britain and would, therefore, wish to share in and contribute to the work involved.

The Inauguration of the BMC

The groundwork by SACOM continued throughout 1944 and the way seemed clear for the inaugural meeting, in the form of the BMC Committee, to be held in London on Saturday 2nd December 1944, when the foundation would be confirmed and established. Those present on that day endorsed the plans drawn up by SACOM, immediately adding 12 further clubs to 13 represented on SACOM as founder members. Three sub-committees were established and arrangements put in hand for the BMC to assume certain national functions currently undertaken by individual clubs. The BMC was afloat. Shortly thereafter other sub-committees were set up, including one to complete the preparation of a draft constitution, which had been circulated. Unfortunately on the same day the SMC was holding its AGM and dinner in Edinburgh and was unable to field a representative in London. On the following day the SMC Honorary Secretary wrote to say that his club had voted unanimously not to approve the draft constitution 'in its current form' though the idea behind the formation of the BMC had 'within limits' the SMC's full sympathy. It was not explained that the main recorded objection was the possibility that matters of prime interest to Scottish mountaineers might be decided by a predominantly non-Scottish body.

Yet another and apparently totally unconnected problem was to emerge. On 21st January 1945 a letter was sent to the President of the AC (then L. S. Amery) by 11 members of the club, eight of whom had previously held high office in the SMC. The tenor was that the scheme to form the BMC had been launched in the name of the AC, though it had not been endorsed by the club's committee or submitted formally to a general meeting for approval. Furthermore, when such a scheme was discussed grave objections were 'certain to be brought forward' and all those concerned with the formation should be advised without delay! The thrust of the President's reply was that the setting up of SACOM and its work constituted 'active consideration' on behalf of the AC, giving the opportunity for some of the signatories to have ventilated their disagreement. However, to be safe, the AC Committee put a motion to a general meeting on 10th April 1945 endorsing the action taken to set up the BMC. Two of those 11 members tabled an amendment regretting that the President and Committee had not sought prior endorsement and disapproving of the BMC's formation as then envisaged. The amendment was lost, 14 votes to 82, and the motion carried with a substantial majority. Furthermore, the meeting presented an opportunity for a number of distinguished mountaineers such as Jack Longland to speak up strongly in favour of the foundation of the BMC.

The Constitution Finally Agreed

Whatever the reasons for the inability of SACOM to reach an agreed draft before the inaugural meeting, one fact was clear. Without the formal support of the SMC the new Council would have had to change its title to the National Mountaineering Council, or the Mountaineering Council of England and Wales. Hardly a new issue for constitutional lawyers, the matter was satisfactorily cleared up during 1945 when amendments were agreed which gave the SMC founder status and the right to nominate a representative on the Committee. There was to be a Scottish Committee of the BMC consisting of representatives from the Scottish clubs belonging to the BMC. The BMC Committee would not reach any decision concerning Scotland until the matter had been considered and reported on by the Scottish Committee, and was enabled to delegate its powers on any matter to the latter, which should also nominate the BMC's Vice-President. The Scottish Committee was also empowered to co-opt representatives of other Scottish clubs which were not members of the BMC, though these were excluded from voting on the nomination of the Vice-President. The final draft of the constitution was agreed at the Council's first AGM on 15th December 1945. The SMC had secured a deal, but this was not to be the end of the Scottish story.

Three main aspects of the first constitution are of interest:

The Object – The Council was instituted to facilitate consultation between mountaineering clubs domiciled in Great Britain or the British Empire, and to take appropriate action on all matters on which the collective experience of British clubs may prove of service to the mountaineering community. The geographical area of interest was probably meant to be the United Kingdom of Great Britain and Northern Ireland, but this was a common error in terminology at that time. In any case the Irish Mountaineering Club (Belfast section) was elected in due course. Inclusion of 'The British Empire' was a throw-back believed to allow for entry of the Himalayan Club, founded in 1928, before the independence of India in 1947, but in general terms was soon to become extinct except in the honours field. In any case international relations were eventually developed by the BMC in a European context, largely through membership of the Union International des Associations d'Alpinisme. There was no reference to Alpine Clubs long established in other parts of what was to become the Commonwealth.

Membership – The Council was to consist of representatives nominated by each constituent club consisting of the following 25 clubs and those subsequently elected by the Committee.

List of Founder Clubs: Alpine Club*, Alpine Ski Club*, Association of British Members of the Swiss Alpine Club, Birmingham University Mountaineering Club, Cambridge University Mountaineering Club, Climbers' Club*, Derbyshire Pennine Club, Fell & Rock-climbing Club of the English Lake District*, Grampian Club, Gritstone Club, Imperial College Mountaineering Club, Junior Mountaineering Club of Scotland, Ladies Alpine Club*, Ladies Scottish Climbing Club, Liverpool University Mountaineering Club, Midland Association of Mountaineers*, Mountaineering Section of the Camping Club, Oxford University Mountaineering Club, Pinnacle Club*, Rucksack Club*, Scottish Mountaineering Club*, Sheffield University Mountaineering Club, Wayfarers' Club*, Yorkshire Ramblers' Club*, (* entitled to nominate a member of the Committee).

To be eligible for election a club's main object had to be mountaineering, owned and controlled by its members and not restricted to those belonging to a particular religion, race or political party. This rule was later waived in favour of the Achille Ratti CC. In the early days there was a small minority view that the Council might be swamped by a mushroom growth of new, small clubs and to placate this minority the rules originally provided for club membership to be at least 50 persons and the club's age to be at least 21 years! Fortunately visionaries such as A. B. Hargreaves carried the day and provision was built in for the

Committee to waive these requirements by a unanimous vote. It was not long before they were removed altogether.

Officers and Committee – In addition to the Vice-President, already mentioned, the officers were the President and Honorary Secretary appointed by the AC, and an Honorary Treasurer and assistant Honorary Secretary appointed by the Council. The Committee was to elect constituent clubs, make representations and take appropriate action on behalf of the Council, to appoint sub-committees and consider and take action on all their reports. It consisted of ten members nominated by the founder clubs plus four members (later to be increased to six) elected at Council by clubs not represented among the nominated members, together with the four senior officers. Thus the Committee was responsible for the management of the affairs of the BMC and accountable to the latter at the Annual General Meeting. The President and Vice-President were appointed for a term of not more than three years. The first to hold these offices were Geoffrey Winthrop Young (AC) and James Wordie (SMC), the Honorary Secretary was John Barford (CC), Honorary Treasurer H L Roberts (WC) and Assistant Honorary Secretary Ted Pyatt (JMCS).

The Nature of the Job

To better appreciate the functions of the BMC over its first 15 years or so it helps to have some idea of the nature of the beast and the job it did. First, the volume of voluntary effort devoted in this country to the administration and development of any sport is not often appreciated. Secondly, one of the main characteristics of climbers generally is their intense individualism reflected in the innumerable clubs of different kinds throughout the realm. Thirdly, it is not possible in the nature of things to calculate how many people hill-walk or climb. The only certain factor is that in total it is far greater than the number of people who belong to clubs affiliated to a national organisation.

Although it was planned as a membership organisation (a federation of clubs) the BMC is perhaps better seen as an 'umbrella' body representing the collective interests of its members and, indirectly through its work, benefiting all those who venture out on the hills and moors. It was not a governing body, had no authority over its members, and there was no rule book of the game. It had to rely on tact, diplomacy, education, a lot of hard work and perhaps a dash of leadership to carry through its programme.

As to the nature of the Council's work in the early years, clearly it was wasteful to duplicate activity best left to individual clubs or more appropriate to another national body, though there was often scope for co-operation or mutual support. The most suitable tasks related to central issues common to all, such as: the production of handbooks, research on equipment, mountain safety, management of a mountain guides' system, environmental issues, external relations and international affairs. Near the top of the Honorary Secretary's list was the encouragement of potential new member clubs. Resources were tight. There were no government grants or paid staff. Clubs parted with their annual subscription with reluctance. Most of the work was carried out through the Committee and by correspondence. This made a heavy load for the Honorary Secretary who, as one retiring President remarked, "was in fact the BMC". Generating about 50 missives a month my only clerical support was a small secretarial agency in Chelsea, run by a Miss Corby, a real treasure.

In time, however, an effective and productive structure of sub-committees was developed along with a small group of assistant secretaries with specific responsibilities. Many individual committee members were a great source of strength. Although each represented a member club, and often belonged to several, they would take on work in a field familiar to them – and go far beyond the line of duty. They also gave the Honorary Secretary a degree of support at a level I have never experienced in any other body. Such were Anthony Rawlinson (CC), Frank Solari (RC), George Starkey (ABMSAC), George Watkins (Mtg Section CC), Nea Morin (PC), Tom Clutterbuck (MAM) and a whole raft of SMC representatives. Except for a couple of Council AGMs, all meetings were held at the AC in London. The Council and Committee representatives came from far and near. No-one charged expenses. There was an austerity about the early years which discouraged socialising.

How did people get directly involved with the BMC itself, given a serious risk that their climbing activities might become curtailed? While representing RAF MA at the Council AGM in 1953, I sat next to John Hammond (CC) who had come to report for the Harrison's Rocks sub-committee. It was a sunny Saturday afternoon and we both agreed we would leave as soon as we could and made a note not to get involved any further in BMC affairs. Within two years John was lost on Mount Cook and I had become Honorary Secretary. People became involved through a mixture of chance and persuasion. Several declined when approached, or shortly found some excuse to leave. Others equally active on the hill found themselves drawn in and most, but not all, were sufficiently altruistic to stay on for some time, coming to realise the relevance of their role for the common good, though with typical British reticence this was rarely alluded to before they finally moved on. Any umbrella organisation is at one stage removed from individual members of clubs and it was, therefore, harder to build up and retain individual loyalties to the central body by name. On the other hand most committee members became dedicated and, in those days, cynics were few.

As for the programme of work itself, in the first issue of the journal *Mountaineering* (June 1947) the first President interpreted the Council's formal object as being 'to collect, harmonise and unite the opinion of climbers and climbing clubs in the country, in all matters affecting our common mountain welfare; and to express them, where need be, with the greater carrying power of a single voice'. He went on to summarise his own view of matters of concern in order:

a) protection for our climbing areas; climbers to be consulted in the 'new planning';
b) provision of accommodation, huts, hostels etc. in the areas, raising funds for this policy;
c) collection of information 'here and abroad' and to investigate scientifically the value of new equipment, ropes, appliances etc., and to locate where different types of equipment could be procured;
d) provision of instructors by clubs to assist with training in other national bodies, and to put individuals and associations seeking help in touch with their nearest local club. *Climbing in Britain* had already been published; regional professional guides were to be regulated;
e) to assist the Mountain Rescue Committee in its long established and vital work;
f) to establish a system of regional committees;
g) to collate and circulate relevant information in the journal.

It will be interesting to see how Young's personal listing was adhered to in the passages that follow. Early meetings of the BMC Committee identified short-term targets such as the acquisition of Helsby Hill, the introduction of an insurance scheme for climbers, an index of current journals, literature and information, and a memorial in some form to those who had died in the 1939–45 war. As time went by the need for such shopping lists evaporated, but the time to bring individual projects to fruition proved to be far longer than at first imagined.

Popularisation of the Sport

It is hard for many people today to imagine how mountaineers felt about any intrusion in their pastime ever since the early development of the 'sport'. Even the latter term was looked on with disdain and was rarely used before the war. Mountaineering was something to do rather than talk about. It was a way of life. In his book *The Undiscovered Country* (The Ernest Press, 1993) Phil Bartlett wrote 'Attempts to delve into mountaineering may be regarded as an affront. When Tilman said that all self-respecting mountaineers should shudder whenever they see anything about it in the newspaper, he was expressing a widespread sentiment'. High-altitude expeditions were traditionally reported in The Times. This ethic was carried forward in a diluted form into the proceedings of the BMC. At a committee meeting in March 1945, when discussing the role of the CCPR, the principle was 're-affirmed' that publicity should not be given to mountaineering and that there should be no 'popularisation' of it. This was confirmed at the next meeting in June, arising from a discussion of a request from the Boy Scouts Association. The Committee was worried in 1947 about the emergence of a training organisation called The Mountaineering Association which had popularisation of the sport as one of its aims, and later in the year rejected a request from the Health and Holiday Exhibition to be associated with the staging of a public demonstration of rock-climbing at Earls Court.

Whatever the BMC then willed, the tide of popularisation was strengthening, so much so that by 1957, writing in the ACJ's centenary edition, A.K. Rawlinson saw it as a positive development. Public interest in 'The Everest story' had assisted fund raising and support for exploration. Many factors continued to promote popularisation. Underlying this was a growing reaction from the factory and office, from the urban life of our age. Wages were higher and holidays longer, but most of all people, especially the young, were taking up climbing because their friends did. The public appetite was whetted by the rapidly increasing supply of books and magazines on the subject, the development of training schools and organised courses for beginners made it easier for the timid or uninitiated, and belief had grown in the virtues of mountaineering as a medium of education, physical and moral. Popularisation meant change which in turn meant more organisation, seen in the multiplicity of clubs and the need for co-ordinating bodies such as the BMC to promote common interests. From then on there was no further adverse comment in the BMC Committee minutes about popularisation of the sport, but popularisation stopped far short of the idea of a single national club to which all would belong. It is not surprising that centralism never got a look-in, and still today most would agree that we do things differently in this country.

Publications
Climbing in Britain — In the early days the only method of communication between the BMC and all member clubs and individuals was by the written word, and the first decision, once the Council was set up, was to

form a publications sub-committee with Young in the chair. In particular this would progress the production of an 'elementary book' on hill-walking and mountaineering. John Barford had already started work. The Council empowered him to co-opt any helpers he needed to compile 'a booklet giving the technical information essential to any beginner in the British hills if he (sic) is to learn to hill walk or to rock-climb safely and efficiently'. He saw an urgent need for this now that the war was over and people found a natural outlet for their energy in the hills. Modest about his own contribution, Barford, in fact, wrote much of the text himself with advice from his many friends. Material was also contributed by A.B. Hargreaves (FRCC), J.H.B. Bell (SMC), A.S. Pigott (RC), Wilson Hey (First-Aid Committee) and G.H. Watkins (Mountaineering Section of the Camping Club). 'Lastly, but most important', wrote Barford in his acknowledgements, 'Geoffrey Winthrop Young has played a great part in moulding an engineer's amateurish first attempt of editing in something approaching a book.'

Within 21 months *Climbing in Britain* was out; a remarkable achievement for those days when delays in the production of almost anything were endemic. With only 160 pages, 18 photographs and many line drawings and lists, it gave the beginner virtually all he needed to know in writing. It sold like hot cakes (125,000 copies) and is remembered by many of the post-war generation as the trigger of a future life of enjoyment on the hills. No such book had previously obtained such a wide circulation.

Mountaineering – The next most important, but more controversial step, was to agree on a house journal, for all clubs and the public, which first appeared in June 1947. In the interim period the Honorary Secretary had issued circulars to clubs about matters of common interest. *Mountaineering* was to have taken over this function, but publication was not frequent enough and the circulars continued. Tony Smyth (foundation Editor and then about to become the first Chairman of RAFMA) described it as a problem child since the aim was to inform rather than amuse, or even interest, but not to run at a loss. Least of all should it be set up in competition with club journals, or diminish their circulation. However, the journal would need a leavening of articles, by prominent mountaineers, relevant to the Council's work. Teething troubles arose from the continual changing of addresses, very common in those post-war years, and problems in the printing industry generally attributed to the shortage of fuel and materials. In 1950 one club formally proposed that publication cease until these problems were remedied, but there was no seconder.

The first issue of *Mountaineering* included the piece by Young on what the BMC was about, and the text of BMC Specification No.1 Natural Fibre Ropes for use in Mountaineering. There was a wealth of other interesting information. Mountaineers intending to visit Switzerland and relying on hostels and huts learned that the maximum amount of Swiss francs allowed was £12 a week per head. Nearer home the reader learned that skis, and snow-shoes provided the only method of travel in many parts of Southern England in the severe snow conditions which lasted for two months in early 1947. The publication of Ted Pyatt's *Sandstone Climbs in S E England* now made it possible to locate Harrison's Rocks since the locals, when asked, were totally ignorant.

The journal [Bulletin] was issued quarterly in 1948 but by 1951 had settled down to a regular twice a year at 2/– (10p) a time. *Mountaineering* ran to over 50 issues until its demise after 1971 on the appointment of a National Officer. It steadily built up in volume, scope and recognition under the guidance of a string of worthy, hard-working and unpaid editors, each with a team of supporters. Occasional swipes at it were made by the odd disenchanted club for being irrelevant and a waste of money. However, the journal presented a continuous, interesting and comprehensive view of the work of the BMC from 1947–71 to all clubs and the outside world and, not least, a record of the hundreds of individuals involved in this. In the last editorial an un-named editor concluded: 'As I see it the BMC is at a most important turning point. Some may regret this; the small group at a club meet on deserted crags; the occasional walker whom one met with glee to pass the time of day. Yet in ten years the change has come. No longer the place for an amateur organisation, mountaineering in Britain needs professional help on equipment testing, a professional secretariat, professional officers ... and a professional journal'.

Other Publications

Early attempts to compile quarterly summaries of newly-published climbing literature, including indexes to current journals and climbing books, proved too big a task and there was no demand for them. However, it was agreed immediately that the preparation and production of guidebooks should be left to the clubs without any involvement on the part of the BMC except to draw attention to the publication of new or reprinted guidebooks. Attempts were made in 1954 to interest Penguin Books in a new work to replace *Climbing in Britain*. Some interest was shown provided that the scope was extended to the Alps. The BMC identified a willing editor, but the publishers subsequently withdrew and indicated that they had reached the end of the line. Instead the Honorary Secretary looked around for an interim replacement. It so happened that Godfrey Francis (AC, CC, ACG) had written a manuscript commissioned by EUP for the Teach Yourself Series, and it was agreed that this should be published under BMC sponsorship, supported by the Scottish Clubs and the Mountain Rescue Committee. The book, called *Teach Yourself Mountain Climbing* was published in 1958 with 192 pages and the minimum of illustrations. This time the text was divided between British and Alpine climbing. This modest handbook proved to be a useful stopgap. Unfortunately 'Goff' Francis died in a mountaineering accident shortly after.

Another Penguin Volume

It was over 20 years before the appearance of what John Hunt described as a worthy successor to *Climbing in Britain*. In 1965 Penguin Books eventually relented, no doubt in view of the further public interest in the subject, by publishing *Mountaineering* by Alan Blackshaw (AC, CC, ACG and later to become President and Patron of the BMC), but it was vastly different from its predecessor. Completely new with the text drafted by Blackshaw himself, it was a prodigious piece of work, embracing almost every aspect of mountaineering. The length (542 pages) and price (18/6) gave a measure of what had happened in climbing in the intervening years. The book was published with the approval of the BMC and ASCC and included the MRC's standard contribution. It underwent a third revision in 1970, and was further revised in 1975.

Club Huts

High up on his list of tasks for the new BMC, Geoffrey Winthrop Young had put the provision of accommodation, huts and hostels in climbing areas and the raising of funds for provision in areas not already served by clubs, or where the latter could not afford them. As he was not a centralist, a species hard to find amongst British mountaineers, he would have excluded any idea that the BMC should take over the clubs' own function to plan, build and manage huts in their own areas. Had he realised the practical and legal problems for an umbrella body to mount a public appeal for such a broad purpose to benefit third parties he might have been surprised, particularly as the senior clubs had individually managed to establish several of their own huts before the war. However it took 20 years to bring to fruition the memorial hut project as the story below illustrates. Subsequently the BMC did not repeat the exercise though in time member clubs themselves have individually adapted or built dozens of properties for their own members and guests. This pattern might puzzle a visitor from abroad, but it is the British way and our decentralised approach has many advantages. Furthermore, the establishment of a category of membership for the BMC and ASCC provided a useful network for arranging reciprocity and use by clubs without huts against a reasonable guarantee and some sanction for users' reliability and good behaviour.

There were other small ways in which the BMC was of assistance to member clubs. Several younger clubs experienced unsympathetic landlords regarding such problems as access or status. In other cases support was occasionally needed to allow a derelict building to be renovated or with a planning application that had been rejected. Those cases on record were settled satisfactorily. As time went by the number of cases declined as new local clubs or regional committees established themselves and local networks, though in some cases a solution was secured through the good offices of a local mountaineering personality with whom the BMC got in touch.

A War Memorial
In 1946 as an aftermath of the war years, a scheme was developed to provide a permanent memorial for British mountaineers who had died in the war. This was well received, but what form it would take, where it would be sited and would the money needed be forthcoming, were questions that remained unanswered for some time. Such a project on a national scale had not been attempted before, although many clubs had, or were doing, their own thing. For an umbrella organisation such as the BMC to tackle such a project raised all kinds of questions. Not least it was discovered that while many might privately have sympathy, it was much harder to command personal loyalties for a centrally run project, as subsequent events were to show. However, other ideas began to trickle in, the first being to purchase an unspecified tract of land or even a mountain which could be kept much as Great Gable is in the Lake District in the care of the National Trust. Later, Cader Idris featured in the story but was dropped apparently due to doubt over future military training needs.

In 1952 a sub-committee was formed under the chairmanship of Harry Spilsbury (FRCC, WC, RC) and an appeal for money launched without a specific project in sight, although it might have provided a fund from which individual club projects could be assisted. Progress was slow, only £1,000 was raised, and no grants were made. The reason for this in part was that the terms of the appeal handed out by the experts were so restrictive and so difficult for individual clubs to accept that they were put off. A change in the conditions was virtually impossible since they could only be made with the agreement of those who had contributed!

A glimmer of hope illuminated the possibility of a single hut as a project, but the problem of looking for a suitable site with access of the kind needed by members of some 90 different clubs posed trying problems of leasing or purchase, security and management. However, in 1956 the SMC, which had put in much hard work in trying to find a suitable project, came forward with an attractive scheme which might

meet all the criteria. This was for a hut in Glen Brittle, by the Black
Cuillin hills of Skye. This soon got the backing of the Committee,
provided that the necessary finance could be secured and a suitable
structure agreed upon. Member clubs were sounded out but the great
majority did not reply. Others countered with alternative suggestions,
each of which had little merit. However, in the meantime, Dame Flora
MacLeod had generously agreed in principle to feu a one-acre plot on
the public road 200 yards north of Glen Brittle House. It was no easy
matter to secure permission to build in Glen Brittle and, apart from the
Youth Hostel, no other dwelling had been added in the Glen in recent
decades. The SMC had done very well indeed, but it was to be another
ten years before the project was completed. Despite the apathy amongst
member clubs there was a very strong feeling in the BMC and ASCC
Committees that this was exactly the right course to pursue.

One of the essential stages was to secure the co-operation of Dame
Flora's tenants, Hugh and Margaret MacRae at Glen Brittle House, which
had become over the years the only watering hole in the glen for those
who enjoyed a little more comfort after a day on the Cuillin. The MacRaes
were concerned, as a result of a 'high pressure' visit to Dame Flora's
lawyer earlier by a BMC representative from the south, as to the
ultimate use of the hut by all and sundry, as there had been a great
increase in the number of undesirable characters visiting the Glen,
some of the worst offenders being mountaineers! The relationship
between landlord and tenant in Scotland, both in law and personally is
rather different to elsewhere in the UK and the MacRae's agreement
to the lease was essential: in the Western Highlands, trust is all-
important in these matters, and the only party outside the Estate that
they trusted was the SMC. However, the problem was resolved locally,
assurances being given by the SMC, and the project was declared a joint
BMC-ASCC affair.

A major appeal and campaign were planned and launched at the end
of 1959, with many innovations, including a poster illustrated by a
drawing of the future hut against a backdrop of the Cuillin by W. Heaton
Cooper (FRCC), the Lake District artist. The sub-committee was
reformed. Harry Spilsbury, who had as much experience of hut
development in England as anyone else, continued as Chairman with
Fred Pigott as Treasurer and Ross Higgins (SMC), who had now become
Chairman of the ASCC, and George Roger convenor of the SMC Hut
Committee; Anthony Medlicott (AC and FRIBA) offered his services as
architect free. Plans were agreed as was a decision to build to a high
standard, in stages, and with borrowing (if needed) until the full sum of
£8,000 was raised. Frequently the BMC found unsolicited support from

The Guardian newspaper which still maintains a healthy interest in the British Hills. At the time Alastair Hetherington was the Editor and on the day the Appeal was issued he ran a leading article: 'What better memorial could mountaineers who fell in the war wish for than a climbing hut from which others might follow in their footholds? And where better than in Glen Brittle, the climber's main base for the Cuillin hills of Skye? Skye is remote and until 1896 the Cuillin could claim the last unclimbed peak in the British Isles, but their great ridge and inexhaustible buttresses should be part of every climber's education now. The projected memorial hut should help to make them so.'

And thus it came to pass. The Glen Brittle Memorial Hut was formally opened on Saturday 5th June 1965 by Dame Flora, on a day which turned to sunshine as the time for the ceremony approached. There was a gathering of almost two-hundred representatives of clubs, other climbers and relatives of those in commemoration of whom the hut was built. Also present were Hugh and Margaret MacRae, representatives of the National Trust for Scotland, the SYHA, the RAF Kinloss Mountain Rescue Team, Chief Constable of Inverness-shire and, appropriately, that great Everester, T. Howard Somervell (1890–1975).

Speeches, short and to the point, were made by Harry Spilsbury who, in introducing Dame Flora, referred to the trials and tribulations that had been endured. She responded in an admirable speech on the beauties of Skye and the Cuillin and on the benefits the Hut would confer on the whole climbing fraternity. Since mountaineers drew such inspiration from their enterprises, this was surely the place to be and the place in which to remember. Ross Higgins, in proposing a toast to the Hut and all who would use it, asked those present to couple it in their minds with the names of all those who had worked so strenuously for so many years to achieve it. These were too numerous to detail individually, but an exception had to be made in six cases; Fred Pigott and George Roger, the two appeal treasurers; Mike Holton and Hilary Sinclair, the two BMC secretaries during the gestation period and, above all, Ruth and Harry Spilsbury without whose indefatigable efforts and selfless dedication, as well as a vast amount of sheer hard practical work, the Hut would never have been built. Unfortunately Spilsbury and Medlicott had few years to see their child grow up as both died in mountaineering accidents in 1970.

Morphia for Mountain Accidents

In the run-up to the foundation of the BMC, support was vowed for the work of those mountaineering clubs which, since the 1930s, had been providing first-aid kits and stretchers at rescue posts in the hills. This was operated by the clubs' First-Aid Committee which became the

Mountain Rescue Committee in 1946. Many were involved in this voluntary effort, but central to it until his death in 1956 was Wilson H. Hey, a Manchester surgeon and member of several clubs.

Before the war the arrangements for rescue and recovery were fairly primitive, although there was rarely a shortage of helpers. For some casualties the process did much more damage than the accident itself, and an essential element for the kits included ampoules of morphia for the relief of pain. Then, as now, except where there was a formal dispensation, each administration of such drugs had to be authorised and carried out by a qualified and registered person. In 1934 the Home office refused Wilson Hey permission to supply the 27 posts with morphia, but he continued to do so on his own authority and at his own expense until 1949 when he learned that it was being supplied for use by unqualified rescue workers both in mines and at airports. Attempts to interest the Home Office in regulating the position for mountain rescue failed, so he formally notified them what he had been doing since 1934. Prosecution followed with gratifying speed. Hey was fined £10 with 10 guineas costs and had thus created the opportunity to draw public attention to the anomaly.

The Home Office eventually relented and agreed to receive a delegation from the MRC and BMC representing all clubs and users. A scheme was worked out. The BMC was to be responsible for its administration – which authority was promptly delegated to the MRC. For his public-spirited action, successfully concluded, Wilson Hey received the grateful thanks of British mountaineers.

Early Equipment

The availability of equipment after the end of the war was dire. There had been no imports or home manufacture for public use. Everything was in short supply and there had been a lot of making do. Almost to make matters worse the Government off-loaded enormous stocks of cheap surplus mountaineering equipment which were little short of useless, if not dangerous. There were boots which heeled over to one side after a week or so of wear, paper-thin cotton anoraks, ice-axes with sharp steel-edged heads that wore through gloves in a few hours or so, and karabiners that opened under low stress. It was, perhaps, fortunate that our trained mountain troops finally went into action in Holland.

Hemp and manilla ropes were available, but knowledge of their safety properties was minimal. About the only good item to come out of the war effort was the commando moulded rubber sole which was soon manufactured in Britain commercially and later to be replaced on the Continent by the Vibram sole. But there was strong consumer resistance, particularly in the North. Even in the late 1950s the advice was 'boots for winter use in Scotland are only safe in all conditions if the soles are edged with tricouni. It cannot be too emphatically stated that Vibram soles are quite unsuitable for Scottish mountaineering at all times in winter and spring and in certain conditions in summer as well'.

Some climbers were also conservative about the use of ropes of artificially made fibres. This was overcome after nylon ropes were demanded for the RAF Mountain Rescue Service in 1951, and people had learned how to handle them. A distinct advantage was their trading value abroad. At least one JMCS member found he could largely finance a season in the Alps by selling a full-length 3/4 weight nylon from British Ropes Ltd.

The Equipment Committee Begins Work

Entering the field early in 1945 to tackle the potential dangers of using surplus wartime equipment was the BMC's Rope & Equipment Sub-Committee, recognising immediately the need to inspect and test what was available, and to draft the first specifications for natural and artificially made fibre ropes for climbing. An enormous amount of voluntary work had to be undertaken quickly to bring about some kind of order before too many climbers were maimed or died in accidents.

For a long period three names predominated in this work: R.P. Mears, W.H. Ward and Frank Solari. The latter, in the Ministry of Supply, was well placed to secure official assistance in testing equipment and co-operation in the production of standards. BMC Specification No.1 for natural fibre rope for use in mountaineering was published in 1947. Publication of the specification for artificially made fibres followed later, to avoid freezing the characteristics of these new materials before they were fully understood. This enabled the BMC to check the ropes on public sale and examples broken in accidents, publishing the results with suitable advice to makers, retailers and clubs. The inadequacies of the wartime equipment were generally self-evident except for the karabiners which had an alarming tendency in use to bend open under serious tension. After systematic testing, a campaign was mounted to warn the

Right: Two years after the Everest triumph (*see frontispiece*), Charles Evans led another expedition to a successful first ascent of Kangchenjunga (28,208ft/8598m) — the world's third highest peak. The summit was gained on 25 May, 1955 by Joe Brown and George Band (the current BMC President). Brown climbed a Severe crack (*inset*) on the final rock buttress to gain the area just below the summit snow cone (*main picture*) — Yalung Kang in the middle distance, with the Makalu/Everest group on the horizon. On the following day the climb was repeated by Tony Streather and Norman Hardie.

Left: Don Whillans and Chris Bonington on the bivouac ledge below the Chandelle (above) of Mont Blanc's Central Pillar of Frêney in August 27, 1961. On the following day they completed their celebrated first ascent (accompanied by Ian Clough and Jan Djuglosz). This was perhaps the most important alpine first ascent made by British climbers in the post-war years, bringing to a climax the efforts to emulate the top alpine standards that had been initiated by the likes of Bourdillon, MacInnes, Brown, Blackshaw, Nicol, McNaught-Davis etc. through the ACG. Both Bonington and Whillans went on to fill key positions in the BMC. British Alpine and Expedition skills have lent our representatives a degree of status and influence on the UIAA and the International Guides.

trade and the public. Other matters were given attention, such as proper use of rope and slings. In over 60% of rope breakages death occurred; 75% in the case of slings. Research also disclosed the weaknesses of the nails then available and of their fitting. Advice was given on the safe use of ropes, slings, karabiners and rubber-moulded soles. These and similar activities in the first ten years of the BMC's life must count as one of the most important contributions to safety and climbing practice in Britain.

Better Maps for Mountaineers
As Geoffrey Winthrop Young expected, in the early days authorities began to seek advice from the BMC. The Ordnance Survey was a case in point. As aerial survey displaced the theodolite, with the use of stereo pairs of photographs and the introduction of photogrammetry, map makers found they could produce a graphic and detailed view of the landscape and abandon symbolic and often misleading representation of physical features used by generations of cartographers. Their problem was what to leave out. Inclusion of all was easy but would present a morass of confusing detail. Following a day at Chessington and a presentation by the BMC, in 1958 proposals were agreed and included in an experimental edition of the Foinaven area in Sutherland, which is reflected to this day in Landranger sheet 9. This brought the reality of buttresses, crags and ridges to all users of the 1: 50,000 and 1: 25,000 series. From then on conventional signs were dead and a sheer face or nasty drop looked like one, but in exchange the old familiar trig points have become examples of industrial archaeology to be cherished as evidence of the good old days.

The Cold War Cancelled in 1956
One of the many spin-offs from Everest 1953 was the beginning of a thaw in the 'cold war' between the communist states and the west, so far as mountaineering was concerned. John Hunt's subsequent visit to Moscow had opened a chink in the Iron Curtain through which was established a link with those who shared a common interest and enthusiasm for mountains. In June 1956 a small Soviet delegation accepted an invitation to visit London, hosted by the AC and BMC. The party included M. Bileski, the leader of the projected joint Soviet-Chinese Expedition to Muztagh Ata, and Yevgeni (Eugene) Gippenreiter of the All-Union Alpine section of the Ministry of Physical Culture and Sport who had translated *The Ascent of Everest* into Russian.

It was intriguing to learn from the visitors how the sport had developed in the USSR over the years without any contact with the West. Local groups throughout the Union were each part of the sports sections attached to factories, offices, universities etc. Climbing practice was controlled by directives and safety regulations, and local committees vetted plans for ascents and climbs, recorded results and awarded titles for achievements. Mechanical aids were widely used as were ropes of artificially-made fibres. No secret weapons emerged, though the visitors' knowledge of individual British mountaineers and their activities and achievements was amazingly extensive and accurate. Before leaving, the party conferred the Award of Mountain Climber of the USSR upon the President of the BMC and other notables.

A larger party visited in 1960 and climbed in North Wales, the Lakes, Glencoe and Skye, the group being joined at different stages by members of the main British clubs. Their hosts found the visitors charming, unreservedly keen to take part in whatever was going on and, perhaps unexpectedly, having similar attitudes to the sport as our own, particularly laced with a strong sense of fun!

Scottish Affairs

The founding fathers of the BMC saw Great Britain as the area of its operation: England, Wales and Scotland. It was assumed that Scottish clubs would aspire to membership and most of them did. Why then should they have left so quickly?

Events did not augur well. The first draft constitution, amongst other things, made no provision for Scottish affairs to be managed north of the border. This had to be corrected in due course with the device of a sub-committee on which all Scottish clubs were to be represented, whether or not they were BMC members, while the BMC Committee would delegate to it any of its powers. Progress was masked by a side issue to duplicate the Scottish Committee in the South-East of England, but while all this was going on over some four years, an informal and independent committee was formed in Scotland by the clubs themselves to discuss matters of common interest.

This committee informally inherited the role of the BMC's Scottish Committee, and by a process of symbiosis continued as an independent body to be known as the Association of Scottish Climbing Clubs. This situation was reached in a mist of some confusion, and soon Scottish clubs began to receive requests for annual subscriptions from both the BMC and ASCC, one of which was cheaper than the other! Before long Scottish clubs began to leave the BMC which hoped that other counsels would prevail and bring them back to the fold. By 1951 only the SMC remained in membership and thus it was until Ross Higgins, then Hon Secretary of the SMC, and myself first met in 1956. A simple solution was engineered; the ASCC would handle all Scottish affairs while those of a 'GB' nature were operated jointly through liaison between officers, together with cross-representation on committees and joint publication of reports to all clubs. An early and happy milestone along the subsequent joint path was the Glen Brittle Memorial Hut, and these amicable arrangements endure into the present age.

Mike Holton

An Afterword

Such is life that the intervention of a cardiologist precluded my writing much more about the early years. Co-operation with others in defence of mountain areas was an increasing task, largely in the National Parks. Elsewhere the development and forging of workable access agreements in the 1950s took time. The greatest success appropriately was in The Peak with its forward-looking national park authority. A scheme jointly with the ASCC was worked out with the Nature Conservancy for access to Rhum. After years of negotiation Harrison's Rocks were bought for £68. A national system was engineered by Robert Folkard in conjunction with local representatives for the registration and regulation of a BMC guides service. Coping with growth was a major task, from answering enquiries about "how to ... " to fostering the formation of new small clubs and bringing them into the BMC. By 1958 there were 69 member clubs with a new one monthly. 18 clubs belonged to the ASCC including the SMC which was a member of both. 30 other clubs in GB were listed. The most important function in the first 15 years was the pooling of knowledge, experience and services particularly of the older clubs for the benefit of all. This went a long way to offset their physical inability to take in more than a tiny proportion of the post-war mountaineering generation, and to encourage local enterprise. Amateurs we were in the BMC then, but on a subscription income of £150 a year, we were at least cost effective!

The Sixties

Between 1960 and 1970 rock-climbing and mountaineering in Britain witnessed rapid change and expansion. The British Mountaineering Council, established in the Forties to administer a modest sport of like-minded clubs, found itself assailed by a growing catalogue of responsibilities and by the end of the decade its traditional approach to the sport's administration was no longer keeping pace with the requirements of climbers.

My own connections with the BMC began in 1969. Throughout the Sixties I had been one of the active climbers-on-the-crags. It was, therefore, fascinating to look back through the records and see what the BMC had been doing on our behalf during that period. It was also delightful to talk to some of those who shouldered the burdens of the sport's administration at this time. [2]

Attendance at Management Committees

I was first struck by the consistency of service from the same group of people. Then, as now, the climbing world relied on the dedication of groups of enthusiasts. We are lucky indeed to have this great tradition of voluntary service to the sport and most climbers are totally unaware of the selfless work done on their behalf. The attendance records of some of the more prolific BMC activists of the period gives a profile of this work. This covers management meetings only, additional area meetings and sub-committee meetings would have greatly added to their workload, all of which was unpaid and done in spare time.

Edwin Hammond, who was involved in BMC affairs throughout the period, recalled the relaxed and very courteous atmosphere of committee meetings with everyone seated around the large conference table at the Alpine Club. In the first half of the decade affairs were much dominated by the traditional clubs, all of which had reserved places on the committee. Other clubs – the new upstarts – were voted in to the few remaining slots. Hammond remembers that the main figures at the time were Anthony Rawlinson (Climbers' Club and Alpine Club) – a top civil servant in the Treasury who exerted a restrained but imperious hauteur; Nea Morin (Pinnacle Club), fizzy and charismatic, much involved with Harrison's Rocks and always keen to defend the women's corner; Frank Solari (Rucksack Club) – steadily competent and tenacious on equipment matters; and Hilary Sinclair, modest and back-room boyish, but a skilful

23

[2] I am indebted to Frank Solari, Edwin Hammond, Bill Murray, Alan Blackshaw and Lord Hunt for patiently trawling their memories of the period to assist me in producing this vignette.

Secretary who made telling and well-timed contributions, and of whom Alan Blackshaw opined: "He was a high-calibre policy-maker who ensured that the BMC correctly identified the key issues of the day and kept it on the right lines".

The Great Presidents

The Presidents of the period were deliberately selected (at that time the Alpine Club chose both the President and the Secretary) as men of standing most likely to impress both the climbing world and the various departments of Government with which the BMC had to deal. Dr Graham MacPhee – diminutive and gentlemanly, exuding the aura of the traditional climbing of the Thirties; Jack (later Sir Jack) Longland, bustling and at times suspiciously efficient; Sir John (later Lord) Hunt, no less efficient than Jack but rather more restrained – skilful at disguising his aims behind a veil of disarming urbanity. Their contributions at that time, in terms of the sheer status they lent to the institution, was of incalculable (but very tangible) value when the BMC was striving to assert itself as the premier body representing the sport.

The Presidencies of Longland and Hunt also coincided with a period of national political upheaval and reform, with the change of Government in 1964 and a further General Election (that increased the new Labour Government's majority) in 1966. As both were sympathetic to the new order they rode the mood and as a result the BMC changed considerably and took on a myriad new responsibilities.

The consequences of the growing workload became apparent by the end of the decade when, buckling under the burden of their greatly increased responsibilities, the energies of the ageing cadre of honorary officials who really ran the BMC began to decline. There followed a hiatus in leadership and a pressing need for a professional secretariat backed by an energetic new breed of competent activists.

Which Direction

Though the Sixties saw the institution establish itself as influential it was still, in truth, enfeebled by lack of money and, in many areas, lacked a clear direction. The final years of the decade saw demands for the BMC to transform itself into a European-style national club with a mass membership but neither the traditional clubs nor, in all probability, the rank-and-file climber, really wanted it to grow in that way. In their heads they knew it was probably inevitable, but their hearts yearned to maintain the status quo of the intimate climbing world of yesteryear. This attitude was nowhere better expressed than in Lord Hunt's (he was ennobled during his period of office) valedictory address in 1968 when he hailed the immense amount of work achieved by volunteers: " ... with a minimum of what might be termed superstructure. Climbers had a healthy aversion to climbing politics and a dislike of being organised. So the Council had avoided the massive hierarchies which control some other sports".

What Hunt failed to take into account was that his own prestige (he was approaching the zenith of his career) attracted many to serve and added an excitement to the dry political grind of the BMC programme – in less heady times the burden must have seemed far greater. The fatigue of the BMC was palpable in 1969 when I attended my first AGM and (along with Dave Partridge who was later to become the BMC's last Hon. Secretary, among others) tossed a few political hand-grenades into the proceedings. A Hunt or Longland administration would have shrugged off the attacks as 'little local difficulties', but in the post-Hunt period they gave a serious jolt to the system and were harbingers of major upheavals that were to follow.

The London Base
The BMC was essentially a London institution – a location dictated to allow it to take advantage of the Alpine Club offices and secretariat. There were experiments in holding meetings elsewhere but these came to nothing. The London base was considered best as there were usually representatives of the major clubs (particularly the Scots) living there and it was thus the easiest place to assemble a cross-section of the climbing world in the absence of funding for travel. It was a shoestring operation – club fees being measured in pence rather than pounds. The decision to accept Government financial support in 1965 (a hotly debated issue at the time) allowed a part-time Secretary to be employed and it also triggered a more realistic attitude to fund-raising. In 1968 the BMC moved to Sports Council offices near Regent's Park and later to Knightsbridge. By the early Seventies its finances had grown to the point where it had two professional officers and consequently the move to Manchester became a viable option.

The Growth and Involvement of Clubs
The BMC was based on its club membership and it was not until 1968 that associate membership was introduced enabling individual (non-affiliated) climbers to join and make a contribution. The Management Committee was large in order to embrace as many clubs as possible. There was also six individual members elected at the AGM (one year when nine stood for election the losing three were all co-opted).

Area Committees were also represented but at that stage these were focused on the three main climbing areas – Wales, the Lake District and the Peak District with the Association of Scottish Climbing Clubs and the SMC covering Scotland. There was also a Harrison's Rocks Committee and specialist committees on Equipment, Safety, Huts and other areas.

By the middle of the decade it was clear that this system was no longer viable because of the growth in club membership. This had practically doubled from 70 club members in 1960 to 135 clubs by 1966. It was seen that a broadened structure of Area Committees was the best way to involve the new clubs in the Council's affairs. A new constitution was enacted in 1968 in the final year of the Hunt Presidency. This stripped direct power from all the inaugural clubs except the Alpine Club, and placed it in the hands of a broadened structure of the area committees, each of which was represented on the management Committee. This had an immediate consequence, though it was not obvious at the time. At a stroke the clubs, particularly the older ones, became less involved in the Council's affairs. A new breed of area representative emerged (often members of the smaller clubs). The transition was, in a curious way, a reflection of national politics where the patrician Tories had just ceded power to the egalitarian Socialists. The traditional clubs maintained a tenuous link by their members getting elected to the six places for individuals on the Management Committee, but their direct responsibility was removed.

The expanded Area Committee system had incorporated a North-East Area in 1966, and a London and South-East Area as well as a South-West and Southern Area in 1968 (Yorkshire and Humberside 1974, the Committee for Wales 1976, Lancashire and Cheshire 1977, and the Midlands Area 1994, were later additions). One immediate benefit was that the areas were able to deal with a plethora of strictly local issues, usually concerning access and conservation matters, thus reducing some of the workload of the Management Committee.

It was hoped that the clubs would focus their energies through the Areas, but the results were patchy. The traditional clubs still maintained some effort in the 'mountain' Areas but it was some time before they showed any interest in regional Areas, where the business is often dry and repetitive.

Club interest in the BMC steadily declined and still remains difficult to rouse, except in times of crisis. Even in the CC (my club) there is, to this day, a constant battle to keep members aware, informed and interested in the BMC's work and this despite the fact that numerous club members have been involved in its committees over the years. Yet the club involvement continues to be important. These are institutions of long-standing that provided, and continue to provide, the firm structure of which the BMC is built. A representative cross-section of the climbing world joins them (sooner or later) and it would be a grave error to underestimate their long-term importance in ensuring the stability of the BMC and protecting it from modish and ill-considered reform.

The AGM, Events, Organisation

During the Sixties the Annual General Meeting was invariably a short affair, two hours on a Saturday afternoon in April. Many clubs were represented but the meetings appear to have been tepid formalities without the present-day compensation of an attendant Meet and Dinner. At that time too, there were no conferences or seminars designed for ordinary climbers. By the end of the decade there was a yearly Mountain Safety Conference which brought together guides, centre wardens, school teachers, youth leaders, Sports Council and CCPR officials in earnest jamborees of safety-mongering. Climbers attended almost by default — a telling indicator of how the impoverished and enfeebled BMC had begun to allow the instructional and safety lobby to push it to one side. Indeed by the end of the Sixties, morale and interest were so low that Frank Solari (acting President, Basil Goodfellow's second stint having been cut short by illness) had great difficulty in finding a new President. As this coincided with a bout of resignations through fatigue, or for other personal reasons, the Council found itself at a low ebb with the stalwarts Frank Solari and Hilary Sinclair desperately casting about for new recruits to fill the key positions.

The Climbing World in the Sixties

During the Fifties the successful Everest and Kangchenjunga expeditions and the media interest in Joe Brown inspired many young people, so that by the early Sixties there was a clear increase in the number of climbers. Yet most were operating at no higher than the V.Diff/easy Severe level, such was the danger of the sport at that time. Those who advanced through the Severes to the VS grade were still in a minority. The top climbers were obsessed with repeating routes such as Cenotaph Corner and Kipling Groove and hoping to move on to tackle the great Brown and Whillans climbs of the Fifties.

Running belays took the form of draped slings or threaded natural chockstones, and nylon ropes (that had first appeared in 1948) were beginning to be widely used. There is a revealing entry in a BMC minute in 1962 where the guides, seeking a tougher qualification standard from the BMC, stipulated full competence in climbing in nailed boots, indeed I sometimes witnessed the BMC guide, Ron James, honing his nailed-boot technique on grades up to HVS at that time. For ordinary mortals, footgear for the crags was something more suitable – the elite wore the rare pairs of PAs (it was considered poor form to be seen in them on climbs less than HVS standard), while others climbed in boots or wore pumps or kletterschuhe. Pitons and karabiners were of poor quality. There were no nuts, harnesses or belaying devices.

There was widespread ignorance about ropes – as nylon steadily replaced hemp   and it was not uncommon to see people leading on 300ft (doubled) of 7mm or even 5mm rope. There were frequent fatal accidents where young climbers misjudged their abilities and slipped while making poorly protected leads – never an Easter or Whit went by without an accident on Lliwedd's Red Wall or the East Face of Tryfan, and then, as now, accidents on snow and ice were numerous.

The yearly pilgrimage to the Alps or the Dolomites was considered essential and under the steadily increasing influence of the ACG, high-standard alpinism was becoming more popular. But in 1960 the Eigerwand still awaited a British ascent and the modest climbs of the Tyrol, Arolla and Saas Fee were the standard fare for the masses, though there was quite a large and experienced group operating in the mid-grades (the legacy of 100 years of Alpine Club activity) while the ACG was preoccupied with the hard rock routes of Chamonix and the Dolomites and organising the first ambitious expeditions to tackle the remaining tougher first ascents in the greater ranges.

One very important influence in the mid-Sixties came from a series of television programmes masterminded by Alan Chivers and Chris Brasher. These were live outside broadcasts from far-flung places such as Anglesey, Cheddar, Kilnsey, the Matterhorn and most notably an epic programme on the Old Man of Hoy which left a deep impression. It seems likely that the ascents of Everest and Kanchenjunga and the Sixties TV epics popularised climbing and encouraged thousands of young people to join the sport.

Another important event was the publication of Alan Blackshaw's instructional tome *Mountaineering: from Hill-walking to Alpine Climbing* in 1965 with regular updates and reprints over the next ten years. This was adopted by the BMC as the natural successor to Barford's 1946 manual Climbing in Britain. It brought together all the accumulated techniques developed on the crags and mountains and combined them with the technical wisdom and safety advice generated by the BMC Committees – it was a timely contribution during a period of rapid development, and was particularly useful for climbing schools and novices, and in sharpening up guiding practices.

A final element of popularisation may have been indirectly introduced by the expansion of tertiary education in the early Sixties – which led to thousands of new students (some of whom joined their college and university climbing clubs) all with grants and a generous amount of leisure time.

During the decade the development of nut protection made the harder climbs less chancy propositions. If VD/Severe was the norm at the start of the decade, VS was certainly the general standard at the end, with many leaders operating well above that level. In alpinism, by the end of the decade, most active climbers had their sights set on *grandes courses* and the whole expedition scene was poised to expand as the alpine-trained climbers began to target the great unclimbed walls of the highest peaks.

Mass Training
Against this background The Scouts, Schools, Duke of Edinburgh's Award, Outward Bound, Holiday Fellowship, Youth Hostels Association and Mountaineering Association were all taking parties of young people to the mountains in organised groups. Local Authority Outdoor Centres were being set up. A process of mass-training was under way. Climbing was seen to be a good thing by young people and the authorities alike – the legacy of the Everest success – but a price was beginning to be paid in terms of accidents that sometimes involved fatalities. As the authorities and the media recoiled with the revelation (always quickly forgotten) that the sport was 'dangerous', the BMC came under pressure to 'make it safe', an unrealistic expectation which in practice meant improving standards of advice, training and equipment. The matter was complicated as members of the BMC were far from convinced that they should do anything to encourage the spread of climbing which was at that time, and still is to a lesser degree, a very dangerous sport.

THE MAIN AREAS OF BMC BUSINESS IN THE SIXTIES
A number of themes emerge when one scans the minutes. The main business concerned equipment standards, training matters, the Glen Brittle Hut, concern about a range of environmental and access concerns, and organisational reform to keep pace with Government initiatives and the growing size of the institution.

The Glen Brittle Hut was a major preoccupation in the early years of the decade. The background to this project is described by Michael Holton in the previous section. It took years to get a suitable contractor with a reasonable quote, and then the process of construction was also frustratingly prolonged. By 1965, when the hut was opened, the BMC Committee (and particularly Harry Spilsbury[2] who shouldered the bulk of the work) must have been exhausted by the whole affair to such a degree that it left the whole matter of huts severely alone for years, this despite the success of the Glen Brittle project in terms of its subsequent popularity and financial surpluses. Initially the hut was heavily used, particularly by Mountaineering Association groups, but with the YHA takeover of the MA in 1968, usage dropped off sharply and the BMC's confidence in the long-term viability of the project was undermined. The Alex MacIntyre Hut at Onich and the Don Whillans Hut at the Roaches were established with far less difficulty in the Eighties and Nineties and one wonders what might have been had the Glen Brittle achievement been immediately followed by similarly ambitious projects.

(left to right) George Steele, Frank Solari, Denny Moorehouse, Don Robertson, and Bill Ward Members of the Equipment Committee at Plas y Brenin in 1973

Equipment Standards

Concern about the quality and design of equipment was another important theme of the period. The BMC Equipment Committee with Bill Ward as Chairman, ably supported by Frank Solari and others, grappled with the technicalities of ropes, tape, karabiners, slings, pitons, helmets and harnesses throughout the period, working in conjunction with Joe Griffin at the National Engineering Laboratory, the British Standards Association and the UIAA. (The highlights of the sub-committee's work during the period have been summarised by Frank Solari in the accompanying box – see opposite page.)

[2] Harry Spilsbury received belated recognition for his work on the Glen Brittle hut by being given a posthumous Honorary membership of the BMC at the 1966 AGM.

Some achievements of the BMC Technical Committee during its first 30 years.

* Preparation of a specification for natural fibre climbing ropes. Issue of test reports on the relative merit/demerit of the available natural fibre ropes – withdrawal from sale of the long-respected 'Alpine Club Rope' with red threads through the strands.
* Publication of the vulnerability of the hawser-laid nylon climbing rope of about 4.25lb/100ft ('full-weight' when nylon climbing ropes first became available in Britain) to damage when rope was dragged over rough rock during falling-leader accidents. More substantial nylon rope of about 5.5lb/100ft was recommended and came into general use, and was so recommended in British Standard 3104:1959 Nylon Mountaineering Ropes – the first such Standard in the world.
* Development of a new 'knotability' test to overcome the tendency of knots in some European 'kernmantel' ropes to become untied while in use. This test was offered to and accepted by the UIAA.
* Publicity for the very inadequate designs and strength of many types of karabiner on the market – particularly of British war-surplus items. Development of a Specification for light alloy and steel karabiners.
* Development of British Standard Specification 4423:1969 for climbers' helmets, which influenced the trade to produce better helmets.
* Published the results of tests on the holding capacity of pitons of various designs on various types of rock.
* Published the weakness of belay loops made of thin nylon 'line' of about 1.25lb/100ft as evidenced by the Cyrn Las fatality. Issued advice to use much heavier rope for such loops. Issued recommendations for stitching belay loops of webbing to retain the strength of the material.
* Issued recommendations for harness designs.

This work derived from studies of ropes and other equipment in use and particularly of items that failed in use and in accidents; from tests in laboratories and in the field; from consultations with experts in specialised fields, with the industry and with the UIAA.

The committee took a technical approach to the problems with testing and subsequent reports, in contrast to the UIAA which relied more on *legal* remedies for ensuring better standards. Each subject was thoroughly examined, problems solved and papers and reports published (usually in Mountaineering). It was an area of considerable achievement for the BMC – an object lesson of what can be done by a small group of dedicated experts. Griffin's departure from the National Engineering Laboratory in 1970 marked the end of an era but the BMC Equipment Committee continued to do effective work (in close collaboration with the UIAA) as described by George Steele in his detailed report.

The BMC Magazine
Mountaineering, the BMC's reliable, though somewhat prosaic, magazine recorded a succession of dry but absolutely essential technical reports of incalculable value. I remember visiting Peter Pirie, the Editor, in his North London home at that time to deliver action photos for publication (carefully following the example set by John Cleare and Rosemary Soper). *Mountaineering*, under Pirie's editorship, was a modest but effective publication. It was later replaced by the more populist *Mountain Life*, a short-lived successor (1972–76). After this BMC information was carried in *The Climber and Rambler* – a magazine that had made a number of overtures to the BMC during the late Sixties – and was transferred to *High* in 1985.

Pump-Storage and Hydro-electric Schemes
In the early Sixties with a nuclear power station at Trawsfynydd and another planned for Anglesey, there was much concern about the attendant pump-storage schemes. The fear was that either the Ogwen/Bochlwyd/Idwal or the Glaslyn/Llyn Llydaw lake systems, or combinations in the Carneddau might be targeted and the BMC gave maximum support to a defence campaign to stop this. The result, linking Marchlyn Mawr to the heavily despoiled Llyn Peris, might be seen in that context as a success given that the Anglesey Power Station was a reality and the authorities were determined to have a pump storage scheme somewhere. The BMC also joined with other bodies to successfully oppose a hydro-electric scheme for Glen Nevis.

Other Access Matters
There was a growing problem of access to the mountains in North Wales exacerbated by the sell-off of the Vaynol Estate in 1966. There were torrid exchanges between climbers and farmers in the Llanberis Pass (access to the Glyders from Nant Peris) and the Nantlle Valley (access to both the Nantlle hills and Craig y Bera). The issue was highly charged as these areas were in a National Park and the Ramblers Association was pushing for a formal access order. The local council and national park officials were more cautious, fearing serious trouble. Lord Hunt was drawn into the problem on behalf of the BMC. In the end the Llanberis matter was solved but in Nantlle there was an uneasy stand-off with the interested parties hoping that time would solve the problem.

1965 was a year of explosions – the Hound's Head Pinnacle at Tremadog was deemed unsafe and blown up, and in Derbyshire another enraged farmer took direct action by blowing up sections of Yellowslacks, an outstanding moorland gritstone edge on Bleaklow, which it later transpired was not even on his own property.

Farmer action was in evidence at Craig Bwlch y Moch where access was threatened. There the problem was solved by the intervention of the Nature Conservancy leading to some timely fence and stile building. It was suggested that the BMC should pay a rent for the cliff but this was firmly rejected because of the broader implications. There was also conservation and natural history concerns about the adjoining Craig Pant Ifan at this time. Climbers were using a variety of gullies for descent and destroying rare loams. Again a successful solution was formed by waymarking a main descent path.

In 1969 there was great concern in Scotland about plans to push a jeep track to Camasunary and an improved footpath beyond to Loch Coruisk in Skye which would involve blowing up the Bad Step. Lord Hunt (now in the role of the BMC's first Patron) wrote a strong protest letter to the Secretary of State for Scotland. Bill Murray (BMC Vice-President) and Sandy Cousins organised a spirited defence – the track was built (luckily avoiding the Bad Step) but proved an embarrassing failure as its bridges were soon swept away (as the critics had predicted), and it was decided to allow it to return to nature. One result of this was that Bill Murray was asked by the planners to identify the key wilderness regions in Scotland and he subsequently submitted a paper identifying forty vital areas which has formed a basis for conservation protection ever since.

The battle to prevent despoliation continues. A successful campaign in the Eighties, vigorously supported by the BMC, was the defence against ski expansion towards Lurcher's Gully in the Cairngorms, but the price was the Fort William ski development to Aonach Mor. To this day landowners wantonly scar the hills with tracks to facilitate forestry and stalking.

In Wales the BMC organised strong (and successful) opposition to the Cambrian Way proposal which was projected to have a waymarked route across key mountain areas, notably the Rhinogs and Cadair Idris.

Other access matters concerned: Stoney Middleton – access maintained to the crag behind the electricity sub-station; Wintour's Leap – access maintained despite conservationist and landowner pressure; Cheddar – constant battle to maintain access; Roaches and Hen Cloud – battle to maintain access; in 1961 the owner of the Roaches tried to charge 2/6d per day (perhaps £2 at today's values) to climb there; Windgather – purchased by the Peak Park; Swanage – threats to ban climbing averted; Avon Gorge – discussions with Merchant Venturers on fencing and gates to preserve access for climbers; Morwell – access maintained by the South-West Area but a Permit System for 'BMC Members only' agreed (something of a failure but probably – in view of the cliff's minor importance – a reasonable fudge).

The Foot-and-Mouth Epidemic
One important success for access and conservation (which was greatly appreciated by the farming community) was the almost total discipline of the climbing world during a national Foot-and-Mouth epidemic during the later part of 1967 and the early months of 1968. This meant no visits to mountain and country areas. Only a few quarries on town fringes were available for climbing – and places such as Heptonstall Quarry and Avon Gorge enjoyed a surge in popularity.

Harrison's Rocks
These outcrops were a constant source of anxiety as their popularity increased. There were clean-up campaigns and other management initiatives but by 1969 severe pressure from the local authority made it clear that a carpark and toilet block were essential if access was to be maintained. This was duly arranged through the CCPR and the Forge Farm access ceased in favour of the longer forest approach from the carpark.

Campsites
The BMC had some success in maintaining camping in the key climbing areas. This was under threat from landowners and National Parks: in the Llanberis Pass (official site set up in Nant Peris); the Ogwen Area (the BMC successfully defended camping at Gwern y Gof Isaf) and Borrowdale (the BMC supported the site at Grange). In 1968 plans were laid for the Eric Byne Memorial Campsite at Birchen Edge.

BMC Guidebooks
Guidebook work was in an early stage of development at that time. The BMC's area of responsibility was the Peak District (the CC covering Wales, the SMC Scotland and the FRCC the Lakes). There was a hiatus after the death of Eric Byne (1968) who had formed the dynamic central figure in guidebook recording and the Peak Guides were in disarray following the winding up of its Printer/Publisher so the CC took them over for a period. Paul Nunn, Nat Allen and Dave Gregory were the key figures who led the revival and the Peak Committee took the first steps on a road that has led to today's stunning success in guidebook work.

Insurance

An insurance scheme was finally introduced in 1969 after years of patient negotiations between Hilary Sinclair and underwriters. First reactions were not enthusiastic as the scheme only covered the UK. The greatly needed overseas insurance for alpine accident and medical expenses followed in the Seventies and this proved a major success.

The Sports Council

The change of Government of 1964 was followed by the formation of this new organisation to encourage more activity in Sport (N.B. though active from the start it did not receive its Royal Charter and operate in a fully comprehensive manner until the early Seventies). Its first job was to identify and organise the various bodies representing each sport. Late in 1965 the Sports Council's Walter Winterbottom asked for a report on the activities of the BMC, past, present and future. Sir John Hunt and Hilary Sinclair met Walter Winterbottom in February 1966. First they stressed that the BMC (unlike the bodies for competitive sports) was not a 'governing' but a 'representative' body. The Sports Council wished the BMC to be opened to individual membership (associate membership was later introduced), hoped that the BMC would have talks with the Mountaineering Association and the Mountain Rescue Committee with a view to representing the whole sport, and finally asked the BMC to submit a five-year plan with expenditure. The minute ends cryptically: 'It was agreed to consider this although reluctantly'.

The matter was complicated as the aggressively egalitarian Mountaineering Association had, somewhat mischievously, also claimed to be a representative organisation, probably in a bid to attract Government grant-aid. It is clear that the BMC, representing an unorganised and somewhat elitist sport, did not fit easily into the Sports Council's scheme of things, whereas the MA, with its training activities, would have looked a far more attractive proposition to the bureaucrats more used to dealing with 'organised' sports.

It may be that the BMC's high-profile President led the Sports Council to conclude that the BMC was the body to back, despite its 'traditional' character. John Hunt was determined that the BMC should be recognised as the representative body but was also clear that it could never be a 'governing' body in the manner that the Sports Council expected.

A number of Area Sports Councils were set up on which the BMC sought representation (this indirectly encouraged the establishment of the BMC's Area Committee system). The BMC's more settled relationship was with the CCPR which was similarly 'disturbed' by this thrusting new body. BMC/Sports Council relations were thus delicate from the start and became more so when it became involved in funding, but efforts were made on both sides to establish mutual confidence. There were various vicissitudes in the Seventies but thereafter relations improved, though there are still times of incomprehension that require adroit diplomacy from both sides.

Training and Safety

The above issues cover the majority of the BMC's concerns but the main theme of the decade was undoubtedly the search for better training standards and safe practice in the mountains. It crops up in minutes under many headings. On the one hand the BMC was seeking to influence the Ministry of Education on the dangers of climbing and the need for schoolteachers to observe various precautions when going to the hills. On the other hand the BMC was being assailed by an increasing number of complaints from the Mountain Rescue teams and the guides about poorly led parties in the mountains. The Ogwen Cottage team dealt with 80 incidents in 1960 of which 35 involved parties from institutions (schools, youth groups, D of E Award etc).

In 1961 the North Wales guides submitted detailed proposals that called on the BMC to toughen up standards of entry for those who wished to become guides (a fairly relaxed informal test being the norm at this time), and also made proposals for a more modest award for leaders of school parties – essentially along the lines of the subsequent Mountain Leadership Certificate. The BMC saw immediately that it would be unable to administer such a system and, therefore, rejected it. Instead it drew up a series of Do's and Don'ts in its Circular 326. This was presented to the Department of Education for circulation to schools.

Soon after this Jack Longland took over as BMC President at a time when he was also Chairman of the CCPR's Outdoor Pursuits Committee and Director of Education in Derbyshire. On the 25th September 1963 a meeting was held at the CCPR under Jack Longland's chairmanship. The critical minute reporting the CCPR discussions was introduced under 'Other Business' (i.e. late) in the BMC's October meeting. It reads as follows:

The meeting [at the CCPR] was of individuals, not representatives, connected with the BMC, Guides, Scouts, CCPR, Ministry of Education and Duke of Edinburgh's Award. All felt that some sort of certificate was needed now that so many people were taking mountaineering courses and going back to their schools, youth clubs etc.

At this meeting it had been concluded that the qualification would lie somewhere between that for the BMC's Mountain Guide and the minimum qualification the BMC circulated as necessary if schoolteachers were to venture into the hills with children ...

It was decided, in principle, that the BMC would work in with such a scheme if this was possible. The situation had changed considerably since Circular 326 was prepared. It seemed possible that the BMC might now participate in the preparation of a scheme without having to handle the large task of administration.

So major policy was decided, without warning and late at night at just one meeting. The background to the CCPR meeting is unclear. Was Jack Longland launching a completely personal initiative, or was he responding to some urgent Government 'encouragement'? The fact that each of the interested bodies had their supposed views expressed by 'individuals' rather than mandated 'representatives' is an unconventional way of formulating policy, to say the least. The exact way the scheme would work and the BMC's role (three representatives on the Board) was clarified by Jack Longland in the BMC Management meetings of 3rd February and 25th May 1964 – no discussion about this having taken place at the AGM on the 18th April (though there was a full account in the annual report). The Mountain Training Board (its name was later changed to the more stirring Mountain Leadership Training Board) was established and the training programme for the Mountain Leadership Certificate was fully operational by October 1964. No formal announcement of the BMC's involvement in a major new training body was made at the 1965 AGM, merely a terse entry about the MTB's business as if it were accomplished fact.

Whether Jack Longland deliberately kept discussion to a minimum or was merely displaying his typical efficient committee skills is difficult to say. He may well have felt that speed was necessary to counter the reactionary attitudes of the traditional clubs that he had fought all his life. In this he was probably mistaken as the BMC was already fully aware of its responsibilities. In hindsight it is clear that it would have been better for the BMC to have had a fuller debate on such a major policy development. Who can say what wisdom might have been added by realistic mountaineers if the subject had been examined more thoroughly – particularly on the whole philosophy of encouraging school parties to advance into mountaineering beyond a basic introductory stage. One can only speculate that had more thorough appraisal taken place, the upheavals of the Mountain Training Dispute in the Seventies might have been avoided. It is relevant to point out that the Cairngorm Accident of 1971, in which five school children and a supervisor died, involved a party led by a qualified instructor (he had the more advanced Mountain Instructors Certificate), operating from the basis of a comprehensive and centrally-planned schools programme run by a highly informed Education Authority headed by a mountaineer. These factors called into question the whole rationale of taking parties of school children into the mountains (particularly in winter) and organising a qualification system to facilitate and encourage this.

Nevertheless in the mid-Sixties school parties were already going to the mountains so the immediate task was to gain an improvement in the mountain skills of their leaders. The MTB trained a large number of people in a very short time and the number of incidents diminished – a clear tactical success which allowed the Board, the Centres and the Authorities to blot out any thoughts of the possibility of the strategic weakness so tragically demonstrated by the Cairngorm incident.

By 1965 another weakness in the hastily formed Board became apparent. There was spirited discussion about who would control the proposed Mountain Instructors Certificate designed to tighten up the skills of the Outdoor Centre Instructors who were running the Mountain Leadership training. There was also concern about how this would impinge on the existing Guides qualification. The BMC (with Sir John Hunt now the President) took the view that it should be administered by the BMC, whereas Jack Longland worked assiduously to get it incorporated into the MTB remit. After negotiation, the latter solution was agreed, but a new constitution for an enlarged Mountain Leadership Training Board had to be enacted to allow this.[3] There were clearly tensions between Hunt and Longland during these exchanges, and these were to re-emerge when Lord Hunt's Working Party made some significant criticisms of the Board's work in its report published in 1976.

It is likely that had the MTB been formed during the Hunt Presidency it would have come under much greater influence from the BMC, instead of becoming, in effect, a self-sustaining quango run solely in the interests of the user groups and with a marked tendency to undervalue broader mountaineering wisdom. It also soon transpired that the CCPR was uneasy about its involvement in the MLTB and saw it as ultimately a BMC matter. In September 1968 a BMC minute recorded the CCPR position as it was understood by the Hon. Secretary, Donald Greenwood:

> As a national body the Council [BMC] should be responsible for any work on a national level in mountain training. Such work was

---

[3] According to Dennis Gray the BMC was unable to find any constitutions for the MTB or the MLTB during the Mountain Training Dispute. Whether they were mislaid, conveniently 'lost' or never written is not clear.

currently carried out by the CCPR via the MLTB. It was not the purpose of the CCPR to become involved with the detailed work of individual sports and it had indicated that when it was in a position to do so, the BMC might take over the work of the MLTB itself. The CCPR had no mountaineering expert on its [HQ] staff.

The BMC hoped that the National Officer position (that it was attempting to get financed at the time) would take over the MLTB administration from the CCPR. In the event it was some time before this transition took place.

The formation of the MTB (MLTB) and its growth, and the subsequent Mountain Training Dispute, offers some valuable lessons for the BMC. When major policy initiatives are proposed they should always be subjected to thorough committee examination and debate. Though it may be impossible to foresee all potential pitfalls, such a process should ensure that identifiable controversial elements are fully thrashed out to everyone's satisfaction before any decision is taken. Securing this procedure is often difficult as major policy initiatives (by their nature) are often backed by vested-interest groups or individuals determined to push them through with a minimum of debate.

This care in policy formation is particularly important in an institution that, rather like a trades union, is a 'one party state' with neither the time nor energy for adversarial politics. It is a procedure that has, I am sad to say, been ignored on several occasions since.

The Mountaineering Association

Although not directly connected with its dealings with the MLTB, the BMC's failure to come to the assistance of the ailing MA in 1967 missed another important training opportunity at that time. For nearly two decades the MA, under the idealistic but somewhat mercurial leadership of Jerry Wright, had given rock-climbing, snow and ice and alpine training to thousands of aspirant climbers in a modest but highly effective way. This training, designed to attract fee-paying individuals, was similar to a traditional club introduction.

Jerry Wright — his *Mountaineering Association* gave climbing introductions to over 15,000 people in the post-war years.

It would have formed a logical extension to the institutional training which the MLTB was seeking to control. But Wright's organisation had been regarded with scepticism by the major clubs and Wright himself was mistrusted as an unreliable socialist maverick (the man who had hosted the fanatical German climbers who placed the pitons in Munich Climb).

Wright's attempt to present the MA as a representative body to the Sports Council was seen as further evidence of his disruptive tendencies. Rather than identifying the MA's decline as an opportunity, the BMC appears to have reacted to its difficulties with a degree of schadenfreude. In the event, after Wright's retirement, the MA was absorbed into the YHA. The MA's decline had been sudden – 1000 people trained in 1965, 600 in 1966 and 400 in 1967 – but this may have been due, in part, to Wright's failing energies coupled with the break enforced by the Foot-and-Mouth epidemic. It is likely that a pared-down operation based on its proven method would have had a continuing relevance, indeed Dennis Gray resurrected MA-style courses for the BMC in the Eighties.

The UIAA

BMC relations with the UIAA were assiduously cultivated throughout the Sixties with our representatives attending main council meetings at Geneva, Madrid and on Crete. The achievements through the decade appear modest though some had a long-term and tangible value. Various so-called 'International Youth Meets' were organised. An international grading system was established which became the standard for the main alpine areas. The Equipment Commission was quite effective with the UIAA standards encouraging a steady improvement in rope and karabiner quality. An international system of mountain rescue signals was also established.

Despite this it is difficult to avoid the conclusion that the UIAA was more preoccupied with establishing itself as a sort of climbing United Nations rather than zealously seeking any particular reform. The main BMC aim – to get reciprocal rights agreed for its members to the main alpine huts systems – remained tantalisingly out of reach and UK climbers were forced to join one of the main European Alpine Clubs to secure the concessions.

Summary

Much was achieved during the decade though some major opportunities were missed. This was a crucial period in the BMC's evolution as it slowly began to assume the role of a representative body for the whole sport. I remain humbled by the contributions of our predecessors and marvel at the cohesion and idealism of the climbing world.

Postscript:
As the final touches were being made to this book there came news of Frank Solari's death and it is fitting that a tribute to his work should be placed here, in the decade in which he was most active. His final contribution to the BMC was with this book. He was tremendously supportive to me in compiling this paper and also made prodigious efforts on the photographic side, securing several key photos and making prints for the portrait line-ups.

Frank was a member of several clubs serving as President (1961-62) and Vice-President (1962-63). His contribution to BMC affairs was immense, spanning nearly three decades. His main work was on the Technical Committee but he also served in other capacities, notably as Vice-President during Basil Goodfellow's second Presidency and as Acting President in the difficult period that followed Goodfellow's death in office. After the BMC left London Frank focused the main thrust of his service through the Alpine Club, and was particularly involved in the restructuring of the library as a charity, and the financial organisational work that stemmed from that decision.

He retained an interest in BMC and UIAA equipment matters and was also involved in countless Alpine Club exhibition and lecture tasks. There never was a more loyal and valuable servant of the climbing world, a contribution recognised by the Honorary Membership of both the BMC and the Alpine Club.

Frank's final contribution to the climbing world was to leave a generous bequest to the Alpine Club, part of which the A.C. has allowed to be used to help finance this history.

Another notable climber who made a significant contribution to BMC affairs in the late-1960s was W.H. 'Bill' Murray and he too sadly passed away early in 1996. Murray was the last Scottish climber to be officially selected as a BMC Vice-President. (W.M. MacKenzie was the final nominee, but never took up office ... shortly after this the Mountaineering Council of Scotland was established). John Cunningham was a BMC selection for Vice-President and did not officially represent Scotland. Murray's particular contribution on Scottish access matters is described in the text. Many will cherish memories of his magnificent speech at the Portinscale AGM of 1984 when he laid out the tenets of high-quality writing on mountaineering in a trenchant and inspiring manner.

THE BMC ORGANISATIONAL FLOWCHART

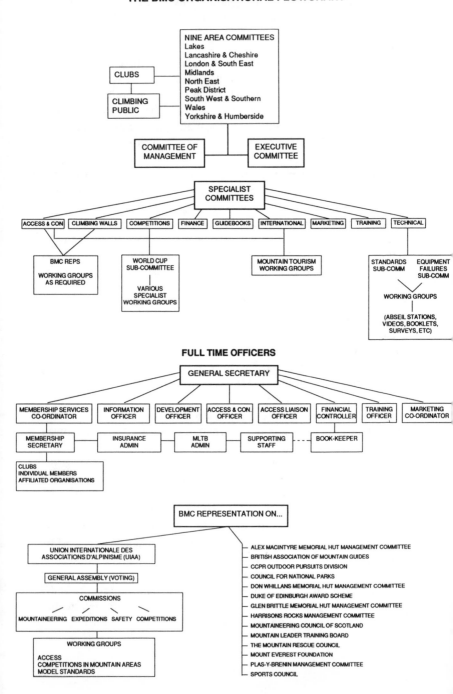

The Seventies

At the beginning of this decade I was away from the domestic climbing scene living in Kenya, but unbeknown to me a group of enthusiastic volunteers was hard at work developing plans which would change the Council irrevocably. The Wolfenden Commission, reporting at the end of the Sixties, had made recommendations to Government that it become directly involved in the funding of sport and, with the acceptance of this report, grant aid was made available to help national bodies improve their administration. Initially this was to be via The Department of Education, but this was soon to be superseded by the setting up of The Sports Councils in January 1972, with Royal Charters funded from the Department of the Environment.

The BMC at that date was firmly rooted in London, with the use of a tiny office in the old CCPR (Central Council of Physical Recreation) HQ in Park Crescent, and the services of a part-time typist. Its overworked Hon Secretary, Donald Greenwood, and President, Lord Hunt, with the support of their colleagues of the Management Committee, had decided to seize the opportunity provided by grant aid and to go 'professional' for it was becoming more and more obvious to these hard-pressed souls that, with the exponential growth of the sport, and the necessity to liaise more and more often with statutory bodies, such as the Forestry Commission, the Water Authorities, the Nature Conservancy Council, the National Parks, and all the educational, voluntary and youth organisations interested in mountain activities, this was creating demands far beyond what volunteers could possibly be expected to meet.

A three-year development plan was started and later completed in mid-1971 by a newly elected team of officers, with Tony Moulam in the Chair and Peter Ledeboer as Hon Secretary. It is only many years after such events that in picking over the bones you realise their significance, but central to the plan was to be the creation for the first time ever in British climbing of a professional officer post, The National Officer, with both technical and administration duties backed up by a full-time office staff and appropriate accommodation and facilities. At least this was the intention, but finance remained a problem for a principle of grant aid was and is that usually a national body must find a good portion of its own overall running costs, relying on Government support to finance specific items, and it is expected that the body in question will raise more and more of its own finances as the organisation grows. This was a hard pill for the then BMC membership to swallow for it meant higher affiliation fees. In the end it was agreed but not without some hard sell by the likes of Jack Longland, John Hunt and Bob Pettigrew in support of the BMC Officers.

Whilst these matters were being finalised, there occurred an event which was to have the widest repercussions in the mountaineering world, namely the Cairngorm tragedy when five children and a student teacher perished whilst taking part in an expedition organised by the Edinburgh Education Authorities in November 1971. This and other follow-on tragedies, particularly to a group of Scouts in Snowdonia, alerted many in the mainstream climbing world to the serious nature of some of these programmes and the need for mountaineers to have more input into their planning and control. The result was to be a massive confrontation between those involved professionally in educational activities in the mountains and the BMC, but I am getting ahead of myself for this was all to be in the future, especially for myself returning just before these events on an urgent visit to the UK for family reasons, but which then led on by a series of coincidences to my applying for and being appointed as the first ever National Officer of the Council.

Before I take the story further I must declare that it is not possible for me to be objective in writing about two decades of BMC history. I can only do this from a personal perspective and if I miss out on any one person's contribution, or place undue emphasis on certain events, I can only apologise, for I do acknowledge that the development of the BMC to its current position in our sport was the work of many hands, some of which is obvious and some not so from the official record in the minute books and from memories. But, when I joined in January 1972 I found many new initiatives had already been planned, such as: the setting up of a Safety Sub-Committee under the leadership of the then Director of Plas y Brenin, John Jackson; the launch of a new mass circulation magazine *Mountain Life* to replace the old BMC house journal, *Mountaineering*; and the responsibility for producing a national edition of *New Climbs* in 1972.

That is how things stood when I commenced work, reporting to the small BMC office in Park Crescent situated in the plush surroundings of the Regent's Park district of London. Our landlord was the Crown, and besides the mountaineers there were many other sports bodies housed in the building, which was also to be the site of the offices for the new Sports Council, the body being set up with responsibility for funding

English and British sport, there being separate bodies for Wales, Scotland and Northern Ireland. Sport in Britain is traditionally run and, despite protestations to the contrary, is a hive of political intrigue with English, Scottish, Welsh and Irish dimensions. Each activity is represented by a national body and there are literally dozens of them, supporting everything from athletics, football and golf to hovercraft sailing and metal detecting. Most of these national bodies are members of the reformed CCPR, which acts as their forum and does its best to represent the needs of sport to Government, provide services such as parliamentary and taxation advice for its members, and generally acting as a lobbying and representative organisation.

I knew nothing of this when I became National Officer, and it was a revelation to me. Thus I started out from an office barely big enough to turn round in, and with a young typist equipped with an ancient machine, a duplicator and a telephone, into what were then uncharted waters for mountaineering. Many had reservations about these developments, including myself, for on the one hand we felt that climbers were not interested in either organisation, rules or national bodies, and that a part of the sport's essential appeal was its sense of freedom and anarchy; on the other hand we could see the need for some support, some planning, and protection if mountaineering were in the long run to preserve its integrity. That turning 'pro' was not to be all serious was brought home to me on my very first evening in London, working late in the office on my own when I answered the phone and the following conversation took place; "Is that the BMC?" demanded the voice of an anxious young female. "Yes". "Well it just will not go!" lady caller. "It will not go?" I repeated totally mystified. "I have already told you so!" lady getting angry. "What will not go?" me also getting irate. "My mini car that I had delivered this morning." lady in surprise. "But why are you ringing us?" I demanded. "You are the BMC and I want it mended now; tonight." she responded. "My dear lady, we are the British Mountaineering Council. You need the British Motor Corporation, good-night!" and I ungallantly hung up on her as she stammered an apology.

In February 1972 both the BMC and the Mountain Leader Training Board (MLTB) agreed that the Council would take over the administration of the scheme. Since its inception in 1964, it had been developed jointly between the CCPR, who had until that juncture provided the administrative back-up, and the BMC and had thrived under the leadership of its Chairman, the former BMC President Jack Longland. It was by then one of the biggest training schemes in British sport. At the setting up of The Sports Council, which was taking on many of the functions of the original CCPR, including the ownership of Plas y Brenin and other existing national sports centres such as Lilleshall and Bisham Abbey, the administration of such schemes was to be handed over to the national bodies concerned. This became one of my first tasks, namely to plan for this extension of responsibilities, for it meant that inevitably the BMC would need more staff and a bigger office. During those early months I was bewildered by the complexity and bureaucracy of sports administration and I was also astounded at the strength of feeling about certain issues, for it was obvious that the Cairngorm tragedy would loom large in debate as the formal enquiry into what had gone wrong got under way.

Looking back now at the record as revealed by the Management Committee minutes of 1972, it was a remarkable year of progress in the history of the Council and many of the later positive developments first surfaced at that period. Investigations began into developing existing insurance schemes, discussions were held with a view to setting up an expedition fund and the Council actually obtained a £5,000 grant from The Sports Council to help fund the Autumn attempt that year on Everest's SW Face, which in part led on to the present BMC/Sports Council scheme of financial support for approved expeditions. Guidebooks and their production took up much thought and time. Two volumes of *New Climbs* were prepared that year and published via West Col, and the idea was mooted that the Council should take on the responsibility for publishing the series of Peak guidebooks (it was already responsible for the compilation of this via a sub-committee of its Area Committee) as previous commercial arrangements had by then totally failed the climbing community.

Mountain Life was successfully launched and within the year was recording a small profit. The Safety Committee was set up, and subsequently re-organised under Ron James's leadership. It was later still to be merged along with the old Equipment Committee into a single Technical Committee on the move of the BMC to Manchester at the end of 1974.

A set of instructional safety film strips, shot by John Cleare, aimed at mountain walking in Summer and Winter, were prepared and successfully marketed, and the BBC, with the Council acting as Technical Advisor, produced a rock-climbing instructional series, *Rock Face*, which was screened on BBC2 and soon repeated to widespread critical acclaim. Doubtless it would make today's hi-tec rock jocks wet themselves with laughter with its old fashioned fuddy-duddy equipment, clothes and techniques.

An event which did have wider repercussions than we realised at the time, was the exhibition by Russian climbers of speed rock-climbing at the Summer 1972 Munich Olympic Games. In tandem with the Games, the DAV (German Alpine Club) organised a climbing meet, to which the BMC sent Mike Butler, Malcolm Howells and Ed Cross. The Germans also organised a televised debate in the Löwenbrau beer hall about whether organised competitions had any place in climbing. After taking wide soundings the Council decided to oppose these developments, and I spoke at the debate against the proposal put forward by the USSR Mountaineering Federation, which naturally wished to promote their type of speed competitions. After the conclusion of the debate a vote was taken and every country present voted against the introduction of organised events except Russia, but this was to be only the first skirmish in a long-running saga that ended towards the end of the next decade with the UIAA formally accepting organised rock-climbing competitions.

So much was happening that it is hard to keep up with the record even now twenty years on. Weekends were organised for club representatives at Helyg to help with advice over their internal organisation problems and, at The Sports Council's invitation, the BMC was invited from thereon to assume a greater role in the development of Plas y Brenin. The recommendations of the Cairngorm Enquiry were published at this time and left many mountaineers feeling that some of the leading questions as to what had gone wrong were unanswered, and there was widespread unease about this in the climbing world. Unfortunately this strength of feeling was not sufficiently noted in the mountain training world, and thus the seeds of future conflict between those professionally involved in instructional schemes and the amateur/ club climber were sown, a conflict that would reach its climax a few years later with the publication by the BMC of the Hunt Report on Mountain Training resulting in the greatest confrontation in the history of British climbing.

Younger activists might wonder now what it was all about, and I will try at the appropriate time to fill in more of the detailed background to the dispute, but it is possible here to illustrate the strength of feeling abroad at that time by recounting the story of a visit paid by the BMC Hon Secretary Peter Ledeboer and myself in the Winter of 1972 to Birmingham, one of a series we were then engaged upon around the country. The purpose was to drum up support from the clubs and members for the many initiatives then intended, particularly in areas such as our ability to combat threats to the mountain environment. We were then involved in opposing the setting up of a new long-distance, high-level footpath in Wales, The Cambrian Way, in which endeavour we were eventually successful on the grounds of safety; the pumped storage scheme at Llanberis which campaign we later lost; supporting The Friends of the Lake District in opposing the A66 road widening scheme; yet another lost cause, but successfully defending the Cromlech Boulders which were threatened with demolition due to road-widening and which were saved for posterity, although this was to be a recurring threat over the next few years. We also intended to increase our role in mountain training, improve our services and so forth: in short we needed more members, and more money to carry out the tasks we were planning. The meeting in Birmingham was organised by the senior BMC club in the area, the Midland Association of Mountaineers, and they had done a good job in getting out the voters for the hall was packed when Peter and I took our places on the platform.

The Hon Secretary of the BMC, a diminutive figure, but a good soul, with nothing but the best of intentions began the evening with a rather over-long introduction, which included reference to the fact that I had produced a plan which would lead to the BMC taking over the administration of the Mountain Leader scheme on 1st January 1973. At this a member of the audience sprang to his feet, ran down the outer aisle, leapt on the stage and began to attack poor Peter, screaming, "Murderers, molesters!". Sitting on the platform alone with Peter, I should have moved to his aid, but I was transfixed. Luckily, others in the audience jumped up to help restrain the apparent madman and Peter was unscathed. We realised later that this outburst had been inspired by the climber's firm conviction that such schemes as mountain leader training were directly responsible for the Cairngorm tragedy. He felt that by providing such certificates the mountaineering world was encouraging those in authority to have a false sense of security and that without such training schemes the Edinburgh school party would never have been allowed on to Cairngorm on the weekend in question. It was a controversial viewpoint, but the incident illustrates the depth of feeling at that time, and why the mountain training dispute later reached such highs and lows of both argument and ill-feeling.

In November 1972 the BMC organised 'A Focus on Modern Mountaineering' and a mountain painting exhibition in the Lesser Free Trade Hall in Manchester. This was an idea I had, which exceeded my wildest dreams in the interest it excited. Over 300 climbers came to it from all over the UK, and we had so many pictures for the exhibition that we could not hang them all. The highlight proved to be the final speaker of the evening, the late Alan Rouse who had to be helped on to the platform, for he was sporting one of the largest plasters on a limb any of us had ever seen. He had fallen the previous week and fractured a leg. His topic that night was 'The Challenge of Solo Climbing' and the success of that evening gave the impetus for us to hold in March 1974 the first of the National Mountaineering Conferences at Buxton.

In January 1973 the BMC did assume responsibility for administering the MLTB, but it was to be the end of the year before sufficient space was obtained to set up a suitable office, which was achieved by the BMC moving, along with The Sports Council, into even more up-market offices in Brompton Road, Knightsbridge, directly opposite Harrod's. An Administration Officer was recruited, and Kip Gilpin joined the BMC in this capacity. Meanwhile a working party under the chairmanship of the late Maurice Bennett was busy drafting a new Constitution, and recommended changing the voting and representative structure of the Council, which up until that date had been rather a hotchpotch with some clubs having historical Management seats, e.g. the Alpine Club, and others sitting on that group as nominated representatives, e.g. the Guides. Maurice's group recommended that clubs should work through Areas, and that in future those forums should elect the Management Committee. This was to be the first of several redrafted constitutions which was to lead finally in the next decade to a one member, one vote (including the ever growing number of individual members) Council, and it might be worth noting that the original shakers and movers, such as the A.C., willingly surrendered their privileged positions in order to widen the democracy of the BMC and, therefore, improve its standing and appeal.

It may seem getting things out of proportion now, but in the early part of 1973 the buzz word was 'Safety', for the result of the spate of tragedies occurring to young people, of which the Cairngorm incident received the greatest publicity, resulted in something like a panic amongst the establishment. Meetings were held with Government departments, The Sports Council, the Training Boards, and the Rescue Services due to the grave public and media concern (this seems to rear its head approximately once each decade) about the number of mountain accidents during that winter. Over the previous few years the CCPR/BMC had held an annual forum on the topic of Mountain Safety, and in March 1973 the BMC took this on board and organised a National Safety Conference at Leeds University. The speakers were drawn from both the 'pros' and amateurs: Sir Jack Longland, Tony Moulam the BMC President, Ken Wilson Editor of *Mountain*, Graham Tiso, Tom Price and Bill March, and it was hoped vainly by organisers such as myself that this might diffuse some of the head of steam then building around these issues. It was not to be, and there were some volatile moments, especially when one of the four-hundred delegates, at question time, after a particularly bruising exchange, offered to 'meet the Editor of *Mountain* outside!'. At the time this was good naturedly dismissed by Nat Allen, who had been brought in to Chair this particular session, as just a bit of good old fashioned plain speaking, but with hindsight it was yet another indication of the unresolved differences that would lead the BMC into a major confrontation.

These demands for a safety campaign also led to the worst constitutional crisis in the BMC's history, for partly originating in an unofficial Sports Council suggestion and partly due to over-enthusiasm on their part, the then Hon Secretary and the President involved the BMC in ambitious plans to make a feature film on Mountain Safety. Before the Management Committee could be informed, a substantial commitment had been made with a trial shooting and the preparation of a script but, unfortunately, finance could not then be obtained and the project had to be cancelled. This led to recriminations and ill-feeling, for the BMC was left with no legal option other than to pay for all the preliminary work, with the sums of money involved being substantial and almost beyond the Council's ability to pay, and Peter Ledeboer and Tony Moulam resigned. This was a tragic outcome for they had meant nothing but good by their actions, and had set in train many initiatives which were to prove sound over the next few years, and they do deserve, however belatedly, a vote of thanks from the membership for their hard work whilst serving the BMC.

At this moment of crisis, *Mountain Life*, which had promised so much in the way of providing improved communications for the BMC and its work, also ran into difficulties. The Council had entered into a publishing agreement for the launch with West Col, but they then made it plain that they had no wish to continue with this arrangement as it was proving so time consuming for such a small business as themselves to provide. The situation was saved by Chris Brasher who, along with a colleague, Anthony Churchill, agreed to take over the magazine and become its Editor, and he was joined by John Cleare as his assistant.

Despite this positive outcome over the magazine, which then prospered under Chris's dynamism until it was merged in 1976 with *Climber*, morale was still at a low point and an obvious lesson of the Safety Film debacle was the need to concentrate on the core requirements of our sport: access work, conservation, equipment testing, guidebooks, expeditions, training etc. and not to become side-tracked by the media or official pressures into knee-jerk, peripheral campaigns. But we had to face the fact that the BMC then was just not up to responding to all these demands. How

BMC PRESIDENTS

Geoffrey Winthrop Young
1945-1947
Alpine Club, C.C., F.R.C.C.

Alfred Sefton Pigott
1947-1950
Rucksack Club, C.C.

Robert Samuel Theodore Chorley
1950-1953
Fell & Rock, A.C.

James Mann Wordie
1953-1956
Scottish Mountaineering Club, A.C.

Basil Robertson Goodfellow
1956-1959 1968-1969
Rucksack Club, A.C.

George Graham Macphee 1959-1962
Scottish Mountaineering Club, R.C.
Wayfarers', A.C., F.R.C.C.

John Laurence Longland
1962-1965
Climbers' Club, A.C.

Henry Cecil John Hunt
1965-1968
Himalayan Club, A.C., C.C., F.R.C.C.

Anthony John James Moulam
1970-1973
Climbers' Club

Alan Blackshaw 1973-1976
Climbers' Club, A.C.*, W.C.

Robert Gavin Pettigrew 1976-1979
Oread, A.C., C.C.

Joseph Walmsley 1979-1982
Rucksack Club, A.C.

Thomas Price 1982-1985
Fell & Rock

John Neill
1985-1988
Climbers' Club, A.C.*

Christian John Storey Bonington
1988-1991
Climbers' Club, A.C.*, F.R.C.C.

Ian Gordon McNaught-Davis
1991-1994
Climbers' Club, A.C.*

Paul James Nunn
1994-1995
Alpha, F.R.C.C., C.C., A.C.*

HONORARY SECRETARIES 1945-1974

GENERAL SECRETARIES 1974-

John Barford 1945-1947
Climbers' Club, A.C.

Alan Stewart 1947-1952
Rucksack Club

Frank Shuttleworth 1952-1955
Rucksack Club

Michael Holton 1955-1960
RAF Mountaineering Assoc., A.C.

Hilary Sinclair 1960-1964
Alpine Club, C.C.

Donald Greenwood 1965-1971
Alpine Club

Peter Ledeboer 1972-1973
*Association of British Members
of the S.A.C., A.C., F.R.C.C.*

Dave Partridge 1973-1974
Farnborough M.C.

Dennis Gray 1974-1989
Rock and Ice, A.C.*, Karabiner

Derek Walker 1989-1995
Climbers' Club, A.C., F.R.C.C.

Roger Payne 1995-
Alpine Club*, C.C.

to achieve this was the challenge which faced the Council at this moment of crisis, and waiting in the wings was the man with the answers, Alan Blackshaw. He moved into the Presidential hot seat and, with the recruitment of the late Dave Partridge as Hon Secretary, began the task of restructuring the Council into almost its present-day form.

A broad-based group of climbers was recruited and a Future Policy Committee was formed with Alan himself in the Chair, and Dave took on the onerous task as its Secretary. Throughout the rest of 1973 and into the early part of 1974, a demanding round of meetings was held the length and breadth of the land. The pace was hectic for it was a race against time in that, after the events of that year, the membership needed to have its faith restored in the efficiency of its organisation. But even in this dark period there were to be lighter moments, especially in attending some of the meetings of the Future Policy Committee.

Alan Blackshaw's stamina was impressive for during this period of great BMC stress he was also embroiled as an Under Secretary in the aftermath of the so-called 'Oil Crisis', when the producing nations decided to more than double the price of the black gold. On one occasion Alan turned up to chair one of our meetings, held in the plush surroundings of a certain London Club frequented by military types, with the latest situation/briefing papers on the crisis for his then boss, Lord Carrington, inside an HMG-marked brief-case padlocked to his wrist! If any terrorist group had decided to have a go at getting hold of these top secret documents, they would have needed first to cut off his hand, and then to make their getaway whilst being obstructed by a bevy of gin-swilling Colonel Blimps and Flying Officer Kites who were ringed about us, amazed as committee member Ken Wilson shouted his message that, "climbing is about dying"!

Before I move on from the events of 1973 there are several other developments worthy of record. The serious problems resulting from the over-use of Harrison's Rocks, perhaps out of necessity the UK's most visited outcrop, were identified that Summer in a report by the late Dennis Kemp, which he undertook at his own expense and time, but which did lead on to corrective action commencing, undertaken by the joint Sports Council/BMC Committee responsible for the Rocks.

A programme which has continued up to this day and perhaps an even more significant event was the appearance of the first ever Peak series guide to be published by the Council, namely *Staffordshire* (The Roaches Area) by Dave Salt. This was made possible by grant aid from the Sports Council, which was also persuaded at the time to provide funds for the Climbers' Club to overcome a similar funding difficulty with their established series to Wales and farther afield. Both the BMC and the CC decided that from thereon they would take on the publishing responsibility for their guidebooks, eschewing commercial houses, but very much helped by the setting up shortly after of the distribution agency, Cordée, via a dynamic member of both guidebook teams, Ken Vickers. A prime mover in these negotiations was one of the BMC Vice-Presidents, John Wilkinson, who as Guidebook Editor for the Fell & Rock series had great expertise and authority in these matters.

Two other important events that happened in 1973, forerunners of many such later initiatives, were when the BMC hosted its first ever International Climbing gatherings. At the end of the summer the Council held a meet in Llanberis for the UIAA, when 57 climbers from 19 countries attended (including three Russians). Shortly after this event 8 members of the prestigious Groupe de Haute Montagne came as BMC guests to North Wales. Both of these gatherings spawned their legends, and the cast lists were like a Hollywood movie, but for me the first was highlighted by the inclusion among our team of helpers of Peter Boardman (then a University student) fresh from his first ever Himalayan trip, and the second by the support of that damned Yankee Boy, 'Hot' Henry Barber drafted in to wear down the cream of French climbing by his incredible enthusiasm to crag and to party. He was, however, to meet his match in the person of Jean Afanassieff with whom I had the good fortune to climb at Tremadog where he insisted that we climbed Alpine style. Such piddling little climbs did not require considerations like belays he decided and as he proceeded to race up everything, coils in hand, he almost had me convinced until I found myself stuck behind him on The Grasper. Help! However, the most historically significant climbing of that meet was to be the performances of Simone Badier. In 1973 few in the UK seriously believed that a woman could climb as well as the men, but we were quickly made to revise our opinion as she floated effortlessly up the test pieces of the day, and her example was to be the start of a renaissance in British women's climbing that has continued to this day.

Meanwhile the Future Policy Group was running into insurmountable problems over reconciling the widely divergent views being expressed to it by interested parties as to the BMC's future role in Mountain Training. It found itself unable to agree on these matters and recommended to Management at the end of that year that such was the complexity of the issues involved that they required a separate group of the highest possible expertise to look at the situation. This recommendation was accepted and Lord Hunt was invited to form a committee, which task he readily agreed to and a 12-member advisory group of outstanding experience from both the field of mountain training and the sport was gathered and held its first meeting in March 1974.

In that same month was held the first Buxton Conference and, apart from the celebrity lecture on the Saturday night by Kurt Diemberger – the first of the now famous 'My Life and Hard Times' series and a last-minute unscheduled appearance by Cesare Maestri, the rest of the speaking talent was home grown. Our Chairman, Ian McNaught-Davis (Mac the telly to us all) and the two overseas speakers set the standard for the many succeeding Buxton's, with Maestri confounding his critics by simply declaring that he could not give a fig for their views, and if he discovered a glue that would help him stick the better to the mountainside he would use it, and Diemberger holding his audience enthralled for almost 4 hours with his climbing life story.

In May 1974 the Yorkshire & Humberside Area Committee was formed in response to the growing importance of the area as a climbing centre, and the AGM of the Council was held in the Peak District at the Maynard Arms in Grindleford. The decision had been taken the previous year to move the annual meeting out of London, and to combine a dinner and a social event in an attempt to beef up both the attendance and the significance of the event. However, on this occasion the live rock band from Manchester we had booked for the after-dinner disco proved to be too much of an attraction, for word of their intended presence had spread far and wide in the climbing world, and several hundred youthful gatecrashers arrived in the hall from many parts of the UK as soon as the band began to play. Unfortunately the loud rock music did have an adverse effect on certain of our members' susceptibilities, and I suffered a terrible verbal drubbing from A. B. Hargreaves (a great opera lover) who was astonished to learn that the BMC was actually paying this band of hooligans to perform. I was not helped in my defensive argument as to what a good idea it was to attract young activists to BMC events by a certain well-known climber, swinging backwards and forwards above the heads of the gyrating bodies, hanging by his hands from a chandelier, like a trapeze artist. That remains the largest crowd I have ever seen at a BMC Annual Meeting, but it did stretch the famous Blackshaw skills of tact and diplomacy as he tried to placate the management who had been assured before the event that only a well-behaved crowd of old buffers ever attended BMC Dinners!

Before the evening's merriment a very interesting proposal did surface at that year's AGM under AOB, namely that 'when activities were concluded in working quarries that the BMC tried to ensure that the faces were left in good condition for climbing'. At the time it appeared a far-fetched proposition, but it seems that its proposer was ahead of the game for this is just what one planning application by a quarrying company, current in West Yorkshire, has agreed it will do on completion if allowed to cut stone.

In the summer of 1974 the Future Policy Group made its interim report to Management, minus any reference to training, and a key recommendation was to move the Council out of London up to Manchester, to be more in the geographical centre of British climbing. In tandem with this was the recommendation for the recruitment of a professional General Secretary and the doing away of the Honorary post; the change in the role of the National Officer to concentrate on the technical/participation areas of the sport; a change in the specialist committee structure to complement these recommendations with an Executive to be set up composed of the elected Officers, plus the General Secretary to deal with urgent situations; and new forums to be set up to deal with finance, publications, huts, training, international affairs, amenities, access and conservation. Any less skilful mover than Blackshaw might have run into major opposition with such radical proposals, but by carefully staged announcements, such as reading a paper at Buxton in the preceding March, and the printing of a discussion document (a green paper) in *Mountain Life*, by the time the report did reach Management much of its radicalism appeared to be by common consent, and in the Autumn it was overwhelmingly agreed that the Council would restructure its organisation and move north. The MLTB agreed to come with us, and the search began for a new HQ.

In September 1974 the first Management Meeting was held in Manchester (at the YMCA) and on 1st October I was appointed the first General Secretary. Shortly afterwards I recruited Rita Hallam, to help plan the move to Manchester and to become the Council's Assistant Secretary/Office Manager, a post she was to fill with dedication for more than a decade during which she became synonymous with the initials BMC. In November of that year Peter Boardman was appointed as the new National Officer and Fred Smith became the Secretary of the MLTB. Meanwhile Rita and I looked at office buildings in Sale, Stockport and Manchester City Centre, all to no avail, until a chance conversation between a member of the Manchester University MC and Ken Wilson led me to approach the University to see if they could accommodate us. They not only could, in their new Precinct Centre then just nearing completion, but they offered us a deal that was hard to refuse with the rent a fraction of that then being paid in London.

It was heartening how the Manchester climbing fraternity of those days rallied to help the BMC move north. A Stockport removal firm run by climbers carried out the physical move, whilst the office was planned for us, and the contracted work of wiring, partitioning, decorating and fitting out was superintended by a member of the Rucksack Club, Stuart Beal. The firm which did this for us was so battened down on their pricing by Stuart that they eventually went broke fortunately not until they had finished kitting out Crawford House. This was completed in January 1975 and the move was made out of London, and the Manchester office opened on 11th February marked by a celebratory party, followed by a public lecture by Kurt Diemberger in the Free Trade Hall. The move to Manchester meant saying good-bye to Kip Gilpin who had served us well in London, but we were able to keep in touch when he joined The Sports Council staff at our departure. I would like here to pay a tribute to the late Fred Briscoe of that organisation who, as our Liaison Officer, supported the BMC strongly in our forward plans, including relocation.

A new HQ meant many new faces, particularly amongst the volunteers. One of the most significant changes besides the setting up of the new structures recommended by the Future Policy Group, was the birth of the Technical Committee chaired by Vin Machin with Peter Boardman as Secretary. Spawned from the old Equipment Committee and the Safety Committee this new forum immediately swung into action. One of its first actions was a meeting with the specialist mountaineering trade from which came various joint initiatives, including: the setting up of an equipment pool for expeditions, run successfully for several years by Ian Parsons; some joint testing programmes, including continuing to test ropes at the National Engineering Laboratory (work already begun by the old Equipment Committee); and the creation of a Trade category of membership. The positive aspects of moving to Manchester was that there was a dynamic climbing scene at the University headed by Joe Tasker and Dick Renshaw who quickly made themselves at home (particularly Joe who loved to sit in my office discussing part imaginary, part definite, mountaineering trips around the globe), that we had many more volunteers to draw upon; we had our own meeting room that we could use day and night (which we did) and much more space to work and move around in. However, we quickly found the downside was that our neighbourhood made our previous home in Knightsbridge seem idyllic in terms of being a crime-free zone.

The most amazing incident of many in this field was when Peter discovered some youths trying to break into the office in broad daylight, shortly after we arrived in Manchester. He chased them and rattled their ear holes a little, but later that day they returned armed with a high-powered air rifle and shot a pellet through our window that missed Rita's head by inches as she sat typing a pile of letters. The hole in the window just above her head left us in no doubt that she would have been seriously injured had the projectile hit her! There are many more such stories to recount, such as when my car was being stolen and I dived in the back as it was being driven away and grappled with the thief; or when Rita walked out to the carpark after working late one night to find her car bricked up in the air and all 4 wheels missing; or even when Tim Clifford and my son Stephen agreed to go to the bank for us one Friday lunch-time and they were mugged as they came out carrying £30 for petty cash. Fortunately, although Tim who was holding the money was beaten up, he recovered, but if it had been the other way round, and they had been attacked before entering the Bank, the thieves would have got away with thousands of pounds, for it was the height of the insurance season.

We were not deterred, however, by these happenings, and the BMC meeting room was henceforth used for everything from literature festivals, survival conferences, to one or two good old knees-ups, particularly when we had our regular get-togethers with the Trade. On occasions one of our Trade members (Troll) would supply a barrel of beer to help lubricate the evening's happenings.

In March 1975 we held our first gathering in the BMC meeting room to discuss climbing walls with interested parties, including architects, planners, local authority centre managers, designers, Sports Council. Over 20 representatives attended, and it was agreed that from hereon the BMC, via its National Officer, would provide an input and take a major interest in the development of any future projects. Discussions also began that month, via a suggestion from the Mountain Guides Association, for another national hut to be built in Scotland, perhaps on Ben Nevis. It was a controversial idea that had both its keen supporters and detractors, but which did lead to a compromise several years later when the Onich Hut was acquired, which sadly became a memorial to a future National Officer, Alex MacIntyre.

The AGM of 1975 was held at Eyam, and the Management decisions were greeted with enthusiasm by the membership, except that a further area was identified that needed a specialist group, namely Public Relations. The Council, via its representatives, was finding itself being called upon more and more to give opinions and to speak to the media in defence of the sport. So a committee was formed to advise in this area and to monitor our performance, with Audrey Salkeld as Secretary and myself in the Chair, and with such media gurus as Ned Kelly, Leo Dickinson, Alistair Macdonald and Tom Waghorn in membership. After the first meeting of this Committee, occurred an incident I will never forget. I was giving Audrey and Ned (both based in Bristol) a lift to Piccadilly Station and we had to stop at a set of traffic lights on the way. Coming to rest behind a large car parked in front of us it became obvious to us that two men in this car were engaged in some kind of furious struggle. Suddenly this spilled out on to the pavement and then: "Watch out, one of them has a gun". It was true, I realised, as the weapon held in the hand of one man was being wrestled with by the other, and it swung back and forth past the windows of my car which, being a summer's day, were wide open. "Duck" and we all three went down on the floor, then up again as we sat mesmerised by the action. One guy was calling out: "Help me, he's trying to rob me". But who was the goodie and who was the baddie? Suddenly it was over and the man who had been trying to grab the gun, managed to overpower the one who was holding it. It transpired that he was the goodie and the other chap had jumped into his car, produced a firearm and demanded his wallet. He had pretended to do this, but as he handed it over, he bravely grabbed at the robber's gun-hand: hence the life-or-death struggle we had witnessed. As the goodie frog-marched the baddie off to find a policeman, with a hand forced up his back, Ned turned to Audrey and me and warmly congratulated us on organising such an interesting first meeting of the BMC Public Relations Committee!

Two other notable events in 1975 were the decisions to form a Committee for Wales, made up of all the clubs and individuals in the Principality, which up until that date had been included in either the North Wales Area Committee or the South-West & Southern; and the success of the National Officer, Peter Boardman, in being one of the three Britons who successfully climbed Everest's South-West Face. The latter gave a tremendous fillip to the standing of the Council. This was further enhanced when the BMC managed to resolve long-standing access difficulties (at least for the time being) at both Cheddar and Swanage where the problems were overcome at both sites by voluntary agreements. But more and more frequently, despite these latter successes, access and conservation matters were occupying BMC voluntary effort, for it was during this period that many regular climbing grounds were being designated as SSIs, which required careful monitoring by the Council. Early in 1976 the BMC, because of its increased fears on conservation grounds, decided that it would oppose the setting up of any new long-distance footpath in the mountain areas of the UK.

The AGM and Annual Dinner in 1976 were held in the Stickle Barn, Langdale, and Denis Howell, the then Minister of Sport, was the guest of honour. Before he was allowed to eat and speak, he was taken climbing for the first (and last?) time in his life by Peter Boardman on Middlefell Buttress, which excited much press coverage. At this AGM it was agreed to appoint a permanent representative to the UIAA, in view of the growing importance of that body, which position the Management Committee decided I should fulfil in order to achieve continuity, as I had been attending the meetings for some while by that date. At this AGM, Bob Pettigrew was elected President to succeed Alan Blackshaw, John Neill was made an Honorary Member, plans for a new insurance scheme were announced (which has since gone from strength to strength), and the merger of *Mountain Life* with *Climber* was agreed. It was also decided to form a Trust to help with fund-raising and a Limited Company to run the BMC's commercial activities (publishing, insurance and other services), in order to avoid undue financial risk to the Council.

It is interesting to also note who were the Vice-Presidents of the BMC at this crucial handing over of the reins of office by Alan Blackshaw. The two retiring officers who stood down with him were John Wilkinson and Don Whillans, whilst Eric Byrom continued to serve. All these three climbers had supported the Council's restructuring enthusiastically whilst the two incoming new Vice-Presidents, Chris Bonington and John Cunningham, were equally committed in their support for change. It is worth noting here that within the first two years of arriving in Manchester the overall membership of the BMC doubled in strength.

1976 developed into a year of mixed fortunes for the BMC. The Buxton Conference was oversubscribed and every ticket sold. The revised insurance scheme was launched and was immediately successful. A new Stanage guide produced by the Peak Area Guidebook Team, aided by the Publications Committee, sold 600 copies in its first week of sales; this was followed by a volume to the Chew Valley which was not so successful. Peter Boardman and Joe Tasker achieved the epic first ascent of the West Face of Changabang. The Council, via its South-West Area, solved the access problems surrounding climbing at Avon Gorge. The Eric Byne Memorial Campsite was set up in the Peak District, partly at the initiative of the Area Committee. And the BMC was one of the prime movers in securing a rejection at the UIAA of a move by the Russian delegates at the General Meeting in Geneva to promote speed climbing competitions internationally. However, everything else was overshadowed by the developments surrounding mountain training.

The Council adopted the Hunt Report as its future policy in September 1976 and, with its radical recommendations particularly that the BMC should have the controlling voice in the policies adopted by the MLTB, it immediately ran into considerable opposition from certain of the existing members of the Board led by their redoubtable Chairman, Jack Longland. Both sides took up strong positions and the scene was set for major confrontation which was exacerbated by the fact that the MLTB had never had a Constitution, It had, up to that date, run on an old chums basis with little or no standing on ceremony, a need for votes, or a legal basis to justify its existence. In retrospect this was one of the key reasons why the situation became so fraught, and why it escalated so quickly. The MLTB rejected the Hunt Report after the BMC had accepted it as policy. This put the Council in a quandary. How to resolve a situation where you had an unelected body, at that date responsible financially to the BMC, and administered by it, but without any formal means of influencing its decisions other than via its own representatives on the Board who were, in any case, a minority of the membership. Several meetings were held and instead of resolving the position, relations worsened, and by the middle of 1977 a stalemate had been reached and so the BMC Management decided to set up a working party to draft a Constitution for the Board.

Many other events were happening whilst this was on-going, and for instance, the BMC met representatives of the Mountain Rescue Committee who stressed the need to keep the service voluntary. The Lancashire & Cheshire Area Committee was formed in September of that year: a serious access problem at Chapel Head Scar was resolved, and agreement reached with the landowners and the Cumbria Naturalists' Trust which allowed climbing to continue.

At a meeting between the Management and the Guidebook/Publications Committee it was agreed that the possibility of a selected guidebook to the Peak District would be considered; this finally came to pass two decades later! Concrete investigations began with a view to obtaining a second national hut in Scotland. The Climbers' Club suggested Ballachulish, but the British Association of Mountain Guides opted for a site high on Ben Nevis at the side of Lochan Meall an t-Suidhe. The Guides were also refused membership of the International Union of Mountain Guides (UIAGM), leading the BMC to support more strongly their application to join the UIAGM. The BMC's influence at the UIAA and with the UIAGM did help them gain this important cachet, which they achieved a short while later.

Besides the Mountain Training dispute and running almost parallel was another difficult area within Mountain Training to resolve the future role within the sport of Plas y Brenin. The BMC had, via its representatives and Management Committee, been voicing concern for a considerable period about the role of the Centre. Under The Sports Council's aegis it had assumed unto itself the title of the National Mountaineering Centre, and high levels of spending were being sanctioned without any clearly defined objectives, or an agreed role in the sports it served. Happily this did not disintegrate into the kind of confrontation surrounding the future of the MLTB, and the situation was resolved partly as a result of a BMC paper written by Ken Wilson and myself, which led to a working party being formed under the Chairmanship of Edwin Hammond, a former Committee for Wales member. This helped to diffuse the situation and led to relations between the BMC and Plas y Brenin eventually becoming one of mutual help and support.

The BMC adopted a Constitution for the MLTB in early January 1978 and called a meeting of all the interested parties, but Jack Longland and most members of the original Board refused to accept this and decided to continue meeting as of old, which they did separately without the BMC being represented. At this juncture Jack was able to play his ace for The Sports Council intervened (he was Vice-Chairman of that organisation) and they cut our grant drastically, claiming that we were no longer administering the Board. This was despite the fact that the day-to-day work of registration, course information and supplying relevant publications to candidates continued as normal from the BMC office. The Council responded by appealing to all its members to write to their MP, which hundreds did, demanding the reinstatement of our full grant. The Mountain Training dispute was by that date national news and even the Sunday Times ran a major feature giving the background detail and, although Jack and his Board may have had the ear of the establishment, the BMC began to win the media battle being characterised as a poor downtrodden national voluntary sports body ill-used by heartless bureaucrats in a David and Goliath struggle.

At this juncture things were getting financially desperate for the BMC. Besides having our grant cut we were having one of our periodic battles with HM Inspector of Taxes, and two burly figures were encamped at the BMC demanding vast sums of money and threatening dire consequences for our poor Hon Treasurer Brian Monk and myself, if we did not pay up. We had to confess that we could not meet their demands and, in retrospect, it is fortunate that we could not for many months later, after many subsequent meetings and an appeal, we managed to reduce the amount to be paid to a fraction of the original figure. At least our standing in the climbing world was rising ever higher, for it was seen by its actions in this dispute that the BMC was not a lap dog of any establishment and that it would defend the sport if it was thought necessary.

Then Denis Howell the Minister for Sport decided to involve himself and sent for me and took me on a three-mile walk to hear our side of the story. "For God's sake call off your MP baiters." he pleaded "I can't go into the bar or the tea rooms at the House without being button-holed by some MP or other demanding I settle the mountain training dispute!". But he could not interfere with the workings of The Sports Council this

(*above*) The BMC's Dennis Gray, lobbies Sheffield Wednesday Manager and Sports Council member, Jack Charlton, during the mountain training dispute — the Sports Council had cut the BMC's grant after it (the BMC) reconstituted the MLTB in order to enact the recommendations of the Hunt Report.

because of its independent Royal Charter, only give advice. "Get hold
of Jack Longland, have a few drinks and find a compromise for goodness
sake; you climbers are all stark staring mad!" A few days later Jack did
'phone me and we did meet in secret in a pub just outside Buxton. At the
meeting we laughed loud and long at how we had tried to blacken each
other's case, and the manoeuvres each side had used against the other,
and I would like to record just how highly I did regard Jack for he, like
us, was standing up for what he saw was right, without malice or
vindictiveness, but we both had to agree that we were in a hole and
needed to find a way out.

Almost immediately after this event, but totally independently, the
Alpine Club, via its President Peter Lloyd, contacted both sides and
offered to set up an arbitration panel if both sides would immediately
agree a 'truce'. On 22nd February 1978 the BMC Management
Committee accepted this offer, as did Jack and his supporters just a short
while later.

Unfortunately just before this happened, Peter Boardman decided to
resign as National Officer as he had been offered the post of Director at
the ISM in Leysin, Switzerland, in succession to Dougal Haston who
had been killed whilst skiing, engulfed in an avalanche. Peter wished to
spend more of his time in writing and climbing, for his ambitions lay in
the fields of Alpinism and Himalayan mountaineering, and though we
were all sad to see him leave, everyone with whom he had come into
contact at the BMC recognised his brilliance and accepted that the job at
Leysin provided him with a unique opportunity. On the 1st March 1978,
Alex MacIntyre was appointed National Officer to succeed Peter and, in
retrospect, it is amazing that the Council had two climbers of such
outstanding abilities both on and off the mountains to fulfil such a key
role within the BMC for almost a decade. Each brought to the Council
different skills, different styles: Peter, diplomacy, thoughtfulness and
caring. Alex was thrusting, pushy, legalistic for his university degree
was in Law, and one of the first tasks he undertook at the Council was to
write a paper on Legal Liability and Climbing (the first of several such
documents to be prepared by the BMC over the next decade).

The setting up of the Mountain Training arbitration proceedings, and
the preparing of the necessary documents to present the BMC's case,
took up a massive amount of time for almost the whole of the next year.
It was agreed by the Management Committee that Dr Will Butler, a Vice-
President and top cancer specialist, would present the BMC's case whilst
Jack Longland's group elected Roger Putnam, Warden of Eskdale
Outward Bound, to represent them. At least one good thing to come of
was that the BMC's full grant was restored and there was once again

only one MLTB serviced from the BMC office, with Dave Humphrey drafted in from Plas y Brenin to serve as acting Secretary until agreement could be reached about the future role of the Board.

In retrospect the 1978/79 period was a hectic one over access and conservation issues, for they were emerging with such regularity that at its Management meeting in November 1978, it was agreed that as soon as financially possible the Council would appoint a professional Access Officer. There were serious problems at Tremadog due to a huge rock fall; and Mrs Williams, the owner of Bwlch y Moch, invited the BMC to take the crag into ownership (which it did a short while later). Hugencroft, our longest-standing access problem, developed and is still on-going at the time of writing; the Roaches area, had been acquired from the Brocklebank Estate by a private owner who insisted on charging climbers to climb; and a vigorous campaign, led by our then Peak Area Secretary, Mark Vallance, was begun to resist this. The North West Water Authority tried to institute a permit system for climbing on its land, and yet another campaign, spearheaded by the Lancashire & Cheshire Area Committee, finally defeated this imposition.

Investigations during 1978 convinced the BMC that the majority of climbers were against a hut high on Ben Nevis. Alex MacIntyre prepared a questionnaire and circulated this widely and it was obvious from the replies that, as agreed by The Mountaineering Council of Scotland, there was a need for a hut to be sited in the valley, not on the Ben. By chance we found out that our neighbours in Manchester, the CHA, had a cottage at Onich, which lay unused in the winter: early in 1979 we agreed to rent this for a trial period during the following winter of 1979–80 to see if there was a demand for such accommodation.

In that same month a national guidebook meeting was held when the BMC took the initiative and called together all the clubs in the UK responsible for their production (CC, FRCC, YMC etc), with a view to pooling expertise and improving our editing and production methods. Also at that time a climbing wall panel was convened, for the burgeoning number of such facilities was demanding more and more BMC effort, and it was agreed that a joint publication would be prepared by the BMC and Sports Council for publication during 1979.

At the AGM of 1979, held in the Lake District, Bob Pettigrew stood down as BMC President, and it is to him more than any other single person that the Council owes a successful outcome to the Training Dispute. An educational advisor himself, he nevertheless identified totally with the BMC's cause and was resolute throughout the whole period in maintaining the Council's position as set out by the Hunt Report. Joe Walmsley succeeded Bob and within a few weeks was faced with the daunting prospect of being one of the BMC's witnesses at the Mountain Training Dispute tribunal. This must have been an event almost unique in climbing history, for it had all the court room drama of a Hollywood soap opera. Held in the Lands Tribunal at the Inns of Court on 30–31 May 1979 in front of the arbitrators, and Chaired by Mr J. H. Emlyn Jones, a distinguished Alpine Club member, and head of the Tribunal, witnesses were called and cross-examined, and papers submitted. Dr Will Butler performed so well whilst presenting the BMC's case that the Clerk of the Court thought he was some Barrister we had retained from the Northern Circuit. Roger Putnam acquitted himself equally well, thoughtfully presenting the other side's case with skill and care, but soon it was all over and both parties had to wait and sweat it out to await the adjudication.

Meanwhile much else was happening at the BMC; a ban on climbing at Pant Ifan, Tremadog was lifted after a meeting between the Committee for Wales and the Nature Conservancy Council. John Bradley, the Brecons National Park Officer and a keen climber, took on the Chair of the Access & Conservation Committee. The BMC set itself up to sell to its members by mail order climbing ropes, manufactured to UIAA standards, by a company within the Manchester conurbation. This was in order to raise extra funds to help finance, amongst other activities, an Access Officer. The effect of this mail order venture was to have far reaching consequences on our Trade relations, for it was greeted by them with dismay; and so at the end of 1979 we convened a meeting with manufacturers and retailers in Manchester to discuss our mutual positions. They objected strongly to the BMC moving into specialist retailing, but after the BMC's needs were explained a compromise was reached. They would help us by joining the Council in larger numbers as Trade members, and in order to help develop our relations with them, they would allow us a free stand each year at the Camping and Outdoor Leisure Exhibition, which is the shop window in the UK for the specialist Trade. Trade sponsors also came forward to underwrite the overseas speakers at Buxton Conferences and helped us with advertising costs. So with these inducements, we retreated from our 'rope trick', and excellent relations have been maintained between the Trade and the BMC ever since.

1979 was without doubt a year of such significance in BMC history that one can declare it a truly historic one to end the decade. During the summer occurred two events without parallel before or since. First was the Christopher Marsh case, which came about as a result of a terrible fatality in the Alps, when 8 climbers died on the Tour Ronde and a 17-year old British climber was initially blamed and threatened with a charge of manslaughter by the French Police. The BMC had by that date very good contacts in France, including the Officers of the FFM and CAF, and with their help, particularly that of Vincent Renard in Paris, a barrister was briefed in Grenoble at the BMC's expense and eventually after a Justice's review the case was dismissed.

The other happening had not so successful an outcome, for by the late 1970s the Peregrine Falcon was re-establishing itself on many of our cliffs due to the banning in that era of the use of DDT. This fact was not widely appreciated, nor had the BMC then such close ties with the RSPB. That summer two Lakeland climbers were prosecuted for disturbing these birds on Rainsbarrow Crag in Kentmere. This had been done inadvertently by the climbers concerned, who were totally unaware of the Peregrines' presence, but it did lead the Council into urgent meetings with the bird protection lobby, and since that date, via a series of voluntary agreements almost universally recognised by climbers, such sanctions have not again been used against us.

At the end of 1979 the arbitrators' report on the Mountain Training Dispute was published and it was quickly accepted by both the BMC and the whole MLTB. Its main recommendations were that the Board should be re-styled the Mountainwalking Leader Training Board, that the Mountaineering Instructors Certificate (MIC) should become the responsibility of the BMC, and that the Mountain Leadership Certificate should be replaced by a log book system that reflected more truly the low technical standard of the award.

The BMC was to have the largest number of seats on a newly formed Board which should be independent in policy making, but continue to be administered from the Council's office with a joint BMC/MLTB administrator to be appointed. This officer would also service a new Training Committee which would be responsible for the MIC and any courses the Council decided to organise for its members, some of which it had already begun to plan in the Alps for novice training in 1980. A further body, the Standing Advisory Committee, was to be set up with wide representation, but answerable to the BMC, to present an overview to the Council (and other bodies) on the policies and developments in the whole field of mountain training. Thus the 1970s after so much fractious debate, argument and dissension were to finish on a note of co-operation and high optimism which was highlighted when the BMC was able to appoint a part-time Access Officer, Mark Hutchinson, who commenced work in December of that year. It was a fitting outcome to a remarkable decade of progress for the BMC.

Dennis Gray

The Eighties

The first part of this decade was marked by the rapid development of several new UK climbing areas, perhaps most significantly South Pembroke. This pioneering led on to a potentially serious conflict between climbers and conservationists which happily was resolved to everybody's satisfaction after a round of meetings between the National Park, the RSPB and the BMC. The BMC's appointment of Mark Hutchinson as Access Officer had been made not a moment too soon, and, working with local activists, particularly Pat Littlejohn and members of the South Wales MC, several voluntary access agreements were hammered out which are still the basis for allowing climbing activity to take place in Pembroke to this day.

There were many other access and conservation issues during 1980, and perhaps the biggest single action surrounded the battle to stop water extraction by the Water Boards and British Nuclear Fuels from Ennerdale and Wastwater. The Council joined together with other amenity bodies (Friends of the Lake District, RA, CHA, etc.) to oppose this, and eventually such was the public outcry, the application was rejected.

The new MLTB held its first meeting in February 1980 and shortly after this event Jack Longland retired as Chairman of the Board (he was succeeded by Wally Keay) and at the same time he also stood down as Chairman of the Management Committee of Plas y Brenin, where the Council held its AGM that year. The BMC representatives on both of the bodies made it plain at these events how much they respected Sir Jack, and it was fitting that a short while later the Management Committee offered him Honorary Membership of the Council which he accepted happily and without rancour at past disagreement. Another long-serving Honorary Officer who stood down during 1980 was the Peak District Guidebook Series Editor, Dave Gregory. During his term of office he had overseen six guidebooks and a recent developments new route book and, along with his successor Geoff Milburn, he was the bedrock on which the unrivalled standing of the series was built.

The National Mountaineering Conference of April 1980 witnessed another full house and the guest of honour, Warren Harding, received an ovation at the end of his talk on the Saturday night which those of us who were there will never forget. Shortly before this event a strong party of Polish climbers visited Scotland as guests of the BMC for winter climbing, and later that year a party of French women came to climb in the Peak District and North Wales, a group which included a brilliant young star, Catherine Destivelle, who impressed everybody with her virtuosity.

The BMC held its first Alpine Training Course that summer in Ailefroide with four one-week courses, staffed by British Mountain Guides and directed by Dauphiné guru John Brailsford, which were very successful. The relations between the Council and the Guides, for whom the Council continued to provide the administration, were further cemented when Peter Boardman, a BMC Vice-President, became their Chairman. Such initiatives, and the provision of insurance, began to lead on to the steady, upward growth in individual membership, a trend which has continued up to the present day. Finally at the end of 1980 Alex MacIntyre decided to leave the BMC in order to further his ambition in the field of lightweight Himalayan climbing, and we had to bid farewell to someone who, like Peter Boardman, had grown so much in stature while working for the Council that on leaving he left a massive void that was hard to fill.

Because of financial considerations it was then decided to combine the positions of National Officer and Access Officer for a trial period, and Mark Hutchinson moved over to Alex MacIntyre's former desk early in 1982 with the General Secretary taking on some of the technical workload. Chris Dodd was appointed the BMC/MLTB's first Training Administrator in May 1981 and besides servicing SACOMT and the MLTB had also to monitor the work of the new Training Committee, chaired by former BMC President Bob Pettigrew, which was expanding rapidly. It is interesting to note that by this date the office was answering over 10,000 letters a year, mainly from climbers seeking advice on everything from expedition planning to climbing wall design.

The 1981 AGM was held at the then home of Lancashire climbing, The Black Dog Inn at Belmont. Joe Walmsley continued as President, but Brian Monk, the BMC's long-serving Honorary Treasurer, retired having served his maximum sentence allowed under the constitution! The Executive of the UIAA hosted by the BMC met at Ambleside in April 1981 and, for once, the weather was kind and the sun shone throughout the whole weekend. Some delegates managed to climb in Langdale and on Castle Rock with masses of daffodils in bloom around their feet, and all the overseas visitors departed believing that the English Lake District was a most wondrous place. That year saw the introduction of the UIAA Reciprocal Rights scheme under which BMC members, on payment of a fee for a Carnet, gained rights in huts belonging to all the major Alpine countries (CAF, DAV, CAS, CAI, OAV etc.), whilst parties from Switzerland and Israel came to climb in the UK as guests of the Council.

Finally, the publication in 1982 of two Peak Area Guidebooks, *Derwent Valley* and *The Staffordshire Area* marked the end of that series, and to celebrate this event and as a thank you, a party for all guidebook workers was held at The Swan, New Mills at which a presentation was made to Dave Gregory, the retiring Editor.

At the 1982 AGM held at Ambleside, Tom Price was elected President, and a new Constitution was adopted which enfranchised individual members. This allowed them to hold office, attend area meetings and gave them the right to vote at AGMs. This was one of the most significant events in the Council's history for this new Constitution also enshrined in its provisions the principal of one member one vote. The Council was further able to increase its services by offering cheap travel on bus routes to Chamonix, the Verdon and other Continental destinations. A great fillip in 1982 was the refusal of planning permission, after the long drawn-out Cairngorm (Lurchers) Inquiry (at which the MCofS/BMC had been objectors) to a further development of ski lifts and another access road, resulting in a successful outcome to preserving one of the major mountain regions of this country.

The BMC hosted two of its most important International Meets in the Summer when it organised an International Women's rock-climbing gathering in June, and in September a strong party of American climbers came to the UK. The climbing achievements on these meets was outstanding, especially by several young participants who have subsequently made a significant impact on our sport. The Buxton Conference of 1982 was yet another milestone in development with more overseas speakers than before. It was the Saturday night lecture 'My Life and Hard Times' by Don Whillans however which, as they say in show business, knocked them dead!

So much happened in 1982 that I can record just a few more of the highlights. The new-style Mountaineering Instructors Certificate was introduced: It was the 50th anniversary of the founding of the UIAA, and the General Assembly that year was held for the first time in Asia in Kathmandu. 1982 witnessed a real surge in the provision of modern climbing walls when new developments opened at both Altrincham and Plas y Brenin. The financial success of the Peak Guidebook series enabled the BMC to help two member clubs with their programmes, and loans were made both to the Climbers' Club to produce a new Ogwen guide, as well as to the South Wales MC to produce a definitive guide to their area.

Looming over the whole year, however, was tragedy; first Peter Boardman and Joe Tasker disappeared high on Mount Everest. Then in the autumn, Alex MacIntyre was killed by stonefall whilst attempting a new route on the South Face of Annapurna. Thus, despite all the other positive developments throughout 1982, it remains a bleak period because of the loss of two of the BMC's most illustrious supporters.

1983 was a much happier year with perhaps the best ever winter conditions in Scotland enjoyed by four top Japanese climbers who visited the UK in February as guests of the Council, whilst the BMC, via its long-running expedition grant scheme, was able to make awards to a record number of groups climbing in remote ranges abroad. Two of the most significant breakthroughs in the field of access for climbing occurred at this time. Hobson Moor Quarry was compulsorily purchased by Tameside Metropolitan District Council in order to secure access for rock-climbing the first time any Council had ever taken such action on our behalf. Then, partly as a result of many years work by our former Hon Secretary, Hilary Sinclair, the amended Occupiers Liability Act was passed into Law. This relieved landowners of liability in allowing free access to land for recreational purposes. Another significant event was the purchase by the BMC/MC of S of the Onich Hut as a memorial to Alex MacIntyre.

The new series Stanage/Millstone guide appeared in April and was a runaway success with over 2,000 copies sold by the end of 1983. Climbing wall developments continued apace, demanding that a working party, chaired by Ken Wilson, be set up to advise the Management Committee on their best future design and management. Ian Dunn was appointed professional Technical Officer on a part-time basis mainly to service this work. It is surprising to recall now that at this juncture Britain probably still led the world in this field, as instanced by the visit paid by a high-powered French delegation, funded by their Ministry of Sport, led by Yves Ballu and including Jean-Marc Blanc and Patrick Edlinger, to study British climbing-wall provision.

Both the UIAA and the BMC set up new Future Policy Groups in 1983 and in the Council's case a group was assembled under the chairmanship of Dr Will Butler with the brief from Management to chart developments for the next five years, in anticipation of preparing the BMC's first Corporate Plan.

At the beginning of 1984 the BMC invited the Standing Advisory Committee on Mountain Training to advise on its future role at Plas y Brenin. It had been voicing concern for a considerable period about the escalating deficit, the safety record and the policies being pursued by

The Sports Council at the Centre. A small working group under Alan Blackshaw was set up, and happily, after discussions between that body, the new Director of the Centre, Dave Alcock, and the BMC, the situation was resolved amicably and a joint liaison group was set up.

The Buxton Conference of March 1984 was the one that climbers still talk about, partly because of its cabaret 'The Miss Buxton Competition', won by Don Whillans, but also because of its galaxy of speakers, which included two of the most outstanding mountaineers of all time, Ales Kunaver from Yugoslavia and the one and only Walter Bonatti. Ales was killed just a few months later in a helicopter crash in the Julian Alps, but anyone who met him could never forget this most international of climbers, nor those who heard Bonatti speak, fail to be inspired. The BMC lost two more of its keenest supporters at this time when Jack Bloor, the former Chairman of the Yorkshire and Humberside Committee, succumbed to cancer, and Bob Gookey, Chairman of the London and South-East Committee, was killed in the Cairngorms.

In May 1984, Rita Hallam, the BMC's long-serving office manager, who had become the Council's major domo, left to move to Scotland and she was replaced later in the year by Lesley Smithson. Another sad event in 1984 was the death of the Yorkshire MC President and Rock & Ice member, John Midgeley. At the request of his friends who raised the necessary purchase price, Aldery Cliff was bought by the BMC in order to secure access as a memorial to this fine climber, whilst the Yorkshire Dales National Park, partly at the urging of the Council, bought Crookrise, which guarantees climbing activities at the outcrop.

During 1984 the Technical Committee was involved in much work, helping to further develop the UIAA standards which had then become widely used, for ropes, harnesses, helmets etc., and two very important instructional publication initiatives were undertaken. The Technical Committee (with Trade support) produced the first of its booklets *Knots* and at the end of the year there appeared *Mountaincraft and Leadership* published by the MLTB and the Scottish Sports Council. As one of the most useful and informative books in mountaineering history this has subsequently sold tens of thousands of copies.

The 1985 AGM of the Council was held in the Peak District and Tom Price handed over to John Neill as President. A controversial issue was the BMC's magazine connection and it was agreed that the Council would move from *Climber* to *High* as its 'official organ' in May of that year. The decision was seen by some as badly advised, but in subsequent financial benefits alone it has proved its worth. Computerisation began in earnest under the direction of our new Office Manager, Lesley

Smithson, whilst the Peak guidebooks were being similarly formatted. The Climbing Wall Working Party reported to Management in June 1985 and its report was approved by them and The Sports Council which agreed to publish their document as a formal guide to the design and management of such facilities. Many new public walls were built in this period (15 in 1985) and so the BMC decided to set up a permanent sub-committee to monitor these developments.

The first National Youth Meet was held at North Lees Farm, Stanage, that summer and 80 young climbers from all over the UK attended. A few weeks later almost unannounced due to a misunderstanding over invitations a party of five Korean climbers arrived in Manchester and climbed in Yorkshire and the Peak District. A short while after they had left, a strong team of French climbers led by Jean Claude Droyer and including Isabelle Patissier and Alain Gherson visited and climbed in North Wales, the Peak and Yorkshire as guests of the BMC. Meanwhile many British climbers continued to attend similar fixtures abroad, for instance, Gill Price, Martin Atkinson, Mandy Glanville and Ben Moon represented the BMC that summer at a climbing meet organised by our French counterparts, the FFME, at Fontainebleau and Verdon.

The Access Committee organised its first ever national crag clean-up day, a follow-on to its adopt-a-crag campaign, which was well supported by dozens of different groups the length and breadth of the country, but it is sad to note that this was the year that the Craig y Forwen access difficulties first developed. The BMC in 1985 once again lost some of its best known members with the deaths of Bill Peascod, a former Vice-President, on Cloggy, Roger Baxter-Jones on the Triolet, Charles Marriott and another former Vice-President Don Whillans. The latter perhaps was the greatest British mountaineer of his or any other generation.

The Future Policy Review was completed early in 1986 and approved by the Management Committee. This was then translated into the BMC's first ever Corporate Plan by the Council's Hon Treasurer Mike Watson and myself, which was then submitted to The Sports Council and by the end of the year it was approved.

The 1986 AGM was held in Llanberis and for once it was a lively affair with a motion of censure being proposed by Ken Wilson and seconded by Audrey Salkeld. It cited poor communications between the various BMC committees, and although this did at least ensure a keen interest in the event there was little or no support for the proposal.

At this time both Mark Hutchinson and Ian Dunn left the BMC, and Andy Fanshawe was appointed National Officer with the same remit as had been enjoyed by Peter Boardman and Alex MacIntyre, whilst the Council continued to negotiate with The Sports Council for the appropriate grant aid to appoint a full-time Access Officer.

In March the biennial Buxton Conference saw yet another full house, and many lectures and events were held during the year on behalf of the Don Whillans memorial fund. In June a strong party of Czechoslovakian climbers visited the Peak District, Cornwall and North Wales and they were without doubt the boldest solo and leading rock jocks that we had entertained to that date, with 6b on-sight solos in Cornwall and ascents of routes such as Strawberries.

Every year, however, seems to have had its share of tragedies, but 1986 was exceptional for in that Winter John Bradley, Chair of the Access Committee and National Park Officer, died whilst traversing his beloved Brecon Beacons, and that summer witnessed the terrible series of events on K2. Amongst others, Alan Rouse, a BMC Vice-President, and Julie Tullis both died. This led to two memorials being set up in their memory: the first was The Alan Rouse Climbing Wall in Sheffield, organised by the BMC which commenced building at Christmas 1986. The other, a camp site at Harrison's Rocks which did not open until 1994, was a memorial to Julie.

The second National Youth Meet was again held at Stanage in July 1986, and attendance was slightly down on the previous year, with 70 young climbers attending. In September three Indian climbers visited the UK as guests of the Council, attended a two-week instructional course at Plas y Brenin and climbed in the Peak District. Many British climbers once again went the other way to meets abroad, the most significant being a Rassemblement at ENSA in Chamonix for women climbers to celebrate the 200th Anniversary of the ascent of Mont Blanc at which Alison Hargreaves and Brede Arkless represented the BMC.

The move to *High* magazine produced an income of approximately £10,000 for the BMC in 1986 and, as the Council did not itself produce any guidebook, other than a National New Climbs booklet, and having funds in reserve, it was able to make a £6,000 loan to the Climbers' Club to produce a new *Dorset* guidebook. It also gave a grant of £2,000 towards the Alan Rouse Wall.

In March 1987 the Council organised a conference at Plas y Brenin, 'Training for rock-climbing', which saw a full house with 200 delegates present. This initiative was followed in the summer by practical training and testing sessions at RAF Cosford and Brunel. In retrospect, that year seems to have been overfull with such events, for a party of Polish climbers visited Scotland that winter whilst Soviet climbers were in the

Peak, Cornwall and North Wales in June. The first International Youth Meet was held in the Peak District in July 1987 and 80 young climbers attended from 11 countries. That year, on behalf of the UIAA, the BMC hosted a meeting of the Technical Commission at Leeds University in April, and the Medical Commission at St Bart's Hospital in London, courtesy of our own Medical Advisor, Dr Charlie Clark. Bill Wright was appointed as our first full-time Access Officer in May 1987, and many initiatives followed including another National Crag Clean-up Day which was well supported with 60 groups cleaning up a total of 80 sites throughout the UK.

The Peak Guidebooks scored a treble whammy during the year by publishing in 3 volumes all the limestone routes in the district, whilst the Publications Committee produced another National New Climbs volume, and a booklet *Ropes* by the Technical Committee. The Climbing Wall Report was finally published by The Sports Council to wide acclaim. The Training Committee, via a working party partly chaired by Peter Livesey, produced a proposal for a supervisors award in rock-climbing, but this was seen as too controversial and it was issued after wide debate in the form of an advisory guidance booklet only. However, this action, just a few years hence, led on to the Single Pitch Supervisors Award which is now so much in demand. Bob Pettigrew succeeded Wally Keay as Chairman of the MLTB and both the Board and the BMC further developed their in-house computerisation, with the installation of a desk-top publishing facility.

A hurricane hit the south of England in October 1987 and did massive damage to woodlands and the sandstone outcrops, particularly at Harrisons Rocks. Fortunately The Sports Council agreed to provide immediate financial assistance to help with remedial work and now, several years later after much hard work, most of the damage has been repaired. A happier event was the setting up of another memorial to Al Rouse in the form of a specialist library of mountaineering books in Sheffield, at the initiative of Geoff Birtles, Editor of *High*, who was joined that year by former Peak Chairman, Ian Smith, as Deputy Editor.

1987 was a successful financial year for the BMC. The Council finished with a surplus and, for the first time in many a year, was able to transfer funds into reserve.

The 1988 AGM was held at Bamford and John Neill handed over the Presidency to Chris Bonington. This meeting was dominated by the issues surrounding competition climbing, and it ended with a directive instructing the Council to embrace this new element of the sport, but only to agree to this taking place on artificial structures. This led to the Management Committee forming a Competitions Committee to oversee these developments under the Chairmanship of Stephen Porteus.

The Buxton Conference of that year was a sell-out in advance with Reinhold Messner giving the traditional Saturday night lecture, and the cabaret raising over £600; with £300 being donated to the Al Rouse Library and £300 towards the Julie Tullis Memorial.

That summer a meeting with the owners was held on Lundy and Bill Wright and other BMC representatives managed to secure an access agreement with a series of voluntary agreements aimed at bird protection. Also the Access Committee produced its well received leaflet *Tread Lightly* which has subsequently needed reprinting.

An International Youth Meet was held at Tremadog at the end of July and 100 participants from many countries attended. Several Czechoslovakian climbers were the stars of the meet, arriving in a 12-year old lorry which broke down and which delayed their departure home by over a week. Andy Fanshawe (fresh from his triumph on Menlungtse) and his next door neighbour chased around scrap yards the length and breadth of Manchester searching for the necessary spare parts to mend the thing.

BMC courses in the Alps that summer were even more well supported than previous years, and 93 participants attended whilst another 60 young people, aided by grants from the Jonathan Conville Trust, took part in a 3-day 'Introductions to Alpinism'. Both the Glen Brittle and Alex MacIntyre huts enjoyed successful years, with a surplus being recorded on both accounts.

Chris Dodd left the BMC at the end of 1988, finishing on a high note with the completion of the new edition of the best-selling booklet *Safety on Mountains*, written by John Barry and Tim Jepson. After over 17 years with the Council I decided in November to 'retire' in June 1989 for personal reasons and in order to make way for a new figure to head the Council's professional staff.

1989 proved to be a year of upheaval, change and new directions for the BMC. Derek Walker was appointed to the post of General Secretary to succeed me, whilst Iain Peter on 1st March was appointed Training Administrator to succeed Chris Dodd. In the summer Andy Fanshawe (who like Peter Boardman and Alex MacIntyre before him) wished to concentrate on 'expeditioning' left the BMC and shortly afterwards so did Lesley Smithson. Andy was succeeded by Roger Payne, and Lesley by Jayne Nicholson a former BMC employee who had been away for two years studying in Higher Education.

A trial Film Festival was held in Leeds on 8th-9th April 1989 which was a disaster in that everything that could go wrong did, with broken projectors and silent sound-bites, but in May the very first UIAA World

Cup Competition was organised by DMM/BMC in Leeds and despite teething problems was a rousing success, especially as it was a Briton who won – Jerry Moffatt. By the end of this series of competitions around the world, another Brit was pronounced the first 'World Champion' Simon Nadin!

The final International Youth Meet was held at Plas y Brenin that summer, organised by Andy Fanshawe as his farewell, for two days after it was completed he left the BMC for Makalu. It was perhaps the most successful of its genre for the sun shone throughout. The Access Committee organised a symposium where the major topic was the effects on our sport of 'Water Privatisation', and the MC of S managed to appoint a part-time professional officer, Kevin Howett, whose post was partly funded by a grant from the BMC.

Finally, work was completed during 1989 on the BMC's second Corporate Plan to commence 1st January 1990. Its major implications were a pressing need for additional professional support with a second Access Officer and a Competitions/Climbing Walls/Youth Officer to be appointed, both of which were eventually agreed with The Sports Council. This event, though boring to the general climbing public, reflected what was apparent at the end of the decade of the 1980s that everything was conspiring to increase participation levels in our sport, with more leisure time, both voluntary and forced, younger participants than ever before commencing to climb in droves, better climbing wall provision, and the effects of much more media exposure etc. This makes a most suitable point for me to finish my review, with a boom under way, and with more and more participants providing a demand for a bigger and more effective National Body, but bringing in its wake more and more work and problems for the BMC.

Dennis Gray

Into the Nineties

1989 – The Year of Change

As a BMC Vice-President in 1988, I was one of the first to hear of Dennis Gray's intended retirement which came at a time when I was considering a career move out of teaching. In recent years I had become more closely involved with the BMC, first as Climbers' Club President in the mid-1980s, and second as the Chairman of the Don Whillans Memorial Fund from 1985. After much thought and deliberation I decided to apply for the General Secretary's job, was successful, and moved into the so-called 'hot-seat' in August 1989.

The two other new men appointed in 1989, Training Administrator Iain Peter and National Officer Roger Payne, were both experienced mountaineers and had been guides since the early 1980s. They were also very committed and ambitious and wanted to make their mark on the organisation. With Jayne Nicholson returning as Office Manager, Iain, Roger and myself joined Bill Wright to make up the new team of professional officers.

At this time the contribution of Chris Bonington was enormous. Chris had thrown himself into the role of President with his customary energy and enthusiasm and this was especially important at a time of so much change. His sheer status as Britain's best-known mountaineer considerably enhanced the Council at meetings, AGMs and conferences, with government bodies and outside organisations and with the general public. He was readily available to offer encouragement and advice and believing strongly in the democratic structures of the Council, was keen that the BMC should move forward in an open manner of trust and stability.

The Second Corporate Plan 1990-93 – the organisation grows

With the onset of competition climbing, the steady growth in the number of climbers, the increasing demand for training, and the associated access problems occasioned by the greater numbers, it had become apparent to the Executive and Committee of Management that the BMC would have to expand its organisation to cope with the growing pressure and problems. My first job as General Secretary was to identify the priorities for the next four years, write them up into a comprehensive plan for presentation to the Sports Council, on whom we were dependent for financial support.

In fact, it was most important to rebuild close and firm relationships with the Sports Council, because these had been threatened by a serious incident in late 1988 before I became General Secretary. A request had been made to the BMC from a club in Brazil for help in organising a course for climbing instructors. The Sports Council was approached for financial assistance for a visit to Brazil and, in turn, requested help from the British Council in Brazil. On investigation, it was discovered by the British Council that the club did not exist and a fake application had been made by an individual climber living in Brazil. An enquiry was held by senior executives of the BMC which, on the evidence presented at that time, concluded that although there had been insufficient care in processing the application, they found no evidence of impropriety or dishonesty. A meeting was held with the Director General of the Sports Council where the results of the enquiry and the steps that were being taken to tighten up procedures within the BMC were explained. It was clear when I started that there was much to do to strengthen relationships with the Sports Council.

The key elements of the 4-year plan were to ask the Sports Council to help fund a full-time Technical Officer for the MLTB, to seek the appointment of a second Access Officer and a Competitions/ Climbing Wall Officer, and to assist in the provision of a 'Development Wall' for climbing competitions, demonstrations and training. The latter was soon to be overtaken by events in the rapid escalation of interest in climbing wall development.

The plan was presented to the Sports Council in early 1990 and at a time when grants to 'governing bodies' were being greatly cut back, we considered ourselves fortunate to be offered £110,000 per annum for the next 4 years, to be divided between training, access, expedition support, and funding for the new British Competition Team. This meant that the MLTB could go ahead with its plans for a second officer, and John Cousins, who had been helping in a temporary capacity for several months, was appointed in 1990. However there were insufficient funds for the second Access Officer or the Competitions/ Climbing Walls Officer and we had to build up our reserves over three more years before making these appointments.

Even with the Sports Council grant, the financial state of the BMC remained precarious. We needed to embark upon a membership drive to raise sufficient funds, not only for the implementation of our plan, but for our continued survival in our present state. The BMC just had to become more self-sufficient. Clubs and individual climbers had quite naturally always been reluctant to pay higher fees to what many saw as a 'bureaucratic' organisation. The key was to improve our credibility, reinforce the element of trust in the organisation, launch a more professional advertising and marketing campaign to gain more individual members and sell more BMC insurance and other services.

By October 1989 the first of a number of promotional leaflets was professionally designed by the Berghaus team on our behalf and widely distributed both through the magazines and by Chris Bonington in his winter lecture series. As a result and by further initiatives, individual membership grew from 5,000 in 1989 to nearly 7,000 in 1990 and doubled to over 10,000 by 1994 with gradual increases in subscriptions over the period.

Meanwhile the Clubs maintained and strengthened their support over the next few years. The Club structure had always been regarded as the backbone of the BMC, and despite a quite substantial subscription increase per Club member from £1 in 1990 to £3.50 in 1994, there were few grumbles and these were mainly about multiple membership. Indeed more Clubs sent representatives to area meetings and most of the larger Clubs such as the Climbers' Club, Fell and Rock Climbing Club, the Alpine Club and Red Rope increased their interest in BMC affairs. By the early 1990s both the CC and the FRCC had joined the BMC Guidebook Committee in making donations to the Access Fund from their guidebook work.

Club membership grew from 260 in 1989 to 312 in 1994, and the larger individual membership and the increased subscriptions enabled the BMC to have a much sounder financial base. Coupled with this, a further grant in early 1993 from the Sports Council, which was naturally keen to support competitions and climbing wall development, led to the appointment of Hugh Harris in May. Good relationships had been built up with the Countryside Commission and the Countryside Council for Wales and these organisations offered similar grants to allow the appointment of Kath Pyke as the second Access Officer in November.

So by the end of the four-year period the BMC had been able to complete the aims of the Corporate Plan. The extent of the BMC's financial growth in these six years from 1989 to 1994 is illustrated on page 321.

New Initiatives in Mountain Training

The appointment of Iain Peter as Training Administrator/MLTB Secretary in 1989 coincided with an increased fear of litigation in the outdoor adventure field and a growing concern that all those involved in taking young people into the hills or onto the crags should have the correct experience and the right qualifications. Relationships between the MLTB and the BMC had steadily improved since the reforms following the Training dispute, partly due to the moderate, diplomatic personality of Training Administrator Chris Dodd, and also because of the influence of the two chairmen of the MLTB, Wally Keay and Bob Pettigrew, the latter having also been chairman of the Training Committee for many years.

The BMC had always wished to minimise the 'aura' of certification and was suspicious of everything that might affect the traditional freedom to climb. This was interpreted, however, by some members of the Training Committee and the MLTB as merely an excuse for stifling further developments in mountain training.

Having been brought up in the instructional world of Benmore and Glenmore Lodge and having worked as a mountain guide for many years, Iain Peter clearly believed that the Training Committee of the BMC had been forced to drag its feet over the last few years and that further reforms had been held up by the more vocal elements in the Management Committee. His views were shared by Dave Alcock, director of the National Centre, Davey Jones of Ogwen Cottage, and others on the Training Committee and within the MLTB.

In January 1990 the Committee of Management agreed to reconvene the Standing Advisory Committee On Mountain Training (SACOMT) under the chairmanship of Alan Blackshaw to 'advise on any changes that may be necessary in the present arrangements for mountain training and qualifications, having regard to recent developments and in view of the Single European Market of 1992'. This committee met on many occasions during 1990 seeking advice and opinion from all those in Britain who had an interest in training matters. By early 1991 the SACOMT report had been accepted by the Committee of Management with some important and far reaching recommendations:

1. The establishment of a United Kingdom Mountain Training Board under the chairmanship of Alan Blackshaw with Iain Peter as secretary, to co-ordinate the activities of the four mountain training boards of England, Wales, Scotland and Northern Ireland. The BMC, the MCofS, the MCofI and Welsh mountaineers would be represented on this new body.

2. The revision of the Mountain Instructor Scheme (MIC) and the creation of a new Mountain Instructor Award (without the winter element), both to be administered by the MLTB.

3. The disbanding of the Training Committee, which since 1979 had responsibility for the MIC and its replacement by a Training Advisory Group, to be chaired by a BMC Vice-President (first John Porter and later Mike Rosser).

That these reforms went through without contention says much for the respect and trust in which Blackshaw was held as well as for the administrative and persuasive skills of Iain Peter. With the formation of the UKMTB much of the earlier hostility between the four training boards disappeared. A year later in 1992 came the formal signing of the European Standard for Mountain Leaders, whereby British citizens who wished to lead groups in Europe could now gain an internationally acceptable qualification – the European Mountain Leader Award.

The Mountain Instructor Award qualification became instantly popular with dozens of candidates applying for this award over the next few years causing a logistical problem for the National Centres which could barely cope with the demand. A new professional body, the Association of Mountaineering Instructors (AMI), was formed which now has over 400 members. Between 1992-94 the UKMTB produced its National Guidelines for all those involved in *formal* mountain training, although the BMC and the MCofS were insistent that these guidelines must not be seen to apply to the normal activities of clubs and individual climbers.

A further major change in the relationship between the BMC and the MLTB took place in the summer of 1991. Because of the cramped conditions of the BMC office at Crawford House, and the expansion of the activities and staff of the MLTB, it was proposed by the MLTB that they open a 'branch office' in the former ski store at Plas y Brenin, where Iain Peter and John Cousins should mainly operate. A further justification for this move was that it would bring the new re-vitalised MLTB into closer contact with the main centres and providers of mountain training.

The BMC Executive Committee of Chris Bonington, Ian McNaught-Davis, John Porter, Angela Soper, Brian Monk and myself had all expressed doubts and concerns about a possible split between the BMC and the MLTB if the move went ahead, and those with long memories recalled that the Hunt Report, following the dispute of the late Seventies, had recommended that the two bodies should remain firmly linked. At what was seen as a crucial meeting at the Rising Sun Hotel, Bamford on April 21st 1991, the day after the BMC Annual Dinner, Bonington, Mac, Porter and Walker were persuaded by Pettigrew, Blackshaw and Peter that their fears of a 'split' were unjustified and that the arrangements for the new office should go ahead.

In the event, the move to Wales worked well for the MLTB. Iain Peter introduced a number of publicity leaflets and made sponsorship agreements for the MLTB, and as a result, registrations for the ML scheme grew over the next few years making more funding available for the Board.

By 1992 the BMC had agreed to allow the Board to drop the controversial 'walking' from its title thus reversing the decision of 1979, although of course 'Mountainwalking Leader' remained the name of the actual award. The MLTB received another boost in 1992 with the adoption by the BMC of the Single Pitch Supervisors Award, which was to be administered by the MLTB on behalf of the BMC. Unthinkable a few years earlier, this scheme had been adapted from the controversial 'Guidance Notes' of the late 1980s and had been strongly opposed by the Committee of Management over the years, because of the continued and natural fear among climbers about climbing 'certificates'. The demand was clearly evident from local authorities and youth organisations throughout the country, and once it was in place, the scheme was popular with over 2,000 registering in the first year, and a continued similar demand since.

The BMC eventually accepted the scheme for safety, ethical and environmental reasons because of the growing and over-use of popular crags by outdoor education groups, many of which seemed to have little knowledge or concern for the traditional values and mores of climbing. Whether this award is the answer or will lead to greater popularisation of our precious climbing areas and a need for more controls in the future remains to be seen.

Meanwhile other BMC training and safety initiatives have flourished, spurred on by a continuing concern about winter and alpine accidents involving young people in particular. From 1990 Iain Peter and Roger Payne began a series of lectures in the autumn and spring of each year around different polytechnics and universities on Scottish winter and Alpine climbing. These helped increase safety awareness to potentially vulnerable young students and also gave them a valuable introduction to the work of the BMC.

The series of lectures was supported by Berghaus and a further initiative in the spring of 1994 resulted in the making of a video, 'The Complete Winter Experience', which was sponsored by Berghaus, whose donation was matched by the Sports Match Scheme. Featuring Iain, Roger, John Cousins and Alan Hinkes this successful 25-minute video was made at the time of great media attention to the large number of accidents in the Scottish Highlands in the winter of 1994. It had its 'premier' at a conference in Dunblane organised by the Scottish Mountain Safety Group, and sold 2,000 copies in the first year. A similar video on Alpine climbing was completed in 1995.

Over the years the courses financed by the Jonathan Conville Trust were increased to allow many young climbers to be introduced to Alpine mountaineering, and from 1991 a similar training programme was introduced in Scotland.

Iain Peter left the MLTB/BMC in December 1994 after initiating and overseeing a series of reforms which gave mountain training a new sense of direction and purpose. He pushed through these measures with a forthright and determined approach, and the BMC, and especially those in mountain training, owe him a debt for his vision and resolution.

However, over the last three years since the establishment of the MLTB

Welsh office, the BMC had seen considerably less of Iain. It was not until the arrangements for his replacement were discussed at the end of 1994 that the BMC view prevailed that their new Training Administrator (shared with the MLTB) should be based at the new office in Manchester, which would remain the administrative office of the MLTB. It was clearly felt that the best long-term solution to keeping the right balance and good relationships between the BMC and the Board was for them to have their main headquarters under the same roof, and for the BMC and MLTB officers to be continually in touch so that ideas, opinions and initiatives could rub off on each other for the mutual benefit of both organisations.

It is also vital that the BMC retains its strong representation on the Board, ideally including lay climbers, although it has often been found difficult for such people to be available for the daytime meetings held by the Board. For the last two years, the chairman of the MLTB, Ian Mc Morrin, has been co-opted on to the BMC Management Committee and this practice of inviting the current chairman to attend management meetings should be continued.

Access and Conservation

Our patron Alan Blackshaw's summing up remarks in the 1989 Access symposium that 'Access and Conservation seemed to be the most fundamental issues facing the BMC' were reflected in the many surveys and questionnaires conducted over the last few years. The majority of climbers and mountaineers who responded were in agreement that access and conservation matters formed the most important part of our work.

As Peter Mould reflects in the title to his article on Access and Conservation *'Plus ca Change'*, there have *always* been access and conservation problems for the BMC to face. What has changed and intensified in recent years is the sheer scale of the problems as more and more people are going into the hills and on to the crags, while many landowners seem ever more sensitive to what they see as overuse.

However the Access and Conservation Committee and officers have continued to enjoy some notable successes and have considerably helped to enhance the reputation of the BMC, both to its own constituents and to outside organisations, as a caring and responsible body.

In 1989 the threat posed by Water Privatisation was eased after a successful campaign which resulted in written assurances from the Minister of Sport specifically stating that climbing and walking would be unaffected by the Water Privatisation Act. In the same year the BMC played a prominent part in the 'Save the Cairngorms' campaign with the

BMC PATRONS

illustrated earlier:
The Lord Hunt of Llanfair Waterdine
K.G., C.B.E., D.S.O.
Alan Blackshaw O.B.E.
Sir Christian Bonington C.B.E.

Sir Robert Grieve
Scottish Mountaineering Club

Sir Charles Evans
Climbers' Club, Alpine Club, Wayfarers'

Wynford Vaughan Thomas
Climbers' Club

BMC VICE-PRESIDENTS

those who later became Presidents or General Secretaries are illustrated earlier:

Dr. J.M. Wordie 1947-53, Jack Longland 1970-73, Alan Blackshaw 1972-73, Chris Bonington 1976-79, 1985-88, Joe Walmsley 1982-83, Paul Nunn 1986-90, 1993-94, Derek Walker 1988-89, Ian McNaught-Davis 1987-90.

Names in the main portrait sections are followed by dates of office and club affiliations (principal club first). A.C.* indicates past or current membership of the A.C.G. as well as the A.C.

Paul Arthur Fletcher 1953-55 *S.M.C., A.C.*

Charles Gorrie 1955-59 *S.M.C., A.C.*

Robert Folkard 1959-63 *S.M.C., A.C.*

Iain Ogilvie M.B.E. 1963-68 *S.M.C., A.C.*

Frank Solari 1968-70 *R.C., A.C., M.A.M.*

Bill Murray O.B.E. 1968-71 *S.M.C., A.C.*

Mike Westmacott 1971-72
C.C., A.C.*

Don Whillans 1973-76
Rock and Ice, A.C.G., C.C.

Dr. John Wilkinson
1973-76 *F.R.C.C., A.C.*

Eric Byrom 1975-78
Rucksack Club

John Cunningham 1976-79
Creagh Dhu

Iain MacCallum 1978-81
Karabiner Club

Dr. Will Butler 1979-81
London Graduate M.C.

Peter Boardman 1979-82
Mynydd, A.C.G.

Bill Peascod 1982-85
F.R.C.C.

Dr. David Roberts 1982-85
M.A.M.

George Band 1984-87
C.C., A.C.*

Alan Rouse 1985-86
Vagabonds, A.C.G., C.C.

John Porter 1989-93
A.C.G.

Angela Soper 1990-93
P.C., F.R.C.C.

Stephen Venables 1990-93
C.C., A.C.*

Jancis Allison 1993-96
C.C., F.R.C.C., Cleveland M.C.

Mike Rosser 1993-96
Gwent M.C., C.C., A.C.

Doug Scott C.B.E. 1994-
Nottingham C.C., A.C.*, C.C.

HONORARY MEMBERS

illustrated earlier:

Donald Greenwood 1971
Fred Pigott 1972
Sir Jack Longland 1973
Frank Solari 1975
John Neill 1976
Bob Pettigrew 1986
The Lord Hunt 1986
Bill Murray 1986

John Llewellyn Jones 1974
A.C.

Dr. Bill Ward 1975
Farnborough M.C.

Alan Hargreaves 1983
*Wayfarers', C.C., F.R.C.C.,
R.C., A.C.*

Vin Machin 1987
Rucksack Club

Maurice Bennett
1991 (posthumous).
A.B.M.S.A.C.

Peter Wild
1991 (posthumous).
Rucksack Club

George Steele 1992
Alpine Club, F.R.C.C.

Harry Spilsbury
1996 (posthumous).
Rucksack Club, Wayfarers'

HONORARY TREASURERS

illustrated earlier:

John Llewellyn Jones
1969-74
Iain MacCallum 1974-76

Note: From 1973 the Treasurer was answerable to the Finance Committee, the chair of which was filled by a Vice-President, an ex Treasurer or a person with particular financial expertise.

Herbert Roberts 1945-51
Wayfarers' Club

Anthony Medlycott
1951-52 *Rucksack Club, A.C.*

Tom Hardwick 1952-55
Rucksack Club

Lt.Col. Ambrose Crawley
1955-57 *Royal Artillery M.C.*

George Starkey 1958-59
A.B.M.S.A.C., A.C.

Joe Della Porter 1960-66
Summit M.C., J.M.C.S.

Jo Kretschmer 1966-69
C.C., A.C.

Brian Monk 1976-81,
1987-92 *Cromlech Club*

Jack Ashcroft 1981-85
Oread Club

Mike Watson 1985-87
Individual

Brian Griffiths 1992-96
F.R.C.C., C.C.

CHAIRMEN OF THE
FINANCE COMMITTEE
and Honorary Auditors

Chairmen illustrated earlier:

John Llewellyn Jones 1973-74
Eric Byrom 1974-78, Iain MacCallum 1978-82,
Joe Walmsley 1982-83, Mike Watson 1988-92,
Brian Monk 1992-95

Hon. Auditors not illustrated:

F.J. Guest 1945-?, R.A. Tyssen-Gee 1956-67,
H.N. Fairfield 1968-72, J.A. Crewe 1974-75

Brian Nicholls (Ch)
1984-87 *Chester M.C.*

Harold Mellor (Ch)
1987-88
Lancs C&C., R.C., W.C.

John Shaw (Ch) 1995-
Lancs. Caving & Climbing

Bob Astles (Aud.)
1976-90 *Karabiner, R.C.*

THE COMMITTEE OF MAN-AGEMENT makes (or ratifies) all key decisions of the BMC except those reserved for the AGM. It meets five or six times a year (here at the Manchester University office in Sept. 1984). Voting members comprise the President, Vice-Presidents, Hon. Treasurer, Gen. Secretary, two members of each of the area committees and co-opted representatives of (currently) the official magazine, the Mt. Council of Scotland, the Mountain Guides, the MLTB, the Joint Services and the Competition Climbers. Observers represent the Sports Council, Plas y Brenin, the Mountain Rescue Association, some specialist officers, and (sometimes) sub-committee reps.

Pat Stevens (SW)
Mark Hutchinson (official)
Tom Price
Denis Gray (Pres.)
(G.Sec.)
Rita Hallam (Sec.)
John Barry (PyB)
Dave Roberts (R.Cossey)
Vice Pres)
Mike (Wales)
Climber & R)
Paul Dewhurst
(Lancs and C

Charles Manning (SW)
Jack Ashcroft (Hon Treas)

Dave Dickson (Peak)
Adj Hubbal (Peak)

Also present
Dave Basketfield (SE)
Colin Knowles (Yorks)
Geoff Fletcher (Lancs and C)
Geoff Fletcher Dunn (officers)
Chris Doddsfan (Guides)
Harold Drasdo

Bill Ruthven (Lakes)
Bob Pettigrew (NE)
Chris Edwards (Guides)
Steve Dervin (NE)

Mountaineering Council of Scotland which successfully opposed a further attempt to develop skiing in Lurchers Gully.

For several months in 1990 climbing was banned at Upper Pen Trwyn following a serious rock fall on to the road below. After protracted negotiations between Bill Wright and Aberconwy District Council, an agreement was reached whereby the BMC took responsibility for the installation of bolt anchors at the top of many routes below the walk off, where the strata was loose and climbers might trigger rock falls. As a result climbing was allowed to continue on this much favoured site and this was seen as a major achievement, highlighted in a popular, promotional full page advertisement which had as its punch line – 'The only thing worse than falling off Pen Trwyn is not being allowed to'.

Similar solutions were sought to deal with the ever-present threat to climbing at Cheddar, and later at the GO Wall at Wintour's Leap. At Stone Farm Rocks belay anchors were installed to prevent further rock erosion. For the BMC to take responsibility for the placement of 'official' anchors (bolts and chains, or large iron rings) albeit for lower-offs and strictly for access and conservation reasons, was a new policy development involving important ethical and legal liability considerations. These actions were perceived to be the best solutions in exceptional circumstances at these particular crags, and the BMC has so far strongly resisted any suggestions that it should be involved in any further bolting activity or re-equipping of routes.

The high cost of the bolts at Pen Trwyn and elsewhere was met by the Access Fund which had been set up in the 1980s to help relieve access difficulties. The most regular income had come from a percentage of the sales of BMC Guidebooks, but in recent years there have also been substantial donations from the Climbers' Club, the Fell and Rock Climbing Club and other guidebook publishers. In 1993 Mark Vallance donated £5,000 from the Wild Country Foundation, and repeated this the following year to sponsor regular productions of Access News. These quarterly newsletters sent to club secretaries, outdoor education centres and official bodies, and distributed at meetings and lectures, have heightened awareness of the access problems facing climbers throughout the country and the steps which the Access team have taken to resolve them.

A major break-through occurred in 1992 in Pembroke when for the first time climbers were allowed into Range West on a legitimate basis, again following protracted negotiations between Bill Wright and the commanding officer at Castlemartin. This followed an access campaign by individual climbers to gain entry into this fabulous area, organised by Dave Cook who had orchestrated the mass trespass of October 1991 which brought considerable media attention to the problem. Tragically,

'Cookie', a leading activist for over 30 years and a staunch advocate of freedom for climbers, was killed in a cycling accident in Turkey shortly afterwards.

Meanwhile on the conservation front, a dream of many years was gradually emerging as by 1992 after years of quiet, persistent diplomacy the British Upland Footpath Trust was set up following discussions with the Camping and Outdoor Leisure Association, the Ramblers' Association and the Mountaineering Council of Scotland. The aim was to channel funds into upland path repair, particularly from hill-walkers and the outdoor industry, and to ensure that path repair was carried out to the highest possible standards in line with the BMC's Upland Footpath Policy. By 1994 BUFT had been registered as a charity, donations were coming in, notably one for £110,000 from the Alec Grant Trust, and four footpath projects had been identified at Coire Lagan in Skye, Redacre Gill in Langdale, Losehill in the Peak District and on the west face of Tryfan. So the BMC had taken an important lead and was clearly identified with footpath improvement schemes and the conservation and protection of the mountain environment. In fact the BMC footpath policy has influenced nearly every major body involved in the management of upland areas.

Bill Wright, who was employed as the first full-time Access and Conservation Officer from May 1987 to December 1993, played a major role in these developments. He was a determined and tenacious negotiator with government officials, local authorities, landowners and farmers, and heightened the profile of the BMC by his media interviews and his articles in the climbing magazines.

During 1993 we were eventually successful in obtaining joint funding from the Countryside Commission and the Countryside Council for Wales for the appointment of an Access Liaison Officer. Further help came from the Guidebook Committee and the Wild Country Foundation to enable us to appoint Kath Pyke in November 1993, one month after Jeremy Barlow had been appointed to succeed Bill Wright.

Much of Jeremy's time in 1994 was spent co-ordinating our campaign to change the Government's plan to introduce the new offence of 'criminal trespass' as part of the Criminal Justice Act. Despite concerted efforts and the support of John Hunt, Chris Bonington, Doug Scott and many others, the act is now in force, although we have been assured that its provisions are in no way directed against bona fide climbers and mountaineers. Time will tell. Meanwhile in 1994, Kath Pyke made great strides in building up and co-ordinating the many volunteer access officers around the country. In 1994 the access team with its volunteer helpers was involved in 117 climbing sites in England and Wales where access issues had been raised – a reflection on the sheer size of the growing problems that have to be faced.

Competition Climbing

To understand the BMC's involvement in competition climbing it is necessary to go back to the beginning of 1988 when the BMC had become isolated in the UIAA Council as the only federation which still opposed competition climbing. Yet many top British climbers had competed abroad and at an open meeting in January they asked the BMC to regulate and organise the new sport at home. The issue was discussed at the AGM in April where the majority were in favour of the BMC's involvement in competition climbing – but only on artificial walls.

In May an attempt by 19-year old John Dunne and former athlete Brendan Foster's Film Nova company to stage an outside competition at Malham set off alarm bells. Foster hoped to show it on the BBC Grandstand programme but there was an instant and almost unanimous hostility from a broad section of the climbing community. The event was prevented by an immense and successful propaganda and telephone campaign organised by the BMC which was totally opposed to this unwanted intrusion on to the natural crags.

Guided by the views of the membership at the AGM and influenced by the Malham affair, the Committee of Management, at a crucial debate in June, decided to support and take over the direction and control of competition climbing though not the actual organisation of events. The highly entertaining first World Cup event at Leeds in May 1989, organised by DMM, converted many former sceptics, especially so with the nail-biting super-final victory for Jerry Moffatt. By the end of the 1989 series Buxton 'stickman' Simon Nadin, in his first year of competitions, became the first World Champion and Jerry Moffatt took 3rd place.

There was considerable initial enthusiasm for the new sport from a number of the leading young climbers, many of whom including Moffatt, Nadin, Moon, Masterson, Dawes, Pollitt and Leach attended the first open meeting for competition climbers at the Marquis of Granby, Bamford in September.

However after the initial success there was disappointment in 1990 when the British round of the World Cup had to be cancelled because no suitable venue could be found for the allotted date in the UIAA calendar. The only British event was the Bendcrete Open in March at Olympia, again won by Moffatt with Felicity Butler as the women's champion. For 1991 there was promise of a world cup event at the newly-built National Indoor Arena in Birmingham, where the management was keen to host the event and the Sports Council offered further grant aid.

In the meantime, however, there was a potential conflict in the early summer when a group of northern enthusiasts, led by Jerry Peel, 'secretly' organised an outside bouldering competition, the 'Burnley Boulder Bash', at Crookrise, clearly contravening BMC policy by staging the event on a natural crag. Fears of further 'fun' events outside were eliminated after a meeting involving myself, Bill Wright, Jerry Peel, Graham Desroy and Gill Kent and Greg Rimmer of *On The Edge* magazine. All agreed that it was more suitable for all competitions to be held on artificial walls, and by the end of the year a number of indoor competitions had taken place, including the Northern and Southern Indoor Bouldering Leagues and the Boulder for Fun competition at the new Berghaus wall in Newcastle organised by Stephen Porteus and Hugh Harris.

With the opening of a large new climbing wall at the Foundry (Dec. 91) in Sheffield, with instant popularity, soon to be followed by other dedicated walls at Bristol, Birmingham and elsewhere, where indoor competitions could be held, there fortunately was no longer the demand for competitions outside. Also by now the UIAA had followed the British example and accepted that no World Cup events should take place on natural crags.

DMM successfully organised the final event in the World Cup at the National Indoor Arena in early December 1991 which the French dominated with Francois Legrand and Isabelle Patissier being the winners. The BMC again took the lead and were granted the final event at the NIA in December 1992.

Funding was offered from the newly set up Foundation for Sport and the Arts of £49,000 towards the event, but DMM was forced to pull out of organising it in late September due to pressure of their own business, only two months before the scheduled date. A crucial decision was made that the BMC officers should take over the organisation itself, although this appeared controversial and risky to one or two members of the Management Committee. Helped by Anna Gregory, chair of the Climbing Wall committee, and Hugh Harris who was seconded for 6 weeks from his job of managing the Foundry, the event was again successful, largely because of the help of the above two volunteers, competition chairman Stephen Porteus and Roger Payne who co-ordinated the whole competition. A British wall made by DR/Bendcrete was used for the first time, and the popular winners were Lynn Hill and Jibé Tribout. The following year after retiring from competitions to resume her normal climbing career, Lynn was to free climb the Nose of El Capitan.

By 1993 some of the initial novelty value of competitions had dissolved and in the tougher economic climate lack of sponsorship forced the cancellation of the World Cup event in 1993, largely because of the difficulties of ownership of the international TV rights which the UIAA was reluctant to hand over until it was just too late to attract a sponsor. Other federations faced similar difficulties and only 6 events took place.

A further substantial grant from the Foundation for Sport and the Arts of £80,000 in early 1994 allowed the BMC to buy 60% of its own wall panels (from Entre-prises), and with the major sponsorship from Snow and Rock, the same organisational team of Roger Payne, Hugh Harris (since May 93 the Competitions and Climbing Wall Officer), Anna Gregory and Stephen Porteus worked hard with the NIA to ensure a further successful event, although audience participation was lower than in 1992.

But the early success for British climbers of 1989 was not to be repeated. Moffatt, Nadin and Moon all lost interest, and although new names appeared, notably Ian Vickers and Fliss Butler as our most consistent competitors, the British team (sponsored by Reebok since 1993) never matched the early success. The men's events in the World Cup Series in the Nineties were dominated by the French, all named Francois – Legrand, Lombard and Petit, while the women's events were won by Isabelle Patissier (France) 1991, Lynn Hill (USA) 1992 and Robyn Erbersfield (USA) 1993 & 1994.

Although the British events have been a success, they have been very expensive to organise and needed a lot of time and effort. Sponsorship has remained extremely difficult to find and without the substantial donations from the FSA it would have been quite impossible to finance these costly events. By the mid-1990s the long-term future of the World Cup Series is still uncertain with a number of federations being forced to cancel, and only four staged in 1994, and no series sponsor forthcoming. As far as British climbers are concerned many of the leading 'crag' climbers do not seem sufficiently interested in the grind and dedication of indoor training that is necessary to achieve real success on the international circuit. Perhaps rightly most are far more interested in the 'real thing' on the crags.

The New Wave of Climbing Walls
The Corporate Plan of 1989/90, written soon after the successes of Nadin and Moffatt in the first World Cup Series, foresaw the need for a 'Development Wall' where the best young British climbers could train and which would be an exemplar of climbing walls in the future. Plans for such a wall at Oldham, with local authority and Sports Council support, were overtaken by events. A consortium of Sheffield climbers, Paul Reeve and Jim Kelly, backed by the enterprising Wild Country/ Outside combination of Mark Vallance and Dick Turnbull, took the

opportunity to buy an old foundry in Sheffield and convert this into the first and most successful of the new generation of modern dedicated tall climbing walls. British climbing was never to be the same again.

The Foundry opened in December 1991 and was an instant success, attracting 60,000 user visits in the first year with many people driving vast distances to climb there. Winter weekends were especially popular with sometimes over 400 climbers a day paying to climb and enjoy the social atmosphere. It is now clear that the success of the Foundry was to have major and long-term implications for the sport. Hitherto most of the successful climbing walls had tended to emphasise solo climbing with its attendant degree of risk and necessity for good judgement. The Foundry instituted large numbers of top ropes on the Belgian model and thus allowed extensive high-powered training free from risk. Later, bolt-protected (and therefore safe) leader climbs were added that had much more in common with European-style sport climbing than the traditional British ethic.

The success of the Foundry was soon to be followed by other commercial enterprises opening up at Bristol, Marple, Birmingham and many other towns and cities throughout the country, nearly all with BMC support and often with Sports Council and FSA grants. As a result a whole new generation of people was being encouraged to start climbing, and with an increase in media interest, climbing was reported to be one of the fastest growing sports in the country. The new walls began to exert a considerable influence on outdoor climbing and undoubtedly they have influenced British climbing attitudes in the Nineties. Climbers became fitter and did much harder routes, but there was also a decline in interest in traditional climbs in favour of sport climbing venues such as Pen Trwyn and Portland. In this period the BMC was inundated with requests for help and advice almost on a daily basis as new plans were formed for walls here, there and everywhere. Whether the success and interest in so many new indoor walls can be maintained remains to be seen.

Bolts

Undoubtedly the most prominent and controversial issue to affect climbers and raise the temperature over the last few years has been the increasing use of bolts on British crags following the invention of the cordless drill in the mid-1980s. The subject has been fiercely debated in pubs, cafés, meetings and conferences and there have been frequent exchanges in the climbing and national press, and on television. To deal with this major issue, the BMC organised a whole series of meetings to give people the opportunity to talk and discuss before policy was agreed.

In January 1991 the BMC organised a seminar on 'in-situ' protection at UMIST in Manchester, where some serious papers were read by Pat Littlejohn, Pete Gomersall, Martin Berzins and others. Then in March the whole subject was hotly debated at Buxton. The audience agreed that indeed 'the traditional ethos of British climbing *was* being endangered by sport climbing'. Jerry Moffatt and Chris Gore failed to make a convincing case for sport climbing against the arguments of Ken Wilson and Royal Robbins, who had felt so strongly on the issue that he had travelled from California just to take part in the debate. Others felt strongly too and Catherine Destivelle was one of many who made impassioned anti-bolt contributions from the floor. The message according to 'Climber' was clear – 'the people have spoken and in large enough numbers to make the message clear: the bolters need controlling if our crags are not to become clinical, sporting playgrounds where all you'll need is a rack of quick draws and a chalk bag'.

Following further open meetings throughout the country it became clear that the vast majority wished to preserve the traditional British ethic of leader-placed protection, and that bolts had no place in British climbing apart from on certain agreed quarried crags and on agreed sections of certain limestone crags, where it was impossible to place normal gear. This was reflected in the Bolts policy which was adopted at the 1992 AGM which has remained in force and generally accepted since.

The concern that climbing worldwide was also being too heavily influenced by French-style sport climbing led to the BMC organising two important international climbing meets at Plas y Brenin in the spring of 1992 and 1994, to introduce overseas visitors to the joys of Welsh climbing and to stress the importance of upholding the traditions of bolt-free adventure climbing. The majority of the visitors applauded the BMC policy, although after Mick Fowler had given one of his particularly gripping 'true adventure' lectures, a young French climber, who earlier in the week had fallen off Cockblock, landed on his backside and could not sit down for the rest of the meet, brought the house down with his remark, "Meester Fowler, I think you are a dinosaur". Unfortunately and perhaps significantly these meets were not graced by the same number of leading climbers from the major European countries as had been the case with the BMC international gatherings of the 70s and 80s.

Although most climbers favour the BMC policy, there is still a minority who seek a proliferation of bolt-protected climbing even to encroach into the easier grades. Sport climbing has become increasingly popular and more and more young people are getting their introduction to climbing through the safe and sanitised world of the artificial wall. It is quite clear that in the future a large task of education is required if new recruits to the sport are to be introduced into the more traditional styles of climbing.

Tensions heightened in the autumn of 1994 after more than twenty bolt-protected routes in the middle and upper grades were developed at a little-known quarry at Harpur Hill near Buxton by two Saddleworth activists Sid Siddiqui and Bill Birch. This caused outrage amongst some local climbers. The Peak Area Committee, after a lengthy and open debate, condemned the bolting and the offending items were promptly removed. But the debate continues with considerable media attention so that Harpur Hill has become something of a cause célèbre about how far bolting will be allowed. Since then other incidents of bolting suggest that this will remain a controversial issue.

A New Hut – Rockhall Cottage
The Don Whillans Memorial fund had started under my chairmanship in the autumn of 1985 and a series of lectures by Chris Bonington, Doug Scott, Joe Brown and Nat Allen, plus a well-orchestrated 'Buy a Pint for Don' appeal, raised a substantial amount of money in the late 1980s. The initial idea was to secure a permanent base or campsite in the Chamonix valley for British climbers, but after many visits and considerable investigation, this project was deemed just too impractical. Not enough money was raised for a property and the only possible camp-site offered by the French authorities was found to be in a former avalanche zone.

The failure of the Chamonix scheme was very disappointing but a second option, much favoured by Don's widow Audrey and the Committee, was to have a hut in Britain dedicated to Don's memory. Fortuitously, in 1990 the derelict and primitive Rockhall Cottage became vacant as the Peak Park Board re-housed the self-styled and legendary 'King of the Roaches', Doug Moller and his wife Annie into a modern property a few miles away. The Peak Park Board then approached the BMC to see if a joint venture could convert the cottage into a climbing hut; they would provide the architectural planning, design and building expertise while the Memorial Fund would supply the money. However, although over £50,000 had by now been raised, this was still insufficient to modernise the dilapidated ruin, but a further substantial grant from the Sports Council and support from the Rural Development Commission made the project possible and the work was carried out during 1992.

The site at the Roaches was especially apt as it was there that Don first met and climbed with his legendary partner Joe Brown and where he first met his wife Audrey. One of Don's first great routes was, in fact, the Sloth which surmounted the spectacular overhang on the Upper Tier and astonished onlookers at the time.

Audrey Whillans officially opened the Hut in January 1993 and a great many of Don's former friends and guests crowded into the Cave to drink champagne. It was a memorable occasion, worthy of the traditions of the cottage, the crag and the great man himself. Since then there have been a lot of bookings and many climbers have enjoyed that very special atmosphere of Rockhall Cottage.

Incorporation – The BMC Becomes a Company Limited by Guarantee

In 1991 our long-term accountant, Bob Astles, suggested that the complex accounting system could be simplified if the BMC and BMC Services Ltd could be combined into one company. On advice from our solicitor Martin Wragg, the answer seemed to be to convert the BMC into a company limited by guarantee, which would protect the President and other BMC Officers for the future and give the organisation a fully legal entity, rather than carrying on as an unincorporated association. This was particularly important as the whole financial base of the Council had grown considerably over the last couple of years, as membership and subscriptions had increased and as more services were offered to the climbing public. Also at this time we suffered the worst fraud in the Council's history with the Lindagate affair when a part-time Book-keeper misappropriated over £20,000 of BMC funds. Criminal charges followed and fortunately all the missing money and their associated costs were recovered, but it was a great shock and a salutory lesson for the staff. Immediately all financial procedures were tightened up. By 1994 so much money was pouring through the office that it was necessary to employ a Financial Controller as well as a full-time Book-keeper.

Incorporation basically involved reaffirming the existing constitution of 1982. We little realised what a long drawn out and costly process it would be, involving hours and hours of debate and discussion at area and management level, and frequent drafts and re-drafts of the memorandum and articles.

The key people in the working group which had to wrestle with the drafting and assist Martin Wragg, were Sylvia Loxam, Andrew McLellan and especially Malcolm Prentice whose precise and carefully expressed views were invaluable. A late objection from Bob Reid, the President of the Mountaineering Council of Scotland and his executive committee – first to our title and then about references to our representation 'for Great Britain' – was averted by a suitably worded joint minute. This was accepted by both Councils which recognised and re-emphasised the role of the Mountaineering Council of Scotland in climbing and mountaineering affairs in Scotland. The Memorandum and Articles of Association for the new company were finally accepted at the 1993 AGM by 5,864 in favour to 1 against, followed by a postal ballot passed by 6,011 to nil. The new company came into effect on 1 January 1994 with members of the Executive Committee becoming the first Directors. From now on the business of the Council would be carried out in accordance with the Companies Act.

At the same time as our own internal constitutional re-examination was taking place, the Sports Council was unveiling proposals for its own future re-organisation. This would involve replacing the existing Great Britain Sports Council with a United Kingdom Sports Council and establishing a separate Sports Council for England, while retaining the existing councils for Scotland, Northern Ireland and Wales. This would almost certainly affect the funding of the BMC and the other national organisations in the future so it was decided to set up a Joint Mountaineering Advisory Group (JMAG) to meet on a regular six-monthly basis to discuss these and other matters of mutual interest and concern. Paul Nunn and I represented the BMC at the first meeting with two representatives of the Mountaineering Council of Scotland, Mountaineering Council of Ireland and Welsh Mountaineers at Plas y Brenin in November 1993.

Our Involvement with the UIAA, the Council Meeting and Everest Celebrations 1993

The first half of 1993 was an extraordinarily busy time as within a four-month period we opened the new Whillans' hut in January, staged an ever popular Buxton Festival in March, prepared for and voted on the incorporation of the BMC at the AGM in April, and hosted the prestigious UIAA Council meeting at Plas y Brenin in May to coincide with the 40th anniversary celebrations of the first ascent of Everest. This was a real baptism of fire for new Office Manager, Katherine Brown, who played a key role in the organisation of these events.

Also at this time the Everest celebrations were orchestrated in London by the Mount Everest Foundation, Alpine Club and Royal Geographical Society under the chairmanship of Patrick Fagan, while a major fund-raising exercise was organised on behalf of the Mount Everest Foundation. A memorable lecture evening and reception was held at the Royal Geographical Society in the presence of the Queen and other members of the Royal family. The BMC was able to invite the President and committee members of the UIAA to the lecture and reception, prior to the UIAA Council meeting at Plas y Brenin. This was the first such meeting in Wales since 1968 and was very well attended and graced by the 1953 Everest team on the Saturday evening for a splendid reception and buffet. They, as usual, were staying along the road at Pen y Gwryd. Ed Hillary was made an honorary member of the UIAA that evening.

It was appropriate that for the first time that year two British women, Rebecca Stephens and Ginette Harrison, reached the summit of Everest by the South Col Route. Also Dawson Stelfox from Northern Ireland became the first Briton to climb Everest by the North Col Route that had confounded so many British attempts dating back to 1922.

BMC influence within the UIAA has steadily increased over the last few years, and our delegates have made an important contribution to the work of the international body. We have been well represented on the commissions with several of our members acting as Chairmen. Dr Charles Clarke was Chairman of the Medical Commission for 6 years until 1991 and achieved an impressive amount of work, establishing the Mountain Medicine Data Centre in Barts Hospital in London which received thousands of enquiries. Alan Blackshaw, whose own involvement in the UIAA dates back to the 1960s, has been Chairman of the Mountaineering Commission for the last five years with Roger Payne as its Secretary. They have tackled many important issues, including compiling the Model Standards for Mountain Leaders which have been adopted in several countries, and conducting a valuable research exercise into the effects of competitions (mainly ski-mountaineering) in mountain areas, which diffused a potentially divisive situation. George Steele, since the early Seventies, and Neville McMillan, have made a major contribution to the Safety Commission, which has produced standards for all kinds of mountaineering equipment. Paul Nunn was the Karakoram expert in the Expeditions Commission while Dave Morris was Secretary of the Mountain Protection Commission for many years. Ivor Delafield has been Chairman of the Competitions Commission since 1991 and has struggled to get this controversial new sport off the ground. Mike Westmacott is the Vice-Chairman of the new Documentation Commission. Finally, since Ian McNaught-Davis became our representative in 1988 he has made his very considerable presence and influence so much felt in the UIAA that he was elected a Vice-President in 1994 and became President in 1995 following the tragic death of Pietro Segantini.

Among the problems to be faced over the next few years are the continued fight for access to the world's mountains and an attempt to reduce peak fees. Sadly at present, more countries are beginning to impose charges on climbers. It is vitally important that opportunities exist within the UIAA to meet with representatives of the 'host' countries from Nepal, India, Pakistan, China and elsewhere to try and resolve these difficulties. From my experience the UIAA has done much valuable

work on behalf of world mountaineering, and the BMC has played an
important and leading part in its development.

The 50th Anniversary Dinner

In April 1994 a large gathering attended a BMC dinner to celebrate the
50th anniversary at the Royal Victoria Hotel, Llanberis. Sadly John Hunt
was unable to be with us, but all the other past Presidents from Tony
Moulam (1970) to Chris Bonington (1991) were there, along with a great
many other BMC luminaries, supporters and guests. That grand old man
of British climbing, A.B. Hargreaves, a strong link with 1944, was there
celebrating his 90th birthday that week-end, while the youngest member
was 11-year-old rock-star Adam Dewhurst. Among the guests were
former secretaries Dennis Gray and Mike Holton who have contributed
so much to this history, Lord Roger Chorley, indoor climbing champions
Ian Vickers, Fliss Butler and Naomi Guy, and Everest climber Dawson
Stelfox, along with many others.

Chris Bonington proposed the health of the BMC and traced its
progress over the last five decades. Then Ian McNaught-Davies gave
his valedictory address. Like Chris before him, Mac had put in a
tremendous amount of time and effort as President over the last three
years. All in all it was an extremely enjoyable and nostalgic occasion.
Earlier at the AGM, another highly distinguished member of the climbing
community, Paul Nunn had been elected President to succeed Mac, while
Doug Scott, soon to be awarded the CBE for his contribution to
mountaineering, was elected as Vice-President to join Jancis Allison and
Mike Rosser.

The New Headquarters

The Future Policy review of 1986 had identified the need for the BMC
to have a permanent home. For years we had been overcrowded in the
offices at Crawford House as more staff were appointed. From the time
of my appointment in 1989 the need for a new headquarters was seen as
a priority, and as we approached the end of our lease in December 1994,
so the search for more suitable accommodation became more urgent. It
had been generally agreed by successive Executive and Management
Committees that Manchester remained the best location for the BMC,
although other suggestions such as a country house in the Peak District,
office accommodation in Sheffield, and a move to Plas y Brenin were
all proposed and considered since 1989. Meanwhile, with Office
Managers Jayne Nicholson and Katherine Brown, I had inspected many
possibilities in the Manchester/Stockport area, and for a while the newly
developed Castlefields area seemed a favourite option.

With the new fever and popularity surrounding indoor climbing walls, which were becoming so much a centre of climbing and social activity, we were diverted in late 1993 to consider seriously installing the headquarters alongside a new indoor complex in Manchester. Despite initial enthusiasm for this project, neither a suitable site was identified nor were any grants forthcoming. Then in early 1994 an office building next to the Foundry in Sheffield was also seriously considered. After meetings involving opinions from all the Area Committees, the central and politically neutral Manchester location was considered best and Claude Davies was called in to help us in a renewed search for a property we could afford. By September he had found a former church in West Didsbury, already converted into office accommodation, and we moved into the new headquarters in March 1995. It had been a long haul to find a permanent new home for the BMC and this had been a fitting way to mark the 50th year.

Postscript (written in 1995)

In January 1995 as we signed the lease for the new headquarters, I announced my intention to stand down as General Secretary. Roger Payne was appointed to succeed me and took over on July 1st. Meanwhile John Cousins had replaced Iain Peter as MLTB Secretary in January and Adge Last became Training Administrator in March. Ian Parnell became the first Regional Development Officer based at Undercover Rock in Bristol in June, and Andy MacNae was appointed to replace Roger Payne. Katherine Brown returned from maternity leave as Marketing Co-ordinator. In a new home with a keen young staff and sound finances the BMC was securely placed to face the next few years with confidence.

Sadly the tragic death of President Paul Nunn with his friend Geoff Tier in an avalanche on Haramosh II in August was a terrible blow for the BMC. He had made a great contribution to British mountaineering over the last 30 years and will be sorely missed. He was the first BMC President to die in office. A day or two before the news of their deaths, we heard that Alison Hargreaves was lost on K2 after realising her ambition in climbing that mountain. In May she had become the first woman to climb Everest solo, from the North side and without oxygen, a great achievement for which she received world-wide media acclaim. Alison had also been a keen supporter of the BMC, had attended a number of international meets, was a member of the International Committee and was the BMC representative on the Mount Everest Foundation.

Two months earlier at the end of June, Nat Allen died after a long fight against cancer. As is evident from this book, Nat was one of the greatest servants of the BMC, especially in the Peak District and on the guidebook scene, and was one of the best-loved characters in the mountaineering community. These deaths and others such as guidebook writer Paul Williams, in June, and the BMC patrons Sir Robert Grieve and Sir Charles Evans at the end of the year have made 1995 a sad year for mountaineering and the BMC.

Under Paul's Presidency and that of his predecessors, Chris Bonington and Ian McNaught-Davis, the BMC had moved forward considerably, and their contributions as leading figures in the mountaineering world cannot be underestimated. The BMC was fortunate that Mac was again available to step in as acting President after Paul's death until the AGM of 1996. During the last few years the Council has made progress in an atmosphere of trust and responsibility with the support of the clubs and individual climbers. Good relationships have been maintained with the Sports Council, the CCPR, the Countryside Commission and a host of other regional and national organisations. As always in the past the BMC has relied heavily on the continued goodwill of dozens of keen volunteers on area and specialist committees who have worked hard on behalf of the Council.

In this period as the BMC has employed more staff, grown more professional and become a limited company, so it has developed to serve the differing needs of climbers and mountaineers, at a time when there is more interest in the sport than ever before and when climbing attitudes are undergoing some fundamental changes. It has been sometimes difficult to keep all the disparate groups of climbers together in the broad church organisation that is the BMC, but this is the challenge that the Council has faced and will continue to do in the future.

Derek Walker

A RECORD of AGMs.

1945	Dec.	15	Alpine Club, London.
1946	Dec.	22	Alpine Club, London.
1947	Dec.	22	Alpine Club, London.
1949	Jun.	11	Central Station Hotel, Glasgow.
1950	Jun.	24	Engineers' Club, Manchester.
1951	Jun.	23	Alpine Club, London.
1952	Jun.	28	Alpine Club, London.
1953	Mar.	14	Alpine Club, London.
1954	Mar.		Alpine Club, London
1955	Mar.	26	Alpine Club, London.
1956	Mar.	24	Alpine Club, London.

A RECORD of AGMs (cont.)

1957	Mar.	30	Alpine Club, London.
1958	Mar.	29	Alpine Club, London.
1959	Mar.	21	Alpine Club, London.
1960	Apr.	2	Alpine Club, London.
1961	Apr.	15	Alpine Club, London.
1962	Apr.	7	Alpine Club, London.
1963	Mar.	23	Alpine Club, London.
1964	Apr.	18	Alpine Club, London.
1965	Apr.	10	Alpine Club, London.
1966	Apr.	30	Alpine Club, London.
1967	Jun.	24	Alpine Club, London.
1968	Nov.	4	Special AGM at A.C.
1969	Jun.	7	Alpine Club, London.
1970	May	9	C.C.P.R., London.
1971	Jun.	26	C.C.P.R., London.
1972	Jun.	17	Maynard Arms, Grindleford (first dinner).
1973	Jun.	23	Royal Hotel, Caernarfon.
1974	May	11	Maynard Arms, Grindleford.
1975	May	31	Bull's Head, Eyam.
1976	Apr.	24	Stickle Barn, New Dungeon Ghyll, Langdale.
1977	Apr.	23	Plas y Brenin.
1978	Apr.	22	Maynard Arms, Grindleford.
1979	Apr.	21	Stickle Barn, New Dungeon Ghyll, Langdale.
1980	Apr.	26	Plas y Brenin. Dinner at Waterloo Hotel
1981	Apr.	25	Black Dog, Belmont (Hot Pot Supper).
1982	Apr.	24	Waterhead Hotel, Ambleside.
1983	Apr.	23	Royal Victoria Hotel, Llanberis.
1984	Apr.	14	Derwentwater Hotel, Portinscale.
1985	Apr.	20	Palace Hotel, Buxton.
1986	Apr.	26	Royal Victoria Hotel, Llanberis.
1987	Apr.	25	Royal Oak Hotel, Keswick.
1988	Apr.	16	Marquess of Granby, Bamford.
1989	Apr.	22	Royal Victoria Hotel, Llanberis.
1990	Apr.	21	Ullswater Hotel.
1991	Apr.	20	Marquess of Granby, Bamford.
1992	Apr.	25	Royal Victoria Hotel, Llanberis.
1993	Apr.	24	Ullswater Hotel.
1994	Apr.	23	Royal Victoria Hotel, Llanberis.
1995	Apr.	29	The Webbington Hotel, Loxton, Somerset.
1996	Apr.	20	Buxton Community College. Dinner at Lee Wood Hotel.

BMC DEVELOPMENT AS SEEN THROUGH MEMBERSHIP STATISTICS

Year	Clubs	Individual	Year	Clubs	Individual
1950	34		1975	176	804
1951	40		1976	200	1,250
1956	46		1977	208	1,753
1957	60		1978	216	2,534
1958	73		1979	237	2,890
1959	82		1980	223	3,157
1960	89		1981	244	3,408
1961	99		1982	244	3,416
1962	109		1983	249	3,860
1963	115		1984	251	4,128
1964	122		1985	261	4,133
1965	131		1986	260	4,358
1966	138		1987	262	4,805
1967	146		1988	267	5,117
1968	146		1989	260	5,703
1969	147		1990	270	6,829
1970	152		1991	270	7,189
1971	148		1992	268	7,674
1972	146		1993	296	9,682
1973	145		1994	312	10,143
1974	145	336	1995	312	10,245

NB: There has also been an Organisation membership for many years numbering over 200 organisations such as schools, mountain rescue teams, youth organisations, etc. A category for trade members was introduced in the late 1970s and grew to nearly 100 trade members. Now trade and organisations form part of a new Associate member category which numbers some 200+ in 1994.

MEMBERSHIP STATISTICS

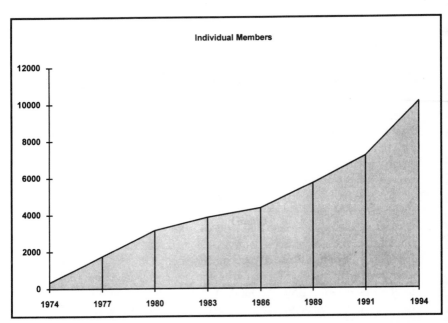

Individual Members

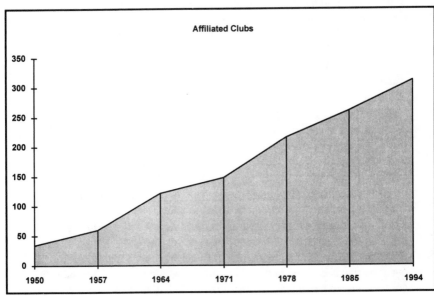

Affiliated Clubs

COMMITTEES

Access and Conservation – Plus ça Change?

[The following quote from the early 1800s, which appeared on a notice board, shows nicely just how far we have come with access in Britain.

'All persons found wandering abroad, lying, lodging or being in any barn, outhouse or in the open air and not giving a good account of themselves will be apprehended as rogues and vagabonds and either be publicly whipped or sent to the house of correction and afterwards disposed of according to law by order of the magistrates']

This article does not pretend to be a comprehensively researched historical account, rather it comprises personal recollections and reflections from someone who was in at the beginning of the Access & Conservation Committee, prompted by sweet inveigling by Derek Walker to contribute to the BMC's 50th Anniversary publication. In fact the Committee should celebrate its 21st Birthday this year, but nobody seems to be able to find its birth certificate – minutes of the first meeting – and therefore we can be no more precise than 'Autumn 1973'.

Before the Committee was formed, ad hoc initiatives by Areas or Committee of Management were the order of the day whenever there was an access problem or conservation threat, or whenever the BMC was invited to comment by Government, or some other national body, on these issues. On the COM, Hilary Sinclair, a former Honorary Secretary of the BMC, volunteered (or got landed with) the necessary research and secretarial work. Alan Blackshaw, the new Presidential broom, proposed that additional sub-committees of COM should be formed to strengthen the BMC by involving more volunteers with expert knowledge and hence 'broadening the base' of the Council. During this time I was no more than a moderately inactive member of the Climbers' Club, but happened to have occasional lunches with Alan because we worked in neighbouring office blocks on Millbank in London. Most of my spare time was taken up with being General Secretary of the Chiltern Society, a relatively new, but rapidly growing, amenity Society. I ventured the view that access to crags and mountains would become increasingly contentious and that, in any case, the BMC should be more visibly associated with access and conservation matters in the same way that the Ramblers' Association (RA) was then becoming. A fatal remark! So I found myself joining Gwen Moffat and Hilary Sinclair at Hilary's London flat for the first meeting of the Amenity, Conservation & Access Committee (ACC). (Amenity was gradually dropped from the title.) I discovered that we had joined the BMC's other fledglings – Finance, Publicity, Huts, Training, International Affairs and Future Policy. My earliest impressions of ACC were ones of seriousness of mission, breadth of topics covered (more of which later), and brevity of paperwork by Hilary (the civil servant) who served as both Secretary and Chair. Being already fully stretched with work, family and Chiltern Society my membership of ACC was hesitant and somewhat tentative. I was happy with the Terms of Reference proposed and duly approved: 'To work under the COM and EC for the protection and extension of mountaineering, climbing and walking areas and for the preservation and enhancement of the beauty of country of interest to mountaineers in combination with other bodies with similar objectives, and Area Committees assisting and advising the latter', but would the degree of delegation from COM in practice enable us to get on with the job and justify the time taken up at Committee meetings? I need have had no fears.

Membership of ACC rapidly expanded to include Bill Kendrick (Friends of the Lake District), Amory Lovins (Friends of the Earth), Mark Vallance, Bruce Goodwin, John Neill, Dave Ellis, John Bradley (National Park Officer, Brecon Beacons) and Paul Sedgwick. Some had detailed knowledge of particular areas and others specialist expertise, but I was struck particularly by the generally strong sense of commitment to 'conserving the mountains' and our access to them. Indeed it was this phrase that was chosen as the theme for a two-day national conference held at Plas y Brenin and organised by the ACC in 1976. The main purpose of the conference was to focus mountaineers' attention on the increasing problems of conserving mountains (including access to them), and to bring mountaineers' needs to the notice of planners and other organisations. It also served as a statement by the BMC that these issues mattered, as least as much as ones of techniques, equipment and safety. Already, in the President's Annual Report for 1974, it had been acknowledged that in dealing with 'the crucial problems of access, conservation and erosion, the BMC, through the ACC and Areas, had a real role to play for mountaineering collectively'. The conference not only underlined the importance of this area of work but, through the generally favourable media coverage and active participation by luminaries such as Robert Grieve, John Hunt and Jack Longland, signalled acceptance by the mountaineering world.

A major constraint to our work in the early days was the lack of any professional secretarial back-up, particularly as Hilary Sinclair was suffering from increasingly poor health. From early in 1977, the COM accepted the need for such support but, partly due to problems over Sports Council funding arising from the training dispute, it was not until the end of 1979 that the Committee had the part-time services of National Officer, Mark Hutchinson, who fortunately had planning qualifications. Mark's arrival on the scene coincided with Hilary Sinclair's resignation as Chairman due to ill-health thus ending services to mountaineering for over 30 years, with the award of the OBE. John Bradley took over the lead, onwards, upwards and sometimes down, until his untimely death on the hills in 1985. I thought that my fairly frequent and largely unpredictable absences abroad on work would protect me from a 'Buggins' turn' inspired stint as Chairman, but with the decision to appoint a Vice-Chair – first Dave Ellis and then, from 1992, Paul Sedgwick – objections could not be sustained and I took over in late 1986.

Although long service and continuity is a strong and valued feature of ACC membership, there have been changes and, as should be apparent from the current roll-call, subject matter expertise is greater than at its formation. And so many have made special contributions to its work.

Mike Browell – landscape architect. Interpretation of landscape issues and mountain users reactions to them. Richard Gilbert – Teacher and writer on topical mountaineering issues. Barbara Jones – Ecologist. Advice on biological matters, both policy issues and site specific. Tremadog management plan. Sue King – Biological Scientist, Head of school science department. Author of report on Peregrines and rock-climbers. Bob Lowe – Planner with extensive experience of National Parks. Investigations and reports on specific issues, especially in Wales. Dave Morris – Countryside campaigner and ecologist scientist. BMC representative and press officer. Mountain Protection Commission of the UIAA. John Neill – Former BMC President and Access Co-ordinator Committee for Wales. Tim Richardson – Planner and various countryside management jobs. Drafting of Access & Conservation Strategy. Paul Sedgwick – Planning consultant. Upland footpath study, BMC representative on BUFT. Matthew Simon – University lecturer in mechanical engineering. Secretarial assistance to ACC when without an Access Officer. Drafted papers on Energy and Long Walk In. Ken Taylor – Agricultural consultant. David Beskine –

Representative of the Ramblers' Association. Kevin Howett – Representative of the Mountaineering Council of Scotland.

Of greater importance, access to professional BMC staff has changed out of all recognition since the early days. Until 1979 ACC (and hence BMC) coped only because access problems and Government public consultation exercises were fewer. Areas were offered less support, communication with the media received less attention and Hilary Sinclair, occasionally supported by other members, put in much hard work. From 1980 to 1986 while Mark Hutchinson was responsible for executive action, the Committee's efforts seemed to run smoothly, albeit at a fairly leisurely pace.

During 1986 and 1987, without professional support, implementation often slipped or never occurred at all, despite members taking on and completing many assignments. At times we seemed to be out of our depth, not least because the tempo of public consultation requests increased to the level of near bombardment. From 1987, ACC had the services, more or less full-time, of Bill Wright. We were able to tackle the backlog of unimplemented Committee decisions and, in particular, strengthen work with and support of Area Committees and their voluntary access and conservation workers. The first annual access symposium was held in 1988 to provide a get-together of ACC members and area access volunteers, an opportunity to share experiences and problems and to learn from experts. Contact with all kinds of national and regional bodies was strengthened, particularly Government and its agencies for countryside, conservation, sport and physical recreation, the National Trust, Country Landowners Association, National Park Authorities, Council for National Parks and Ramblers' Association and the Mountaineering Council of Scotland. To secure a stamp of approval as a conservation organisation we sought and obtained for the BMC membership of the International Union for the Conservation of Nature. Contact with the mountaineering press and national media was also stepped up.

Early on in my Chairmanship I realised that to be really effective in conserving the mountains the BMC needed a network of volunteer access and conservation workers at the level of individual mountains and major crags. The one or two per Area, which we were then aspiring to achieve, would be nothing like enough. In the early days of the ACC we had promoted an 'adopt-a-crag' scheme linked principally to keeping litter down and ensuring access, but it was clear that many adoptions had been abandoned or neglected, presumably due to the lack of organisational structure and central support. It was obvious that one

Access Officer who was being run off his feet maintaining Area level contacts and developing and maintaining liaison with numerous national bodies, could not possibly take on the task of building up a large network of volunteers. It seemed possible, if unlikely, that once established, the network could be sustained on a part-time basis by one national Access and Conservation Officer, so the idea was born of an Access Liaison Officer, initially as a one-off contract position, and this recommendation of the ACC became incorporated into the 1990-93 Corporate Plan of the BMC.

However, as the months and years ticked by we had to face the fact that, despite pestering Presidents and the ever cheerful Derek Walker, the BMC's existing finances were not going to permit an appointment within the Plan period. So we sought dedicated funding and happily applications to the Countryside Commission and the Countryside Council for Wales for 50% grant for a three-year appointment proved successful. Added to this there were generous contributions from the Guidebook Committee and the Wild Country Foundation (Mark Vallance). The post was advertised, along with that of the Access & Conservation Office in 1993 and both brought in a wonderful bag of applicants, talented both on and off the rocks. Near the end of 1993 Jeremy Barlow took over the ACO post, coming from Oxfam with experience that included campaigning, and Kath Pyke filled the new ALO position having previously worked in countryside management and nature conservation.

And now for a quick scramble through the main issues and types of problem that were dealt with by the ACC in its first 3 years. How do these compare with those we faced some 20 years on? Are we into new country, or is the terrain much the same?

Reports of Government Committees and Commissions

There was the Sandford Committee on National Park Policies, the DOE's Countryside Review Committee on problems and policies, the DoE appointed Stevens Committee on Minerals hot on the heels of the discredited developer – rigged Zuckerman Commission - the Nugent Committee on military land and various policy position statements on footpaths and access. All these required scrutiny and discussion to formulate BMC views and to decide how these should be conveyed. On major topics like Sandford, ACC did comment separately on behalf of the BMC. For others we supported the views of national bodies such as the CCPR and the Standing Committee for National Parks (later Council for), of which the BMC was, or became, a member, or of CPRE with which we established liaison. A frequent pattern with reports of Government-appointed committees, as is well illustrated with Sandford, was long delays both before Government's official response and afterwards in implementing decisions, especially those related to strengthening countryside protection. This required vigilance and vigorous follow-up action by voluntary bodies to press for fulfilment of promises.

In the 1990s we are seeing history being repeated over 'Fit for the Future', the report of the 'Edwards' National Park Review Panel. For the BMC we were able to support most of the recommendations of this thorough review except that we did not like the rather flabby compromise stance on access to open countryside. Government eventually accepted many of the more important recommendations, such as independent boards for National Parks, and revision of Park purposes to stress that they should be places for *quiet* enjoyment, and included the measures in its 1992 party manifesto. These good intentions were not matched by provision for legislation in either the 1992 or the 1993 Queen's speeches. However, professional campaigning by the Council for National Parks, in which Council President Chris Bonington played a visible role, culminated in Lord Norrie's Private Members Bill with full Government backing. But, due to a procedural objection in the Commons, the Bill failed on the last pitch and, as I write, there are signs of cooling off by Government and doubts whether legislation will feature even in the 1994 Queen's speech. This prevarication – welcoming of a report followed by promises without fulfilment – as in the 1970s, raises serious doubts about how sincere the Government really is in protecting our countryside, even the best of it.

Over the last three years too there has been a mixed bag of policy consultations from Government on nature conservation, wind farms, super-quarries, means of controlling hunt saboteurs and New Age travellers (new laws on aggravated trespass), EC's agri-environment package and other topics. In a relatively new trend other national organisations have been seeking the BMC's views on their policy proposals: the Country Landowners Association on 'Access – New Way Forward', the Ramblers' Association moving in BMC territory on upland access in its 'Harmony in the Hills', the National Trust on access to its properties, and the Himalayan Environment Trust on its code of conduct for trekkers and mountaineers.

Government Planning Framework

In the early and mid-1970s, County Councils were busy preparing structure plans which established the planning policy framework – in line with Government legislation and guidelines – and National Parks were designing national park (management) plans. For the first time voluntary bodies were being invited to make representations early in the planning process, before preparation and after survey work, as well as at public hearings to review draft plans. This placed a potentially heavy work load on the BMC which had to be left mainly to Area Committees. The newly established ACC, lacking an executive officer, could not offer overall guidance or effective co-ordination of views, and only one Area had established a conservation sub-committee by early 1974. No doubt there are some 'old hands' who can remember how comprehensive and thorough was the scrutiny and the topics which provoked the most comment. Certainly at the ACC level one of the issues was which sites, even in National Parks, should receive the dubious accolade of 'honey pot', that is a popular location at which people should be encouraged to congregate to take pressure off other areas.

Two decades on, the need to scrutinise plans is still with us as the planning cycle requires these to be reviewed every five years (although the frequency usually stretches to 7 or 8 years) and there is a call for continual vigilance to check that planning, decisions and management activities do actually comply with policies. This is still very much the work for Area Committees and fortunately all have at least one voluntary Access & Conservation Officer and some have members who are also on National Park Committees and Boards. Attitudes to conservation and amenities have changed. For example, many question whether there is a case for classing any site – certainly any new site – as a 'honey pot' in our National Parks.

Access to Crags

This is at the heart of the BMC's work on access and conservation and, as such, every ACC agenda features a number of problem crags and mountains and, no doubt, such are raised at most Area meetings. Early on, the ACC sought to spell out principles which should guide decisions on individual sites such as no permits, no payment for access, no booking in, voluntary 'no climbing' agreements to protect fauna (birds) and flora where justified, and quiet negotiation (rather than confrontation) with landowners and occupiers to resolve conflicts. As far as possible protection of and negotiations over access were to be left to Areas with ACC providing guidelines and back-up support in difficult cases. In fact, it has been possible for ACC to be involved in individual cases only since the BMC has employed Access Officers. Thus individual case work has grown, particularly during Bill Wright's time because of more staff time available and growing pressures to stop or restrict access. More recently the underlying causes have often been hard-pressed landowners and occupiers seeking alternative cash generation opportunities, rather than keeping out beastly climbers, or avoiding the risk of legal liability. Certain crags such as Cheddar, Hugencroft, Craig y Forwen and Rainster Rocks are perennial problems or a frequent outcrop! In particular the failure to secure access agreements to the last three of these crags is a matter of concern which is constantly in the committee's area of unfinished business.

Threats to Mountain Areas from Development

As with access problems, proposals for road, energy, water and quarry projects have always been with us. From the start, the ACC has been able to follow the lead of national environmental organisations such as the Council for National Parks and the Council for Protection of Rural England. Sometimes our opposition has been implicit by virtue of membership (of CNP) or affiliation (MCofS). At other times, to counter major threats, we have been vocal in our own right or jointly in collaboration with other organisations such as the Ramblers' Association and individual National Park Societies. Either way, discussion of the issues and what line to follow on behalf of the BMC takes committee time. Thinking back over the years, it seems that more often than not the development goes ahead, but frequently modified in ways which minimise environmental damage as with powerhouse undergrounding and landscaping on the Llanberis pumped storage scheme. Also the mere fact of reasoned opposition on environmental grounds has undoubtedly influenced the designing of at least some future projects. And there have been successes such as the saving of the Cromlech Boulders.

In the early days, the ACC, backed up by Area Committees, applied its mind to the A66 trunk road widening in the Lakes and to proposals for the Manchester-Sheffield motorway and the Ambleside by-pass; on energy to the Llanberis pumped storage scheme and other possible projects; on water to plans for new reservoirs in the Peak and Dartmoor; and with quarries, to china-clay workings in Cornwall, limestone excavation in the Yorkshire Dales and fluorspar extraction at Middleton Moor. Twenty years on the themes are much the same – developer's desires to use wild and attractive land to build or extend infrastructure and services, or provide materials required by our relatively affluent nation – except that today it is more likely that the developer will be a private company rather than a public sector agency.

Area Committees continue to be the vigilant front-line, but ACC has involved itself in proposals to remove the Padog Bends on the A5; the general principle of wind farms and also specific developments; access to Water Authority land on privatisation; proposals for a massive extension of Swinden Quarry being pedalled as a means of landscaping existing excavations; and both the general principle of super quarries and specific proposals for such a quarry at Kentallen in Glencoe.

Cars and Traffic

From the start of the ACC this was seen as a complex matter on which there was much scope for conflicting views. On the one hand, mountaineers are only too willing to use roads or permitted access on tracks to reach their intended crags, or get as high up the mountain as possible. On the other hand, other people's cars create noise and visual intrusion which diminish the wilderness experience. Taking a responsible line, however, ACC came out in favour of traffic management schemes, including complete bans as introduced for the Goyt Valley to cope with excessive numbers of cars. It also advised Area Committees to support restrictions on indiscriminate parking to avoid blocking farm gateways and to oppose vehicular use of green lanes and similar tracks in mountain country. (Note recent events on the track up to Cloggy!)

Today this is an issue of growing significance and increasing complexity. Where traffic is restricted, as recently at the Roaches, is the alternative public transport provision adequate for climbers? How should we react to landowners and farmers providing small carparks near crags? Oppose on the grounds of unacceptable 'sub-urbanisation', or should we welcome on grounds of serving mountaineers' needs, reducing scope for conflict with landowners and, consistency with the BMC's policy of no payment for access while providing opportunities for landowners and tenants to recoup some of the costs of recreational use of their land?

Recreational Use By Others

Again this was seen as, and still is, a tricky area. By being too vociferous against grouse shooting, power boating, horses on paths, or off-road vehicles, we could be accused of hogging the best belays. Hence the ACC took, and has continued to adopt, the cautious stance of backing Government policies and regulations that restrict use of the countryside by noisy sports and seeking to enforce the proper use of the rights of way network. Hence, ACC supported the ban on power boats using lesser lakes in the Lake District. Today the main problems are mountain bikes and off-road vehicles. The ACC has strongly supported the Edwards Committee recommendations on redefining National Park objectives to stress recreational use for *quiet* enjoyment. However, this has not been without considerable agonising whether other visitors would regard a crag full of cussing, lycra-clad sport climbers as being quiet!

Forestry
The blanketing of the hills with evergreen forestry has been one of the environmental blights of the mountains in recent years. In the early days of the ACC, forestry in Britain was still reeling from a critical Government review which catalogued damage to landscape and views, restrictions on access, limited employment of generations and low return on capital, despite subsidies and tax concessions. Opposition to 'blanket afforestation' became quite emotive, particularly in the light of plans to increase plantings and the BMC certainly joined in the chorus against intensive upland forestry.

Ever since, forestry has been an active issue for ACC. We took the lead, along with other national recreation and conservation bodies, in successfully lobbying Government in 1988 to end the tax relief arrangements that granted subsidies, effectively up to 70% of the price, on land purchases for forestry. By 1991, we had a specific, clear-cut BMC policy on forestry advocating forestry and woodlands, mainly on lowlands and urban fringes, with fellings and new plantings to give a mixed age, mixed species structure as part of a multi-purpose countryside. Fortunately attitudes and practices within the forestry industry were rapidly changing at the time and, by the early 1990s, much public sector forestry was in line with BMC policy. The main concerns in recent years have been over privatisation, whether the private sector will demonstrate the same degree of attachment to environmental sensitivity and how to prevent the substantial losses of informal and permissive access on Forestry Commission properties on their sale to private landowners.

Limitations on Access to Open Countryside
Rather surprisingly, given the Committee's terms of reference and the fact that access to a high proportion of crags and mountains is above the fence or wall line, restrictions due to military use apart, this was not seen as a major issue at the first few meetings of ACC. Thus the absence of general 'rights' to roam at will on open land or to cross cultivated land to reach specific crags (in many cases) was not a matter of great concern. Initially ACC took a fairly passive stance welcoming access agreements and ranger services wherever Local Authorities provided them, but leaving Areas or Clubs to settle access problems, whenever they occurred, at local level through direct negotiation.

However, ACC did alert Areas to the possibility of problems in future and invited them to review whether the usual routes to main climbing locations were along public rights of way and, if not, to consider taking action to have those routes added to definitive maps during periodic statutory Rights of Way reviews. The resultant consultation, along with wider BMC work on future policy in the mid-1970s, sharpened strategy for achieving the BMC's principle aim of 'preserving and extending freedom of access to mountains and crags'. Thus ACC adopted the right to roam over open countryside while respecting the rights and interests of owners and other users, including wildlife, as the bedrock of BMC policy on access. These consultations did raise the question whether an established rock-climbing route could, or should be, regarded as a public right of way on the grounds of regular, unchallenged usage. ACC's legal boffins advised that this question had never been tested in law and that any action might fail. COM did, however, advocate a test case, but no action materialised.

For the last decade at least, achievement of a right to roam has been continuously on ACC's agenda. It was the basis of our enthusiastic lobbying for implementation (promised by Government but broken under pressure from the powerful Moorland Association) of the recommendations of the Common Land Forum. It formed the cornerstone of our response to the Edwards National Park Review Panel. It became the main issue in pre-election dialogues we sought to establish in 1991-2 with the political parties (most successfully with Labour resulting in a lengthy meeting between Bryan Gould, their Environment spokesperson, Bill Wright and myself). It has also been a key element in our reaction to the never ending flow of consultation documents about the countryside, access and recreation - for example, Countryside Council for Wales 'Threshold 21', Ramblers' Association's 'Harmony in the Hills', and Country Landowners Association's 'A Better Way Forward.'

Footpath Erosion

From the inception of ACC, heavy wear and tear on popular mountain paths, access routes to certain crags, and long-distance tracks was seen as a 'crucial problem' for BMC members. However, other than the obvious course of urging highway authorities, including National Parks where powers had been delegated, to carry out their maintenance responsibilities, ACC was not sure how to tackle the problem. By the mid-1980s ACC, through its publication '*Tread Lightly*' was advocating to all who venture into the uplands ways in which individuals could reduce their impact, perhaps the most visible of which is on footpaths.

A further initiative in the late 1980s came with Paul Sedgwick's study of the problem of footpath erosion, sparked off by growing concern among climbers that spilled over into the national press, about footpath construction work and inappropriate technologies and materials being used. This led to policy recommendations by ACC and a BMC policy on the repair and maintenance of upland footpaths which has become widely accepted. For example, its universal adoption was recommended by the Edwards Report on National Parks. In 1990 a conference attended by a wide spectrum of outdoor organisations also endorsed the policy and proposed setting up of a fund specifically to aid footpath repairs financed from sales of guidebooks and equipment. Somewhat protracted negotiations have led to the setting up of such a fund, under The British Upland Footpath Trust, sponsored by the Camping and Outdoor Leisure Association, the Ramblers' Association, the Mountaineering Council of Scotland and the BMC. BUFT became registered as a charity in June 1994 and benefited from early donations from the Wild Country Foundation and Berghaus. BUFT finally became a fully functioning and effective agency in upland path repair later in that year when the Alec Grant Trust donated £110,000 to be used in four major path repair projects on the West Face of Tryfan, Losehill in Derbyshire, Redacre Gill in Langdale and the Coire Lagan footpath in the Cuillin of Skye. On a temporary basis the BMC is shouldering the administrative burdens of BUFT.

Waymarking and Cairns

This was another issue addressed by the ACC. In order to conserve and protect the wilderness character of our uplands it enunciated a policy of 'keep to the minimum' consistent with safety, which has remained unchanged over the years. ACC applied, and continues to apply, this approach to long-distance trails advocating that these 'spoon-fed' paths should keep off rocky places and the highest ground. For example, it opposed a N-S Wales trail crossing all the highest peaks in Snowdonia.

Climbs Wrecked by Excessive Use of Ironmongery

This, along with excessive wear and the case for rationing access on the most popular crags, was raised as possible issues by ACC in its dialogue with Areas. Were they serious problems? Now, 20 years on, they most certainly are! The question of deciding on which crag bolts should be allowed and which (where bolts have been placed) should be cleaned up, remains fairly and squarely with Areas. Nevertheless, ACC has a real interest in the application of the BMC's policy on bolts; the sight or even the thought of 'rock jocks' dangling from top-ropes and drilling away at rock faces is not compatible with our image of climbing as quiet enjoyment to either the general public or to countryside managers. ACC is currently engaged in a major exercise to enunciate a comprehensive BMC strategy for access and conservation. Among the issues it is grappling with in thought, discussion and consultation are how to regulate and manage use of crags by groups, especially so that individual climbers are not 'crowded out', and whether (and in what ways) the general policy against paying to climb should be refined or qualified.

Litter and Eyesores on Mountains

From the start of ACC these were seen as serious problems for which all users of the hills were at fault. Applying the principle of 'putting our hut in order', ACC launched the 'adopt a mountain/crag' scheme under which individual clubs were encouraged to clean up and care for a particular mountain or crag and at the same time monitoring access to it. Areas were also encouraged to identify eyesores and lobby the owner or appropriate Local Authority for its removal. Influencing and educating mountain users in good housekeeping has remained a continuing if low-key activity, the main means being ACC's publication '*Tread Lightly*'.

We don't hear much about either litter or adopted crags these days. Are mountaineers heeding advice and taking litter home? Perhaps we need to pay more attention to cleaning up eyesores like the Pen y Gwryd petrol station?

Effective Action

Finally, the young ACC had to address the question of effectiveness. In theory it was there just to advise COM and Areas, although in practice it had or assumed considerable delegated authority from COM. First it sought to offer sound and intelligent advice, both on technical aspects of access and conservation issues and on tactics for resolving problems and getting the BMC's voice heard. On the latter it needed to be in tune with climbers' thinking and to recommend or undertake action in keeping with the BMC's 'style' on other issues. It urged Areas to develop good relations with local landowners and farmers and with other recreational users and their representative bodies. ACC encouraged quiet negotiation over problems rather than aggressive confrontation. ACC sought to develop regular liaison with its natural allies, RA, CNP and YHA and to build good relationships with national bodies such as Countryside Commission, Country Landowners Association and the National Trust. One means of laying the foundation for effective action was through organising the major conference at Plas y Brenin in 1976, already referred to, on Conserving the Mountains. It was well attended, not least by top mountaineering brass, had good speakers and, through signalling that the BMC was serious about access and conservation, helped to build the fledgling ACC's credibility and influence.

At an early ACC meeting it recommended that the BMC should recruit a number of influential people as its Vice-Presidents, especially who could carry weight on environmental matters. Also it sought to establish a list or panel of 'tame' Lords and MPs who should receive BMC material on access and conservation issues. Although neither of these proposals was rejected, in the absence of even a part-time A&C Officer, action was a long time in materialising, and we still have a lot to learn from the Ramblers' Association.

Three formal meetings of ACC a year for 21 years, much reading and study between meetings and attendance at seminars, conferences and even site meetings. Has it all been worth the efforts of ACC members and latterly the BMC staff? Certainly there have been a number of notable successes such as the undergrounding of plant and landscaping of the Llanberis pump storage scheme, the successful opposition to ski development in Lurcher's Gully on the Cairngorms and, latterly, gaining access to MOD's tank firing range, Range West at Castlemartin. Many access problems have been resolved, often with the help of the Access Fund, not just the more visible ones such as the re-opening of Pen Trwyn and keeping going climbing at Cheddar. National credibility has undoubtedly grown over the years, particularly with the Countryside Commission, Countryside Council for Wales, The Sports Council, Department of Environment, National Parks and some of the political parties. The proverbial grapevine tells us that, in these organisations by and large, we are looked upon as a responsible and reasonable body. And then there is the wider influence of numerous individual members of the BMC and its clubs who show a love and respect for the mountain environment, not just the activity of climbing. Some are visible as senior members of public bodies, including National Park Authorities, but in the final analysis it is the mass of rank and file climbers and hill-walkers, many heeding advice in *Tread Lightly*, who have greater impact.

So the answer to the question is 'Yes', albeit guardedly because there have been some failures, it has involved much activity and the task seems to be never ending. Undoubtedly, but for the BMC's work on access and conservation through the ACC and the growing army of volunteers in Areas, there would be many more Craig y Forwens; and landowners, countryside managers and the general public would have a much less favourable view of our beloved sport.

Peter Mould

ACCESS & CONSERVATION COMMITTEE
(Originally called Amenity, Conservation and Access Committee, then Access, Conservation and Amenity Committee).

Chairman
1973-79	T H Sinclair
1979-86	J H Bradley
1986-	P S Mould

Secretary
1973-79	T H Sinclair
	(also Chairman)
1979-86	M Hutchinson
1987-93	W Wright
1993-	J Barlow

Vice-Chairman
1986-92	D Ellis
1992-95	P Sedgwick

From 1986 to 1987 secretarial duties were undertaken by a working group of members of the Committee.

The Official Opening of the Glen Brittle Memorial Hut on June 5, 1965

After many years of fund-raising and negotiations the BMC, working in partnership with the Association of Scottish Climbing Clubs, eventually brought this ambitious project to a successful conclusion. The building of a new hut below Britain's finest mountain range, was perhaps the greatest achievement of the BMC's early years. The photograph on the right shows the three principal figures involved — Dame Flora Macleod of Macleod and Harry Spilsbury (centre) and, partially hidden behind Spilsbury and Dame Flora's daughter (Mrs Joan Wolrige Gordon), the redoubtable Ross Higgins of the ASCC, all receiving the deserved congratulations from the assembled climbers and dignitaries.

CHAIRMEN OF THE HUTS COMMITTEES

illustrated earlier

H.L.Roberts 1948-1952   Harry Spilsbury 1952-1968

Bill Wallace 1968-1973

Don Morrison 1974-1977

Tom Meredith 1977-1988
(MacIntyre)

John Foster 1985-
(Glenbrittle)

Dave Ellis 1989-
(MacIntyre)

Rod Hewing 1993-1995
(Whillans)

BMC HUTS   Three memorial appeals (for the climbers killed in World War II, Alex MacIntyre and Don Whillans) have allowed the BMC to acquire climbing huts in Glen Brittle (1965), near Ben Nevis (Onich, 1983 — *left*) and in the Peak District (1993) - a Neo-Gothic cottage below the Roaches, previously the home of the colourful recluse, Dougie Moller (*above*). Another acquisition (1995) was a former church in Didsbury (*below*) bought for the BMC's administrative, archival and social functions.

Nea Morin   Terry Tullis

ACCESS AND CONSERVATION A vital BMC task is maintaining access to cliffs and taking action to preserve, tidy or repair the mountain environment. The BMC's great achievement in its early years was to secure permanent access to Harrison's Rocks in Kent (*above*). These were acquired in 1958 (to be administered by a CCPR/BMC Committee) — a long-running saga in which Nea Morin, Terry Tullis and Maurice Bennett played leading roles. On the conservation front the BMC also supported the fight to stave off Draconian post-war hydro-electric plans for the North Wales valleys.

In 1979 Tremadog's magnificent Bwlch y Moch cliffs (*left*) were acquired by the BMC. The Roaches (1980, Peak Park), Earl Sterndale (1984, BMC) and Hobson Moor Quarry (1983, Tameside Council) were also saved for climbing, the latter after being clogged with tons of illegal landfill that was only cleared when climbers protested — an example of the need for constant vigilance.

Access and conservation were in conflict during the development of the sea cliffs where. ornithological factors placed major responsibilities on climbers. Red Wall, Anglesey *(right)* and Boulder Ruckle, Dorset were cliffs where BMC diplomacy retained access in the Seventies. BMC Officers have since been constantly involved in sensitive negotiations to maintain climbing access to sea cliffs.

CHAIRMEN OF THE ACCESS & CONSERVATION COMMITTEE plus BMC Access Officers
illustrated earlier:
Hilary Sinclair 1973—79
John Bradley 1979—86

Peter Mould 1986—

Mark Hutchinson
1979—1986

Bill Wright
1987—1993

Jeremy Barlow
1993—

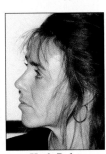

Kath Pyke
1993—1996

Above: Dave Cook (on the gate & inset) at the start of the 1991 mass trespass he organised, to gain access to the cliffs in the Range West military area of Pembroke. Army and BMC officials later worked a temporary compromise to allow climbing.

Spontaneous climber action has always played a role in access and conservation matters. In 1973 climbers squatted on top of the Cromlech boulders to prevent their demolition for road-widening. Bolts were removed in Pembroke, Cornwall, Lundy and the Peak by climbers determined to maintain ethical and environmental standards. In Yorkshire, in 1988, spontaneous outrage (fronted by the BMC) prevented Malham Cove being used for climbing competitions. In the Peak, in 1991, painted graffiti and chipping on Froggatt's Great Slab was cleaned and repaired *(below)* by a hastily convened team in which Jerry Moffatt *(below right)* played a prominent role.

Alex MacIntyre (N)
1978—1980

Andy Fanshawe(N)
1986—1989

Kip Gilpin (O)
1973—1975

Fred Smith (O)
1975—1977

Ian Dunn (O)
1983—1985

Hugh Harris (O)
1993—1995

Dave Humphries (T)
1977—1980

Chris Dodd (T)
1981—1989

Iain Peter (T)
1989—1994

John Cousins (T)
1990—1996

Caroline Robertson (S)
1968—70, 1971—73

Sonya MacMillan (S)
1970—1971

Rita Hallam (S)
1974—1984

Hilda Elford (S
MLTB) 1976—1993

Lesley Smithson (S)
1985—1989

Jayne Nicholson (S)
1989—1992

Katherine Brown (S)
1993—1995

Liz Guest (S)
1995—

EQUIPMENT AND SAFETY Climbers examine damaged helmets at the 1973 Safety Conference (*above: l to r*) Tom Price, Herbert Hartley (MRC), Bill March, Tony Moulam and Noel Kirkman (MRC). In its earlier years BMC testing revealed technical faults in ropes, helmets, karabiners, wire swaging, ice-axes, pitons, tapes etc. With the growth of specialist manufacturers standards improved but there are still examples of poor design and weak material, and Sport Climbing and Climbing Walls have brought new problems. The sagacity, vigilance and impartiality of the Technical Committee therefore remains of critical importance - e.g. in 1985 a poor nut design was revealed by drop tests (*below*), the sheath of the sling being stripped.

THE TECHNICAL COMMITTEE
Equipment Sub-Committee
Safety Committee
Chairmen illustrated earlier:
Technical Committee
Bill Ward 1945-1974
Vin Machin 1975-1987
Safety Committee
Charlie Gorrie 1954-1961
John Jackson 1971-1972

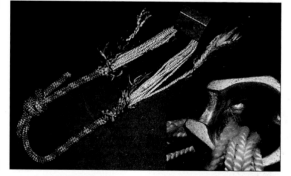

Neville McMillan 1987-

Ron James (SC) 1973

Johnnie Lees (SC) 1974-77

Mountaineering
The Official Journal of the British Mountaineering Council

Vol. 1   SEPTEMBER, 1947   No. 2

MOUNTAINEERING

PUBLISHED BY
THE BRITISH MOUNTAINEERING COUNCIL

MOUNTAINEERING

September, 1963   PRICE 2/-

Vol VI   No 4   1971   Price 12p

Mountaineering, the BMC's house magazine, was a model of crisp reporting and interest during its early years. Don Aldridge's functional 1959 redesign (*above*—showing John Cleare's elegant Bosigran cover) allowed climbing photographers to make telling contributions through the Sixties. In 1968 a fashionable graphic style was introduced (*left*) which undermined the photographic thrust. The publication was wound up in 1971.

Wing Cmdr.Tony Smyth
1947—1948

Ken Pearson
1948—1950

Herbert Coates
1950—1955

Don Aldridge
1958—1960

Dick Brown
1967

Kevin Fitzgerald
1968—1971

Bruce Bedford
1972—1973 *Mountain Life*

Chris Brasher
1973—1975 *Mountain Life*

John Cleare
1975 *Mountain Life*

Walt Unsworth 1976—1985
Climber and Rambler

Geoff Birtles
1985— *High*

Mountain Life

No. 3 AUGUST 1972
65 PENCE $1.35   NATIONAL MAGAZINE OF MOUNTAINEERING COMMENT AND CURRENT EVENTS

Mountain Life marked the BMC's bid to join the cut-throat world of commercial magazine publishing — a venture done in partnership with entrepreneurs Robin Collomb (1972—73) and the Chris Brasher / Anthony Churchill partnership (1973—75). Despite the acquisition of *Rocksport* in 1975 the magazine failed to achieve viable profitability and was incorporated into *The Climber* in 1976 where BMC news was thereafter squeezed into one or two pages a month.

Mountain Life +Rocksport
DECEMBER/JANUARY 1976
30p
23

Boardman on Everest
Cunningham on Ice

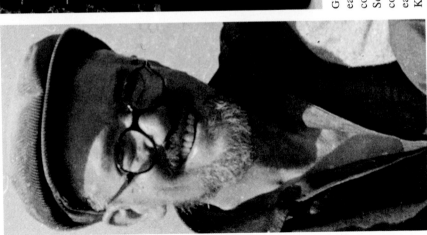

GUIDEBOOKS Eric Byne (*left*) recorded Peak District new routes in the post-war years and edited early guidebooks thereby laying the foundations of the BMC's guidebook tradition. Byne's work was consolidated by Tony Moulam, Paul Nunn and Dave Gregory. Gregory was General Editor during the Seventies and Geoff Milburn took over in 1980. The current nine definitive guides (front row, *above*) cover the busiest climbing region of Britain. They exist because of long-term cumulative effort, with each edition based on the field-work of a group of climbers – a typical team celebrates the 1990 Kinder guide publication (*below*). It is a tradition of service for which we owe them all a great debt.

Mark Clark
Harry Venables
Jed Sturah
Keith Ashton
Geoff Milburn
Con Carey
Dave Whitely
Adrian Hughes
Adam Longson
Craig Samuels
Marc Baxter
Loris Doyle
Jim Moran
Dave Gregory

GUIDEBOOK EDITORS AND OTHER KEY WORKERS

Editors illustrated earlier:

Eric Byne 1962-1968
Tony Moulam 1968-1969
Paul Nunn 1969-1973

Dave Gregory 1974—1980   Geoff Milburn 1980—

Nat Allen

Ernie Marshall

Tony Howard

Malc Baxter

Steve Bancroft

Carl Dawson

Gary Gibson

Dave Farrant

Phil Gibson

Keith Sharples

Graham Hoey

Malcolm Taylor

The need for regular and *definitive* guidebooks is epitomised by the saga linked to Cratcliffe's Fern Hill. This climb proved to be an alternative start to the 1951 route Nutcracker, climbed by Vin Ridgeway (died, 1956) and Peter Harding, but their route was missed from the 1970 guidebook and the apparent gap was filled in 1972 when Keith Myhill led Fern Hill (right). Later Harding questioned the originality of Fern Hill and a period of confusion followed. It transpired that Ridgeway led a lower traverse to gain, and climb, the edge of the buttress. Ridgeway stunned himself on the upper overhang so Harding completed the climb by the route taken later by Fern Hill!

Peak District Guidebooks

Without fear or favour I intend to begin this history lesson on Peak District rock-climbing guidebooks and how the BMC became responsible for creating stability in the Peak, with the guidebook *Laddow Area* Climbs on Gritstone, 1948, 4/- (20p). This most important of guidebooks to Peak climbing was produced by a group known as the 'Gritstone Guide Committee', formed in the summer of 1946 mainly of Manchester, Sheffield and South Midlands climbers. The Karabiner Mountaineering Club and the Manchester University Mountaineering Club had made the first moves, but they then joined forces with the Peak Climbing Club and the Rucksack Club. Encouragement came from S.M. Beal, H.J. Cooke, N.L. Horsfield, N. (Plum) Worrall, Arthur Birtwistle, J.E. Byrom and A.J. Lowe. By the winter of 1947 they had a manuscript, edited by Harry Parker, with the printer/publishers, Willmer Bros, and this was in the shops by the Spring of 1948. Volumes 2 and 3 of this series were under way by the summer of 1948. Meetings held in Manchester allocated areas to field workers, with Birmingham-based Eric Byne taking charge of the Sheffield teams when he began to meet them on the Edges. Volume 2, *The Sheffield Area*, 1951, was written by members of: The Valkyrie M.C., Sheffield University M.C., the Oread M.C., Midland Association of Mountaineers (M.A.M.), and the Peak C. C.

The third volume was edited by Allan Allsopp who, with the Laddow Area team, joined by various Lancashire and Yorkshire activists produced a remarkable guide to crags ranging from Windgather to Almscliff – this book had everything between its covers and was entitled *Kinder, Roches and Northern Areas*. These guidebooks appeared in the shops during the summer of 1952 at the princely sum of 9/- each (45p), hardbound with photographs, printed and published by Willmer Bros. (a remarkable achievement when there were no phones or typists, 2nd in the age of hand-written text, twopenny stamps, and big envelopes).

The production of these three guidebooks (including a revision of *Laddow Area* in 1956 and a revised edition of *Kinder and Roches Area*, 1957) and a reprint of the *Sheffield Area* book (1956) easily filled the

Left: Those involved in the ethical arguments about the use of bolts *appear* to agree on one point — that the Gritstone outcrops should remain untouched. Yet bolting and pegging on gritstone in the Fifties and Sixties shows that nothing can be taken for granted. The most notorious of these climbs used bolts and pegs on the main central wall of Wimberry in 1964. It was finally led free (left) in 1987 by Nick Plishko (Wristcutter's Lullaby, E6, 6c) as one of the finest free climbs on grit.

needs of the post-war climber. This period saw two other guidebooks appear which were produced privately, mainly due to lack of communication between clubs, climbers and the Guidebook Committee. Pete Harding and the Climbers' Club put out a large format soft-covered guidebook to *Black Rocks and Cratcliffe Tor* (1949). To *Brassington Rocks* (and Harborough), 1950 (being limestone then seen as presumably an alien rock) the Midland Association of Mountaineers gave a small hardback guidebook edited by Eric Byne. New crags and new climbs continued to be found and climbed. The now 'with it' field workers pushed the information through to the unstoppable Eric Byne who continued to catalogue and store it all.

1957 saw the appearance of volume 4 Climbs on Gritstone entitled *Further Developments in the Peak District* (edited by Byne and Wilfred White), price 10/6 (52p) printed and published by the ever faithful Willmer Bros. and Haram who were subsequently unable to see their way clear to support the Peak series again. *Further Developments* had a foreword by the old gritstone warrior Alf Bridge, and it contained an appeal to 'stop damaging gritstone edges with nailed boots', and from Eric Byne the statement 'that perhaps gritstone had now reached its peak in the standards of difficulty that has been attained'. The book contained many new crags and details of a dastardly development: 'artificial' or 'aid climbing'.

With the passing of Willmer Bros., Eric Byne continued the search for a publisher, generally without success. The development of crags continued and information on climbs flowed in unabated to Byne, while the guidebook work took on a *go slow*. Impatience by some of the younger element caused concern and a printed soft-cover supplement came out, produced by Rodney Wilson (and edited by C. Buckley) for the Manchester University M.C. If nothing else *Recent Developments on Peakland Gritstone* reactivated the guidebook team.

The British Mountaineering Council seemed eager to get involved in Peak District problems, while The Peak National Park was aware that climbers were all over its patch. This in turn involved the President of the BMC, Sir Jack Longland, who convened a meeting at his Matlock County Council offices where the Peak Area of the BMC had a Committee. Inspired by Jack Longland the meetings were enthusiastically attended by the Peak's greatest characters. It was at a 1960 meeting that the next important development happened. Into the meeting walked a troublesome-looking bearded craggy, Graham West. He had with him a completed manuscript of a guidebook to 'Mountain Limestone' and what was more important he had a publisher. The Peak Committee gave West and his book their blessing and in 1961 the revolutionary *Rock-climbs on the Mountain Limestone of Derbyshire* appeared, edited by Graham West, published for Manchester Gritstone Climbing Club, 1961, by Cade & Co, price 12/6 (62p). The enthusiasm of West and his artist mate, Malc Baxter, created the impetus required. Eric Byne was asked by Longland to form a committee to produce guidebooks to Peak climbing in 1962. This done it was seen that to contain Peak development on both gritstone and limestone 8 volumes would be required.

Arms were twisted and field workers set about the job leading to volume 1 of the new series *The Sheffield-Stanage Area* Rock-climbs in the Peak, edited by Byne, published by Cade & Co, price 12/6 (62p) which came out in May 1964. Again, something new – a plastic cover with in-bound pictures and produced for the Peak Committee of the BMC. Technically that should be the end of the story, however, the impoverished BMC, drastically short of funds, leaned heavily on Byne to keep the publishers sweet, an amazing arrangement still requiring no cash layout.

The romance with Cade & Co continued. In February 1965 *The Saddleworth – Chew Valley Area* came out, edited by Byne, published by Cade & Co, price 15/- (75p). Much of the work was done by the Rimmon M.C. and the Manchester Gritstone C.C. Following this came *The Sheffield – Froggatt Area*, 1965, price 17/6 (87p). This was Cade's last guidebook and Byne was again without a publisher. Sadly, almost surrounded by manuscripts, Eric Byne died on 2nd January 1968. The death of Byne and the absence of a publisher gave the opportunity to any taker with the means to produce a pirate guidebook. Roaches was out of print and not due until 1970. John Smith edited a paperback edition, sponsored by Bryan Stokes in Sheffield, *A Climbers' Guide to the Staffordshire Roaches and Hen Cloud Area*. This contained little exploration with its 162 routes compared to the 257 climbs in the official guidebook, but it provided the necessary challenge.

Dave Gregory collected all the Peak material available from Eric Byne's widow, Ivy, finding a complete manuscript for volume 4 *Chatsworth Grit*. The Climbers' Club Guidebook Committee was approached and through John Neill, Series Editor, it was agreed that with Tony Moulam as C.C. Editor and Paul Nunn for the Peak, the Climbers' Club would publish the guidebook. Volume 4 appeared in 1970, *The Chatsworth Gritstone Area*, published by the Climbers' Club for the BMC Peak Area Committee, jointly edited by Moulam and Nunn. It was the first Peak guidebook to cost £2. Paul Nunn took over the Editor's job, an arrangement that suited both the Climbers' Club, as publishers, as well as the BMC Peak Committee.

Volume 5 *The Northern Limestone Area* (1969) was compiled by Paul Nunn, as was volume 8 *The Southern Limestone Area* (1970). The manuscript for volume 6 *The Bleaklow Area*, had almost been completed by Byne, and the guidebook came out in 1971, published by the Climbers' Club. This was the last guidebook to have the support of the Climbers' Club and its distributor Moac.

Volume 7 was produced by a massive team effort and fortunately Eric Byne had laid out a manuscript before his death. Tony Moulam, CC, then Paul Nunn, took a bite at editing this book, gathering as they did all the new developments on Kinder. The withdrawal of the Climbers' Club support was due in the main to an overstretching of their fragile resources and the Peak guidebooks were in the mire once more. The BMC Management was approached and agreed to try, as the sport's governing body, to have a go at applying for a grant from the Sports Council. A meeting was held where our case was put, with existing guidebooks produced and evidence of their urgent need to climbing which impressed the gathering. In short a grant was made. Triumphant we returned to Kinder. Paul Nunn resigned the job under pressure from his own work. A troika was gathered to edit the guidebook with Gregory (brains), Vickers (publicity/distribution), and Allen (plumbing) forming the team.

The Kinder Area, volume 7 of the series finally appeared in 1972 after the original photographs had unfortunately all been lost. To supply some of the replacements, Dave Gregory roped in Geoff Milburn and the duo promptly dashed from crag to crag – discovering in the process that a white crash hat and a white anorak do not necessarily create the best black and white photographs. The troika sent out the guide dedicated to Eric Byne and under the name of Paul Nunn who had done much of the work on it. It was the first guidebook produced and financed under the BMC banner with the BMC logo on its spine. So began a whole new ball game for the guidebook team.

The final volume to this series, volume 9, *The Staffordshire Gritstone Area*, appeared in 1974, price £1.70; Dave Salt compiled the work with the trio of Gregory, Vickers and Allen overseeing it. The guidebook work for the BMC Peak series was never the same again. An Executive to the General Committee (the Open Meeting) was formed, responsible to the Publications Committee of the BMC. No longer HB pencils, erasers and exercise books … word-processors, floppy discs and a touch of the IBMs, and we were in business. My story ends here, and I'm pleased to say, grey hair, 20 guidebooks and 20 years later, 'They all still live happily ever after'.

The story however continued … the third series of guidebooks to the Peak District (Rock-climbs in the Peak) was overseen by Dave Gregory, starting with *Stanage Area* (edited by Brian Griffiths and Alan Wright) and *Chew Valley* (edited by Bob Whittaker) in 1976.

1977 saw Steve Bancroft's 'Bumper Fun Book' a.k.a. *Recent Developments to Rock-climbs in the Peak*, which brought many of John Allen's new routes to the notice of the climbing world. The 1978 *Froggatt Area* guidebook raised some criticism of the grading of climbs, and a Guidebook Executive was created with the chair person of the Peak Area Committee chairing its meetings. Lyn Noble filled this position for several years, followed briefly by Dave Dixon and then Ian Smith. The series continued with *Northern Limestone* (1980, edited by Chris Jackson), before a controversial decision was made to incorporate both limestone and gritstone crags into subsequent volumes. This led to *Derwent Valley* (1981, edited by Jim Ballard & Ernie Marshall).

At the end of the series Geoff Milburn took over as Series Editor, starting with volume 6, *Staffordshire Area* (1981, Mike Browell, Dave Jones & Nick Longland). The 1980s saw the fourth series (Peak District Climbs) which began to chart a complete record of all first ascents in the Peak District – a mammoth task. After the classic *Stanage-Millstone* (1983), a *Peak Supplement* (Gary Gibson, 1983) and *Derwent Gritstone* (1985), two limestone volumes finally expanded into three; *Peak Limestone – Stoney; Chee Dale*; and *South* (all 1987). *Moorland Gritstone – Chew Valley* (1988, compiled by Carl Dawson & Chris Hardy) was a particularly fine achievement and the series closed with *Staffordshire Gritstone* (1989, Gibson).

By 1988 the BMC Peak Area Guidebook Executive sought autonomy and after a short, sharp skirmish it eventually became the Guidebook Committee – a main committee in its own right with Terms of Reference and a Constitution specified by the Management Committee of the BMC. Its first (and so far only) chair person is Dave Gregory; the Series Editor is still Geoff Milburn, and little has changed.

The fifth series (Peak Rock-climbs) began with the flagship, *Stanage* (1989, Graham Hoey) and the long-awaited *Kinder and Bleaklow* (1990) which had taken 16 years to come to fruition. This was followed by another *Peak Supplement* (compiled by Chris Hardy, 1991). The *Froggatt* guide (1992, Keith Sharples) was the most recent of a sequence to be turned out by a hard-working band of volunteers.

The culmination of efforts was in 1993 with *On Peak Rock* – an encyclopaedic single volume to the District's best climbs for which the main driving force was the compiler Carl Dawson who shared the editing with Geoff Milburn. The launch of this event saw another milestone. Nat Allen, who began this brief history, bowed out from the last of his many guidebook functions, that of chairing the Guidebook Open Meetings, the infamous Shouting Matches. No-one has a longer connection with Peak District climbing and 'Uncle Nat' deserves more

than this brief mention. The challenges are greater than ever with access
to computer publishing methods making private ('pirate') guides easier
to produce. The Committee has also begun a series of topo guides to
ward off any threat from outside agencies starting with *Stanage* in 1993
by John Street helped by Dave Gregory. At present the Committee is
about to complete a volume to the gritstone of the Derwent Valley as
well as two to cover the Peak's limestone crags. After those the cycle
will doubtless begin again. Volunteer workers are harder to find in these
materialistic days but as to the future – optimism rules.

Nat Allen (with Dave Gregory and Geoff Milburn)

Note: During completion of this publication in 1995, Nat Allen lost the
battle against cancer, but had been climbing just a few days before his
death. Tragically Paul Nunn also died in an accident in the Karakoram.

GRITSTONE GUIDEBOOK COMMITTEE
This was inaugurated in November 1962 and consisted of the following
members: J.R. 'Nat' Allen (Rock & Ice), Peter Bamfield (Alpha M.C.),
Malcolm Baxter (Manchester Grit), Derek Burgess (Oread), Eric Byne
(Editor/Chairman), Keith Chadwick (Rimmon), Alan Clark (Peak C.C.),
D.M.E. Dickson (S.U.M.C.), John H. Fearon (Peak C.C.), Harry Gillott
(Peak C.C.), Les Gillott (Peak C.C.), Dennis Gray (Alpine C.G.), David
Gregory (Peak C.C.), Ray Handley (M.A.M.), Albert Hattersley (Peak
C.C.), M.P. Hatton (M.U.M.C.), Tony Howard (Rimmon), Barry Knox
(Mountain Club), John Loy (Peak C.C.), C.B. Machin (Peak Comm.),
Ernest Marshall (Oread), Martin Graham (Mountain Club), Donald
Morrison (Canadian A.C.), Paul Nunn (S.U.M.C.), Neil Parker (Gritstone
Club), David Penlington (Oread), K.J. Rhodes (M.U.M.C.), Mrs R.
Townsend, Ron Townsend (Peak C.C.), Graham West (Manchester Grit),
Mike Wild (S.U.M.C.), Ben Wilson (Peak C.C.), also a Black and Tans
member (later Mike Simpkins).

General Editors
1962-68   E Byne
1968-69   A J J Moulam
1969-73   P J Nunn
Replaced by Guidebook Committee Executive.

GUIDEBOOK COMMITTEE EXECUTIVE

Chairman

1979-84	L Noble
1984-85	D Dickson
1986-88	I Smith

Guidebook Series Editor

1974-80	D Gregory
1980-87	G Milburn

Business Manager

1979-87	M F Browell

Replaced by Guidebook Committee

GUIDEBOOK COMMITTEE

Chairman

1988-96	D Gregory
1996-	G Hoey

Secretary

1988-93	C Dawson
1993-94	H Lawrenson
1995-	A Wood

Guidebook Series Editor

1988-	G Milburn

Business Manager

1988-	G Hoey

Treasurer

1970-87	J Llewellyn Jones
1988-	B Griffiths

Other Current Members (Nov. 1994): Dave Farrant (Computers), Chris Hardy (New Climbs), Kath Pyke (BMC Access Officer), Geoff Radcliffe (Chatsworth Guide Compiler), Keith Sharples (Artwork), Malc Taylor (Limestone Guide Compiler), Chris Wright (Limestone Guide Compiler).

How Not to Produce a Guidebook

The BMC has several, even lots of committees. Most of them are composed of quite normal sociable individuals beavering away for the good of the Council and its members. The Guidebook Committee is not quite that. As with all the BMC committees, its members are all unpaid volunteers with wives and husbands who think that they ought to be putting the shelves up in the kitchen instead of spending all their time scribbling and going to meetings. All that as well as going climbing. They share the responsibilities; Field work, Photography, Diagrams. Marking the routes on the diagrams, Editing, Proof-reading, Word-processing, Pagination, Printer link, Business Manager, Treasurer, Access details, Computer Whiz.

Its members are mainly drawn either from Sheffield or the misty areas extending from Glossop to the wilderness of the Chew Valley. Its meetings take place alternatively in the two areas, frequently in the residences of the larger-housed, and occasionally in private rooms in public houses. When this occurs the landlord asks the regulars to be tolerant of the visitors and waters down his stronger beers, for the Guidebook Committee is beset by tribulations, the vicissitudes afflicting the production of guidebooks being legion.

Vital field workers emigrate to France and when encountered busking on the Champs Elysées cannot remember what happened to their notes. You have all the new routes written in your guidebook which is on top of your sack. Someone borrows your guidebook and it's gone for good. But one, having an address on it, it came back by post. You lend an irreplaceable old green Stanage guide to an artist. He gets a contract in the Emirates and the irreplaceable is seen no more. You have finally finished the work on your crag and the editor wants the routes numbered from the other end of the crag. You make that final (huh) visit to check that it reads correctly the other way round. Temptation wins and you put the typed sheets down while you boulder about for a while. The sudden gust blows the better part of the script into the Derwent. You are back at the car after the last visit to that unpopular crag. A passer-by wishes to know directions for his walk. You put the sheaf of notes on the car roof while you point out his way and drive off forgetful. Some primitive sense reminds you half a mile down the road but by your return the sheets are a muddy mâché.

All the summer the weather has been good and the photofile is brimming. The instant the photos disappear into the room where the

Post Office keeps winning pools entries, notices of unsuspected legacies, and other delights, the weather breaks and you have to rush round with unwilling leaders, seconds and photographers in rain and frost. The photographer and/or the artist takes flying time, falls off their bike, has an argument with a drunk/car/lamp post/falling rock and is walking about with their arm plastered in an horizontal right angle. And all the while the people you meet who know that you are connected with the guidebook scene (a fact you keep very quiet indeed, but evil secrets will out) wonder loudly why the guide is so overdue.

It is no better when the evolution brings it indoors. The final script rests in the printer's safe hand but the premises are bombed. The manuscript, typescript, galleys, ozalids or photographs get lost in the post. The post being proved unsafe the stages of the growing guide are transferred by cars which are broken into and the documents stolen. One stage of the proofs is like a large toilet roll. Your dog or child or wife has seen too many telly adverts and it finishes up wrapped round the table legs. Another stage has 32 pages printed on a large sheet of photo-paper in a complex order, half of them upside-down. You slip a neck disc trying to read the pages upside-down. The printed text is cut out and stuck in the form for the final pages. Bits of text slip off and get in the middle of a diagram. You don't notice that one of the diagrams has no numbers on it. There are Neb Buttresses on two of the crags and the diagrams appear on the wrong crag. One of the newly working-out quarries is filled in as the guide comes out. Immediately after publication of the guide, access problems develop on the newly popular crags. The owner of one blows it up. That of another covers it with tar.

Two things make it all worthwhile: The guides, when they see the light of day, and them, the members of the committee with whom you argue and protest. Who are stubborn and will not see your very reasonable point of view. With whose ideas on ethics and bolts you completely disagree. Who work like beavers for nothing, who turn up cheerfully for meeting after meeting. Who you count as mates and who get a tremendous kick out of climbing and who are putting so much back.

You're a competent crag artist or a keen climbing photographer. You're doing some guidebook work already? You've found some old quarries and all the locals are going mad with crowbars and bolt guns and you're collecting the descriptions and you need some help in getting them into print? Don't contact me through the BMC; contact the Hon. Editor, Geoff Milburn. He's younger and saner than me and his hair isn't grey. But think on, once he gets his claws into you, you could be still writing guidebooks in 30 years time.

Dave Gregory

History of the BMC Technical Committee

The BMC Technical Committee has always been one of the foremost and, to some, the most mysterious of the BMC Committees. It started life as the BMC Equipment Sub-Committee in about 1947. During the next 40-odd years it carried out many tests of equipment and provided representatives to standard-making bodies both in Britain and on the world scene. Its members have a reputation for longevity, both on the Committee and on this earth. Four of the thirteen Honorary Members have come from the Technical Committee. Awards obviously made partly for long service because those four people have given 93 years of service among them.

Over the years many people have contributed to the work and only a few are remembered here. Apologies to anyone missed. Your contribution was always appreciated. Among those remembered are scientists, climbers, instructors/guides, retailers and manufacturers.

BMC Equipment Sub-Committee

The Equipment Sub-Committee was formed in 1947 with Bill Ward as the first Chairman, a post he held for 27 years. He was joined in 1948 by Frank Solari who later served as Vice-Chairman for many years. Other stalwarts included Stanley Thomas and R.P. Mears, who was an early expert on ropes and karabiners. Frank Solari remembers that there were never enough people for the work to be done but, nevertheless, much was achieved.

In 1947 the Committee produced a specification for *Natural Fibre Ropes for Mountaineering*. This was used henceforth as a reference when testing ropes whether new and unused or damaged in accidents. Reports on accident investigations were published in *Mountaineering* until a breach occurred over the way Mr Mears handled the results of tests of ropes from several dealers. Soon after the Committee reformed without him and sales of the *Alpine Club Rope* were stopped as by now it was well below the standard of the best available.

Nylon ropes were starting to appear, but early ropes were not substantial enough and doubts were expressed about nylon until it was discovered that the problem was caused by abrasion while dragging the rope over rocks. (Some things never change.) Hemp and manila ropes of the period were substantial enough to cope with such treatment. The problem was solved by beefing up the nylon ropes which then quickly became universally accepted. This led to a British Standard for *Hawser Laid Climbing Ropes BS3 104:1959,* the first standard for a climbing rope anywhere in the world.

Soon kernmantel ropes began appearing from the continent, but their physical properties were initially unsatisfactory. Later, when the UIAA Safety Material Commission produced a standard involving a drop test, this problem disappeared. A subsequent problem of kernmantel ropes tending to become un-knotted during use was solved by the use of a knotability test devised by Graham Tiso.

Brittle karabiners and soft karabiners from European manufacturers were studied and a standard was devised to control their performance. A major problem was inadequate control of the metallurgical aspects of manufacture and the test facilities at the National Engineering Laboratory, East Kilbride, were put to full use in testing karabiners.

Work with the Institute of Aviation Medicine at Farnborough helped in producing a British Standard for *Climbing Helmets BS4423:1969* based on a draft standard for motor-cycle helmets.

Ice-axes were studied with a view to standards, but designs were too fluid and the work was inconclusive.

Joe Griffin at NEL, East Kilbride, conducted field tests on soft steel pitons and highlighted some of their weaknesses. When hard-steel pitons became available he was able to demonstrate their superiority by repeating the field tests.

In my own early days on the Committee we met either at the BMC's Park Crescent office in London or at the Alpine Club. Meetings started soon after 6pm and always went on until about 11pm. My earliest recollection is of the enormous length of time spent going over the minutes of the previous meeting for accuracy.

BMC Technical Committee

When the BMC moved to Manchester in late 1974 it was realised that the Equipment Sub-Committee must also move. The opportunity was taken to reform it with a wider role and to call it the BMC Technical Committee. A new Chairman was sought and, after a couple of false starts, Vin Machin was invited to take on the task. Initially Don Whillans was invited to be Deputy Chairman, but he found difficulty in attending meetings so, in 1976, I became Deputy Chairman.

The first Secretary was the new BMC National Officer, Peter Boardman. Over the following years this post has had a list of distinguished holders – Alex MacIntyre, Neil Grandison, Roger Payne, and now Andy MacNae.

Meetings took place at the BMC offices for many years until we became fed up with cars being broken into. We then moved to the NNC Clubhouse at Risley where meetings still take place. Meetings usually start by 7.30pm and often go on well after midnight. In the last few years the present Chairman, Neville McMillan, has re-organised the Committee into sub-committees and working groups. This cuts down the range of work at any one meeting, but long hours are still the norm.

One of the major successes has been a reporting scheme whereby shops and individuals can inform us of equipment failures where they wish us to carry out some investigative work. This sub-committee is always the busiest and investigations can take up to a year to complete.

UIAA Commissions

The BMC Technical Committee has always played a significant role on the international scene. They sent representatives to the first meeting of the *UIAA Safety Material Commission* in 1951. Frank Solari became President of that Commission in 1970 and held the post until 1974. When the *Safety Methods Commission* started in the 1970s, representatives were sent and I attended first in 1973 becoming Vice-President in 1976 to 1977.

In 1975 both UIAA Commissions merged to form the *UIAA Safety Commission* but the BMC Technical Committee continued sending two delegates. I have been one of the Technical Directors since 1978 and served as Vice-President again from 1988 to 1990. The BMC has hosted meetings of the UIAA Safety Commission in 1976 (Plas y Brenin), 1979 (London) and 1987 (Leeds University).

Standards

Early achievements included British Standards for *Hawser Laid Mountaineering Ropes* and *Climbers' Helmets*. The Committee also sent representatives to the committees preparing British Standards for breathable fabrics and for sit harnesses.

Our representatives have been leaders of working groups and major contributors to UIAA standards especially for karabiners and harnesses.

Neville McMillan represents the BMC on BSI work for CEN (European standards). The BMC acted as co-host (with BSI) to meetings of the CEN Working Party on Mountaineering Equipment in 1992 (Manchester Airport) and 1994 (Denshaw).

Communications with Climbers and the Trade

Over the years many different methods have been used to communicate with climbers, manufacturers and shops. In the early days much use was made of the BMC's publication *Mountaineering*. Later a Trade Newsletter was produced and circulated about 3 times each year. It was a limited channel but allowed the trade to keep abreast of our work. After the move to Manchester, first Tom Waghorn and later Steve Ashton, wrote up the work of the Committee in their regular columns in *Climber and Rambler* (later in *High*). This was successful while we had the services of those professionals. Such writing, however, is really a specialised task for which most of the Committee's members are not trained.

Public Meetings

In the late 1970s we experimented with public meetings. The initial demand was so great that two were held each year for about 3 years. The first-year audiences were more than 60 at each venue. In the first two years one meeting was held at Leeds University and one in London. Unfortunately by the third year, when one was held at Plas y Brenin, we attracted only 9 people.

In 1992 these meetings were revived with a meeting at Plas y Brenin. Over 60 people attended. Last year the audience grew to over 150. Only time will tell if we can continue to attract such numbers. In addition the Technical Committee has tried other channels of communication such as booklets and videos.

Booklets Produced

Three booklets have been produced all of which have been a success. *Knots* was produced in 1986, *Ropes* in 1990 and *Crampons* in 1992. *Knots* and *Ropes* are now being revised ready for re-issue. Other booklets on *Bolts*, *Helmets* and *Belaying Devices* are planned.

Videos

Even more successful has been the venture into videos. This started when Phil Dickens was able to borrow a camcorder from Nottingham University to record the re-enactment of an accident in which the rope broke due to abrasion. The final video was impressive and we realised the tremendous potential of this medium. A subsequent video on rope damage (*Fall Back*, 10 min) has been equally successful.

ABMEM
In 1991 the UK manufacturers of mountaineering equipment formed themselves into a pressure group in response to the impending legislation from Europe. ABMEM, the Association of British Mountaineering Equipment Manufacturers, has the full support of the Technical Committee. Through ABMEM manufacturers now have a greater representation on the Technical Committee and on the BSI Committee on Mountaineering Equipment.

Key Personalities
The Technical Committee has always had a good core of scientists and engineers. There has never been enough for the potential work which could be done nor was there ever enough money. Among those who have contributed the following is merely a selection:

Scientists: Dr Bill Ward from the Building Research Establishment; R.P. Mears early expert on ropes and karabiners; Frank Solari from the Aeronautical Inspectorate Directorate Laboratories, MOD; Dr Joe Griffin from the National Engineering Laboratory, East Kilbride. Carried out fundamental test work on karabiners and pitons; Dr Stanley Thomas from the National Physical Laboratory; Bob Robinson from the Royal Aircraft Establishment, Farnborough; Geoff Borwick from the National Engineering Laboratory. Carried out tests on ropes and karabiners; Dr Phil Dickens from Nottingham University, who also carried out development work on camming devices and testing of karabiners. He also got the Committee started making videos.

Climbers: Vin Machin, Chartered Engineer, later instructor; Tony Barley, Chartered Engineer; Neil Grandison, Metallurgist; Don Whillans; Alex MacIntyre; Andy Fanshawe.

Instructor/Guides: Peter Boardman; Rowlands Edwards carried out work on belaying devices; Bill March helped with organising of UIAA Safety Commission meeting in 1976; Colin Firth representing the BMC Guides; Roger Payne.

Retail Representatives: Graham Tiso devised the knottability test which is still part of the UIAA and CEN standards; Tony Lack helped to organise UIAA Safety Commission meeting in Leeds 1987; David Sprossan; Dave Brown helped with the *Knots* booklet;

Manufacturers Representative: Denny Moorehouse

Journalists: Tom Waghorn: Steve Ashton

Present Technical Committee:
Neville McMillan, Chartered Engineer; Andy MacNae; George Steele, Chartered Engineer, Chairman of Standards Sub-Committee; Dr John

Keighley, originally a scientist from Leeds University – textiles expert and now a helmet manufacturer; Paul Seddon, harness manufacturer and long time support on standards work; Hugh Banner, Chairman of ABMEM, hardware manufacturer; Alan Huyton, Chartered Engineer; Dick Peart, lecturer and specialist in engineering and production management at Nottingham University; Neil Grandison, engineer and contracts specialist; Vin Machin, engineer and chief instructor at Crowden Centre; Jane Blackford, engineer from Sheffield University; Ben Lyon, caving specialist and equipment distributor; Brian Molyneux, retail expert.

George Steele

An Account of the Life on the BMC Technical Committee and the UIAA Safety Commission

During more than twenty years on the BMC Technical Committee and the UIAA Safety Commission I have spent many hours trying to find new ways of advising climbers. The problem is often as simple as how to avoid them simply misusing their equipment. I have joined enthusiastically with my fellow committee members in worrying about how best to get the message over. Because as Jonathan Swift put it 'How is it possible to expect mankind to take advice when they will not so much as take warning.'

We often have to theorise about what might have caused the problem and thereby consider many possibilities which might never happen. The fact that many of the things about which we worry may never come to pass was foreseen by Oscar Wilde when he said, "the old believe everything, the middle-aged suspect everything, the young know everything". Needless to say the above committees are not short of relatively middle-aged and old men!

The main driving force in our work comes from a belief in Murphy's Law which states that *if something can go wrong it will go wrong; and not only will it go wrong but it will go wrong at the worst possible moment.* Consequently we spend a lot of our time worrying about potential problems or investigating equipment failures which caused or contributed to accidents. Despite this emphasis on safety and avoiding problems I have a personal point of view which I hope you will find refreshing.

Imagine driving along a road with an unmarked bad bend just ahead. It is of great importance whether you know about the bend or not. If you know about it you can be expected to take appropriate action and to negotiate the bend safely. If, on the other hand, you are completely unaware of the bend, you may well be in for a very nasty surprise if not much worse.

Similarly if I explain the potential dangers of not wearing a helmet or using a chest harness alone, and afterwards you go off and climb without a helmet and with only a chest harness, I will not be worried by your decision. Your actions will have been taken in the full knowledge of the dangers and I believe that in itself can considerably reduce those dangers.

This is not a view held universally, especially in some international circles, where safety is often considered to be an area where personal freedom should not be allowed. We find considerable problems because of the different philosophies in other countries. The Germans and Austrians, for example, feel a great responsibility to make climbing safer for their countrymen and to that end may impose restrictions on the use of equipment or techniques through their ability to withdraw alpine club membership or insurance cover if anything goes wrong.

The difficulties are compounded by our relative inability to speak the other European languages with any degree of fluency. On the other hand perhaps this is not such a great problem. Benjamin Franklin described a man who was so learned that he could name a horse in nine languages but so ignorant that he bought a cow to ride on.

It is vital to work towards harmony in international standards because most of the equipment we use in climbing is of foreign origin and even where it is British the manufacturers require an international market for the product to be economical in production. Nowadays we need to have European standards to meet legal requirements.

Some of my international colleagues are very learned men who try to apply their learning to the safety field. Unfortunately many of our problems are caused by a lack of hard facts upon which to base our recommendations or decisions. As A.E. Mander put it *'the fewer facts someone has the simpler the problem seems to him. If we know only a dozen facts it is not difficult to fit a theory to them. Unfortunately that theory may have little validity when more facts are discovered.'*

In the absence of adequate information proposals are often based upon distorted personal opinions by people who should heed Mark Twain's advice – 'get your facts right first then you can distort them as much as you please'.

This can lead to another situation obviously well known to Benjamin Franklin who said, "the learned fool writes his nonsense in better language than the unlearned, but 'tis still nonsense", and as Bertrand Russell put it 'even when the experts all agree, they may well be mistaken'.

Because of these problems, working to improve things at the international level is a very time-consuming task and we must ask for patience if we seem to take a long time over it.

In a slightly lighter vein I can tell you that my colleagues on the UIAA Safety Commission do not always practise what they preach. Much of our time at meetings is spent deliberating over the fine print in standards and recommendations. Sometimes after the work is finished we manage to have one day climbing. On occasion I have had cause to be amazed at the relatively poor standard of safety practised by my colleagues.

On my first meeting in 1973 in Andermatt we spent three days carrying out tests of belaying methods to determine those suitable to be recommended. The work was performed with great attention to detail and careful consideration of the safety of climbers. After the meeting we had a day's climbing on the south pillar of Grosse Schjien (a 250-metre Hard Severe). I was climbing with a Swiss Army Guide and Wolfgang Weber, a representative from the Swiss rope manufacturer, Arrova Mammut. The guide tied on to one end of the rope, tied Wolfgang on about 20 feet from the other end and asked me to tie on at the end. He then climbed until the rope ran out and belayed. We followed climbing together. Everything went well until we reached the crux which was a short blank wall about 4 metres high with a peg in its middle. The idea is to hang away from the peg until your feet are high enough to allow you to reach the holds at the top of the wall. The guide went ahead and disappeared round a corner above the wall. The rope was taken in and Wolfgang had a good tight rope as he climbed.

When the rope in front of me went taut I followed but mistimed my move at the peg as a result of which my feet slipped causing me to slide down to the ledge below. Because of the consequent tug on the rope Wolfgang appeared suddenly round the corner above looking rather startled and wondering what was happening. At the second attempt I made the move and the rest of the climb involved no more problems.

At the top I taxed the guide with the comment that we had worked so rigorously on safe belaying the last few days and now he was using quite unsafe methods. He shrugged his shoulders and said that he had watched me throughout the meeting and had seen that I was a good climber so he had ignored me altogether on the climb and had concentrated his attention on Wolfgang who was doing his first climb!

You will see from this that my colleagues are probably following Oscar Wilde in thinking that '*the only thing to do with good advice is to pass it on and never to use it oneself*'.

Speaking of advice reminds me of the time when we decided to try to get a Government Minister to visit a UIAA Safety Commission meeting we were organising in London. At that time I worked in the Department of Prices and Consumer Affairs (DPCA). One of our Ministers included 'walking' in his hobbies in Who's Who. We, therefore, decided that he might be interested in attending the meeting. The first step was to sound out the Minister informally. My own Director was supportive and the response from the Minister's Private office was positive. Next I had to draft a letter of invitation for Dennis Gray to send formally inviting the Minister to attend the meeting. On its receipt Private Office sent the letter to my Director for advice and he, of course, passed it on to me. Of course, the resulting advice was that he should accept. Two weeks before the event, Private Office was asked by Director to write the Minister's speech for the visit. Guess who was asked to do the first draft!

When the meeting started I advised the President of the Safety Commission, Georges Moissidis, that we would have the Minister visiting on the last day. He immediately asked me to write a speech for him to respond. The Minister's visit went off very well and his speech, would you believe it, was very praising for the work of the BMC Technical Committee. Work which otherwise would fall to his Consumer Safety Union of which I was a member. After the meeting Dennis Gray asked me to draft a letter of thanks and to ask the Minister for an opportunity to discuss with his officials the possibility of funding from DPCA for the work of the Technical Committee. The letter was eventually received and Private office sent it to my Director for advice. Guess who was consulted!

This time there was some opposition but eventually a meeting was arranged. The BMC was represented by Alan Blackshaw and Vin Machin. I sat across the table with my Director not being sure which hat I was supposed to be wearing. The outcome, unfortunately, was no funding. The Government had changed since the Minister's visit and there was now no policy for supporting safety work in the voluntary sector. Never mind we tried, oh how we tried.

EQUIPMENT SUB-COMMITTEE

Chairman			Vice-Chairman	
1945-74	Dr W H Ward		1946-66	F Solari

Secretary

1945-47	A R H Worssam
-53	R P Mears
1954-60	G W Hall
1961-63	E Lloyd
1963-66	F R Robinson
1966	A M Kragh (acting)
1966-73	J A Holmes
1973-74	F R Robinson

Wound up and replaced by Technical Committee in 1975.

SAFETY COMMITTEE

Chairman		Secretary	
1954-61	C C Gorrie	1971-72	R G Pettigrew
		1973	J R Lees
Lapsed. Reformed in 1971.		1973-77	P C Shone

Chairman

1971-72	J A Jackson
1973	R James
1974-77	J R Lees

Disbanded in 1977 and work taken over by Technical Committee.

TECHNICAL COMMITTEE

Chairman		Vice-Chairman	
1975-87	V Machin	1975-76	D Whillans
1987-	N McMillan	1976-	G Steele

Secretary

1975-77	P D Boardman	1978-80	A MacIntyre
1981-92	N Grandison	1992-95	R Payne
1995-	A MacNae		

The BMC and Mountain Training

In his autobiography *Life is Meeting*, Lord Hunt, himself a former President of the Royal Geographical Society, the Alpine Club, and the British Mountaineering Council, reveals that he was inspired to take up mountaineering at the age of 14 by the classic climbing book *The Making of a Mountaineer* by George Ingle Finch.

At about the same age I too discovered Finch's book in the library at Nottingham High School, whence I had been despatched to study a quite different topic. From that first encounter I developed a voracious appetite for mountain literature which, according to my tutors, was in inverse proportion to my appetite for academic scholarship(!) but I had gained the key! The torch was ignited for this adolescent. Britain's incomparable mountain heritage is mirrored, naturally, in the richness and variety of its mountain literature. What better educational foundation could any sport possess? Such a literature has produced scholar mountaineers in their turn. A rare breed. We have at least one – Robin Hodgkin – who is still active. When researching for this article I discovered that Geoffrey Winthrop Young's valedictory address in the Alpine Journal for 1944 was followed immediately by Robin's article on exploring the Ala Dag in Northern Turkey. As a Headmaster of Abbotsholme School in Derbyshire, Robin followed the redoubtable Reddie who was a pioneer of outdoor education in the 1930s!

Despite the profound influence of *The Making of a Mountaineer* on generations of young climbers, George Ingle Finch would have shied from the term 'Scholar-Mountaineer' – he was a pragmatist and came straight to the point:

'Man's heritage is great.
There are the mountains;
He may climb them.
Mountaineering is a game second only to the greatest and best of
   all man's games – life.'

For a more lyrical summary I must summon the master – C.E. Montague:

'In such a sport as mountaineering, vicissitudes of heat and cold are again, for a few make-believe hours, the hazards that they must have been to the houseless man of the prime; sunset and dawn are re-charged

with the freshness and wonder that they might have had on the morning and evening of the first day. Rightly to perceive a thing, in the fullness of its qualities, is really to create it.'

In this article on mountain training I shall seek to demonstrate that it was the Alpine Club, oldest and premier mountaineering society in the world, then acting as a representative body of sport, which first promoted training in mountaincraft when it responded positively to a request from the War Office to organise and operate a course in mountaincraft skills for army cadets with the aim of personal and social development, then described as 'Character Building'. The course, which was very successful, was held in April 1944. Amongst the team of Alpine Club members acting as instructors were Sir Jack Longland and the legendary A. B. Hargreaves. When I discovered this I telephoned 'A.B.H.', much to his astonishment! and he sent me the following note:

'Yes, we instructors, who included Dr Charles Warren and Ivan Waller, were recruited by the Alpine Club and Climbers' Club to help them with this, which we were pleased to do, though being in wartime, getting to and from Wales was very difficult for us because of petrol rationing. We were in Llanberis for 10 days and were accommodated in the Llyn Padarn Hotel which had been taken over for the officers of an infantry visit which was in camp in that area. I rather think they were commando troops and the cadets were accommodated with them in camp. These cadets were an excellent mixture of 17-year olds – some of them from public schools – who responded well to the daily activity on the hills, often in poor weather. I never saw the piece about this in the Alpine Club Journal, but was glad to have your photocopy of it. All I would add is that we (the instructors) had with us on various climbs, the Army NCOs, who knew it all (!), but didn't. One or two of them were more of a problem than the boys! The only accident there was occurred to me when I was doing a climb on Lliwedd called the Purple Passage, when some of the young soldiers moving about above kicked off a small stone fall which fell on my head and knocked me out, with the result that I was put into Bangor Hospital for a week with a hole in the head. The accident could have been much more serious if I had not landed on the firm level ground on that terrace across the East Peak where I had various people, including Ivan Waller, to get me up to the Terminal Arête and so home.

The most frightening part of the whole 10 days was having to be driven around in army transport by young soldiers who made great fun of it, though they did not actually have any smashes but only a few runs out of road and near misses. We got on well with the army unit commander who was enthusiastic about the idea and amongst the top brass who came to see what was going on, was Geoffrey Winthrop Young.'

Of course, in this informative period between 1937 and 1944 it will come as no surprise to learn that a number of kindred bodies were acting in parallel, but with no convergence. A British phenomenon! There appears to be no doubt, however, that the principle driving force in the movement towards the use of mountains as an education medium and vehicle, which gathered such momentum as to be irresistible even to Government and programmes of legislation, was the Alpine Club led by the redoubtable Geoffrey Winthrop Young, doyen of Alpinists, Her Majesty's Inspector of Schools, President of the Alpine Club and the British Mountaineering Council, poet, visionary and educationist.

In his seminal valedictory address read before the Alpine Club on 7th December 1943, more than half a century ago, Geoffrey Winthrop Young, during the course of an inspiring philosophical treatise, alluded to demands being made on the Alpine Club, in its specialist area of mountaincraft, from various quarters official and semi-official. He classed these under three headings, and emphasised the third, as a new character of demand, arising out of the rapid changes proceeding in the structure of society, the fresh attitude towards national education which was resulting from the changes, and the part which hills and climbing seemed now destined to take in such training.

He went on to enlarge the theme of the three categories, dwelling for a short time on the second which we now know as conservation of the mountains. He referred to our larger protective projects such as the great national parks scheme, and lamented that where such schemes were in conflict with powerful centralised interests, mountaineers were unable to protest on their behalf with a powerful, united mountaineering voice. Even when he had succeeded while President of the Climbers' Club, in securing a consultative committee, divergence of regional interests led it to commit a fantastic suicide by opposing, as its first act, the access to the mountains bill! But it is the third category which is of direct significance to this historical account and which was to lead directly to a 'new national heritage within a natural heritage', our LEA residential mountain centre. The demands of this category grew out of the rapidly changing social structure, and consciousness of the British people, and out of the establishments' progressive acceptance of a collective responsibility for the preparation for life and for good citizenship of their fellow countrymen.

Winthrop Young averred that, in compressing the experience of 45 years of study into what his contemporaries alluded to apologetically as 'education' into a sentence, he had long discovered with alarming certainty that they were paying far too much attention to the training of the mind alone, and far too little to the psycho-physical processes by which qualities, latent in every individual, and which he summarised as the chivalrous virtues: self-reliance, endurance, alertness, hardihood, daring, mutual service, self-sacrifice, were brought into the dominant position in controlling conduct. It took War to make the problem suddenly vital, and to secure implementation of measures to improve the fitness and physical well-being of young people both in the short and long term.

Gradually it became to be accepted that boys and young men first, girls and young women later, must spend some part of each year at least under conditions which would encourage them to realise themselves physically, and as individuals, in forms of adventure demanding resource, courage and endurance, and to realise themselves socially by service for and in a community. It was emphasised that the conditions of training must be those of reality. There had to be real hardship, real endurance, real risk, above all, real service. For these conditions, Young argued, the sea had in the past been the school of the race, the first school of the British people, which produced in them their historic quality. Sea schools with practical sailing had already been started under the auspices of the Outward Bound Trust. Aberdovey was founded in 1942.

In conclusion, Young averred that mountaineering, as he and his contemporaries had found in their own lives, afforded the like conditions for discipline and for adventure. The mountains and the sea the uneven surface of land and water, irregular, unforeseeable, but with dangers mitigated by experience, stood alone as training schools of manhood. Young reported that, of the two, mountain-climbing was found to exercise the greater fascination on young minds. What was the fascination? Can it even be expressed in words? Does C.E. Montague come near it again?

'Unless you are a mountaineer, an engineer, or a surveyor, the odds are that the great illumination will escape you all your life; you may return to the grave without ever having known what it is like when the contour lines begin to sing together like the biblical stars.'

This section concluded with the reporting of a request from the Army Cadet Force, which had proposed to introduce mountaineering as the 'peak' subject of its physical training and mental incitement, to affiliate to the Alpine Club for all mountain guidance.

In the meantime the Alpine Club was proceeding apace to set up an infrastructure. On Saturday 4th March 1944 the President announced the formation of a standing advisory committee on mountaineering, which had been effected since the club last met. This committee had met for the first time that afternoon. The President also mentioned that the club had been approached by the War Office in the matter of training selected members of the Army Cadet Force in rock-climbing and mountaineering. Imagine my surprise when recently I received an attractive new brochure for the Army Cadet Force describing mountain training and entitled 'Young Achievers'. I had a strong sense of déjà vu!

So from the very inception of what was to become the British Mountaineering Council, it was tasked with training youth! In the same journal Geoffrey Winthrop Young concluded an article on mountain warfare with this paragraph: 'In this connection it is to be hoped that the recent experiment of a short mountaineering course for a small picked body of army cadets will be followed up and become a permanent institution. (He was a visionary – hence Plas y Brenin and Glenmore Lodge, the National Mountain Centres.) While it may be true that only a few hundred a year can be trained in that way, a large proportion of those so trained will become keen climbers on their own and teach others.' The cascade had begun!

Philosophy was rapidly translated into practice as this account shows. The club agreed to advise the Army Cadet Force on all matters regarding hill climbing and mountaineering and, secondly, to provide instructors for an experimental training camp to be held in North Wales in April 1944 when a selected party of boys would be given a 10-day course in hill-walking, mountaineering and elementary rock-climbing. Hence the involvement of A.B. Hargreaves and other luminaries referred to earlier.

The Standing Advisory Committee was translated into the British Mountaineering Council and, as its first act, published the first training manual for climbers, written by the indefatigable J.E.Q. Barford – it was *Climbing in Britain* and was immensely popular. It sold 50,000 in the first edition. At the AGM of the Alpine Club held on Tuesday 5th December 1944 the President informed the meeting that the inaugural meeting of the British Mountaineering Council took place at the Alpine Club on 2nd December 1944 when 32 representatives of 23 clubs, representing about 7,000 mountaineers, were present. The officers of the Council are a President and an Honorary Secretary, both nominated by the Alpine Club, and a Vice-President nominated by Scottish Club representatives on the Council. Methods of election and powers of the Committee of the Council were described:

'The Council, not yet a year old, has in hand the following:

(i)   The publication of a book, under the auspices of the Council, entitled *Climbing in Britain* containing in concise form all the would-be climber and novice mountaineer should know. It will be cheaply priced and widely available (Spring 1946).

(ii)   An investigation of and report on the best modern climbing equipment and rope, including nylon rope.

(iii)   A furtherance of the national parks scheme as proposed in the recent white papers.

(iv)   The giving of advice and assistance to individual clubs and other bodies interested in mountaineering. In this connection the Council was responsible, at the request of the Central Council of Physical Recreation, for organising a number of mountaineering courses for interested young men.'

The Alpine Journal of 1944-45 carried the report of an experimental mountain course for army cadets held in North Wales during 10 days in April 1944. The course was held under the auspices of the War Office and was based at a military camp. The Climbers' Club kindly lent Helyg as an advance base. The instructors were N.G. Wykes (Commandant), T.A. Brocklebank (Chief Instructor), P. Bicknell, A.W. Bridge, A.B. Hargreaves (whose account is reproduced earlier), J.L. Longland and A.P. Sinker. Part-time help was given by A. Henderson, B. Donkin, N.E. Odell and C.A. Elliott. 'Many valuable data (sic) were gained in this important experiment, which there would be some hope of using in future courses if certain difficulties could be overcome.'

A very full programme was carried out. On Lliwedd, the Horned Crag, Route II, Central Gully and East Peak, and several West Peak routes were climbed, nearly all in rather slimy conditions. Several parties visited the Idwal Slabs (one cadet went up the Tennis Shoe climb), the Central Arête of Glyder Fawr and various Glyder Fach climbs. The Tryfan buttresses were all teeming with cadets almost daily, and it was here that some cadets led some rock-climbs towards the end. Very nearly half of their available days were spent in rock-climbing. It was also the aim of the course to teach cadets to move and find their way confidently and safely; for this were compass games, a manhunt, and expeditions to the Cnicht and Silyn groups as well as to Snowdon, the Glyders and the Carnedds. Weather was kindly, but nevertheless the cadets' achievement was no mean one, since they were not carefully picked, their average

age was barely 17, and they nearly all came from industrial towns. Signs of strain had to be expected, but the instructors' vigilance was such that every cadet was fit to take part in a final expedition over Snowdon by groups using five different routes, without any help from the instructors. The confidence, self reliance, eye for country and powers of leadership, which can be gained in the hills, as nowhere else, did not need stressing to the cognoscenti! It was hoped that all this and more was demonstrated to the War Office authorities by this course and that means would be found to build on this promising foundation.

Those 'means' did not materialise until six years later in 1950 when Derbyshire Local Education Authority became the first Authority to open a residential outdoor education centre. Whitehall Open Country Pursuits Centre on Longhill, Buxton, was officially opened on 28th December 1950. I am proud to report that I was there! I was then enjoying National Service in an RAF Operational Mountain Rescue Unit at Harper Hill, Buxton, and for that first weekend I was seconded to Whitehall as a voluntary instructor. The foundation of Whitehall was an historic development which saw the philosophies of educationists such as Geoffrey Winthrop Young and Jack Longland, then Director of Education for Derbyshire, translated into practice. The Outdoor Education Centre movement was born! Longland had strongly advocated the formation of the British Mountaineering Council, had instructed with A.B. Hargreaves and others on the first ever climbing course for youth organised by the Alpine Club, and was a member (and later Chairman) of the Outdoor Pursuits Committee of the Central Council of Physical Recreation. A distinguished former 'Everester' Jack Longland was visionary, bridge-builder and practitioner extraordinary. He played a seminal role in the growth of the outdoor education movement for more than 40 years and maintained a vigorous interest until his death in 1993.

Parallel to the progressive acquisition by many Local Education Authorities of residential centres, the Central Council of Physical Recreation established national residential mountain centres at Plas y Brenin and Glenmore Lodge. Both centres from their inception gave priority to the training of trainers and today are solely responsible for the training and assessment of the mountain instructor award (Summer) and the mountaineering instructor certificate (all seasons). Their principals are co-opted members of the MLTB and the United Kingdom Mountain Training Board. At the same time (1956) the County Badge Scheme (which I had met on teaching practice at Derby School) translated easily into the Duke of Edinburgh's Award and found an immediate national operational HQ for the expedition section at Plas y Brenin, where Lord Hunt, the first Director, was also Chairman of the Committee of Management. The Duke of Edinburgh Award flourished and flourishes still!

During the next decade three influential reports endorsed the work of the residential outdoor education centres and gave encouragement and impetus to the movement away from conventional sport and recreation to the 'sterner, freer pastimes' advocated by George Ingle Finch and his contemporaries of the Alpine Club. The reports were Albemarle (1960), Wolfenden (1960) and Newsom (1963). The Central Council of Physical Recreation had appointed the Wolfenden Committee which reported specifically and cogently on mountain activities. The message of Wolfenden was that the mould of tradition is irretrievably broken.

'We can no longer look to the well-established clubs to guide the steps of all those who, trained or not, are determined to have a go at one or other outdoor pursuit, and there is difficulty and danger here. In most other sports beginners can at wish or need teach themselves by simply trying and practising. Trial and error will not usually lead to disaster, but in many outdoor activities there is an element of danger. In fact this element of danger may be not only integral to the sport but part of the attraction to those who wish to pursue it. It is not that the actual danger is enjoyed for its own sake; its presence usually means that the situation has got out of control. What is clear is that the means of mastering potential dangers is to be found only in technique and applied experience. Supervision in this type of activity demands a high ratio of instructors, and there is therefore considerable need for greater numbers of experienced volunteers.' 33 years on we must argue that the 'considerable need' is for greater numbers of experienced and qualified volunteer instructors. Among the recommendations of the Wolfenden report were:

1. There should be a governing body for each sport.
2. There should be a national coach or training officer.
3. There should be a graded coaching or training scheme.

Following hard on Wolfenden was the foundation of the National Sports Council in 1965 spearheaded by Denis Howell in his capacity of Minister with special responsibility for sport; the year before had seen the foundation of the Mountain Leader Training Board. The final impetus for the rapid growth in the provision of LEA residential outdoor education centres came in 1970 when Sir Jack Longland highlighted the development as: 'An astonishing drift of the whole range of subjects which we call physical education towards outdoor pursuits, towards mountains and moors and rivers, lakes and the sea'. Why was this? Can C.E. Montague explain it again?

'Bodily safety, a treasure charmless to the mind in ordinary life, regains the piquant value of a thing that will not just come of itself; it has to be wooed; the winning of it depends on the right exertion of some faculty not too perplexing to be joyous – the yachtsman's handling of his craft, the climber's hold on rock, the swimmer's sureness of himself across half a mile of deep water, best of all when the security of everyone in a party depends upon the alertness and fitness of each of the others. Then you revivify all human comradeship too; it comes back cleared of the blur that may have dulled your sense of it at home.'

Lord Hunt in the same report referred to the establishment in 1964 of the Mountain Leader Training Board, born of necessity since:

'Apart from general education in primary and secondary schools, to make future adults aware of their mutual heritage it was also necessary to provide training in the actual skills and the know-how required for the safe use of facilities and for the development of more awareness of the danger of accidents inherent in adventure in wild country and on inland water. The work done by recognised centres in this field is very great, but not great enough. Above all we need to develop higher standards of competence among the adults who organise adventure activities among young people, and recruit more such organisers. The Mountain Leader Training Board was established to undertake this work for mountaineering generally. The use of leisure was still not highly enough regarded as a subject of education. Outdoor activities should have a larger share in the curriculum of teacher training colleges and schools.'

There is no doubt that in the 30 years since its foundation by the Central Council of Physical Recreation and the British Mountaineering Council, the Mountain Leader Training Board has profoundly influenced the nature and content of training schemes which has enabled trained, qualified and experienced adults from a range of professional backgrounds to safely and enjoyably introduce young people to mountain and moorland countryside. Through a continually developing programme of courses the MLTB has since its inception overseen the training and assessment of many thousands of teachers and youth workers who, in turn, have taken an active part in introducing many more thousands of young people to the educational rewards of living and working amongst the mountains. Local Education Authorities, recognising the need for safe practice have, over the years, given the MLTB active support in allocating in-service training funds to those field staff interested in working with young people in this challenging and adventurous sector of education. The MLTB is vitally concerned, therefore, that the training and assessment of leaders at present encouraged by the LEAs should continue to be encouraged, for example, by those schools which may have sought grant maintained status, or which have received the maximum delegation of resources, in particular Department for Education Funding for training, from Local Education Authorities now much diminished in size and influence.

The MLTB is particularly concerned that the Government appears to expect that the private sector will step in to provide the services previously provided by the LEA, and whilst not entirely opposed to the private sector offering both training and assessment opportunities, considers that such a step will result in a reduction in the number of people proceeding through the scheme, simply because it will become more costly for them to do so. The MLTB considers that such a proposal will also threaten the contribution and future involvement in mountain training of the LEA maintained residential outdoor education centres, many of which offer both training and assessment opportunities. The annual report of the MLTB for 1990 lists 156 courses offering training to 1,827 candidates. 61 of these courses and 535 trainers were provided by LEA centres. Of the 39 approved and licensed assessment centres, 27 were LEA maintained. The 1992 booklet on MLTB centres course provision lists 96 approved centres of which 43 are LEA maintained. The 1993 booklet on MLTB centre courses provision lists 86 approved centres of which 42 are LEA maintained. The LEA centres then are clearly crucial to the continued existence of the MLTB's training and assessment scheme and any threat to the centres, such as that contained in the Government's proposal for maximum delegation of the discretionary exception, threatens the scheme itself.

The MLTB voices a related concern that the Government, having demonstrated wisdom and foresight in adopting the statutory curriculum for physical and outdoor education, should now adopt a policy which inevitably limits the further training of teachers and youth workers who might have been expected to actually deliver the outdoor education curriculum and, in consequence, reduce the opportunities available to young people to experience the physical, intellectual, social and moral challenges inherent in an active participation in mountaineering.

The MLTB will continue to press the Government to make provision which will ensure that the training and assessment of mountain leaders will continue apace unaffected by recent legislative changes which have adversely affected the ability of LEAs to continue to fund in-service training of teachers and youth workers and to endorse the work of the UK Mountain Training Boards recently published booklet *National Guidelines*.

The outdoor education residential centres comprise a unique facility for mountain education, networked all over Great Britain, which is the envy of the world. Undoubtedly the greatest single contribution was made by the British Mountaineering Council when it endorsed training as a main priority as the first act of its foundation in 1944.

Bob Pettigrew

TRAINING COMMITTEE

Chairman		Secretary	
1974-75	Lord Hunt	1974-75	D D Gray

Disbanded. Re-established in 1980

Chairman		Secretary	
1980-87	R G Pettigrew	1981-89	C Dodd
1987-92	V Machin	1989-92	I Peter

Disbanded and replaced by Training Advisory Group in 1992.

Chairman		Secretary	
1992-93	J Porter	1992-94	I Peter
1993-	M Rosser	1994-95	R Payne
		1995-	A Last

STANDING ADVISORY COMMITTEE ON MOUNTAIN TRAINING POLICY

Chairman		Secretary	
1982-86	A Blackshaw	1981-89	C Dodd
1986-90	T Price	1989-92	I Peter
1990-92	A Blackshaw		

The Climbing Wall Committee

Although climbing walls had been in existence in Britain since the early Sixties, they first began to make their mark when they aided the surge in climbing standards in the early Seventies. Yorkshire climbers made good use of the Leeds University Wall (designed by Don Robinson) while Pete Livesey (perhaps the most influential pioneer of the period) built up his stamina in rock-starved Scunthorpe by remorseless traversing on the old-style wall at West Common Sports Hall.

Up to that point climbers had regarded these structures as something of a joke – tedious monstrosities of brick, concrete and wood that were useful only for the most simplistic of instructional tasks. BMC representatives (mainly from the training sector) had advised two Sports Council working parties in the Sixties and Seventies. The subsequent booklets and reports led to scores of unsuitable walls being incorporated into the new leisure centres, schools and universities – it was a sad catalogue of failure and a waste of resources.

I had visited a number of the climbing walls in the Sixties and found them of minimal interest. The first wall I used that offered some degree of sporting interest was the backyard wall at City University in London which was opened in the mid-Seventies. This was 10 metres high, brick-built, designed for leading and with a descent from the roof down into the building. Climbing there had the added interest of weather and seasonal variation – a not unwelcome factor, largely overlooked in the current obsession with indoor walls. The main problem with the wall was the very tiresome regime of regulations that was applied by the University staff for which they were frequently berated.

On one occasion Pete Boardman, the new National Officer of the BMC visited. Just the man to bring the manager to his senses I thought.

"This is Pete Boardman who has just climbed Everest – if you won't believe me that these rules and regulations are unnecessary, perhaps you'll believe him." The poor man, punch-drunk from weeks of complaints pleaded for mercy – "Leave me alone ... it's not my fault. Why don't you go up to the Sobell Centre: the manager there wants advice on a climbing wall – go and pester him."

The Sobell's Director was Stuart Cameron, a jaunty retired RAF Officer. He seemed impressed by this pair of intense mountaineering zealots who had come barging into his office and he gave us a conducted tour of the building. We immediately identified a long back corridor as

ideal for a traversing/soloing wall and we also discussed a bigger wall
for the sports hall that he was planning with his friend Gordon Bendall
(the founder of Bendcrete). The corridor wall was constructed with great
speed: a load of rocks (cobblestones, chunks of limestone and river pebbles)
bought from the local garden centre and a few days of intense effort in
partnership with the Sobell maintenance crew and we had a wall – this
owed something to Leeds University but also something to the training
wall established in Plas y Brenin in the Sixties. After advice, the Sobell
sports hall structure was designed as a leading wall with provision for
nut placement but with some bolts, and a belay bar, walk-off ledge and
ladder at the top. Both walls were free from administrative interference,
though initially the sports hall wall suffered from conflicts with badminton
and other sports. The Sobell facilities enjoyed instant and continual success.
For me this was a seminal learning experience. It was clear that with climber
direction on both administration and design it should be possible to get
new climbing walls established in an acceptable manner.

Other walls were built or modified in a more acceptable mould around
that time: the Robinson walls at Guiseley, Bradford, Rothwell and (a
few years later) at the Ackers in Birmingham; Brunel near Uxbridge
was modified by Bendcrete, a company also associated with a new
wall at Kelsey Kerridge at Cambridge. In the early Eighties a Sobell-
corridor-style-wall was built in Altrincham by a voluntary effort
spearheaded by Dave Pearce – this time using three sides of a large
dedicated room, with a full covering of judo-style matting and far
harder climbing. Another important development at that time was
the wall at Charlotte Mason College, Ambleside built with mainly
voluntary effort. This was in a dedicated building in the college grounds
with climbing on all facets, both inside and outside.

All of these ventures were popular and it was thus now clear that
climbing walls did have a major role to play, not for instruction, but as
potent new training aids for established climbers. It was also obvious
that unless the BMC took the initiative, new walls erected in the wake
of these successes would probably still fall short of the required design
and administration requirements. The better climbing wall manufacturers,
though able to influence design to some degree, were not well placed to
press for a freer form of administration – that had to come from the
climbers themselves.

Thus in the mid-Eighties the BMC got three-year funding for a special
development officer (Ian Dunn was appointed) and I was asked to preside
over a survey and set up a working party. Ian and I collaborated in an
energetic round of wall-sampling and fact-finding. We then convened a

PLAS Y BRENIN Major G.I.Milton, the first Director, with his deputy, John Jackson *(left)*, the politician Sir Hugh Dalton (*centre right*), and Sir John Hunt (*right*) at PyB in 1958, three years after its establishment as the National Mountaineering Centre. The BMC is formally involved in PyB's management, providing support and advice in shaping and updating its policies — a necessary though not always harmonious relationship. Under five Directors, PyB, in addition to instruction, has been involved in key training developments and has hosted climbing delegations, lectures and conferences.

| John Jackson | Bill March | John Barry | Dave Alcock |
| 1960—1975 | 1976—1977 | 1977—1985 | 1985—1995 |

(above) Architects of early training initiatives — Sir John Hunt and Geoffrey Winthrop Young confer at Eskdale Outward Bound School in 1954. *(below)* Participants in the first Mountain Leader Course, held at Plas y Brenin in 1964 and led by instructors Barbara Spark *(left)* and Ray Greenall *(front centre)*.

TRAINING POLICY

The BMC played a central role in establishing the main mountain-training programmes in Britain through the Guides and the Mountain Leader Training Board (MLTB). Although the guides now administer their own qualifications they remain closely linked to the BMC. The summer and winter Mountain Walking Leader Awards, the Mountain Instructor Scheme (MIC and MIA) and Single Pitch Super-visors Award (SPSA) are qualifications the use, structure and content of which remain important areas of BMC concern and policy-making.

(below) UIAA notables examine framed sacks at PyB in 1960: *(left to right)* M.Sottsaux (Belg.), M.Brilleand (Fr.), Jo Scarr (PyB), (the first woman to lead Cenotaph Corner) M Van den Berg (Holland), Dr Muhlman (Ger.) and Murray Scott (Glenmore Lodge).

THE UIAA (Union Internationale des Associations d'Alpinisme) was established in 1932. The BMC gives it maximum support, periodically hosting meetings or sending delegates abroad — *above*: Joe Walmsley (*front centre*) and other BMC officials hosting the 1980 Council meeting at Ambleside; *below:* Alan Blackshaw (*right*) at the 1991 Barcelona Mountaineering Commission meeting. The Commissions carry out the bulk of the practical work giving advice to the Council and General Assembly where policy decisions are made. Of late the UIAA has been much occupied in responding to access threats contained in proposed European legislation concerning mountains and sea cliffs. With the growth in international climbing the UIAA has also sought to maintain and develop its diplomatic links with the main mountainous countries to ensure that climbing can continue unimpeded, while still being alert to attendant ecological and sociological problems. The UIAA was drawn into organising international competitions in 1989 and under the Presidency of the late Pietro Segantini (*above:* dark-suited, front right) gained Olympic recognition in 1995.

BRITISH MOUNTAIN GUIDES The BMC certified the first Mountain Guides (Messrs. Wilson, Hudson, Cameron, Dwyer and Taylor) in January 1947. Though VS skills were required (assessment being on classic Severes) most early guides were involved in giving simple rock-climbing instruction (*top left*: George Dwyer demonstrates the bowline to a novice). The growth of mountain centres during the Sixties led to the instructor qualifications MIC and MIAC. These prompted the guides (by then an autonomous group, though still linked to the BMC) to toughen their standards by adding alpine, winter-climbing, and mountain-rescue skills.

There followed a bid to enter the International Guides Association (UIAGM). The photo above shows the British delegation of Colin Firth (*left*), Peter Boardman and John Brailsford (*right*) flanking the French delegate Guy Martin (*centre left*) at the 1977 meeting in Aosta when recognition was gained. This diplomatic triumph was followed by a visit to Britain in 1984 by leading European Guides (*below*) including Anderl Heckmair (*front right*), who had strongly supported British entry, the top French climbers Claude Jager and Guy Dufour (*centre*), and Antonio Carrel and Siegfried Messner (*back row, right*), scions of two famous Italian climbing families

John White
Kurt Sterchi
Austrian delegate
Alan McHardy
Alun Hughes
Herr Immer
Walter Stolz
Malcolm Creasy
Martin Barnicot
John Brailsford
Geoff Arkless
Alan Kimber
Claude Jäger
Guy Dufour
Franz Rasp
Swiss delegate
John Ellis
Xavier Kalt
Roberts
Les Ayres
Nev Collighan
Tim Jepson
Ola Engang
Antoni
Terry Taylor
Sigfried Messner
André Hechmair
Leo Taylor

Ken Wilson 1983-1985

Dave Pearce 1985-1986

Anna Gregory 1991-95

CLIMBING WALLS The BMC / SC manual (*left*) discouraged litigation and officious management and gave technical advice during a period of growth in climbing walls. In the large photo the BMC's Ian Dunn (*right*) discusses design issues with Mike Gilbert (Gwydyr M.C.) one of the developers of the Ellesmere Port soloing wall (opened 1985). The bigger commercial walls of the Nineties led to startling rises in fitness, but also brought high charges, top-roping, competitions and sport climbing which all posed problems for traditional climbing mores.

Development, Design and Management of
CLIMBING WALLS
A Technical Information Manual
for Architects, Leisure Managers and Climbers

CLIMBING COMPETITIONS   The Malham Cove competition scare forced the BMC to join the UIAA in supporting an international circuit of competitions on artificial structures. Commercially organised events (supported by the BMC) were held at Leeds (1989) and the National Indoor Arena in Birmingham (1991), but in 1992, when the sponsor withdrew, the BMC was drawn into organisation. The event (heavily subsidised) was again held in Birmingham (*above*) and repeated in 1994 and 1995. Stephen Porteous (Chairman of the Competitions Committee), Anna Gregory, Roger Payne, Hugh Harris, and the BMC staff shouldered the considerable organisational burden.

Initially the climbing was dominated by Jerry Moffatt (Leeds winner) and Simon Nadin (*right*) who became the 1989 World Champion. Later British participants (all fine climbers) fared less well, despite being organised into a Reebok sponsored squad (*below*: squad members Ben Moon, Felicity Butler, Tony Ryan and Ian Vickers).

AREA COMMITTEES The BMC's Area Committee meetings offer regular opportunities to deliberate on climbing affairs. All are welcome. In a formal vote one must be either a club 'representative' or a BMC individual member but, in practice, general discussion and opinion-sounding is the norm. The agenda usually involves regional cliff and access issues and consideration of national business prior to Management meetings. When there is a pressing local or national issue, special meetings are held to gain a broader sounding of opinion. This 1995 meeting of Lancashire/Cheshire climbers was held to vet a proposal to bolt gritstone climbs on the neglected Lester Mill Quarry. After impassioned debate the plan was rejected.

group of lay experts comprising: Hank Pasquill, Pete Livesey, Ivor Delafield, Mike Browell, Rick Graham, Ian Parsons and Dave Pearce. Our initial recommendations to the Management Committee (which were approved) were that we should draw up a major guidance manual which should be published in collaboration with the Sports Council to maximise its influence. We also noted the need for major new facilities in Sheffield and Birmingham which at that time had no adequate indoor walls.

The main message of the document would be a call for more climbing walls with better siting and design (both indoors and outdoors) and a total freedom from regulations. The focus should be on fitness training for experts, rather than basic novice training. It would also be candid about the dangers of climbing while showing that climbers alone were the best people to manage the risk – free from the distractions of overzealous management. We took evidence and advice from a number of sources. The drafting of this document occupied many sessions of painstaking work and debate. It was structured into three carefully tailored packages – one for architects and developers (with design and location in mind), one for centre administrators (to try to discourage restrictions, registration, sessioning and excessive payments) and the final one directed at climbers (to try to stiffen their resolve to demand the sport on their terms and not allow themselves to be pushed into the patterns of conventional sporting management). We were also aware of the need to give proper advice on the insurance and legal implications involved.

The manual was submitted to the BMC Management Committee in 1986 and provisionally approved pending the critical insurance, legal and Health and Safety ratification. The Management Committee also decided to set up a permanent Climbing Wall Sub-Committee. By this time I was battling with the General Secretary and the Executive on a range of unconnected political matters so, to ensure that the manual was brought to a successful conclusion, Dave Pearce took over the chairmanship of the new committee.

Dennis Gray and Alistair Macdonald (Chairman of the P.R. Committee) had expressed reservations about the length and detail of the proposed manual advocating a shorter, more targeted advice leaflet. They also had reservations about the legal and insurance implications of the manual's key aim of establishing (on walls) the freedom of decision that climbers took for granted on outdoor crags.

After some debate these concerns boiled down to whether the policy would conform to the Health and Safety at Work Act. The crucial meeting was when Dave Pearce met the Health and Safety Executive's Sports Centre representative (who had already studied the draft document) and secured his full support. Dave carefully explained that the manual allowed climbers the freedom to solo or lead whatever height they judged suitable, with or without ropes or harnesses as they saw fit. The official confirmed that this point was fully understood and accepted.

Throughout this period, the new Sub-Committee (which now included trade representatives) had remained united in its faith in the manual approach and their confidence was vindicated by this ruling. The Health and Safety Executive's view was incorporated in the carefully worded clauses on page 32 of the manual '... apart from groups under instruction they [the HSE] do not feel it appropriate to lay down strict rules and regulations for the use of climbing walls. They have examined this report and are in accord with its aims and objects and a copy has been circulated to all HS Inspectors. Stringent Rules and Regulations are therefore unnecessary'. With the Health and Safety uncertainty removed the Management Committee approved the manual for publication.

In hindsight it is clear that this was the key point when climbing walls got the green light to develop in a manner harmonious with the mainstream sport.

Meanwhile I had been liaising with the Sports Council design experts to ensure that the publication conformed to their housestyle and design criteria so that in every respect the Sports Council would see it as its own policy. With the BMC and Sports Council ratification secured, the manual was finally printed and published in 1988 entitled – *Development, Design and Management of CLIMBING WALLS: A Technical Information Manual for Architects, Leisure Managers and Climbers.*

The manual proved to be the tool that was required. It has ensured that the scores of new walls developed since that time have avoided most of the problems of the past, and it has also been highly influential in discouraging vexatious litigation. It is clear that the firm partnership between the BMC, the Sports Council and the Health and Safety Executive was the critical element in securing the authority which the manual has enjoyed. The main weakness of the manual was its rather modest vision of the future, though such were the problems in getting decent new walls built at that time, it was difficult to predict the explosion of interest that was to follow.

Once the manual was published Dave Pearce stood down from the chair which was then taken over by Mike Rosser. Ian Dunn's short term contract had ended and he moved into climbing wall construction though he remained on the committee as a trade representative.

Mike Rosser's Committee had the job of using the manual to secure reforms. The Area Committees each appointed climbing wall representatives as delegates to the Sub-Committee. Their job was to use the manual to get the bulk of the petty restrictions removed from walls all over the country. A list of towns and cities was drawn up where a climbing wall would be of use and eventually this was published as a National Climbing Wall Development Plan. Successive National Officers have been able to give advice (based on the manual and the national plan) and thereby encourage and guide new projects and then recommend them for Sports Council grant aid. The manual removed many anxieties but it was really the financial viability of the more popular walls that was the key to expansion. It was seen that they could earn enough money to be able to quickly recoup any modest capital expenditure (though the BMC policy was to insist on moderate pricing linked solely to administrative and capital costs). It was also seen that walls required virtually no direct administration. As a result dozens of new walls were soon available the most notable being: Newcastle, Sheffield Poly (BMC Financed), Keele, Ellesmere Port, Preston, Blackburn, Huddersfield, Rochdale, Oldham, Broughton and Southport – all of these being small, soloing-style, walls. The Mile End facility marked a further development where a large building was devoted to climbing.

At the end of the Eighties the craze for International Competitions began to push a new type of tall overhanging wall into the limelight. Initially these were cheaply built with specially produced mass-market holds screwed into plywood panelling.

Paul Reeve and Jim Kelly planned one such wall in Sheffield. Hearing that Jerry Moffatt, Mark Vallance and Richard Turnbull had similar plans they joined forces to build a major new facility at the Foundry in December 1991. This was not so much a climbing wall as a large climbing hall with scores of climbs all to be top-roped (ropes in-situ) several of which were overhanging sport-climbs in the European mould. A smaller bouldering wall was also added. In some respects this marked a departure from the advice in the manual in that top-roping was the presiding regime with in-situ ropes, lower-offs rather than gantry walk-offs, bolt-protection on bigger routes (where leading soon became the norm) and higher entry charges. A month later a similar facility – Undercover Rock – was opened in an old church in Bristol.

These were the first real commercially-based walls, previous ventures having been added to existing government, local authority or charitable institutions. This brought mixed blessings. Their main value was the immense amount of climbing that could be done. In this respect they were tremendously successful for training 'existing' climbers. They also proved to be great social focal points as well. They rapidly established themselves as a role models for the next wave of climbing wall development. The Rope Race (Marple), The Rock Face (Birmingham) and The Edge (Sheffield). Facilities have also been opened in Gloucester, Leicester, Hull and locations in Scotland and several existing walls – notably: Preston, Huddersfield, London (Sobell) and Warwick University – added overhanging competition-style leading walls.

The sheer dynamism and scale of these new walls may be blinding people to their defects, particularly their tendency to glamorise European-style sport-climbing and thereby undermine the loyalty to British-style adventure climbing. Climbing can apparently be conducted in complete safety (though subtle dangers still lurk). The soloing walls impose questions of judgement on climbers whereas here the stress is mainly on power and determination. Their influence is already apparent with the growing incidence of novice top-roping on the natural crags which may indicate a growing disinclination to face up to the challenges of the conventional sport. There is also frustration when new climbers find that their climbing wall performance is not easy to transfer, grade for grade, to the traditional crags.

The most insidious problem with the new-style walls is their appeal to people who have hardly any connection with outdoor climbing. These users have minimal experience and regard climbing walls merely as 'get fit' leisure facilities. Such users are often less aware of the underlying dangers of climbing that can still be found in a climbing wall setting. Even experienced climbers, distracted by the light-hearted atmosphere, can easily overlook some crucial belay or equipment check, a matter emphasised by several recent climbing wall incidents one of which involved a fatality.

The proprietors of these walls have also found that they have been compelled to tout for custom (particularly in the summer months) amongst schools and youth groups with the corresponding need to stress safety aspects and employ suitably 'qualified' instructors (a concern given extra edge in the aftermath of the Lyme Regis tragedy). There are now whimpers that even the lowly Single Pitch Supervisor Award is structured at too high a level for climbing wall training. The manual had advised that youth groups and scouts would come to walls with their own arrangements for supervision. This advice was given specifically to discourage Centre Managers from becoming directly involved with training in a dangerous sport. The physiological implications of encouraging minors to advance beyond basic sampling of the sport into regular forms of extreme exercise is another area of concern as is the lemming-like rush to set up climbing competitions for every age and every degree of skill. During 1995 there have been two Youth Festivals of climbing (at Huddersfield and Bristol) with children as young as six climbing and competing!

All of these aberrations are a far cry from advice contained in the manual. They pose major problems for the BMC in acting as a guardian of British climbing mores. Basic climbing instruction (beyond an initial sampler) is most efficaciously conducted to those who are fully motivated in a 'balanced' outdoor location where the dangers are self-evident. Commercial climbing walls are now peddling the myth of climbing in safety in a controlled environment to impressionable parents and children alike, with realistic outdoor introductions now being bypassed. Thus the pressures for total safety (always an illusion) have increased along with requests for new quasi-qualifications. Will we soon be faced with a broad demand to process the crags to be more like climbing walls?

These revived concerns, which had largely receded in the era of the soloing walls, now present a complex range of administrative puzzles. In resolving these matters the BMC will have to work harder than ever to maintain climbing freedoms. Paradoxically the answer may be by promoting walls that are more obviously challenging with a range of climbs (in all grades) where leader-placed protection is required so that new adherents to the sport have the opportunity to observe and practise traditional techniques. There may also be a renewed push, particularly in rock-starved regions, to establish outdoor 'crags' 'boulders' and 'edges' free from rules, payment and bolt-protection as potent trend-setters for the traditional sport. Such facilities would be ideal contenders for Foundation for Sports and the Arts, Lottery or Millennium funding.

The International Climbing Competitions had one useful spin-off when, in 1989, Simon Nadin (an outstanding all-round climber) became the first so-called male 'World Champion'. Not surprisingly this attracted Sports Council and commercial sponsorship with the terms 'competition' and 'national team' immediately striking sympathetic chords. Funding was made available for 'development walls' on which competition climbers might practise (the Foundry being an early recipient). The manual had somewhat ironically stated that climbing was free from organised competition, the intention being to discourage Sports Centre administrators from trying to invent them. Many climbers despise the whole idea of formalised competition but there was a spontaneous demand from others for bouldering competitions on the soloing walls ('games climbers play'). The more elaborate international sport-climbing competitions involving performances of breathtaking athleticism on large and fiercely overhanging structures did make a general contribution in forcing the pace on hold design and spectacular climbing wall architecture. Simon Nadin also noted that they compelled participants to lead climbs on sight which schemed against the growing tendency to only 'work' and 'red point' hard climbs rather than 'flash' them. He regarded this as a good thing.

Anna Gregory, who had replaced Mike Rosser in the Chair of the Sub-Committee in 1991, also became involved in the organisation of climbing competitions. Apologists in the BMC have justified the involvement in competitions with the excuse that the BMC was in control of the activity and preventing it from spreading to natural crags and outcrops. Others took the view that it was force-feeding an activity that without its support would have died a natural death. When the BMC moved from its original stance of mere support to full scale organisation and promotion in 1992, it took a controversial political step and also added a major new task to its workload. This became so onerous that by 1993 the BMC was relieved to at last get the funding for a specialist officer – Hugh Harris – to concentrate on youth, competitions and climbing walls. But International Climbing Competitions (which, apart from the final stages which can be sensational, have long periods of tedium for spectators) have not developed as expected and in recent years Hugh's time has been increasingly taken up with giving advice on new climbing wall projects, some of which are very large and complex.

Other activities of the committee are as follows:

* It has advised the UIAA on international wall standards.

* In 1994 the committee, in collaboration with *High* and Reebok, completed a gazetteer entitled *Climbing Walls* – a very useful booklet for the travelling climbing wall user.

* It has taken part in two I.L.A.M. Conferences and the Recreation Managers Show organised by the Sports Council in 1992 to advise and debate on climbing wall matters.

* It is currently working on the draft for a new manual.

* It has investigated physiological problems attending climbing wall use – a growing area of concern – and is drawing up an advice poster to encourage sensible practice.

These and many other tasks rest on the shoulders of the committee and its new Chairman, Tony Bird, who took over from Anna Gregory in 1995.

The BMC's energetic involvement with climbing walls from the mid-Eighties has been a major factor in their rapid development and popularity. Time alone will tell whether its involvement in competitions and promotion of competition-type walls has been equally beneficial. The whole future direction of climbing walls is now being keenly studied and the new climbing wall manual will need to steer a wise course through conflicting aspirations. Few can deny, however, that in recent years the BMC, for better or worse, has been necessarily engaged with this dynamic new technology and played an important role in its development.

Ken Wilson

Climbing Wall Competitions

The late Don Whillans once said, "climbing walls, climbing walls, there is no bleeding adventure on climbing walls". Well I agree that there is not a lot of adventure on most climbing walls; however, this does not preclude excellent fun, competition and enjoyment. There are some walls which can provide an enormous amount of adventure. A good example is at Sale, in Cheshire, where there is a wall situated on the north-east face of a building in Britain's wettest city. The wall starts 15ft off the ground with a catwalk of man-eating iron railings along its base. Just to climb to the first bolt runner is an adventure and you are in for another once you clip it and the bolt turns around!

The other adventure at Sale is gaining entry to the climbing wall. In 1983 as a newly appointed technical officer to the BMC, Dave Pearce and Ken Wilson advised me to visit the wall and agreed to hold my ropes. I rang the centre to find out whether a visit was possible and they duly advised me that I had to have a letter to prove I was a competent climber. I asked if such a letter from the BMC would be OK and subsequently wrote one minutes later. I also asked for permission for Dave and Ken. On arrival at the wall Ken decided that the letter of competence was totally unacceptable anyway and informed reception that he was Chris Bonington and had no letter of competence. This little adventure proceeded to lose us valuable (!) climbing/adventure time.

Competition is an exciting spectacle that happens on climbing walls. There can be few who were present at the 1989 Grand Prix in Leeds who were not overtaken by emotion with the tremendous performance of Jerry Moffatt when he jumped to the hold below which Didier Raboutou had fallen in trying to reach. On completion of the route he descended to non-stop applause. Critics of competitions can ask what were climbers doing inside on a glorious day in May when Almscliff and Caley as well as Kilnsey and Malham were all bone dry. Well I was there and I enjoyed the event and the memories of that climb will be as entrenched in my mind as much as any ascent I have ever witnessed.

Another memorable competition was at Lyons in the same year when Simon Nadin won the first World Championship. My memories from this event were not Simon's excellent ascent, but the ladies super final which was held on exactly the same route as the men. The crowd in Lyons was enormous and as Lynn Hill started to climb, the expectation that a memorable attempt was about to take place filled the Palais des Sport. Her ascent, only bettered by Simon Nadin and Jerry Moffat and coming ahead of J.B. Tribout and Stephan Glowacz, was exceptional.

1989 was started by another competition that also was extremely memorable as it took place on the 2nd April, my birthday. It was the DR Open and Claudie Dunn won the ladies event, taking a £50 cheque from DR Climbing Walls and a trophy to sit on the mantelpiece and remind me of my competitor in business. It also ensured a memorable birthday celebration.

Since the early Sixties there have been many climbers having fun on climbing walls, from Alex MacIntyre's Brick Edge Cruisers in Leeds in 1974 to the athletes at purpose built climbing centres at Sheffield and the one in Birmingham. This aspect, as both an introduction to our rewarding sport and a valuable training aid, is essential to the development of climbing. It was quick and futuristic of the BMC to realise this needed monitoring in 1983 and may it continue for many years to look after the developments that are happening around the country.

Ian Dunn

CLIMBING WALL COMMITTEE
Started life as the Climbing Wall Working Party

Chairman		**Secretary**	
1983-85	K Wilson	1983-85	I Dunn

Climbing Wall Committee set up in 1985 and reformed in 1986.

Chairman		**Secretary**	
1985-86	D Pearce	1986-87	E Jones
1986-91	M Rosser (after reform.)	1988-89	A Fanshawe
1991-95	Anna Gregory	1989-93	R Payne
1995-	A Bird	1993-95	H Harris

COMPETITION CLIMBING COMMITTEE

Chairman		**Secretary**	
1988-94	S Porteus	1988-89	A Fanshawe
1995-	G Desroy	1989-93	R Payne
		1993-95	H Harris
		1996-	J Arran

Public Relations

This committee was first mooted by Alan Blackshaw in 1973 and was formally launched in 1975. It was charged with scanning the whole spectrum of BMC activities and giving publicity advice and ideas, particularly to aid the General Secretary (Dennis Gray) who was also its Chairman.

It was hoped that this would result in a better coverage for mountaineering in the press, radio and television and also improve 'presentation of BMC policy' to the climbing world at large by keeping climbers aware of all the activities which the BMC was undertaking on their behalf (many of which are worthy but lacking in interest).

It drew its membership from climbers with media connections – in the early days there was Audrey Salkeld (who acted as Secretary for the duration of the committee), Tom Waghorn (another long-standing member), Ned Kelly, Leo Dickinson and Gordon Stainforth. The Editors of the national magazines were invited to attend but rarely appeared. I joined the committee in 1979 along with Ronnie Faux and later members included Mark Hutchinson (National Officer), Alistair Macdonald, Roger Durban, Jim Perrin and Chris Bonington. The Chairmanship was taken over by Alistair Macdonald in 1985 and the committee was finally wound up in 1990. Meetings (often barely quorate) were usually held on a mid-week afternoon in the Manchester HQ. These are best characterised as amiable discussions ranging over the whole area of BMC policy, though in the later stages some meetings were more heated. Tom Waghorn noted that the General Secretary's comprehensive briefings on what had been going on in the BMC and the climbing world were of great value to him in his capacity as a journalist on the *Manchester Evening News*, and Ronnie Faux (*The Times*) and Alistair Macdonald (*BBC TV North*) also brought direct national press and media involvement. Others were present less as recipients of information than of shapers of its presentation. The main subject headings that were covered over the years were as follows:

* *The Magazines:* The coverage of the BMC in the various magazines was a regular item of discussion and constant suggestions were given on how this might be improved. After *Mountain Life* ceased publication in 1975 the BMC placed its news in *The Climber and Rambler* but the partnership began to deteriorate in the mid-Eighties. In 1985 *High* took over as the official magazine. The magazines carried official BMC news and the committee advised on its presentation.

* *BMC Publications:* The presentation of BMC policy in its various documents and its annual report was a standard item of business. The committee could do little more than advise – in practice these publications usually relied on the literacy and wisdom of the writer with very little editing. Jim Perrin was specifically invited to lend his skills as a sub-editor though he was soon employed (in a fee-paid capacity) as the BMC's journalistic scribe and hatchet-man in chief dealing with the regular magazine columns as well as in-house publications.

Roger Durban (working in consultation with Jim Perrin and myself) produced the BMC's first concise colour publicity leaflet designed to attractively and succintly reflect its work and policies.

The committee also advocated a more graphic presentation of facts and figures in the annual report.

* *The Press:* Shock/horror stories about mountain accidents and rescues were a constant source of anxiety particularly in the winter months. The General Secretary, the President or some other spokesman (often Chris Bonington, Doug Scott or Lord Hunt) were invariably approached to comment to the Press, Radio or Television. The committee was a useful forum for considering how matters had been handled and how they might be improved. There was concern that some Mountain Rescue leaders could advocate restrictions on winter climbing. It was seen to be essential that good relations were maintained between the BMC and the Mountain Rescue Committee. Accordingly a delegation (Gray, Salkeld and Macdonald) attended a Mountain Rescue Committee's AGM and Dinner in Exeter in 1988 where there was a 'frank and businesslike' exchange of views.

* *National Conferences:* These biennial events were regularly considered and the committee gave many suggestions on who to invite. The BMC Conference had much potential for positive publicity. Initially they had a range of serious contributions on important issues but slowly the entertainment aspect began to dominate and they became, in effect, sparkling jamborees of films, panel games and slide shows for the faithful. The committee advised on how good publicity might be achieved with such things as press handouts, photos, photo-calls and interviews. In practice the sheer exertion of organising these events sapped most of the BMC's energies and subsequent publicity was usually confined to a photo report in the official magazine and modest press comment. A photo-call of all the guests became standard practice. The committee specifically advised that the BMC should run a Conference aimed more at mountain walkers than rock-climbers and mountaineers, to reflect the breadth of its constituency. This was held at Buxton in 1985 and was a qualified success. For some reason the experiment was never repeated.

* *International Meets:* Consideration was given to these events – particularly those involving invitations to Britain and ways in which they might be publicised. The idea of women's meets originated from the committee and had its consistent support. Three of these were held and they proved a great success. Later four International Youth Meets took place – here the General Secretary was reviving a UIAA activity that was much in vogue in the Sixties – again they proved a great success. The idea of an Ethnic Minorities meet was floated but rejected.

The P.R. Committee, composed of amateurs, was confined to giving periodic advice. The enlarged secretariat of the Nineties took over the whole PR burden working in close consultation with a graphic design company and cultivating contacts with a range of specialist journalists. As a result the corporate image of the BMC has improved (particularly evident in the annual report) though publications remain varied in style and content (perhaps no bad thing). The coverage of BMC affairs in the magazines has also improved and the climbing world is briefed about events and the broad areas of policy. However, by the mid-Nineties, it had become clear that something extra was needed to give BMC news a more in-depth coverage. Accordingly *Access News* (a pamphlet dealing with access and conservation matters that had been published sporadically from 1988) began regular publication in 1994, and 1996 will see the launch of *Summit*, the first BMC house magazine since the demise of *Mountaineering* in the early Seventies. These two periodicals, together with the BMC News in *High* and exchanges by E-Mail and the Internet together with greater activity in BMC Area Meetings should allow a fuller discussion on complex BMC and climbing matters in the future. Targeted press campaigns also have a role to play. In October 1995 the BMC focused press attention on the threat of Council of Europe environmental climbing bans on cliffs with landscape or biodiversity importance and a month later a Press Conference was held in London in an attempt to pre-empt some of the alarmist media coverage of winter accidents. Concerted BMC efforts have also injected a greater degree of accuracy and balance into press reports of recent high-profile Himalayan accidents.

As a national organisation the BMC now recognises the critical importance of accurate and positive publicity and is constantly seeking more effective ways of conveying its message and reflecting the climbing world in a positive light. The current Access and Conservation Officer, Jeremy Barlow, had ten years of campaigning experience with Oxfam before joining the BMC and the recent appointment of an Information Officer (Andy McNae) is a further indication of that resolve. While the modern methods are a great improvement on the patchy amateurism of the past, there is a danger that ordinary climbers will fail to become actively involved and leave it all to the officials. A broad and regular sounding of lay opinion is essential in our loosely organised sport to give policy presentation greater insight and ensure that it remains in touch with the hopes and fears of the broad mass of the climbing world. In this context it is possible that new ways of sounding lay opinion will need to be devised as the BMC's affairs grow in complexity.

                                                              Ken Wilson

PUBLIC RELATIONS COMMITTEE
Secretary
1945-46   J E Q Barford
Lapsed. Set up again in 1973 and in due course took over activities of Publicity and Films and Visual Aids Committee.

Chairman		Secretary	
1973-75	D W Partridge	1975-88	Audrey Salkeld
1975-85	D D Gray	1988-89	Lesley Smithson
1985-90	A Macdonald	1989-90	Jayne Nicholson

Wound up in 1990 and replaced by Marketing Committee.

PUBLICITY COMMITTEE
Secretary
1973-?   Audrey Salkeld
Wound up and work taken over by Public Relations Committee.

FILMS & VIDEO COMMITTEE
Chairman
1974- ?   N Kelly

Secretary
1974-?   J Hartley
Wound up and work taken over by Public Relations Committee.

MARKETING COMMITTEE
Chairman		Secretary	
1990-95	D W Walker	1990-92	Jayne Nicholson
		1992-	Katherine Brown

OTHER BMC COMMITTEES

HUTS COMMITTEE
Secretary
1945-46   J E Q Barford
Lapsed. Changed to Central Hut Fund

Chairman & Treasurer
1948-52   H L Roberts
Changed to Hut Memorial Fund Management Committee in 1952.

Chairman		**Secretary**	
1952-64	H P Spilsbury	1952-55	H C Parker
		1956-61	Mrs M L Files
		1962-64	W Wallace

Honorary Treasurer
1952-55   I H Ogilvie
1956-64   A S Pigott
Changed to Hut Management Committee in 1964.

Chairman		**Secretary**	
1964-68	H P Spilsbury	1964-68	W Wallace
1968-73	W Wallace	1968-69	D D Stewart
1974-77	D Morrison	1969-73	J Simpson
		1974-75	T Meredith
		1975-77	P Roscoe

Honorary Treasurer
1964-68   A S Pigott
1968-73   Y E Yule
Superseded by Glenbrittle and MacIntyre Hut Management Committees.

Chairman of the Glenbrittle Hut Committee
1985-   J Foster

Chairman of the Alex MacIntyre Hut Committee
1977-88   T Meredith
1989-   D Ellis

Chairman of the Don Whillans Hut Committee
1993-95   R Hewing
1996-   D W Walker

INTERNATIONAL COMMITTEE

Chairman		Secretary	
1973-75	A Blackshaw	1973-83	A Heppenstall
1975-85	M H Westmacott	1983-94	R Rutland
1985-92	Wing Cdr N Ridley	1995-	A MacNae
1992-95	P J Nunn		
1995-	Lindsay Griffin		

SKI MOUNTAINEERING & TOURING COMMITTEE

Originally run by BSF and taken over by the BMC in 1990.

Chairman		Secretary	
1990-	M Burrows-Smith	1990-94	I Peter

FINANCE COMMITTEE

Chairman			
1973-74	J Llewellyn Jones	1984-87	B Nicholls
1974-78	J E Byrom	1987-88	H Mellor
1978-82	I MacCallum	1987-92	M Watson
1982-83	J Walmsley	1992-95	B Monk
		1995-	J Shaw

Secretary			
1975-77	F A Smith	1989-95	D W Walker
1978-89	D D Gray	1996-	A Heron

FUTURE POLICY COMMITTEE – set up 1965

Chairman	
1965-	I H Ogilvie

Disbanded and set up again in 1973.

Chairman		Secretary	
1973-77	A Blackshaw	1973-77	D W Partridge

Disbanded in 1977 and set up again in 1983.

Chairman			
1983-84	D D Gray		
1984-86	Dr W Butler	Disbanded	

PUBLICATIONS COMMITTEE

Secretary	
1945-46	J E Q Barford

Lapsed. Set up again in 1973.

PUBLICATIONS COMMITTEE (continued)
Chairman

1973-75	Dr J Wilkinson	1989-90	B Atkins
1978-89	D D Gray		

Secretary

1973-74	K S Vickers	1986-87	D Gregory
1974-75	Dr J Wilkinson	1987-89	D D Gray
1977-85	G Milburn		

Replaced by Marketing Committee in 1990.

THOSE WHO HAVE CHAIRED BMC SUB-COMMITTEES
AND ARE NOT ILLUSTRATED ELSEWHERE IN THIS BOOK

Norman Ridley	Lindsay Griffin	Alistair Macdonald
International 1985-92	International 1995-	Public Relatns.1985-90

Ned Kelly	Martin Burrows-Smith	Bruce Atkins
Film/Video 1974	Ski Mntng 1990-95	Publications 1989-90

AREA AND NATIONAL COMMITTEES

The Area and National Committees were first formed as follows:

1945	Lake District	1968	South-West and Southern
1945	Committee for North Wales	1970	Mount. Council of Scotland
1947	Peak District	1974	Yorkshire and Humberside
1965	North-East	1978	Lancashire and Cheshire
1968	London and South-East	1994	Midland

The Lake District Area - A Look Back

"History" said Derek Walker. "Just a few notes on the BMC's Lake District Area Committee since its inception in 1945. Sorry about the short time limit and it being Christmas, any chance it being ready early January?"

Out came the tape player, but who to call? Who that's still alive to tell of those early years. Sid Cross came to mind, Bill Ruthven and Di Hampton, all ex-Chairpersons able to give flavour to any story. I progressed, meetings organised; Sid Tuesday, Di Wednesday, then down to Bill's at Warton on Thursday and, of course, Andy Prickett, the present Chairman, on Friday.

I gleaned a wealth of enthralling information, so much so that cups of tea stood until cold by my intense interest. I was immediately struck by the make-up, the 'legends' of Lakeland brought together in 1945 with the common aim of furthering good mountain practices and for the vetting of those mountaineers endeavouring to attain a Guide's Certificate.

A letter from Geoffrey Winthrop Young to A. T. Hargreaves invited him to a dinner in London. They were both joined by Johnny Jenkins and John Barford (first BMC Secretary). 'Black ties to be worn!' Sid said that he would not have been able to attend. He did not have a black tie!

The formation of the Lakes' Area Committee was tabled. A. T. H. came back to Lakeland's Langdale Valley and formed the first committee made up primarily of Fell and Rock Club members. A. B. Hargreaves (who stayed a member until 1979), John Appleyard, Dick Plint, Sid Cross and A. T. H. came together in the Wayfarers' Robertson Lamb hut, a momentous occasion. They quickly came to an impasse over who should chair the meetings, for none of them wished to do so. Suggestions came slowly until A. T. H. proposed the well known hotelier from the 'Old Hotel', Cyril Bulman, a knowledgeable, congenial man who knew everyone who climbed in the area, including those likely to attain Guides' Certificates. For Secretary, Cyril cajoled A. R. Wells, a Liverpool man who was much involved in the Scout movement and who had recently built Heron Crag House in Langdale.

The members, other than Chairman Bulman, were foremost mountaineers and rock-climbers; there was a feeling in those days that if it was anything to do with mountaineering one should be a mountaineer. Bulman was acceptable for being born and bred in Eskdale, backed up by his extensive mountain walking prowess.

Truly a formidable first committee with a wealth of first ascents and climbs of quality and daring between them, the right people in the right place at the right time.

When you consider some of those Guides' Certificates, awarded in those first years to other 'legends' like Jim Cameron, Jim Birkett, Len Muscroft and Chuck Hudson, they could only have been sanctioned by such memorable foundation members.

Meetings were often concluded on the crags. Access was not a problem in those early years. Sid Cross and A. T. H. stood down from the Committee when they had a joint venture, owning a hotel in Eskdale. (A.T.H. was later killed in a skiing accident whilst on holiday in Austria in 1951.) Eric Arnison, a Penrith solicitor, took over the chair in 1957, keeping the Fell and Rock tradition, followed by Sid Cross on his return to Langdale, the O.D.G., as 'mine host'.

One of Sid's comments to me was that 'they were lucky to belong to their day and were most fortunate!'

I wonder if he still felt that way when access did become a big problem at Chapel Head Scar, a limestone escarpment 4 miles east of Newby Bridge at the south end of Windermere. A beautiful, hard crag to climb on, quiet and secluded where sunshine graces the crag throughout most of the day, likened by some to Tremadoc (*Climber* December 1976).

Trouble never comes alone, Trowbarrow Quarry in Silverdale followed, luckily for the Lakes' Area they were able to spread the load with the Lancashire and Cheshire Committee claiming this one!

The owner of Chapel Head Scar Crag, Michael Stanley of Witherslack Hall, banned climbing; he was distraught by the drastic gardening undertaken by some climbers in the hunger for new routes; trees had been savaged, ivy stripped and rare plants trampled. Cumbria Naturalists Ltd owned the land at the crag top and the area was designated as a Site of Special Scientific Interest. There had also been some verbal abuse. Chairman Sid used all his knowledge and considerable diplomacy to defuse the situation, very ably assisted by the then Lakes' Secretary, Bill Ruthven (Wayfarers' Club), enabling all the involved organisations to come together at Witherslack Hall. The Cumbria Naturalists were backed by the Nature Conservancy Council and, of course, BMC Lakes brought in the 'big guns' from Manchester!

Many meetings followed; progress was laborious. The Lake District National Park Ranger, Pete Rogers, joined the group. It took until 1979, two years after Sid retired, before the final agreement was signed under the Chairmanship of Percy Howard (Wayfarers'), a practical conclusion which has stood the test of time (abseiling bolts installed 1990), seasonal restrictions, but a right to climb. 1978 was the year when agreement was reached for car access through Ennerdale Forest to Gillerthwaite as far as the zigzag path below Pillar, not free, but enabling more daytime on the hill. The make-up of the Committee has always contained headstrong personalities whose strength enabled mutual advantageous involvement with other strong Lakes-based organisations, a need brought intensively to the fore at Chapel Head.

Bill Ruthven became Chairman, setting a precedent of Secretary to the Chair, meetings were held at Staveley until another ex-Secretary, Bob Dawes, took over from Bill and moved the meetings to The Golden Rule, Ambleside, only minutes away from a climbing wall and a very convivial venue; there the present meetings often start on the wall but end up in the bar! Membership grew with the involvement of those organisations we'd once had conflict with and the extended openness to all interested members, plus those individual or Club orientated.

A consensus was sought and with it a stronger voice helped to protect the environment, encompassing lakes, hills and crags. Any adverse proposals and developments that became agenda items were fought and, in the main, defeated (we were ably helped by Jack Kenyon FRCC, who gave up a vast amount of his time on our behalf).

Networking became a lot easier by knowing those people from outside bodies; the BMC's relations and profile grew. The movement also helped to convey to the grass roots membership that the BMC was working for them. Not that there has always been success; we still do not have agreement on parking below Shepherd Crag in Borrowdale.

There was much scepticism and resistance to footpath building made necessary to allow vegetation to regenerate where extensive footway erosion had occurred. Neil Allinson of the National Trust helped allay most of the fears by site visits with the Chairman, initially below Ravens Crag then over many other sites,

Concern about footpath building has declined and in general we accepted the need for change. Neil retired in the early '90s and Jim

Loxham has taken over the project, including a space in The Golden Rule.

Climbing walls have become very important for training and wet day climbing venues. Since 1984 walls have been constructed at Ambleside, Carlisle, Cockermouth, Barrow, Keswick, Egremont, Penrith and Kendal.

Overheard at the Wyndham Wall, Egremont, a very elderly man was thrutching along the wall enjoying himself immensely; with him was a young tiger. He commented to the boy: "If we'd had these facilities when I was your age, we'd have done an awful lot more climbing in Lakeland!"

Looking back, it's just as well that they did not have the wall - there would not have been much left for today's climbers.

Rick Graham has been in the forefront of what's going on in climbing for some time, so became the Committee's climbing wall representative. Ably supported by those towers of strength, Al Phizacklea and Ron Kenyon, who have regularly been at the sharp edge of thinking on climbing Cumbria, keeping the membership informed throughout a decade of developments.

In 1991 Di Hampton was elected to the Lake District National Park Committee which, in itself, boosted the BMC's profile. Di, a very able, approachable lady, quickly made people take note; her wide interest base was a coup on our behalf. Twice, Di had taken her pen up as Lakes' BMC Secretary so it came as no surprise when she became Chairperson in 1992 when Bob stood down.

Di helped convey the Committee's points of view to the Northern Sports Council and other august bodies and until 1995 she also held the access officer post which Colyn Earnshaw now fills. Meetings carried on in their quiet way as of old. The membership has remained strong, notable mountaineers still attend to voice their and their Club's opinions. Chris Bonington, Tony Greenbank, Doug Scott and Colyn Earnshaw form part of the old school, but the strength is in today's young climbers whose attendance is nurtured and fostered by the present rock-climbing Chairman, Andy Prickett. The meetings are kept short, though everyone has their say — once! The Golden Rule is a place for congenial discussions whether they be on climbing, conservation, access, where to holiday, or just the price of a pint.

The make-up of the Committee has had many, and still has, more hard working members not mentioned. Derek did not allow me to write the whole book, so unfortunately I don't have space other than to thank them all.

The Lakes' Committee goes from strength to strength. There is much to do but as always the right people are in the right place at the right time.

(Oh! How Times Change)

'Wanted. Secretary to serve on the British Mountaineering Council's Lake District Area Committee. Those interested contact the BMC office, Manchester, or Mr P. Howard, in own handwriting!' Just a small ad in Climber Magazine, it being at that time the BMC's platform for news. It seems just yesterday, not 1978; time flies when one gets older!

I applied and was instructed to attend Percy Howard's home near Grange for an evening interview one week later. I entered Mr Howard's impressive house; his good lady led me into the study where three elderly men sat around a table. I was seated facing into the circle of sages! Percy, as I later became to know him, shook my hand firmly, smiled, then formally and with some reverence introduced me to his fellow Committee Members. Firstly there was Mr Jack Kenyon, then A.B. Hargreaves. I wondered what A.B. stood for, or was Abe his name? Mr Hargreaves looked small in stature yet large in personality and confidence, a bit terrier-like. Later on my first impressions were confirmed, especially if I'd misquoted him in the minutes, he had the knack of being able to remember every word he'd said and in the order of saying! (Percy, Chairman, and Jack Kenyon were staunch BMC members of long-standing. A.B. a Lakeland legend in mountaineering; and still is).

I'd spent my life walking the British hills, beginning as early as I could walk, a bit of a climber but no aspirant legend! A fell-runner, footballer, cricketer, played badminton but not graced a climb harder than HVS, a miss in my education which became very apparent early on in my interview.

"Oh! By the way," as I was quickly informed, "just checking if you are the right sort of chap, can't have just anyone you know, must be reliable, honest, dependable and have a love and sympathetic feel for the rock and hills. Have you led any climbs?" "Well, an odd one, Westmorland's Route, Dove Crag, Kneewrecker, been on Gill Slabs, Greenow End and Eagle Crag, been climbing in Borrowdale and Langdale, no real classics". At this point I began to feel that the route to the Secretary's post was looking a bit thin. "I've done Little Chamonix in the wet!" I paused, all went quiet. I'd just grasped a finger-hold enough to thrutch upon, enough to rest before the next crux.

Education, schooling, GCE's? The belay collapsed. I slipped, my mind racing to retrieve the situation. No qualifications until I went to day-release college from work; I'm now a member of the Institute of

Highways Engineers. The downward spiral ceased. I pendulumed then swung gently with some relief to the floor. I at last had found firm ground and good going. I must be the right sort of chap.

"How is your spelling? Have you been secretary of an organisation before?" "Yes, Patterdale Mountain Rescue Team." Another good move! "What of car, transport, family, wife, children, father, mother, home? When can I come to see you?" Percy turned up a week later, checked me out finally, then sent me the formal invitation two days later.

My first meeting was in the Eagle and Child, Staveley. What a disappointment it turned out to be; three people, none of them taking drink.

Well the years passed quickly. The meetings in those early days had few attendants. I got invited along with the Chairman to attend management meetings in Manchester where the business went on into the late night, discussing such topics as training, access, funding, members etc., where debates were long and intense and, of course, much of the evenings were spent listening to Ken Wilson!

A few years later, I myself become Lake District Chairman and the first thing I initiated was moving the meetings to the 'Golden Rule', Ambleside, where my golden rule was that all business had to be completed before 9.30pm; this allowed our members chance to continue discussions informally over a drink and to firm up on acquaintances and friendships. We invited other like-minded organisations to our meetings and it soon became a good constructive night out, the only problem became that of difficulty in raising one's arm!

The BMC Lakes still has this openness where members have a friendly platform to air their views and opinions. We lost the 'Mr' bit (more so since Di Hampton took over the Chair!), but the firm ground early formulating members built up has been substantial and beneficial to our growth. Many of us cannot attain the legendary status of those pioneers, yet the girth of today's young climbers displays athleticism that even those early pioneers would have difficulty matching.

Well, nothing stands still; remember Napes Needle was once taller.

Bob Dawes

LAKE DISTRICT AREA COMMITTEE
Formed in 1945, revivified in 1960.

Chairman		Secretary	
1945-56	C G Bulman	1945-56	A R Wells
1957-72	C E Arnison	1957-61	G B Spenceley
1972-77	S H Cross	1961-68	R G Plint
1978-82	P Howard	1968-75	J A Baxter
1982-87	W Ruthven	1975-78	W Ruthven
1987-92	R Dawes	1978-82	R Dawes
1992-95	Di Hampton	1982-85	G Causey
1995-	A Prickett	1985-90	Di Hampton
Access Representative		1990-92	Lesley Wornham
1990-95	Di Hampton	1992-93	J Gaukroger
1995-	C Earnshaw	1993-95	A Prickett
1996-	R Kenyon	1995-	Sally Clark

The Committee for Wales

The Committee as currently constituted dates only from 1976. Prior to that Welsh climbing interests had been divided between a Committee for North Wales, which looked after North Wales as far south as to include Powys, and the South and South-West Committee which looked after South Wales. Later Shropshire was added briefly to the North Wales Committee. The North Wales Committee dated from the early days of the BMC; at that time the road conditions were less good than they are now, transport was less easily available and there was little of climbing interest in the south. Climbing mostly meant the north; indeed, in this context, Cardiff probably had more in common with Bristol than with Bangor. In the event, as we shall see, the formation of a single Committee for Wales was as much driven by political pressures as by climbing interest. In what follows, 'Committee' stands for either the North Wales Committee or the Committee for Wales, depending on the context.

There are comprehensive Minute Books available for most of the period from 1960 to date but unfortunately there seems to be almost no documentary record of the period before this. Many of the principal characters of the time are, of course, no longer with us and personal recollections are hard to come by. For the first years of its life the North Wales Committee was a relatively unchanging body only representative of a limited group. The membership consisted of representatives from a selection of the more senior clubs in the area; if a member stood down he was replaced by someone from his club. Other clubs had no representation, though if a specific problem came to light an invitation to attend was issued. Apart from occasional open meetings there seems to have been little communication with the majority of the mountain users. The Committee tended to be on rather a stand alone basis and communications with the BMC centrally tended to be few; the officers of the BMC were, of course, 'amateurs' doing the job in their own spare time. The weight of the Committee tended to be that of the senior clubs in the area such as the Climbers' Club, the Rucksack Club and the Midland Association of Mountaineers, and acted through them. However, it is clear from the nature of the 'watching briefs' held over climbing interests, coupled with the contacts made with other authorities and bodies, and the overall concern shown over representing climbers' interests, that issues were vigorously pursued for the good of the whole climbing community.

One major activity in which the Committee became heavily involved in these first years was the whole matter of hydroelectric power generation and the spread of unsightly power cables. An example of a scheme which went through is the pumped storage system at Tan y Grisiau, but more were mooted; there was even a suggestion of a tunnel through the Devil's Kitchen cliffs with a linked reservoir somewhere, perhaps even in Cwm Idwal. To co-ordinate objections to such schemes the North Wales (Hydroelectric) Protection Committee was formed. The North Wales Committee was well represented on this; one of the Chairmen of the NW(HE)PC was the late Tom Clutterbuck who was the representative of the MAM on the Committee. Indeed, his name crops up as one of the driving forces of the North Wales Committee at that time and perhaps elsewhere both in the context of the NW(HE)PC and in other matters.

Another major activity was that of overseeing guide qualifications. In the early 1950s, largely on the advice of Geoffrey Winthrop Young, the Committee was charged with assessing the worth of aspiring professional guides in North Wales. This was done by a BMC Guides Sub-committee for North Wales 'reported to the Committee' whose recommendation was then forwarded to the BMC centrally which, if it also saw fit, issued an appropriate certificate. This activity continued into the early 1960s when the system changed in order to address the matter in what we would now judge to be a more professional manner, though the worth of the earlier system in raising the standard of accreditation must be acknowledged.

In 1961 the Secretary of the BMC sent out a letter to all areas suggesting that all interested BMC clubs should be invited to send delegates from time to time. It appears that the rather closed method of conducting affairs was not solely confined to North Wales. The nature of the problems addressed at that time seems to be very little different from those addressed nowadays, and in just the way things are now, many issues seemed to drag on over years, sometimes with a good outcome, sometimes surrendering to the inevitable unfavourable outcome and sometimes just fading off the agenda. Access and amenity considerations have always been stock in trade for Area Committees, and while any area is bound to feel that its own problems are the ones which matter, it can be fairly said, I think, that Wales has faced a succession of threats of considerable magnitude. The next few years saw the ongoing break up of the Vaynol Estate. This had enormous implications for access as there were considerable fears that a change of land ownership would lead to access difficulties. At this time, and continuing for some years, the Committee was heavily embroiled in identifying the recognised public access points; they often turned out to be far less in number than had been assumed, even in places as popular as Ogwen, and much effort went into 'policing' some of the more unfortunate activities of a minority; such as painting graffiti on boulders, leaving litter etc. – so as not to antagonise the landowners or tenants. Some access gave real problems such as the long-running saga of defining an agreed way from near Nant Peris up on to the mountain to traverse over to Idwal, a route which had hitherto been in use for longer than anyone could remember, and the whole issue of access in the Rhyd Ddu area where some of the confrontations between climbers and landowners looked set to end in violence. I remember heated debates between a gun-carrying farmer with his dog and climbers who were trying to cross the fields to Castell Cidwm!

Another, related, major issue of the time included the prohibition of much roadside camping in the Llanberis Pass; agreed it caused traffic congestion and was highly insanitary but alternative provision had to be made.

The Committee has always been relatively good at co-opting outsiders to the hoped for mutual advantage of all parties; in 1962 the first of these was the then Caernarfon County Planning Officer, obviously a useful person to have around even if not always necessarily on one's side, and since that time co-options have continued, either of individuals with special knowledge or skills or of various statutory and non statutory bodies, to mutual benefit.

Tremadog seems to have featured in some way or another throughout the whole life of the Committee up until the present day. It started in 1964 with parking problems and there were discussions even then over the possibility of buying Bwlch y Moch. This was caused by problems over defining the ownership of the very top of the crag, and responsibility for erecting stock-proof fencing. Perhaps there is no need to dwell further on Tremadog, other than to mention that it really does seem to be one of the hardy perennials of the agenda. Over the years the Committee has worked hard to provide stiles and notices, in addition to providing Trustees when the crag was given to the BMC. From trying to sort out the one-time ban on access to Pant Ifan we have reached the rather ironic point that we now have problems in getting off (not up to) the rocks, with tree damage from abseil descents (which can also be highly anti-social on a crowded crag).

One matter with which Wales has had to contend and which has not affected any other Area Committee has been the simple fact that Wales has certain administrative structures of its own and in this context the one which has had the greatest effect is the existence of the Sports Council for Wales (SCW). Knowledge of this Council surfaced in about 1967; the understanding was that the BMC had a representative on it, supplied by the South Wales MC and as that was the case everything was fine. It was not until 1974 that it was found out that this was far from the case, the SWMC being represented on only one of the SCW's bodies and then only on its own behalf, not on behalf of the BMC. This probably reflects what seems to have been the continuing relatively poor communications between the Committee and the BMC office in London and with other Area Committees. The SCW had more influence on the Committee over the next few years.

In 1968 the Committee underwent a fundamental change in that the membership became a wholly elected one with three officers and eight members elected from all interested clubs at the AGM. An obvious effect of this was an influx of new blood. With hindsight this was just as well; it was far from the case that the previous Committee had been in any way inadequate, but the times they were 'a changing' and the number and variety of problems was on the up and up. The first of many very constructive and fruitful liaison meetings with the Nature Conservancy Council took place, discussing matters such as restrictions for climbers during the bird nesting season and putting over the notion that the climbing community is responsible and not just a load of anarchists.

The Committee Minute Book covering the period 1969 to 1973 seems to have gone astray, but by 1973 it was obvious that the interests of climbers in North Wales were under a barrage of new threats; looking back, they felt as if they might have been overwhelming. The Chairman of the day pointed out that the amount of work was becoming too much for the few stalwarts who did most of it and specific areas of interest were given to members to share the load; conservation to Gwen Moffat, access and paths to Ron Shotton, while Peter Wild acted with enormous diligence as the scanner of newspapers and asker of questions to all and sundry about possibly suspicious goings on. It is not really possible to itemise all threats and advisory activities which were alive at this time; a short list might include: the threat of large-scale copper mining in the Coed y Brenin by RTZ; early clashes between climbers and bird conservation interests on Anglesey; the grandiose scheme for a totally rebuilt Snowdon summit area with landscaping, etc.; the first concerns about access to what later became the scene of a notorious failure –

Craig y Forwen; and the Gwynedd County Structure Plan. Three major events which had started running at that time will serve to illustrate the diversity of the threats and the enormous efforts required by the Committee and many others to achieve a measure of success.

The first event can fairly be said to be almost entirely to the credit of the Committee, but it was not finally resolved until 1981. In December 1973 workmen were found drilling holes in the tops of the Cromlech Boulders, and rumour has it that they were only stopped by two members of the Committee occupying the Boulders and daring the drillers to throw them off! It emerged that the Boulders (or parts of them) were to be blown up as part of a scheme to widen and realign the road so as to smooth out the tight bends over the bridge. The Committee led the objectors and in doing so suffered considerable and probably ill-considered abuse ('selfish', 'blinkered', 'arrogant') and even that champion of the liberal cause, the Guardian newspaper, railed against the Boulders as not worthy of preservation. Harry Sales, a barrister specialising in Town and Country Planning and Bob Dewar, a consultant highway and traffic engineer were recruited to the cause. The cost of presentation at a public enquiry needed fund raising and the preparatory work required activities such as traffic censuses (in the pouring rain, of course). Bob Dewar drew up plans which both widened the road and left the boulders intact; eventually the County Surveyor accepted these and the Public Enquiry with which it all finished was a mere formality.

The second issue put the Committee in the unusual position of siding with the planners and objecting to the objectors. The old A55 along the North Wales coast was long overdue for replacement by the road which is now the Expressway. The draft line was much as it is now which resulted in quite a lot of destruction of existing property in the Colwyn Bay area. An objection was mounted to this, advocating an alternative line into the Conwy Valley, up the flanks of the Carneddau above Ro Wen, over the Bwlch y Ddeufaen where the Roman road went and then diagonally down to sea-level near Aber. There were many reasons given why this was not practical such as loss of deciduous woodland, high construction costs, weather problems and the simple fact that it was just not appropriate for an area of National Park's mountains. The objectors mounted a vigorous campaign, quite properly from their point of view. In the end it all went to Public Enquiry at which the Committee was represented. The original draft line was accepted, as expected, but it was a worrying time.

The third item was a complicated part of an even more complicated whole. The CEGB was planning what is now the Dinorwig Pumped

Storage Scheme. In order for it and any associated work to go ahead an Act of Parliament was required. With the benefit of hindsight it is clear that it was going to go through but at the time much effort was going into lobbying to prevent it or at least to reduce its impact, partly due to the very real threat of further similar schemes following, including one which would probably have resulted in the destruction of Carreg Alltrem. Apparently, independent of all this, a team of workmen was found turning the green footpath which ran from near Helyg to Ffynnon Llugwy into a wide tarmac road. They were extremely evasive about why they were doing it or even as to who they were; however it was obvious that they were providing all-weather access, and over the top at that, to the lake. Eventually it became clear that it was the CEGB and that it was all being done on the back of the Dinorwig scheme. Things became rather heated as it became even more clear that the CEGB had not sought any type of permission or any advice on a sympathetic method of construction, and perhaps worst of all had started work which could only be authorised as a result of the Act receiving Royal Assent at a time when it was still lumbering through Parliament. There was much indignation from all sorts of bodies including the Committee, but by the time details emerged the work was done and the day was lost. In attempts to recover a shred of respectability the CEGB offered to return the road to its original condition once engineering works were complete (hollow laughter) or to surface it with chips chosen to blend with the surroundings. Needless to say these were never done. A minor degree of belated satisfaction came when Dave Roberts used copies of the Committee's minutes and correspondence to convince his MP that the work had started ahead of the Act and therefore unlawfully. Questions were asked in the House and in the end the Minister responsible admitted publicly that wrong had been done and gave an undertaking that such an incident would not happen again.

Feelings had been growing that the BMC's division of Wales into two areas was not very satisfactory, the more so when the south looked as though it was regarded as only an offshoot of a large English area. The BMC itself was looking at this and minor cosmetic moves, such as trying to ensure that the Secretary of the North Wales Committee had a Welsh address, were carried out. In 1975 the SCW suggested that there should be a Welsh Committee but it became apparent that its agenda was not the same as that of the BMC. The SCW-backed body would not be affiliated to the BMC but would have more power and autonomy. It was not really clear if it would be for the benefit primarily of 'Welsh' climbers, however defined, or for all users of the Welsh hills, and in any event would not be able to avail itself of all the advice and support available to the other Area Committees from the BMC centrally. In the end rival open meetings were held, one by the BMC to establish what is now the Committee for Wales and one fronted by an official of the Snowdonia National Park to establish a Mountaineering Council for Wales. In the event it was a case of no contest, as only the BMC meeting attracted any sort of interest. The new Committee was formed with Edwin Hammond as Chairman and Ron Shotton as Secretary, and with the remit to consult with and if appropriate to co-opt members from a wide variety of Welsh-based bodies. Unfortunately though, this started a long period of rather cool relationships between the new Committee and the SCW. The Committee was still an elected one from interested clubs, and while the larger number of members were from the old North Wales Committee it marked the integration of north and south and the introduction of active members from the south, particularly from the SWMC and later the Gwent MC.

This might be as good a point as any to give another short representative list of activities in which the new Committee became embroiled; work on the Caernarfonshire Definitive Footpath Map, co-ordinated by John Brailsford; the quality and nature of the roadworks and fencing on the A5 at Ogwen and the saga of the missing Milestone; access to Cwm Silyn; the Working Party on the future of Plas y Brenin; parking at Pen-y-Pass and the provision of stiles by the Clwyd MC at Craig y Forwen on behalf of the BMC. Also well to the fore at this time was what turned out to be one of the longest-running topics of all, the plan for a Cambrian Way, a sort of Welsh Pennine Way, linking the south coast of Wales with the north.

One of the prime functions of an Area Committee is as a forum for the BMC to disseminate information and to seek the views and advice of the climbing community. Up to about this time the Committee had been relatively uninvolved in the politics of the climbing world outside its own area or in the politics of the BMC at large. When the BMC moved to Manchester, and as it took on more staff and as numbers of climbers grew and their interest diversified, so did the requirement for the Committee to become more involved in wider issues grow also. One of the first of these issues was the major one of the Hunt Report which was as keenly debated in the Committee as anywhere. This is not the place to go over this particular piece of history but it did have one unfortunate effect on the Committee. It will be recalled that a serious rift grew up between the BMC and the MLTB to the extent that the Sports Council withdrew some of its grant to the BMC. The Committee

sided strongly with the BMC, but its Chairman, Edwin Hammond, and
its Secretary, Ron Shotton, sided with the views of the MLTB. For Ron
there was an additional problem as he was an employee of Plas y Brenin
and therefore of the Sports Council which took the MLTB side. He was
given to understand that he could not serve two masters and tended his
resignation from the Secretaryship. Edwin felt that he had no alternative
but to do the same. Edwin had been a leading activist for the Committee
ever since the days of the original North Wales Committee and Ron was
greatly respected and had been the prime mover in the Battle of the
Cromlech Boulders. Their places were taken by John Neill and Dave
Roberts.

The SCW had money which it could use for grant-aid purposes for
Welsh Clubs and in 1974 had agreed that the Committee would be
recognised as the sole governing body for Wales and therefore the only
one with whom to discuss such grant aid and from whom to seek advice.
By 1978, however, it was becoming clear that the Committee was being
specifically excluded from all meetings and discussions on outdoor
pursuits and it was learned that the SCW was intending to set up an
Association of Welsh Climbing Clubs. This was despite having only
recently rejected a suggestion from the BMC to do just that and the
failure of the two sides to arrange a meeting to sort the matter out. The
SCW also intended to establish a Welsh MLTB and a Welsh Mountain
Rescue Service. The Committee reacted by calling a meeting of all Welsh
Mountaineering Clubs and founding its own Association of Welsh
Climbing Clubs (AWCC). This was open to all clubs in Wales, whether
affiliated to the BMC or not, as a forum providing a unified approach
rather than a divided one, and, as a wholly-owned subsidiary of the
Committee, providing for the overall interests of all climbers living in
or visiting Wales. The SCW accepted this compromise, but at the same
time withdrew some of the support it had been giving. For example,
some of the grass roots relationships between the two bodies had been
good, with the SCW providing a free typing service via its Wrexham
office for the Committee's minutes. This service vanished.

However, despite the acceptance of the AWCC as the body whose
members the SCW could give grant aid to, matters did not really improve,
and the AWCC slowly withered and died. The SCW persisted with its
Welsh MLTB and its 'Certificate of Advanced Competence' with no
reference to the MLTB or to the BMC which, even so, they still
acknowledged as the governing body. There seemed to be a total
breakdown between the SCW and the rest of British mountaineering,
and by 1982 it became clear that it boiled down to a basic difference of

view, that of the BMC being that the governing body in Wales should cater for all climbers in Wales and that meetings should be open to all, while the SCW view was that such a body should be of Welsh clubs and for Welsh climbers only. This was not really an illogical stance by either party but reflected their different origins and responsibilities. It is a relief and even a pleasure to record that from this low point, relationships slowly improved so that the situation now is one of considerable accord, with the Committee, now an open forum, advising on grant aid, etc. and the problems of the past now being consigned, hopefully, to history.

All this went on against a background of access and other issues. One of the great running issues of the time was that of the Arans and Cwm Cywarch, which became positively Byzantine in its twists and turns as time went by. It had at least three interlinking strands. The first was that of access to the Arans for walkers linked to access to the excellent crag of Gist Ddu. The Arans are almost entirely devoid of Rights of Way, and the farming community took exception to people crossing their property, to the extent of forming a body called the Society for the Two Arans with the express purpose of preventing access. Tempers became frayed, the Farming Unions were involved, mass trespasses were threatened, open meetings became heated and frankly vituperative letters were published in the press. In the middle of it all the National Park Authority did its best to calm troubled waters with David Archer, the Assistant National Park Officer, himself a climber and a valuable co-opted member of the Committee often uncomfortably to the fore. Eventually an uneasy compromise was reached with a few Courtesy paths and agreed access to Gist Ddu from the main ridge at the top of the crag, but strictly speaking there are still large no-go areas.

Meanwhile, in Cwm Cywarch at the southern end of the Arans, the second part of the story was being acted out. The Stafford Mountain Club has a hut there, Bryn Hafod, largely built by their own efforts on an old long-abandoned quarry site. It was always assumed that they had title to the land but this was called into question by a neighbouring farmer who embarked upon a campaign of harassment; this was all compounded by parking problems as the only parking space is on common land. Again the Farming Unions became involved, the title to the land did not appear to be as sure as had been assumed and much support was given to the club in sorting out their difficulties.

The third parallel piece of the drama was the oddest, one which dragged on until about 1991. Cwm Cywarch is a beautiful, relatively unspoiled cul de sac, where the farming community seems to have needed to change very little. The climbing there is often excellent and there is a lot of it, though due to its rather out of the way location it is not all that heavily used. Much of the cwm was in the ownership of a single absentee landlord, the farmers being tenants. The owner had a strong wish to see that the life of the valley was not unduly altered and that flora and fauna were undisturbed. In this I think we would all have common ground. However, the landlord sought to achieve these ends by restricting climbing. As the BMC stance was one of free access for all there was obviously room here for a difference of opinion. Positions became entrenched with neither side being able to convince the other, largely because of the inability of the landlord to understand the nature of climbing and climbers and her wish for adherence to a long list of impractical demands (the Stafford Club to submit lists of all climbers three months in advance, etc). Mostly everything was conducted in the most civilised of fashions with Bill Wright, the then BMC Access Officer, involved in one-to-one negotiations over sherry in London. One of the odd things was that over the whole time there was no actual restriction on climbing with climbers coming and going as they pleased, though admittedly in fairly small numbers, and despite the fact that there was much debate over the absence of Rights of Way up to the rocks and on the routes themselves, relationships between climbers and farmers mostly remained quite cordial. Eventually the whole thing fizzled out and climbing continues.

New climbing venues bring new problems. Major new venues tend not to be big mountain crags with no access problems but rather cliffs where climbing may impinge on the activities of others. One of the refreshing things about the negotiations over access to such cliffs is the way in which new names come to the fore, usually climbers with local interest and knowledge but with no other obvious connection with the BMC or at least the Committee, but prepared to act in the name of the BMC for the benefit of all climbers. The prime example of this at the end of the Seventies was that of Range East in Pembrokeshire where the prevailing situation of running the risk of being accosted by the military and perhaps reported to the police was steadily converted to the access we have now. This was achieved by long and patient negotiations spearheaded by John Harwood, Pat Littlejohn and, from the Committee, Dave Parsons.

Serious feelings of déjà vu were experienced when news came of plans to build another road from the A5 up into the Carneddau, this time to the head of Llyn Cowlyd, not by the CEGB this time but by the Welsh Water Authority. It was all about redistribution of water resources, more being sent west towards Bangor via the Afon Dena and a new holding reservoir in the flat-bottom land of the Nant Ffrancon. Despite assurances

THE LAKE DISTRICT AREA COMMITTEE

Cyril Bulman 1945-56
Unaffiliated

Eric Arnison 1957-72
F.R.C.C.,

Sid Cross 1972-77
F.R.C.C.,

Percy Howard 1978-82
Wayfarers' Club

Bill Ruthven 1982-87
Chamois, A.C., Wayfarers' Club

Bob Dawes 1987-92
Over the Hill Club

Di Hampton 1992-94
West Cumbria M.C.

Andy Prickett 1995-
Climbers' Club

NORTH WALES
AREA COMMITTEE,
THE ASSOCIATION OF WELSH
CLIMBERS & THE
COMMITTEE FOR WALES

illustrated earlier:

John Neill 1964-76, 1977-84,
Dr. David Roberts 1984-88

*Note: The Welsh Committee has undergone several changes and
titles since 1945 to satisfy changing political circumstances.*

During the decade
1954-64 several access
sub-committees
confronted Welsh
problems.

Tom Clutterbuck 1954-c.60
M.A.M.

John Poole 1960-64
Climbers' Club

Edwin Hammond 1976-77
Yeti, C.C., A.C.

Dave Parsons
1979-82 *South Wales M.C.*

Stuart Thompson 1988-93
Gwent M.C., C.C., A.C.

Andy Newton 1993-96
Climbers' Club

THE
PEAK DISTRICT
AREA COMMITTEE

illustrated earlier:

Jack Longland 1956-75

Note: Machin was frequently described as Area Secretary in early BMC documents but was seemingly the de-facto chairman or convenor between 1948 and 1955.

Bob Davis 1947-48
Derbyshire Pennine Club

Cyril Machin 1949-55
M.A.M.

Lyn Noble 1975-82
Rucksack Club, A.C.

Dave Dickson 1982-87
M.A.M.

Ian Smith 1987-88
Climbers' Club

George White 1988-91
Lichfield M.C., C.C.

Roy Bennett 1991-95
Individual

THE NORTH-EAST AREA COMMITTEE

illustrated earlier:

Robert Pettigrew 1979-87

Donald Barr Wells 1965-73
F.R.C.C. Alpine Club

George Slee 1973-74
N'umberland Mt. Instructors' Club

Eric Walker 1974-75
Northumberland M.C.

Mike Chapman 1975-79
Wanneys M.C.

Steve Derwin 1988-90
Cleveland M.C.

Stephen Porteus 1990-95
N.M.C., F.R.C.C.

Pete Hay 1995-
Cleveland M.C., F.R.C.C.

THE LONDON AND SOUTH-EAST AREA COMMITTEE

illustrated earlier:

Donald Greenwood 1968-c.70
Maurice Bennett 1970-75

Hugh Jordan 1975-80
J.M.C.S.

Peter Watson 1980-84
Camping Club

Bob Gookey 1984
Croydon M.C.

Ivor Delafield 1985-87
London Graduate M.C.

Tom Phillips 1987-92
Maidstone C.C.

Andrew McLellan 1992-96
Red Rope

THE SOUTH-WEST AND SOUTHERN AREA COMMITTEE

illustrated earlier:

Robert Pettigrew 1974-78,
Mike Rosser 1992-

Note: South Wales was originally part of this area but was ceded to the Committee for Wales in 1976.

Mark Hogg 1968-72
Wessex M.C.

John Bradley 1972-73
North London M.C.

Audrey Salkeld 1978
Alpine Club

Bob Robinson 1979-81
M.A.M., Farnborough M.C.

Major Charles Marriott
1981-84 *C.C., A.C.*

Stewart Bondi 1984-87
N. Devon M.C.

Richard Scantlebury 1987-92
Avon M.C.

THE YORKSHIRE AND HUMBERSIDE AREA COMMITTEE

illustrated earlier:

Angela Soper 1989-94
Dennis Gray 1994

Pete Swindells 1974-75
Yorkshire Ramblers' Club

Roy Pomfret 1975-77
Yorkshire Ramblers' Club

Jack Bloor 1977-82
Gritstone Club

Jo Light 1982-83
Pinnacle Club, F.R.C.C.

Dave Smith 1983-86
M.A.M.

Ian Howat 1986-89
Leeds Outdoor Pursuits Group

THE LANCASHIRE AND CHESHIRE AREA COMMITTEE

illustrated earlier:
Brian Nicholls 1978-83

Charlie Vigano 1983-84
Creagh Dhu, C.C.

Paul Sedgwick 1984-90
Individual

John Mason 1990-95
Climbers' Club

Paul Dewhurst 1995-
Climbers' Club

THE MIDLANDS AREA COMMITTEE

Mike Ratty 1994-
Lichfield M.C., A.C., C.C.

that the road would be landscaped, considerable opposition was voiced. Everyone objected to the road and associated pumping houses and other constructions; farmers worried over loss of land and interruption to their activities; the Midland Association of Mountaineers worried that the increased flow in the Afon Dena would damage their conifer plantation which already had a rather tenuous grasp on the land; they and the National Trust worried about damage to the bridge for which they have joint responsibility and which is the access to Tal y Llyn Ogwen farm and altogether it was a worrying time. Eventually the scheme was withdrawn on the grounds that a fresh look at projected water demands in the Bangor and Anglesey area no longer warranted it. The finding that a vein of arsenic-bearing ore ran right through the area of the projected new reservoir helped, perhaps. We can be sure that these plans are on file and could be resurrected if it is deemed appropriate.

The Seventies closed with Wales being specifically represented at a meeting held in Glencoe (where better?) between representatives of the BMC centrally, the Committee, the Mountaineering Council for Scotland and the Federation of Mountaineering Clubs of Ireland. Apart from the high level of socialising and climbing (the weather was excellent) the BMC was able, by using Welsh and other experiences to warn of the directions England and Wales were going in the areas of access restrictions, fears over owners liability etc., problems which did not really seem to exist much then for Scotland and Ireland. I am not sure about Ireland, but it is clear that Scotland is now experiencing some of these problems; there must be a good case for ongoing meetings of this type to pool experiences and resources.

As we started to run through the Eighties, some of the big issues presenting were concerned with the new areas, two of the most troublesome being the Great Orme where the close proximity of some of the climbing to the road inevitably caused the local authority to have considerable misgivings about the wisdom of allowing it at all, and the rapid opening up of the slate quarries as climbing grounds of prime importance. Once again local activists came to the aid of the party for the greater good of us all. Particularly worthy of mention are the long discussions over restrictions at the Great Orme involving also the Country Park Warden Service and the emergence of Andy Newton as prime mover in the debates over the slate quarries, not only in persuading the CEGB that the appearance of climbers in what they probably considered as the vast heap of dangerous rubbish that they had acquired posed no threat to them, legal or otherwise, but also in other slate matters such as the proposed development at Glyn Rhonwy.

Another list of activities for the Eighties shows that while new problems always occur, their natures differ little. It is to be hoped that we all learn from each event so that our voice of reason is more effectively presented each time. Unfortunately, the pressures on the areas of our interest seem not to diminish. Some examples; widening the A470 in the Lledr Valley; access to Llangattock; rebuilding the Cwm Dyli pipeline; the Foel Grach refuge (to rebuild or not to rebuild); the mega-mess caused by the WWA in upgrading the track to Llyn Anafon, and of course the saga of the ban on climbing at Craig y Forwen, a prime example of owner power which is perhaps a salutary lesson to us all. In 1986 the Committee moved one meeting a year from North Wales to the south, an excellent idea; it is difficult to imagine where in the north we would have climbed stripped to the waist as some of us did at St Govans on an afternoon in November! The idea of a South Wales meeting had been tried out at the inception of the unified Committee for Wales but had been a bit of a flop, being held mid-afternoon in Cardiff. Pembrokeshire or the Beacons is a much better idea.

Committee participation in national affairs such as the debates engendered by Walls and Competitions and the furores engendered by bolts (perhaps I should say BOLTS) has continued, but these are best documented elsewhere as they are not primarily Welsh affairs. As we are now in the Nineties recent history becomes current affairs and there are less secure historical contexts in which to review current concerns such as Range West etc. The same old problems recur, such as Llangattock and Craig y Forwen which are still going in 1995, and there are bound to be new ones.

In writing this review it has become clear that a lot has gone on. If the reader feels that some events have been given undue prominence and others have been under-played or left out altogether it is because personal involvement at the time made details more readily recalled or perhaps certain issues just felt bigger at the time. The only real test of the worth of all this activity lies in the question "have the results been of benefit to us all?" No administrative body of an activity such as climbing is going to satisfy everyone even some of the time, and there are many who would look upon us (and the BMC in general) as irrelevant. What we cannot get away from, like it or not, is that freedom to climb in an environment as congested as ours is not an unqualified freedom. It is a freedom that exists only in so far as it does not interfere with the freedoms of others. In seeking to safeguard those freedoms we can reasonably claim (and, to be honest, having a go at pinching a bit more than that at times), I suggest, to look upon the work of the Committee as watchdog, negotiator and thorn in the flesh of the unreasonable, as having been well done and effective. Triumphs, yes, but disappointments too; but it will always be like that.

This has not been an exhaustive list of Chairmen, Secretaries and activists; some names have cropped up in the text, but there have been very many more who share in the credit. Naming names can be embarrassing both to those named and those left out, but special mention should be made of a few of the most persistent and effective members of the Committee; Tom Clutterbuck, Edwin Hammond, Ron Shotton, Peter Wild, Dave Parsons, Andy Newton and also Bill Wright during his term as the BMC's Access Officer. But each is only a case of *primus inter pares*. Head and shoulders above all of us, however, has been John Neill; Chairman, emergency Chairman, acting Chairman, solver of problems, host of liaison meetings with the Nature Conservancy Council, member of more review groups and liaison bodies than I suspect even he can remember. This review is really a tribute to him.

Dave Roberts

NORTH WALES COMMITTEE
Formed in 1945, but seemed to turn itself into the North Wales Hydro Electric Sub-Committee (which represented the BMC on the North Wales (Hydro Electric) Protection Committee).

Chairman		Secretary	
1945--54	T Clutterbuck	1947-48	R G Williams

Abolished in 1961.

NORTH WALES AREA COMMITTEE – revived 1960

Chairman		Secretary	
1960-64	J Poole	1961-67	G Barker
1964-76	J Neill	1967-68	G D Roberts
		1968-71	H Drasdo
		1971-74	D Roberts
		1974-76	W R Shotton (also Treasurer)

Treasurer
1968-72	J E Jones
1972-76	W R Shotton

Wound up in 1976 and activities taken over by Committee for Wales.

COMMITTEE FOR WALES

Formed in 1976 to take over the activities of the North Wales Area
Committee, and activities concerning South Wales, from South-West &
Southern Area Committee.

Chairman		Secretary	
1976-77	E Hammond	1976-77	W R Shotton
1977-84	J Neill	1977-82	Dr D M Roberts
1984-88	Dr D M Roberts	1982-84	R Owen
1988-93	S Thompson	1984-85	J G Thomas
1993-96	A D Newton	1985-86	S Thompson
1996-	E Jones	1986-88	I Waddington
		1988-93	R Lowe
		1993-94	D R Hatcher
		1994-	Christine Simpkins

Treasurer			
1976-78	G G Jones	**Access Representative**	
1978-81	J Llewellyn Jones	1988-93	J Neill
1981-84	J Byam-Grounds	1990	A Newton
1984-90	P Wild	1993-96	R Bennion
1990-95	B O'Toole	1994-	J Custance
		1994-	M Damford
		1994-	P de Mengel
		1996-	G Dickinson

NORTH WALES GUIDES COMMITTEE set up in 1959

Chairman		Secretary	
1959-62	Dr R C Evans	1959-62	A J J Moulam
	(later Sir Charles)		

Wound up in 1962 and activities taken over by Guides Sub-Committee
of Area Committee.

Chairman
1962-65   J A Jackson

Wound up in 1965 and responsibilities assumed by Area Committee itself.

ASSOCIATION OF WELSH CLIMBING CLUBS

Formed in 1979 as a sub-committee of the Committee for Wales

Chairman		Secretary	
1979-82	D Parsons	1979-82	M A Orton

Wound up in 1982.

Twenty-five Years of
the Mountaineering Council of Scotland:
The Start and Early Years

Having been asked, or persuaded, to record the origin and early days of our Mountaineering Council, I can only give a personal history. Unfortunately the well-kept files and Minutes I passed on have not been kept, a tradition which seems to be continuing, which is a pity and not really acceptable for a National Body. Thus I must rely on memory, with help from others.

The MCofS was preceded by the Association of Scottish Climbing Clubs. For several years volunteers from the Clubs got together to pursue matters of interest to climbers in Scotland. They ran winter hill-walking courses and liaised with the Mountain Rescue Committee of Scotland. Much of their work concerned the conservation of our mountain areas.

As with our MCofS, documentation for the ASCC has vanished in the mist. While I can remember several of the good people of the ASCC and those in at the founding of the MCofS, I feel it would be invidious to name some if I cannot give due credit to all. I hope those concerned will forgive me. We only started it and trust others to follow, and do it better.

In the late '60s Bill Murray, then a member of the Countryside Commission for Scotland, saw the need for a strong conservation (not preservation) body to further the public interest, perhaps best expressed by the informed outdoor fraternity, and so the Scottish Countryside Activities Council was formed.

As membership covered many outdoor recreation interests, such as caravanning, horse-riding, rambling and mountaineering, it gave information, advice and comment to the CC for S, which itself was in its infancy.

Then in 1968 that farce of lies, intrigue and incompetence by officials, public bodies, etc. – The Coruisk Affair (Scottish Mountaineering Club Journal No. 160, May 1969) – landed flapping at our feet like a grassed salmon. I became aware that bodies such as our Government, Scottish Sports Council, CC for S, Scottish Landowners Federation and the Media needed some recognised body of expertise on mountaineering matters: such as safety, conservation, the ethos of the sport, etc. Indeed we needed a National Body for the sport. Other sports had Governing Bodies (as they had rules and competitions), but we should have none of that. The ASCC, while the efforts of sincere volunteers were appreciated, was insufficient.

At the 1968 AGM of the ASCC I proposed it be wound up and reformed as the MCofS to be in due course the National Body for Scotland, in partnership with the British Mountaineering Council in England. The BMC would represent the UK internationally, while on internal UK matters it would defer to and support the other three countries on matters of concern to them. Each club climber would pay the same subscription; provision to be made for non-club members; representation to be sought on and from other organisations such as the National Trust for Scotland, Scottish Mountain Leadership Training Board, Mountain Rescue Committee for Scotland etc., and generally to be the voice for the interests of mountaineering in Scotland.

This outline was unanimously agreed and a Steering Committee formed. I drafted a Constitution which was knocked into shape, and this, with some modification, still survives today. We widened our remit in various directions and so in 1970, our MCofS was constituted – I think in May in Perth. We tried hard to get Committee members from as wide a spread of climbers as possible and had, as I recall, climbers from Aberdeen, Inverness, Fife, Edinburgh, Perth, Glasgow and elsewhere.

I had a system of mountaineering contacts in the various climbing areas, who reported about quarterly on anything of interest coming up, so we could try to be ahead of the game. These were busy times in our lives with work, families and climbing, but all contributed various talents to establishing the Council. We had some fifty clubs at the start and much work contacting other organisations. I maintain that we were as busy then as is the current Executive Committee. There is more work now, but more people to share it. We were learning and made a fair job of it. As I recall the Hon. Secretary represented MCofS to the BMC, BMC Technical Committee, SSC, MRCS, SMLTB, SCAC, SLF, SNSC and other representations included: MBA, FC, NIMC, NTS etc.

We ran for about three years, building up our authority and experience, then advised the SSC that we should be named as the National Body for Mountaineering in Scotland. We realised that though we felt our sport was best served by keeping a low profile, we needed the official recognition and possible financial assistance.

Now at that time the SSC felt that the SMLTB was, or should be, the best representative body. This shows how they did not understand our sport. However, I explained the ethos of our sport and that while the excellent SMLTB work was a part of the link with the sport and education, the MCofS was the core of our sport, and was formed by us for us. It was really for those outside our sport to turn to, a way, as we saw it, of protecting and furthering the well-being of our sport and our mountains.

After being unanimously supported by the then Scottish Standing Conference of Sport (all the Governing Bodies), now the Scottish Sports Association, of which we are a full member, we were fully recognised as the National Body for the SSC.

Throughout our first eight years, when I was Hon. Secretary, we had an excellent partnership with the BMC, personified by their Secretary, Dennis Gray. We had a working agreement exactly like the recent Memorandum, restated when the BMC recently became Incorporated. This restated the BMC/MCofS partnership, the BMC representing the UK internationally with agreement of MCofS on matters affecting Scotland and, while working together internally, matters concerning Scotland are dealt with by the MCofS.

Most of our work concerned access and conservation of areas of concern to us. At that time, with the apparent risk of education doing its own thing regarding hill-walking, I found my seat on the SMLTB useful to try to bring the MCofS view into training and safety. To link education and professional use of our mountains with the individual or club climber I started the MCofS training weekends at Glenmore Lodge. In this we had the enthusiastic help of Eric Langmuir and later Fred Harper and this continues with Andy Anderson and his staff.

Most of us on the Executive Committee were new boys to an organisation like MCofS and we were greatly helped by chairmen guiding good organisation and practical politics! Some climbers viewed us disdainfully as bureaucrats and mountaineering politicians, failing to realise that these volunteer amateurs were giving their time to conserve climbing for everyone, despite pressure on all sides to inhibit or spoil their day on the hill. Personally I didn't think of our Executive Committee as a pyramid of officers and other ranks, but rather as a rugby team of various talents aimed at winning for our sport. The Council is the membership, the Committee simply the work party.

When, after some fifteen years away from the Committee, I was asked back I found the Council's field of work greatly enlarged with new elements in mountaineering activity and interest reflected in the work of the sub-committees, representations to and from other bodies, the introduction of staff and, of course, a greatly enlarged membership and hill-going public.

The Council works for all recreational hill-goers, illustrating the SSC 'Sport for All' policy, but perhaps the non-competitive tradition of our sport sets it a little aside from their 'prestige and medal' way of measuring success. However, understanding, reflected by their financial support is improving despite the present difficult times. I feel that they are willing and it is up to us to explain ourselves.

The Council has always been very conscious of the interests and welfare of those who live and work in the countryside. We try to balance a desire in some places for mountain wilderness with the aspirations of local folk and the National interest.

In today's scene, having the MCofS is more vital than ever to protect our interests. This usually puts us in a defensive role, but perhaps by our work over the last 25 years we have earned the ear and goodwill of folk within the SSC, SNH, NTS, Scottish office, etc., and we can now move towards a role which involves more initiative.

So it's on to the future and I'm sure that all of us involved in the past wish all the best – to those now involved, as well as to those who will be part of the future management of the MCofS.

Sandy Cousins

SCOTTISH COMMITTEE

Chairman		Secretary	
1945-51	H D Welsh	1945-51	J K W Dunn

The Scottish clubs represented by the Scottish Committee formed the Association of Scottish Climbing Clubs and in 1951 the member clubs of the ASCC (except the SMC and the London section of the JMCS) withdrew from BMC membership. In 1970 the ASCC became the Mountaineering Council of Scotland (which included the SMC).

The Peak District Area

I was talked into writing about the first 50 years of the Peak Area Committee because I have attended meetings fairly regularly since I came south to the Peak to work, on April Fools Day 1966. Unfortunately my memories have become fuddled by having to write minutes of recent meetings, so I hope you will have some sympathy, as I have, for the previous Hon Sec of this Committee who wanted to look after her baby (too right) instead of recording such exciting climbing news as Mountain Training, Future Policy, Limited Companies and where should the BMC have its HQ?

The most important aspects of walking and climbing in the Peak may well have been done already through the efforts of previous members, especially Jack Longland, Cyril Machin and Eric Byne.

My comments on the earliest days are based on minutes, which only go back to 1958, or conversations with those 'activists' I can talk to – preferably over a beer which may lubricate 'the little grey cells'. When I came to work for the Peak National Park (with the grand title of Warden Service Officer) there was a BMC file which I did study (having been a supporter of G.W.Y.'s ideals for many years) and the earliest correspondence was an answer to the senior National Park Officer, John Foster, in October 1955 from my old friend Michael Holton (just back from the RAF expedition to the Himalayas) who was then Hon. Sec. of the BMC working from his home! One has to remember that Winthrop Young's idea of a BMC only came into being post-war, not so long before the 1949 National Parks and Access to the Countryside Act, and, as now, voluntary workers were not that thick on the mountains! We might climb, but letters were a chore – one thing that hasn't changed in 50 years.

The first National Park, the Peak, didn't emerge immediately after the Act was passed (December 1949) because of political arguments about the representation of county councillors on the new National Park Authority from the different parts of the Peak District – Staffordshire, Cheshire, West and South Yorkshire, as well as a lot of North Derbyshire (and even now you hear ignoramuses talking about the Derbyshire Peak District!) so the new Joint Peak Planning Board didn't meet until November 1951. I apologise for sounding like a history text-book, but today's mountaineers should appreciate the context then – there was not one paid BMC officer, and access to mountains, although talked about for the previous half-century, had only just got onto the statute book; and that with many reservations and conditions.

Mountains in the Lakes and Snowdonia in particular were accessible to mountain walkers and climbers (did not poets and writers help here?) whereas in the Peak the high moors had been protected from walkers by owners of grouse moors, who had to be convinced that allowing the public to walk over them would not ruin their income from grouse shooting. Irrespective of whether you think "huntin', shootin' and fishin'" are acceptable, you have to recognise that grouse moor owners pay rates, employ gamekeepers to burn the old heather so more grouse can reach, and eat, the young shoots, take on local lads as beaters and have a considerable financial interest in an area which will not grow much else – even massed conifers don't like the altitude and sulphur dioxide! So the National Parks Act enabled the Peak National Park to negotiate (note the word) with moor owners to allow the public to 'wander at will' subject to good behaviour and withdrawal of access for 10 or 12 days a year during the grouse shooting season. I always thought that we, mountaineers, got a bargain – true from 12th August one couldn't always go on certain moors, but on those days one could go on others. True, they had some financial compensation from the Exchequer, but we had gamekeepers keeping the heather height down for us to walk over (and chest-deep heather is dreadful).

The history lesson ought to end here but there is another tolerant side to climbers; recognising the skill element of other sports. In the RAF I had to do 'annual musketry' (what a nice old phrase) although I was a PTI and then a Mountain Rescue Team Leader (yes, the mind boggles!). Those who criticise grouse shooting as a 'sport' ought to see grouse flying low and fast over a moor and imagine being in a butt at the bottom of a clough and trying to hit a small bird going over fast, which you couldn't see until it comes over a brow 50 yards away(!) (most escape). The Peak N.P. commissioned a survey about 25 years ago and the Nature Conservancy then reckoned that most owners don't shoot enough, or burn enough strips of heather, and that many of the surplus birds not shot would starve the following winter irrespective of public access! (I'd rather have chicken, free-range.)

The Peak N.P. was well aware of the pressure for access to the Dark Peak moorland and by the end of 1953 had negotiated access agreements to half of Kinder Scout and two years later the rest – 8 owners and umpteen tenants – and by 1961 much of Bleaklow.

The letter from Mike Holton to John Foster mentioned earlier was about BMC priorities for access to crags on these grouse moors, but the question had been asked whether climbers would help in a voluntary warden scheme. Some clubs, e.g. Barnsley MC and Oread MC, were very helpful in those days, but many clubs were known to remove litter after their meets, if not prepared to commit themselves to dates when they might guarantee their presence as voluntary wardens. Yet the Park having promised owners that wardens would always be present, needed a guaranteed attendance; so part-time paid wardens were needed.

In January 1958 Cyril Machin sent a circular to clubs saying that the BMC was *reviving* the Peak Committee with Jack Longland as Chairman and himself as Hon Sec and invited representatives to a meeting at County Offices on Saturday 18th January 1958. He listed crags where access was difficult and put The Roaches and Hen Cloud at the top of the list. In a letter inviting John Foster (NPO) to come to that meeting Jack Longland referred to a meeting of Peak BMC clubs held on 22 March 1957 regarding access priorities and a possible wardening scheme e.g. on Stanage (then in private hands), the success of which would help in discussions with neighbouring owners. An access agreement to Stanage was signed in September 1962 – but not High Neb. (Since then the Peak Board has purchased the North Lees Estate, inc. the Edge.)

Jack also convinced the National Trust agent for the High Peak that high camping overnight by small numbers of members of BMC clubs would not lead to fires and litter, but they would 'play the game and do the right thing'. This gentleman's agreement was a notable breakthrough in the Peak over 35 years ago and worked satisfactorily for many years, despite a much more recent policy statement by the BMC nationally that they could not negotiate exclusively for their members. Fortunately the National Trust has been very sympathetic and in recent times has accepted that such an agreement is for about four people who will clear up and leave early in the morning, and be particularly careful about not causing peat fires.

Possibly the greatest achievement of the Peak Committee is the provision of guidebooks, with Eric Byne the early driving force, but a host of enthusiastic voluntary workers carry on the good work – too many to name here but you can read their names in the individual guides. A history of Peak climbing is there too, and there is the classic book *High Peak* by Eric Byne and Geoff Sutton which is a must – but my copy has disappeared! I was amused to find recently, in the old BMC file in the National Park office, a draft paragraph on access for the first of the new series, written by someone whose name should be included here – Harry Brunt – a keen hill-walker as well as a planner, who did the majority of the initial work in getting access agreements as John Foster's deputy, though the senior officer usually gets his name in lights! Harry was a natural negotiator, he even got around the owners of Yellowslacks after one of them had tried to blow up the crag! The man was so annoyed and frustrated with bad-mannered climbers – modern climbers beware, owners of crags get fed up with constant wall climbing and trespass through their lambing fields and 'stroppy repartee' – getting down to the pub the quickest way. Fortunately much of the crag survived, but it could happen elsewhere if all mountain users don't see the owner's viewpoint and leave no signs of their visit.

Of course the Peak Committee was very fortunate in having Jack Longland as Chairman from the early days until October 1975. Dave Gregory, who was Hon Sec for nearly as long, will tell you how Jack kept the Peak Committee on the right lines with masterly tact and good humour. Yet it is odd now to think that Jack's 'first' – White Hall Centre for Outdoor Pursuits – set a trend for such activities throughout the education world here which has since embarrassed individual 'fun climbers' and the Peak Committee at times more recently. For instance some imitators have been taking over climbs for top-roping incompetents and polishing routes by abseiling down them, or using Jack's agreement for high camping for their own ends instead of seeking specific permission. The Principal at White Hall, Lyn Noble, succeeded Jack as Chairman and carried on the good work, but before him previous principals at the centre, Geoff Sutton, Eric Langmuir and Kim Meldrum had been involved in pressing the Peak N.P. for access to crags. (Kim's greatest contribution may have been his article in the Climbers' Club Journal 'The White Hell Outdoor Pursuits Centre). For some years Lyn Noble chaired the Open Guidebook meetings and the guidebook committee, from which more and more Peak guidebooks appeared – Eric Byne would have been gratified to see the extent of Peak influence here – even now having money to spare for access needs.

After a meeting of the committee at White Hall, I remember going out into a wonderful winter night with Larry Lambe and saying that I envied him his walk across the frozen snow to Windgather Youth Hostel in the light of a full moon. As I drove home the moonlight faded and I realised that there was an eclipse and visualised Larry having to get out his head-torch after all! A memorable evening to be walking across the Goyt Valley – and I didn't hear the end of the tale for some time – the hostel was shut for repairs and they recommended Buxton! After some discussion he was able to stay – but no water.

Looking back one tries to list the achievements. In the early days the Peak N.P. and our Committee were usually working towards the same ends – access for mountaineers – but one aspect of this, from an N.P. viewpoint fell short – voluntary mountaineer wardens to ensure good behaviour – a feature of the 1949 Act. The N.P. had to convince landowners that access agreements would not permit thoughtless members of the public to harm their interests by leaving litter, letting dogs chase their tenants' sheep, or leaving cigarette and pipe 'throwaways' to start fires – and all the other things that might annoy landowners enough to blow up crags! So, very early in the correspondence were requests for help from responsible mountaineers to act as voluntary wardens, but numbers were not sufficient nor dates guaranteed. I was very pleased when I persuaded Dave Gregory, then Hon. Sec., to take a Warden Training Course.

I had hoped that he would set a trend – a voluntary warden may well be worth more than 10 paid men (as they say) but he or she does need some training – if only to learn to say "You may be right" instead of, "go away" in the vernacular. Unfortunately Dave wasn't able to persuade other Peakland climbers to do the same, although I'm sure he helped to influence other mountaineers of the need to look after their own interests (in the long term) in these areas. Certainly some clubs and individuals do recognise the need to speak out when they see 'anti-social behaviour', but unfortunately many tend to think 'its now't to do with me' – but it is! Quite recently representatives of this Committee have moaned about a group taking over part of a crag for top-roping or abseiling, or leaving litter, or allowing youngsters to rampage unsupervised all over the place. Yet rarely have they spoken to them, identified the leader and talked to him (rarely her!!) and found out the organisation, and quoted 'chapter and verse' so, if nothing else, the BMC office can send them some information, e.g. on the Single Pitch Supervisors Award, which I hope any voluntary warden I trained would have done (without showing a notebook or licking a pencil).

Dave may well have done some good in this direction, but later on in 1990 when he stood in for an absent Hon. Sec. to do the minutes, he recorded a complaint from the Peak N.P. about litter on Stanage (5.11.90) ... 'the point was made that the Rangers who are frequently on the Edge could help by carrying such bags of litter collected by climbers on their usual patrols, instead of just looking pretty' ... and taxpayers please note, the majority of rangers on Stanage are paid from public funds!

However, way back in 1967 foot-and-mouth disease outbreaks around the Peak changed attitudes to access completely. We supported the premise that our feet might just spread the disease northwards through the Pennines from Edale, and helped the Peak N.P. in promoting a 'Keep

Off the Moors' policy. Their Information Officer then, Don Aldridge, (himself a climber and a previous voluntary Editor of the BMC Magazine *Mountaineering*, and well known for his cartoon-type illustrations in the first MLC booklet) maintained that the support given to this policy by all mountain walkers was responsible for the few outbreaks within the National Park compared to the many in the surrounding areas. (Throughout the area of the N.P. wardens and information staff were stopping people and asking walkers to keep off all agricultural land.) Whether the Ministry vets were convinced of the negative statistics or not, the BMC was thanked by the N.P. Officer for its support and the members' forbearance when it was over. (The Annual Report of the PDNP 1968 statistics is quite complimentary to laymen walkers.)

Unfortunately the good relationships between the BMC and Peak N.P. officers have declined since then, mainly over the closure of the access moors due to high fire risk. Agreed, if there were no people on the moors the fire danger would be minimal, although there may have been a few arsonists at times, it was believed. However, one big fire in the Swains Greave area of Bleaklow started mid-week, the day after a sheep gather of the headwaters of the Derwent!

The BMC has consistently held that before such draconian measures as blanket-closure are acceptable, public footpaths across these moors should also be closed, but first ask all smokers to leave their habit at home. Legal arrangements for closing rights of way could be argued in advance with various government departments, quoting possible public danger, ecological effects, damage to property etc., so that the principle could be established well before there is an extreme fire risk. The ridiculous situation of climbers having their right of access to crags withdrawn, yet people still walking on a right of way nearby, able to throw their fag ends down, does not get climbers' support.

The BMC has argued the Alice in Wonderland nature of the moor closures, citing the benefits of static, non-smoking climbers as fire watchers, without any success. It was even suggested at a Peak Committee meeting by a smoking climber (me) that smokers *only* should be barred (for the psychological impact – it worked on the majority during foot-and-mouth) and this was translated into a suggestion that the access Bylaws should be amended to cover this point, but the Home Office disagreed. So the daft situation still applies every time we have a dry summer: people can walk along the top of Froggatt and Curbar Edges quite legally whereas climbers can't or shouldn't climb there. I must admit to having amassed 15 stars on Stanage one fine day (celebrating my first year as an OAP) having parked away from the banning signs and leaving fags in the car, but there was a fairly constant stream of walkers, some smoking, along the top of the crag! On the other hand, some years earlier, coming down from the Edge just as the light was failing, I encouraged a few other late climbers to help me pee on a small patch of smouldering peat which would soon have been a major fire.

There are many similar situations in the Peak such as Kinder Downfall and Laddow Rocks, with the Pennine Way not so many yards away. Small wonder that the Peak BMC has lost much of its sympathy towards the present officers of the Peak N.P.

One wonders if there are nowadays more officers who are not keen hill-walkers like Harry Brunt, who did so much of the early negotiations for access, backed by the Board's solicitor, R.N. Hutchins, another hill-walker. Are they now career local government officers only? Or is it that there are fewer members of the Peak Board with sympathy for walkers, as the members should direct the policies that officers follow? When I first started as one of the Board's officers my immediate boss was Harry Brunt, but amongst the members (one third of them were appointed by the government, the others from the County Councils) who were very keen on access to mountains were Phil Daley (Ramblers' Association), Gerald Haythornthwaite (CPRE), Rev Ernest Turner (keen walker as well as Rector of Eyam), Patrick Monkhouse of Guardian fame and author of *On Foot in the Peak* and, just retired, Steven Morton (Sheffield Ramblers' Association). Even the NFU representative, Ivor Morten, with a degree in agriculture, was a very forward looking farmer, and Vice-Chairman of the Board, whilst a famous Peakland walker, Fred Heardman, was a co-opted member. Owning the Nags Head at Edale, Fred was known by owners and gamekeepers as well as walkers and could amuse as well as enthuse with his fund of stories about the moors and wildlife, and was often called 'Bloody Bill the Bog Trotter' by gamekeepers, but he was an asset to the early members of the Peak Board.

The Chairman of the Peak Board then was Alderman Norman Gratton, appointed by Derbyshire County Council, a local man with a Trade Union background, held in some esteem for his down-to-earth attitudes – yet he was still at times an old working man of pre-war days. He supported Ivor Morten's enthusiasm for using the new legislation for access and agreed with the importance Ivor placed on educating the post-war public in environmental awareness, in multiple land use, and appreciating the agricultural benefits to hill farmers of outdoor recreation, and the provisions in the 1949 Act for their compensation.

I apologise if I seem to be writing more of the history of the Peak National Park Board than of the Peak Area Committee of the BMC, but they were very closely related in the earlier days of both, and both were growing up in the new post-war Britain, with the 1949 Act available to use for its idealism. I have mentioned Dave Gregory who has done so much for the Peak BMC that he must (DV) end up as successor to Nat Allen (who has also worked so hard since the early days, yet I haven't mentioned) as the 'Grand Old Man' of the Peak, but we should also honour two men from what is now sometimes looked upon as 'the other side' at the National Park Authority, who have since died.

As a climber working for the Peak Board I was in the middle and was gratified to find how close the personalities of Peak BMC and Peak N.P. were on many of the issues of the day. I recall being in Harry Brunt's office on several occasions when Ivor Morten came in and said "Harry, can't you interpret the 1949 Act so we can get (Exchequer) grant for this?" Harry could quote most of the Act word for word. There would follow a debate on the Dower Report which set out the ideals of the Act and the subsequent Hobhouse Report which suggested the mechanisms, and they would agree to use all three to convince the Minister that what the Peak Board wanted to do could be fitted into the intention of such and such a section of the '49 Act – even Hansard would be quoted by Ivor! I used to spend quite a few evenings at Ivor's house (at his invitation mark you) discussing tactics for resolving problems, and knew that he would spend hours on the telephone with many of the appointed members (and others from various counties) so that the recommendations penned by Harry Brunt, and agreed by John Foster, received their support. Nearly all of these were to do with access to moors or crags, or even their purchase to guarantee access, such as Windgather Rocks or later Stanage Edge and the North Lees Estate – to demonstrate the multiple use of a hill farm. We, as mountaineers and users, also need to ensure that it remains viable, and litter free.

Back to the Peak BMC – it is interesting to note that in 1985 the Chairman, David Dickson (MAM), had done some research and that this Committee represented 'some 70-80 clubs, most of which didn't bother to send representatives ... 'but the point is made that the Peak Area is very likely representing more members of BMC clubs than any other area'. (In fact, the L&SE Area Committee represents 110 clubs. The Peak & Midland (formed 1994) together represents 69. Ed)

When I sit on my doorstep nearly half a century after the formation of the BMC, trying to think of how to write this article, having come from the PH with a 'carry oot' and waiting for an almost full moon to come round and shine on the south of the cottage, I wonder whether more has changed, insidiously, since those days, than we realise? The 'peace and enjoyment of a National Park' as envisaged by John Dower is still here, to some extent, but I can't hear if a hedgehog is coming down the lane, snuffling amongst the roadside vegetation for slugs because lots of commercial aircraft go over. Should not National Parks be 'no go' areas for them or military aircraft? (It's worse in Eryri!) Anyway my neighbour is a townie from Derby who poisoned the laneside over a month ago, doubtless killing small tortoiseshell butterfly larvae as well as the nettles! Most villages are suffering from incomers.

Then there are the sodium lamps; 15 in Stanton, more in Youlgrave, others in Elton and Winster and one in Over Haddon at the top of 'our' lane preventing me from enjoying my roses in the moonlight of a calm summer evening. Why does my Council tax have to pay for all these superfluous lights? Yes, I remember struggling to light an oil lamp or a Tilley, but I didn't have it on all night! Do we really need these to deter burglars – are there statistics available – don't burglars have overheads like torch batteries to set against their tax!

Times have changed in this half century. Peak BMC meetings are now (apart from where the HQ should be) about climbers disturbing rare birds. Is this because the BMC has always been reasonable and not shouted too hard? Surely picnickers, dog walkers, runners and organised groups of ramblers (e.g. CHA or other clubs, not necessarily Ramblers' Association) can disturb even more – and BBC TV identified car rallyists causing kingfishers to leave a young brood recently. Why waste petrol and drive round the countryside when you could walk *on your own* and see and hear more? The pendulum has swung the other way now, Peak mountaineers are very suspicious of officers from the N.P. trying to convince them that keeping away from all potential nesting sites will encourage hawks, falcons, etc. to breed there – surely it is a suitable food supply in the right habitat. Now it is ring ouzels, declared a dirty word by the acting chairman at the last Peak Committee meeting to curb reiteration – apparently at the southern edge of their range on Hen Cloud, despite ornithologists' evidence that they have declined here and the South West for the last century anyway!

So the Peak Committee (which included a lot of Midlands clubs until recently when a Midlands Committee was formed) has been in the forefront of action on access, guidebooks and BMC principles for the last 50 years; they still have to fight more battles for the climbing public (see Editorial in *High* and letter from Hathersage Parish Council, July 94. Don't forget, *we* are the BMC, with a responsibility to future climbers. Enjoy your climbing as much as I have done over the last 50 years even though I couldn't make my leader hear 'take in more' on Beeston Tor the other day, because they had a compressor going at the farm below for their sheep shearing. Then they were *working* while we were playing!

Still to be resolved is access to Brassington (East Hill, Rainster Rocks) where you can only trespass now because a few people (some may have been climbers) told the owner to "go away". (It is outside the boundary of the Peak N P and Derbyshire County Council aren't interested in an access order; the owner not in an agreement, and he has been known to take rucksacks as ransom.) A climber who likes these pleasant little rocks, who is a solicitor, should come forward to argue the case for a public right of way up those climbs recorded in the MAM guidebook of 1950. I will certainly stand as a witness to doing most of the Long Climb variants each year since 1966 (if not The Snuffer Chimney so frequently) and I'm sure Keith Gregson could get more from the Oread Club.

The first job is to convince the Peak National Park officers and members that we protect the hills, not set fire to them, and appreciate the wildlife (lots of us are members of RSPB, NT etc.) but we need a mountaineer appointed to the Peak Board – any offers: it requires time!

J R Lees

PEAK DISTRICT AREA COMMITTEE

Chairman		Secretary	
1947-48	C B Machin	1947-48	R E Davies
Re-established in 1956.			

Chairman		Secretary	
1956-75	J L Longland	1956-63	C B Machin
1975-82	L Noble	1963-72	D Gregory
1982-87	D Dickson	1973	R H Jeal
1987-88	I Smith	1974-78	S M Beal
1988-91	G White	1978-82	M Vallance
1991-95	R Bennett	1982	I Smith
1995-	M Richardson	1982-84	A Hubbard
Access Representative		1984-85	G Birtles
1980s-93	C Hooley	1985-88	G Clare
1988-95	B Wilson	1988-92	Hilary Lawrenson
1993-95	M Trafford	1992-	J R Lees
1995-	D Bishop		
1995-	A Ekins		

The North-East Area

There are no records of the early years of the Area Committee but it appears that it was formed in the mid-Sixties and the meetings were held at Newcastle Polytechnic 3 to 5 times per year. The meetings were generally well attended particularly in the 1980s but in the 1990s the numbers attending declined, so in 1993 the venue was changed to Eldon Leisure Centre in Newcastle which houses the Berghaus Wall, where it was hoped that more climbers would attend the meetings. This did not materialise so the venue has been changed again to the Seven Stars Inn at Shincliffe near Durham which is both more central and ambient and will hopefully attract more members.

One of the first topics discussed was the Hunt Report on the MLTB, and training in one form or another has been on the agenda every year.

In the early days of the committee there were few access problems and one of the main aims was to foster good relations with the various public bodies in the area. This policy has continued to the present day and over the years representatives from many organisations including the Sports Council and Ramblers' Association have attended our area meetings.

Committee members have also attended as BMC representatives, meetings of other organisations such as the Standing Conference of Northern Sport & Recreation and North-East Instructors' Panel.

The committee's views on the running and planning of the Northumberland National Park were put forward to the consultative body in the 1970s, and in the late 1980s and early 1990s a similar exercise was carried out for the North York Moors National Park with particular reference to rock-climbing. It was agreed that campaigning for unlimited access in National Parks will not always benefit rock-climbers. The committee is also opposed to direct action to gain access to crags.

Consultation took place with the Nature Conservancy in the early years and continues with English Nature whenever problems in connection with SSIs arise.

Discussions also took place in the 1970s with the RSPB long before the formal agreements were drawn up.

In the late 1970s the committee's views were put forward to Hadrian's Wall Management Committee as one of the area's important stretch of crags lies immediately under the Wall.

The committee was dealt a severe blow in 1989 when the Chairman, Steve Derwin, was involved in a tragic motorbike accident leaving him partially paralysed. However through sheer determination Steve has recovered sufficiently to enable him to go canoeing and hang-gliding.

The single pitch climbing award and third party insurance were both subjects for which the North-East committee opposed the views of Manchester, but it appeared that they were in the minority.

Malcolm Prentice, the area secretary in the early 90s, gave considerable assistance to Headquarters with the drafting of the Incorporation document.

In the 1970s the North-East was much more fortunate than other parts of the country as it did not suffer from overcrowding on the crags and hills and hence did not experience many access problems. However with the large increase in the number of young people and groups climbing in the 1980s, the area was suddenly faced with numerous access problems some of which still rumble on today. During the last 10 years the majority of committee time has been spent discussing and dealing with access problems arising from litter, parking, dogs, bivvying, fires, language and anchors. We have even had an access problem on a viaduct wall!

Jesmond Dene in Newcastle was one of the first access problems dealt with. Holwick Scar was also an early problem (due to climbers setting fire to the crag) and has still not been resolved; originally there was a hostile farmer and an amenable landowner but now it is a case of a hostile landowner and an amenable farmer.

Many crags in Northumberland developed access problems mainly due to over-use by groups. Most of these were solved by Nigel Jamieson liaising with the landowners, farmers and the organisations concerned. However at East Woodham an education authority turned up unannounced with over 500 people and not surprisingly climbing is still banned. Nigel produced a Crag Care letter and poster which was circulated to all Clubs, Education Departments, Police Groups, Youth Groups and Activity Centres.

The owners of the Grinkle Park estate, Bass, have banned climbing on their crags since 1980 despite many meetings. The only agreement so far is to allow climbing between November and March.

At Peak Scar many years of negotiations eventually led to an Access/ Management agreement, although as this involved banning abseiling and large groups not everyone was pleased with the outcome. However alternative abseiling venues on disused railway viaducts have been found and these are now in regular use.

Several landowners have suggested that the BMC either buy or lease their crags but unfortunately this is contrary to BMC policy.

The threat of nuclear waste dumping in the Cheviots arose in 1979 and the area committee was active in opposition to the proposals, joining forces with the Ramblers' Association. Fund raising was arranged but because the proposals were abandoned the area committee still has £800 in the bank to help fight any future problems.

Over the years the area committee has staged lectures in part to promote the BMC. Speakers have included Alex MacIntyre, Don Whillans, Alan Rouse, Stephen Venables, John Barry, Andy Fanshawe and several lectures by Alan Hinkes. Most of the lectures were held at Newcastle University and supported by the LD Mountain Centre, Berghaus and the Sports Council.

Two of the member clubs in the area have produced definitive guide books, *Northumberland* by the Northumbrian Mountaineering Club and the *North Yorks Moors* by the Cleveland Mountaineering Club. These books have been revised and updated over the years.

Committee members collated information for the BMC Crag Database in 1989 and submitted the details to Manchester and it is hoped that this information will be readily available one day.

Climbing walls have been constructed in many parts of the region during the last 25 years but the first major wall was built at the Dolphin Centre in Darlington in 1983. The BMC Area committee was involved for the first time in giving technical and administrative guidance resulting in the best and most accessible wall in the region at that time. Other well-designed walls were subsequently opened, in particular the wall at the Billingham Forum in 1989. The Berghaus wall was opened in Newcastle in 1990 and is generally regarded as the best wall in the area. However a wall was opened last year in Newton Aycliffe which is also extremely popular.

Steve Crowe, the area's climbing wall representative, produced in 1991 a Regional Plan for climbing walls for the Sports Council which should help to shape future plans.

Competition climbing was hotly debated in the late 1980s but the opposition died down when it was agreed that it would only be on artificial walls. In 1991 the first of many bouldering competitions was held at the Berghaus Wall in Newcastle and it was a great success.

Also in 1991 the first meeting in the area was held to discuss bolting and sport climbing following the insertion of bolts at a popular crag in Northumberland. The meeting was very well attended and resulted in the agreed policy for the area being 'no bolts' apart from lower offs at one crag. Further bolting occurred on a 'grotty' crag and resulted in another well-attended meeting in 1995 where the policy was slightly amended to 'no bolts without prior consultation' [among local climbers] .

Discussions have taken place on the BMC Footpath policy. Serious erosion at the crags has become the problem of the 1990s, especially at Bowden Doors and Scugdale. There has been a spectacular collapse of a large part of the crag at Park Nab, Kildale, caused by erosion. Discussions are currently under way with the National Park and other bodies to try to alleviate the problems and obtain funding to carry out necessary work.

Over the next 50 years there will undoubtedly be a need for many more climbers to put something back into climbing by joining the North-East Area committee and assisting with solving the many problems that will inevitably arise.

Peter Hay

NORTH-EAST AREA COMMITTEE formed 1965

Chairman

1965-73	D R Barr-Wells
1973	G Slee
1974-75	E N Walker
1975-79	M Chapman
1979-87	R G Pettigrew
1988-90	S Derwin
1990-95	S Porteus
1995-	P Hay

Secretary

1965-67	A Taylor
1967-69	B Lane

Secretary/Treasurer

1969-73	G J Jackson
1974-75	M A Griffiths
1975-79	M B Anderson
1979-87	S Derwin
1987-90	S Porteus
1990-92	M Prentice
1993-	P Tweddle

Access Representatives

P Hay
N Jamieson

The London and South-East Area

It is tempting to think that when the founding fathers of the BMC long ago carved up the map of England and Wales into its present representative areas, they demonstrated much the same sense of humour that governments sometimes show when creativity takes over from common sense on local authority boundaries. "Let us", perhaps they said, "create a huge area containing most of the climbers, but none of the mountains."

To be fair, the geographical and socio-economic map of the country probably had *something* to do with it, but the end product remains – the London & South-East Area. Draw a line roughly from Kings Lynn to Bognor Regis. Everything to the right of that line is L&SE territory. Enormous, 'innit'? You can fit almost any of the other BMC areas into it several times over, whether you use square mileage, human or climbing population (there is a difference) as your measure.

By another measure, the area must have the lowest mean elevation of all of the areas, where '1000 feet above sea level' is a celebrated landmark. We're on a hiding to nothing really. With little save sandstone (and we must save sandstone), to offer the rest of you, the statistics must suggest that we are also a greater than average proportion of the crowds on 'everyone else's' crags, responsible for a big share of erosion problems, traffic jams, litter, and so on. And I will stand the objections of certain devotees and campaigners and say that we don't even have any climbing walls of renown to offer. We housed the BMC HQ in South Audley Street days, but we lost that as well!

So, who would want to have anything to do with the London & South-East Committee? Well, whatever the lack of other gifts, I am proud to boast the track record of that Committee.

A well-thumbed, creaky volume charts the activities and pedigree of the current Committee back to the late 1960s. We still have a few links with the progenitors of the modern Area Committee, and have grieved over the loss of others who served so faithfully for so many years. But the Area has never been served by a bunch of old fogies. It is the Area's proud and justifiable boast to have one of the best-attended meetings and active and knowledgeable membership. This has always made for good and pertinent debate, and London & SE can be relied upon to speak its mind. It isn't cussedness, but on a good many issues we have found ourselves on the opposite side of the argument to the mainstream view in the BMC.

'Scruffy climbs, but 'ard', that's how Don described southern sandstone. It's a unique scene and not to all tastes, but it has played its part in the climbing background of many of 'the great and good'. In Harrison's Rocks we have the first crag the BMC took formally under its wing. The absence of comparable, careful management of some of our other precious small crags has sadly led to serious access and erosion problems in recent years, with the risk that one or two crags could literally be 'loved to death' in the next 50 years of the BMC. We must pay tribute to all who work to deny that outcome. The successful management at Harrison's owes much to the happy partnership for over 25 years of the BMC with the Sports Council.

As we in the south and east read in the climbing press of yet another 'state of the art' climbing wall opening in an area (i.e. any area) already blessed with far greater natural facilities than ours, we muse on a curious situation that this huge area, rich in sports facilities compared to many, cannot yet boast a single truly modern climber-dedicated training facility. OK, we have walls of national renown, such as Mile End, Sobell and Brunel, but where is the next 'Foundry'? It isn't for want of need, potential or virtually guaranteed patronage. [Major new walls at the Castle and Calshott Activity Centre were opened in 1995.]

Thanks to Nea Morin, Maurice Bennett, Bob Gookey, Hugh Jordan, David Abbott and the other pioneers, some now gone, but some happily still with us, we're still doing it.

Tom Phillips

LONDON & SOUTH-EAST AREA COMMITTEE

Chairman		**Secretary**	
1968-75	M Bennett	1968-69	E J N Brooke (acting)
1975-80	H Jordan	1969-73	J Collins
1980-84	P Watson	1974-78	D Abbott
1983-84	R W Gookey	1978	P Watson
1985-87	I Delafield	1978-84	R W Gookey
1987-92	T Phillips	1984-87	R Lowe
1992-	A McLellan	1987-90	Anna Gregory
		1990-95	Daphne Pritchard
Access Representative		1995-96	H Jordan
1980s-94	D Abbott		
1994-	T Daniells		

Chairman of Harrison's Rocks Committee
1954-56   C C Gorrie

In 1958 this was superseded by a Joint Management Committee set up with the CCPR (later The Sports Council).

The South-West and Southern Area

The South-West encompasses a large and diverse climbing region that extends from the limestone of Gloucestershire's Wye Valley to Cornwall's granite.

Many of the major figures in the development of British climbing have left their mark on the region's crags. Some such as Chris Bonington, Paul Nunn, Mike Banks, Pat Littlejohn and latterly Martin Crocker have also been committed to the BMC.

The area committee began its life as part of the South Wales and South-West area. In the Seventies the Committee for Wales was formed and the South-West and Southern area was born.

In the early years when Mike Banks was cutting his teeth in Cornwall and later in the Fifties and Sixties when Bonington passed through the region, picking off the plums of Malbogies in Avon and Coronation Street in Cheddar, the number of climbers was low and their impact small.

Later on Littlejohn and friends began the next wave of development. The sport's popularity began to grow and with it so did the many access problems that have become a feature of the committee's meetings which have taken up so much volunteer and National Officer time.

The region has some of the great adventure routes of the UK on the Culm coast and some of the best sport climbs on Portland and in Torbay. The BMC, a body which seeks to represent all interests within the climbing world has in the South-West held a series of debates as to where bolts are acceptable. A consensus has been reached and those who seek to work outside the guidelines have found that the opinion of the majority of climbers wins through.

Over the years the Committee and National Access Officer – first Bill Wright and latterly Kath Pyke – have helped build good working relationships with the National Trust, National Parks, RSPB, English Heritage and a host of County and District Councils and local landowners. The perfect climbing solution has not always been the result, but by negotiating and putting a reasoned and well-researched case many friends and new climbing ground have been won.

In April 1995, the South-West Region broke new ground for the BMC with the appointment of the organisation's first Regional Development

Officer. With the support of the South-West Regional Sports Council and Undercover Rock in Bristol, Ian Parnell is now established in the BMC's southern outpost.

This regionalisation of resources and personnel cannot but help: make the BMC more accessible to its membership: help ensure that there is access to crags; and that indoor facilities and training will be developed for not only the next 50 years but for all future generations.

Mike Rosser

SOUTH-WEST & SOUTHERN AREA COMMITTEE

Chairman		Secretary	
1968-72	M A P Hogg	1968-70	P Leyshon
1972-73	J H Bradley	1970-72	R D Moulton (also Treasurer)
1974-78	R G Pettigrew	1972-73	D W Partridge
1978	Audrey Salkeld	1973-75	M T Hodgson
1979-81	F R Robinson	1975-78	D Marshall
1981-84	Major E H Marriott	1978-79	D Taylor
1984-87	S Bondi	1979-83	F R Brooke
1987-92	R Scantlebury	1983-85	Miss P Stephens
1992-	M Rosser	1985-87	M Riddell
		1987-91	Pamela Holt
		1991-93	Diane Oakley
		1993-94	R Scantlebury
		1994-	J Willson

Treasurer		Access Representative	
1969-72	R D Moulton	1986-87	I Day
1977-78	M T Hodgson	1987-93	A Allonnay
1984-86	Pamela Holt	1994-96	M Raine
		1994-	J Willson
		1994-	N Coe
		1994-	S Taylor
		1994-95	I Parnell
		1996-	S Elliot

The Yorkshire and Humberside Area

The Yorkshire and Humberside Area Committee was formed in 1974 in response to a specific threat. National Park Officer, Wilf Proctor, alerted the Yorkshire Mountaineering Club (YMC) to proposals for developing the Cow and Calf Rocks above Ilkley. They included levelling the quarry floor, arranging the boulders for picnic tables and chairs, and taking the main footpath into the quarry and out at the back by a staircase. Fortunately the climbing world was made aware in time to prevent these 'improvements' and the formation of the new Area Committee was justified straight away.

P.C. Swindells of the Yorkshire Ramblers' Club was the first Chair, Bev Barratt of the YMC the first Secretary, Mike Bebbington of the YMC the first Access officer; the BMC professional officer was Dennis Gray, and the new Committee received valuable assistance from the Y & H Sports Council Officer, Ken Gill. In the BMC Annual Report of 1974 the Committee made its mission statement – to intercept any schemes which might affect the interests of climbers, and to deal with access problems at Yorkshire crags.

For the next few years problems mainly occurred at gritstone crags, Almscliff, Crookrise, Ilkley, Guisecliff and Widdop. Mostly they were solved amicably, but Roy Pomfret wrote in 1975 'the problem at Hugencroft continues to be difficult and may be for a long time'. How right he was: twenty years later we are still trying to reinstate climbing there.

Fears arose that the National Trust could 'tame' Brimham Rocks, which led to meetings at national level between the BMC and the Trust, so that each could understand the other's point of view. Crummackdale was a limestone crag needing intervention with the farmer, and there were problems at Kilnsey where climbers were unfairly held responsible for congestion on the narrow road beneath the crag. Peter Ball volunteered to help Mike Bebbington by covering access problems in North Yorkshire, while Bren Jones contributed to the work of the secretary.

By the late Seventies some ten Yorkshire clubs were represented on the Area Committee. Tony Jones, a Lancastrian in temporary exile, did a spell as Secretary. When Roy Pomfret left Yorkshire, Jack Bloor of the Gritstone Club, climber and fell-runner, took over as Chair and gave us the benefit of his experience for the next five years, supported for most of that time by David Atherton as Secretary. Eddie Lesniak, YMC guidebook Editor, became Access Officer when problems were emerging at Gordale Scar. Since Gordale and Malham were of national importance, Eddie was assisted by the BMC Officer, Mark Hutchinson, and a satisfactory outcome was reached through meetings with the Yorkshire Dales National Park.

The first climbing wall issue occurred in 1979, when the Committee had to intervene at the Leeds University wall on behalf of 'outsiders'; until then Don Robinson's original wall had been accessible and free to all climbers since its construction in 1965. The first voluntary bird restrictions were agreed in 1981 for peregrines nesting at Blue Scar.

From its inception until 1990 the Area Committee met in the Yorkshire Ramblers' Library, inner sanctum of the central Leeds public library. This was an attractive venue because members could browse among the books and journals and research mountains anywhere in the world. Business had to proceed quickly, as the building closed at 9.00pm, and we would adjourn informally to the 'Victoria' across the road. It was a disappointment when restricted library hours forced us to meet elsewhere.

The early Eighties saw Mrs Jo Light of the Fell & Rock Club and David Smith taking the Chair, and Geoff Coupland of the Leeds MC as Secretary. Then came Ian Howat and Nigel Shaw of the Leeds Outdoor Pursuits Group. Ken Tilford began a decade as Access Officer, keeping this crucial position in the YMC. Being the club which publishes the Gritstone and Limestone guidebooks, the YMC is always concerned about maintaining access to crags, and Ken inherited several problems, particularly at Guisecliff. The approach of Access officers is to get to know the landowner, discuss the problems, negotiate a solution, and spread the word to climbers. Normally this works, but unfortunately the farmer at Guisecliff met visitors with a gun. During the years Ken was trying to negotiate, Yorkshire's biggest gritstone crag reverted to jungle, and we no longer hear of climbers going there.

In 1986 the Area Committee appointed its first Climbing Wall Officer, Ed Jones, to monitor the new walls at Guiseley, Rothwell and Bradford, as well as Leeds University, and to represent us on the BMC Climbing Wall Committee. A year later the Committee co-ordinated the first crag clean-up, part of a national BMC effort, and volunteers removed much litter from ten gritstone and limestone crags. Climbing competitions and qualifications to teach rock-climbing were issues of national importance which appeared on the agenda. Making input to the next BMC five-year plan, Y&H decided that the highest priority was to appoint another access professional, but that there was also need for more staff to look after training, indoor climbing and eventually competitions.

Student involvement in the Area Committee peaked in the late Eighties, with Stephen Holroyd then Nick Wood of the Leeds University Union MC acting as Secretary. Angela Soper replaced Ed Jones as Climbing Wall Rep. A threat to hold a climbing competition on Malham Cove was contained by timely action on the part of Ken Tilford and Bill Wright of the BMC, and the first indoor events were held during 1989 in Leeds. The DR Yorkshire Open took place at the University, then the historic International Competition at the Queens Hall, and the Committee talked Angela into having a go at the women's and veterans' events, which turned out to her distinct advantage.

A Climbing Liaison Committee was set up between the BMC, the Yorkshire Dales National Park, the Nature Conservancy, and the Yorkshire Naturalists Union, meeting at least annually, and this has worked well ever since. Relations with the Regional Sports Council were also enhanced by having as officer, Pippa Manson, a keen climber, who regularly attended our meetings.

By the time Angela Soper took over the Chair from Ian Howat in 1990 there were too many climbing walls for one person to cover, so we advertised for volunteers at walls and climbing shops, and formed a Climbing Wall Team, led by Tony Vangrove and Eric Rhodes. These new members promoted the National Plan for Climbing Walls, with particular success at Huddersfield Sports Centre where an existing 'white elephant' was converted into an excellent modern facility.

The Committee organised crag clean-ups at Caley, Shipley Glen and Woodhouse Scar, sponsored by climbing shops Centresport and Wilderness Ways, which are always willing to promote the work of the BMC. Environmental problems arose at Almscliff where the farmer persists in wintering cattle at the crag, ruining the grass. Ken Tilford drew on the BMC's Access Fund to put up signs at Pot Scar showing the agreed access to the crag; it is essential that climbers respect it. At Blue Scar Ken not only re-negotiated access, but inspired the landowner to take up climbing.

Triss Kenny of the Craven MC was the Secretary for our best attended meeting in April 1991 when bolting was on the agenda. The meeting was disrupted by a fire alarm – was a saboteur at work? – but reconvened nearby. It was unanimously agreed that there should be no bolts on gritstone. Then the meeting identified a limited number of limestone crags where bolts were considered acceptable, including the Central Zone of Malham Cove and Kilnsey, which are now of international importance.

Another big meeting was the 100th in March 1992, which the Committee celebrated by considering how to be more effective, then going out for a meal together. From this emerged the Handbook Project. By January 1993 the BMC Yorkshire and Humberside Handbook was ready for distribution to individual members, clubs and key targets in the area. We thank all the sponsors who made it possible to publish this source of information and are pleased to record a profit for the BMC of over £500.

The work of the Access officer had also become too much for one person, so again we advertised for volunteers to help and eventually replace Ken. The Access Team is now John Belbin of the Craven MC, looking after limestone country, Robin Costello of the Fell & Rock, responsible for the gritstone, and Vicki James (YMC), who will write the access notes in future guidebooks. Persistent effort by John and Bill Wright achieved an access agreement for Penyghent, where climbers were being aggressively turned away from the gritstone crag near the summit.

Richard Morgan (Fell & Rock) is the present Secretary and we have a replenished Climbing Wall Team led by Neil Sawyer of the Rucksack Club. Guidebook Editor, Dave Musgrove, and Mountain Rescue Team Member, Doug Brill, are regulars at our meetings and Mieszek Konrad-Kosicki of the Sports Council keeps in touch. Original members, Mike Bebbington and Dennis Gray, still attend, and long may they continue to do so.

Over the years the work of the Area Committee has grown steadily. We now deal with many access problems, monitor more climbing walls and competitions, write detailed development plans for The Sports Council, discuss national issues and contribute to BMC policies. We care deeply about bridging the gap for new climbers between the indoor scene and the real thing. About half of the BMC-affiliated clubs in Yorkshire send representatives to our meetings and there is a good blend of experienced contributors and new faces. Volunteers for specific roles have always come forward. We would still like to see more members, especially individuals, coming along and contributing to democratic decision making within the BMC.

Angela Soper

YORKSHIRE & HUMBERSIDE AREA COMMITTEE

Chairman		Secretary	
1974-75	P C Swindells	1972-78	B J Barratt
1975-77	R E Pomfret	1978-82	D J Atherton
1977-82	J Bloor	1982-86	G Coupland
1982-83	Jo Light	1986-88	N Shaw
1983-86	D Smith	1988-89	S Holroyd
1986-89	I Howat	1989-91	N Wood
1989-95	Angela Soper	1991-93	T Kenny
1995-	D Gray	1993-	R Morgan

Access Representative

1975-80	M Bibbington
1980	E Lesniak
1981-89	K Tilford
1990	K Tilford/C Atkinson-Smith
1991-94	K Tilford
1994-	R Costello
1994-	J Belbin
1994-	Vicki James

The Lancashire and Cheshire Area

My first encounter with the BMC was about 17 years ago, not long after the Lancashire & Cheshire Area Committee had been formed to deal with access problems in the North West which until then had been mainly looked after by the Lakes Area Committee. But well before the BMC had moved to Manchester I had a few brushes with landowners, who had tried to stop access to climbing in the area.

When the Wilton Quarries were owned by the Borough of Bolton in the late Sixties prior to the forming of the North West Water Authority, Bowdon Black and myself had organised a climb-in as a protest. I can always remember a lone policeman appearing over the graveyard of Wilton One, taking one look at about 20 climbers on the 'Prow' then beating a hasty retreat: that was the last we heard.

Les Ainsworth was the first secretary, but after about 3 meetings Les got a job teaching in Aston University near Birmingham, so he 'conned' me into being the Secretary saying that all you have to do is take a few notes and turn these into minutes, that I would have to be elected first, but he would propose me and there should be a couple of people who would second me.

When I first heard of the BMC I thought they made cars, so I couldn't understand what they had to do with climbing, but I went along with Les anyway. One thing I did learn fast was that a Secretary's lot is not a happy one and found myself involved with quite a few access issues. Some of which haven't changed much even to this day. Hoghton Quarry being an example.

Around this time the Mountain Leadership dispute with Sir Jack Longland was going on, and this involved a lot of 'burning the midnight oil' with the Committee of Management. I got fed up with missing the pub, meeting after meeting, so I started taking a few cans of beer with me much to the consternation of some members. Around about this time I confessed to Dennis Gray that it might well be a good idea if I joined the BMC as I was on the Committee of Management. I think this must have been a first. A climber, not even in a club, on the COM.

The Black Pudding team was formed in 1978, the name was a strike back against the 'Cream Team' formed by Ron Fawcett and the Yorkshire lads. One thing I did use the 'team' for was to try to introduce a wide and fragmented group of climbers who had never been involved with a climbing club to the BMC. Through this we organised 'crag clean-ups', trespasses etc. We encouraged climbers to attend meetings as individuals.

CONFERENCES Walter Bonatti's visit in 1984 marked the zenith of the BMC's 'conference era' that brought many famous mountaineers to Britain. A Bonington / Whillans welcoming committee gave his appearance added significance because lingering Frêney Pillar sentiment had, in European eyes, given the Italian semi-spiritual rights to complete that climb. Mirella Tenderini *(centre left)* persuaded the reclusive hero to make the visit and skilfully translated his speech.

Between 1974 and 1993 the BMC held ten rumbustuous mountaineering conferences. Initially designed as serious debating events, they soon evolved into populist jamborees of exotic entertainment — a rich mix of earnest message, political statement, thrilling adventure, slide and film presentations, polemic, panel game, hip-hop, falderal and beerfest. A cross-section of the world's most famous and infamous mountaineers attended, adding cosmopolitan flavour to home contributions and an irreverent, good-humoured audience involvement.

The photos depict: (*right*) an audience vox pop on ethics; (*above*) regular conference anchorman Ian McNaught-Davis, with Dennis Gray and Chris Bonington, side-tracked into energetic discussions on the fringe of the packed bar; (*top right*) a prial of American aces — Tom Frost, Pat Ament, and bouldering guru John Gill.

The BMC Conference was a forum for those espousing the major ethical and controversial positions of the day: Cesare Maestri (*top left*), despite notoriety, was warmly received; Tomo Cesen (*top inset*) raised more questions than he answered in an enigmatic contribution. Royal Robbins's (*far left*) concern about bolting propelled him from the USA (at his own expense) to attend a key debate. At the 1993 event, Peter Croft, Claude Remy and Lynn Hill (*centre left*) reflected the divergence of climbing styles. Bill Tilman (above) enthralled the audience in 1976 and Reinhold Messner (*near left*) opined on high altitude tactics in 1988.

Ed Drummond's poetry oration (*left*) from a twenty-foot tripod squeezed into the Buxton auditorium was, arguably, the finest creative contribution during the conference years. Somewhat more Rabelaisian was the entertainment provided by the *High* beauty competition to raise money for the Alex MacIntyre Memorial Fund: (*top*) John Barry, John Stevenson, Don Whillans and Barry Alsop in ravishing display and (*above*) a befrocked Nat Allen sets about compere Alistair Macdonald.

Denny Moorhouse demonstrates equipment-testing machinery — one of the many displays organised by BMC trade members that lent added interest for conference goers.

Conference guests frequently sampled the local climbing — here Johnny Dawes 'spots' Catherine Destivelle on a Roaches boulder, while Jeff Lowe studies the 'numbers'.

In 1985 the BMC organised a conference with the focus on mountain-walking. This catered for mountaineering activities that fell outside the normal rock, ice and expedition focus of the biennual events. Though rather more restrained and serious, the event was successful, packed with interest, and greatly appreciated. Unaccountably it was never repeated. The photo depicts some of the main conference personalities (*left to right*) Richard Crane, Bill O'Connor, Tom Weir, Dennis Gray, Mike Cudahy, Joss Lynam, Chris Smith M.P., conference organiser John Allen and Richard Gilbert. Other contributors included Mike Harding, John Wyatt, Vin Machin, Brian Hall and Steve Ashton.

Our first dinner attracted over 160. Dennis Gray was our first guest speaker (Bob Pettigrew who was the BMC President also attended). This was a very lively affair that set the scene for many a dinner to come. Team dinners made a small profit which was donated to the BMC fighting fund. A number of incidents during this time stick in my mind.

The initial meeting between the two gun clubs which had established shooting rights at Wilton Quarries and the BMC to work out a suitable timetable to allow both interests to co-exist together. The meeting was organised by the North West Sports Council which had booked a small room for the meeting. Brian Nichols and myself attended on behalf of the BMC with two representatives from each gun club being invited, as well as Brian Perry and various Sports Council people. This room quickly proved to be far too small as every member of the 250-plus of both gun clubs turned up, so the meeting moved into the large lounge bar next door – that was filled to capacity. We were outnumbered at least by 100 to 1. Although I was usually not one who would go in lightly, I was invited to speak first and then we would negotiate upwards. I asked for a total ban on shooting in the quarry. I can still hear the gasps of amazement going round the room, and the noise of guns being 'cocked'.

We organised regular 'Lancashire Weekend Meets' cleaning-up crags, and Paul Sedgwick helped by organising 'skips' for us via Bolton M B Council which often ended up filled to overflowing. One clean-up was at Hoghton Quarry. The owner, Sir Bernard DeHoghton, was talking to Dennis Gray about our 'Colonial Friends' when the two 'Sids' walked in!

Several climbers, including Al Evans, Brian Cropper and Les Ainsworth, were looking at possible access to a quarry at Horwich near Bolton, although in the guidebook it said that it had recently gone 'live' again. We arrived at dusk and climbing over the fences we saw a notice 'Keep Out Dogs', We carefully manoeuvred around a large fierce dog chained up by the entrance, then made our way into the quarry. In the distance, silhouetted against a red sky above the quarry, we noticed a black horse. We were all unconcerned as it galloped along the top of the quarry making its way towards us ... then the horse 'growled'.

During my first year as Secretary for the Lancashire & Cheshire Area Committee it was decided that an organised trespass (but not through the BMC) was needed in an effort to get access to Den Lane Quarries. So we organised one massive trespass of a couple of hundred climbers. The landowner got wind of this via the local papers and tried to serve me with a court injunction. Unfortunately he got my name wrong as Ian Loonsdale! (maybe he was right?) so he couldn't serve it. As the fateful weekend approached it snowed so hard on the Friday that the whole of the Chew Valley was cut off, but for a few weeks after, the owner paid visits to the Bolton Tech climbing wall looking for me. On one occasion little £ signs registered in his eyes when he realised climbers were paying for the use of the climbing wall.

Over the years it has been a pleasure to work with and be associated with the BMC and its professional officers, past and present. You meet a lot of people and make a lot of friends. The present Committee of the Lancashire & Cheshire area is just as dedicated and busy as its predecessors and this can only be a healthy sign.

A lot has changed since I started climbing, and the BMC has always appeared to be at the forefront. We all hope it will be so for the next 50 years.

Ian Lonsdale

LANCASHIRE & CHESHIRE AREA COMMITTEE

Chairman		Secretary	
1978-83	B Nichols	1977-83	I Lonsdale
1983-84	C Vigano	1983-86	P Dewhurst
1984-90	P Sedgwick	1987-94	C Beveridge
1990-95	J Mason	1994-	Sylvia Loxam
1995-	P Dewhurst		

Access Representative

1988-90	B Goodwin
1993-95	J Hancock
1995-	L Ainsworth
1995-	J Mason
1996-	G Smith

MIDLAND AREA COMMITTEE

Formed in 1994.

Chairman		Secretary	
1994-	M Ratty	1994-96	Jo Butler
		1996-	A Rich

Access Representative

1994-	R Law
1994-95	J Lockett
1995-	D Oldroyd
1996-	B Davies

The Buxton Conferences

Somebody, somewhere must still have copies of all the programmes of the inimitable Buxton Conferences, which reached their peak during the 1970s and 1980s. I thought I had, but discover mice have gnawed into and nested in my BMC memorabilia box. These highlights of an important era have been assembled from an assortment of printed sources.

In the late 1960s the Central Council for Physical Recreation hosted a number of Mountain Safety Conferences in London, which were largely for and attended by those involved in the then-burgeoning 'industry' of mountain training. When, in 1971, the BMC entered the scene as co-organiser other venues were tried: first Manchester, then two years later Leeds, where, with speakers Ken Wilson, Tom Price, Graham Tiso and Bill March, emphasis was carefully manoeuvred away from safety. To be preoccupied with caution, it was felt, would very soon distort the traditional spirit of climbing.

By 1974, with a new look, government-funded BMC just about to move north from the capital and consciously reaching out to the climber on the crag, something fresh was called for. Billed as the 'Event of the Decade' the first National Mountaineering Conference attracted hundreds and set the style for the exuberant and (mostly) biennial Buxton beer-and-talk festivals which have since entered folklore. From the beginning the policy was to parade folk heroes and air divisive issues. It was entertainment first, but at the same time a moral and spiritual redefinition. A statement of affinity. Dave Cook kicked off that initial Conference with a spirited examination of the climber in a changing society, to be followed by Robin Campbell, astringent Editor of the SMCJ, railing against the whole notion of outdoor activity as a character-training tool in conventional education. 'Don't be mountain pimps', he warned instructors. BMC President, Alan Blackshaw, outlined his master plan for the new, democratic Council, and sought to allay fears that Sports Council funding represented just another form of prostitution. Colin Mortlock spoke up for the educationists. Jack Longland chaired a heated Any Questions panel. Six films were shown over the course of the day and the international stars for the evening's titillation were Cesare Maestri, defending his Cerro Torre bolt climb (to an unexpectedly warm reception), and the inimitable Kurt Diemberger, putting his and the audience's endurance to the test with a 4-hour film and slide spectacular illustrating his climbing vagabondage. The whole stimulating bag of tricks was held together with characteristic irreverence by the Big Mac himself, Master of Ceremonies Ian McNaught-Davis.

The momentum continued in 1976. Bill Tilman, 78-years young, offered a wholly delightful anecdotal (and unillustrated) celebration of the lightweight ethic, urging his audience, 'Get back to real climbing. Forget such frills as sponsors and expedition notepaper, computerised menus and all that oxygen nonsense!' Peter Habeler, echoed the lightweight motif in telling of his climbs on Yerupaja, Eiger, Matterhorn and Hidden Peak with Reinhold Messner. Pete Livesey spoke on the Hard Rock scene, Chris Bonington advocated Capsule Ascents (which are apparently lightweight attempts springing phoenix-like from heavyweight beginnings) and we also heard from Robin Brook of the Sports Council and Wynford Vaughan Thomas of the Land of my Fathers. Those who wanted to put all the theory to practice shied outside to the mobile climbing tower imported into the Pavilion Gardens for the day.

'Commitment' was the theme in 1978, the year the great Anderl Heckmair came to Buxton to tell of his 1938 Eiger epic. With his lovely wife Trüdl, he quickly won the hearts of Conference-goers. As, too, did Rudi Homberger, who with rare and understated humour outlined the trials of being a hard rock man in a conservative Swiss climbing society. Henry Barber raved about Saxony sandstone, Al Rouse confessed to having fallen out of love with solo climbing (on which he had been advertised to speak). Peter Boardman, after three years' committed devotion to the BMC, was gloomy about the problems besetting modern climbers, but John Porter urged uncompromising resistance to all outside influences. The historian Ronald Clark gave a masterly talk on Whymper, Geoff Birtles took his trousers off, Bernard Atha of the Sports Council sought to plaster over the yawning cracks between his authority and the BMC on the matter of mountain training. The programme now spread over Friday evening and Saturday, making room for George Steele on equipment and Malcolm Pearse's lyrical audio-visual on the Drakensberg.

In 1980, the opening speaker was Lord Hunt, who said that as a society we paid great attention to reducing risk in life ('Risk' being this year's theme). There was a case for scaling it down for novices, particularly in non-voluntary training programmes, but it was an essential ingredient for the full enjoyment and adventure of climbing. Examining what he considered 'justifiable risk', he was clearly signalling where he still stood, notwithstanding the vexed training debate. Excessive sponsorship and advertising could influence judgement in risk-taking, he said, and awards for valour were totally inappropriate. This was a contemporary allusion, which found echo later when the recipient of the year's International Award for Valour in Sport, Jean-Marc Boivin showed films on extreme ice climbing and hang-gliding. With translation difficulties, Boivin managed to side-step questions on the valour issue, asserting only that he did what he did because he enjoyed it. Patrick Vallençant showed El *Gringo Eskiador*, a fantasy film about skiing down Artesonraju. McNaught-Davis remained Conference Chairman, and other speakers included South-West rock-ace Pat Littlejohn, John Barry (Mr Riské himself), Hot Henry Barber, back by popular request to introduce a film of his heart-stopping solo climb of Strand at Gogarth. Harold Drasdo found instructors more at risk than other climbers, and all at much more risk driving to the crag than climbing on it. Mike Thompson's paper on Risk in the Himalaya was delivered in his unavoidable absence by Mark Vallance. But the real star of the show was Yosemite demon pioneer Warren (Batso) Harding. Tanned, tense and by turns manic and haunted, he flashed up the signposts of a long and controversial career. Here were the stove legs, Dolt cart and other items of El Cap folklore, the 26 days on the Wall of Early Light which brought instant fame, he said, but not much fortune ...

The 1982 Buxton Conference was billed as the last – with the accent this time on 'New Dimensions'. It would be dominated by a wizard with dimensions a-plenty, but (at pushing-fifty) scarcely to be described as new. Still, that is to jump to the plum first, when the initial slice of pudding was John Disley, retiring Vice-President of the Sports Council. 'Toe the line, reap benefit', was his message, as he told climbers that for better or worse, the BMC walked the corridors of power on their behalf. (Honestly, that's what he said.) And he added that by the same token, the BMC had to be responsible for the 'great unwashed out there', had to make provision for them without having their confidence, their allegiance, or their dosh. Competitive rock-climbing could bring rich financial rewards, he said, urging the BMC, 'Get into the Olympics! Save your belligerence for fighting access battles'. The overriding problem in future was going to be getting on to crags and mountains, he prophesied. And he was certainly right about that.

Naoe Sakashita, who embraces competitive speed climbing and Himalayan mountaineering with equal enthusiasm, explained how the Japanese Mountaineering Association similarly supported both: the one helped the other. Chris Baxter took us climbing in Australia, Tim Leach went alpine style to Alaska, and Mick Fowler lauded his favourite loose rock. Pete Livesey proffered advice on fitness and training, Andrej Zawada tackled Everest in winter and Jeff Lowe conducted a worldwide ice tour before showing film of climbing Bridalveil Falls. We also saw

Devers, incredible cine-action with Patrick Bèrhault at Verdon and Buoux. And to round off a star-studded day, the roundest star of all: Don Whillans with his *My Life and Hard Times*. Even a streaker dashing across the stage could not interrupt the flow of what was perhaps Don's all-time great performance. Fuzzy black and white slides showed scrawny lads shinning up Froggatt and the Roaches in the Fifties, partnership with the Human Fly, the motor cycle days. We heard tell of snatching Alpine prizes from under the noses of 'furriners' and Brian Nally from the Eigerwand. What days they were. Buxton was certainly going out on a high.

Only it didn't, of course. Two years later, there we all were again. This time with Nigel Gifford as the twinkling master of ceremonies. From home and abroad, assembled the usual astonishing line-up: Denis Howell (former Minister of Sport, founder of the Sports Council), Bill Birkett, Ales Kunaver, Pat Ament, Andreas Kubin, Eric Jones (presenting Leo Dickinson's film of his – Eric's – solo Eiger climb.) Wanda Rutkiewicz put in a surprise appearance and in an animated Question Time featuring Jill Lawrence, Ian McNaught-Davis, Gary Gibson, Al Rouse, and Don Whillans, Ken Wilson played the Robin Day role. Walter Bonatti topped the bill and tugged the emotions; and for a ribald finale, a beauty contest, put on by *High* in aid of the Alex MacIntyre Memorial Fund. It was won by a little rotund bearded lady in fetching floral frills, one Donna Whillans. (Much was seen also of writhing stripper Joanna Barry.)

In an effort to reflect the wider meaning of 'mountaineering' a National Hill-walking Conference was held in October 1985. This was chaired by ex-folk singer Mike Harding and the opening address was delivered by Chris Smith (MP). The star-studded cast of speakers included John Allen, Tom Weir, Richard Gilbert, Joss Lynam, Bob Beighton, Bill O'Connor and Richard Crane.

1986 featured Alistair Macdonald as ringmaster and Jonathon Porritt of Friends of the Earth kicking off in fine style. Speakers included Doug Scott on Adventure versus Achievement, Miri Smid from Czechoslovakia, Thierry (Turbo) Renault on Speed Alpinism, Tony Howard on Desert Climbs, Rowland and Mark Edwards (Cornish gold), Jean-Claude Droyer, Tom Frost and the legendary John Gill. The forum feature was Competition Climbing with panellists Jim Ballard, Bernard Newman, Geoff Milburn. And a programme of films ran concurrently in the Paxton Suite. Pat Ament accompanied his own songs on the piano and Ed Drummond performed his extraordinary *Between a Rock and a Soft Place* – poetry from the top (and sides) of a 25-foot tripod. The evening's Cabaret was memorable for the BMC Follies and the mad Leeds juggler with his ice-axes – all playing their hearts out for the Don Whillans Fund, for Our Don had sadly passed away in the intervening year.

Reinhold Messner made it at last in 1988, along with Randy Leavitt who, having climbed El Cap, then base-jumped off it. The current Minister for Sport, Colin Moynihan provided the token Establishment link, though failed to impress with his praise of climbing frames and the role he saw for retired climbers in running the show for the rest of us. The Conference's overall emphasis was on the Environment, which John Beatty's audio-visual *The Pure Land* admirably celebrated. Most of the speakers were quick to flaunt green credentials. We saw Stefan Glowacz, Wanda Rutkiewicz, Voytek Kurtyka and popular returns from Rudi Homberger and Pat Littlejohn. Craig Smith and Mick Ryan delighted with their fresh audio-viz-whizz. The debate was on Training for Climbing with the fatties ranged against the fitties: Mac in the Chair, and Jim Curran, Phil Smithson, Pete Livesey, Dennis Gray. Among several films was Destivelle in *Seo*! ('Bourgeois hype meets subsistence culture' – Mountain.) As boisterous as ever, the Cabaret featured apt ditties from Rosie Smith and troupe, and the mad axeman, Martin Wilson, now graduated to a unicycle.

1990 – pass. With fresh faces at the BMC, 'Buxton' was delayed, to return in 1991 in new guise as the British Mountaineering Festival. 'Huzza!' trumpeted Ed Douglas in his report for *Mountain* ... 'more rock stars than Woodstock'. Well worth the wait, all were agreed. Paul Piana gave an hilarious account of his Free Salathé climb, Ed Webster struggled against laryngitis and projector failure to present superb desert climbing slides. There were Catherine Destivelle and Jeff Lowe introducing the latest films they starred in, Lord Hunt and Ade Burgess both putting pleas for the environment; Tomo Cesen, but without too many pictures to support his climb of Lhotse's fearsome South Face. The vaunted Bolting Debate proved less sparky than envisaged, Ken Wilson and Royal Robbins winning the polemical battle against would-be advocates Jerry Moffatt and Chris Gore. All the usual jollity around the bar, to which The Cabaret was added as floorshow.

Which brings us to 1993, the year of the Everest Jubilee. Again, the festival – with 'Freedom' as its theme – drew speakers from around the world. Ian McNaught-Davis, by now President of the BMC, opened proceedings with an incisive look at threatened freedoms, Kazbek Valiev, from Kazakhstan, outlined the enormous climbing potential freed up in the former Soviet republics; Canadian Peter Croft shared his particular brand of free love – speedy and often remote soloing; Harish Kapadia told of hidden sanctuaries in the Himalaya; Claude Remy confessed to a bolting bonanza in his native Switzerland, where he and his brother had put up around a thousand new rock routes; Lynn Hill explained how interacting with rock brought her expressive freedom; and there was a double-act on the Freedom to Roam by the BMC Access Officer, Bill Wright and landscape photographer Gordon Stainforth. Mick Ryan gave a presentation of slides and edited interviews, and Mark Vallance took the word a stage further by handing over a cheque from the Wild Country Foundation for £5,000 towards funding BMC access work. An anarchic look at freedom was provided by Larry Locke's *Free Fallin'*, a vigorous and funny prize-winning student film of a base-jump off the World Trade Centre in New York. Finally, Stephen Venables and Chris Bonington, venerable Everesters both, rounded off the formal programme with a look at 72 years of Everest history.

And that, like 'dust in the air suspended', marks the spot where the story ended. There have been no more Buxtons. Perhaps they will be resurrected, who knows? Even though one is saddened over the years by untimely losses, well-loved characters whose absence leaves holes in the social fabric, so noticeable at 'dos' like this, there is surely still a need for some regular shindig and communal discourse? Still a desire to rubberneck among celebrity performers?

It has only been possible to list speakers and some of the films seen over the years. Buxtons are rather more than just the theatre programmes. There have been trade shows and exhibitions and competitions and rummage sales. Art and music, poetry and song – and a lot of late night conviviality.

Audrey Salkeld

CCPR/BMC MOUNTAIN SAFETY CONFERENCES

1967	London	1971	Birmingham
1969 Oct. 25	London	1973	Leeds

NATIONAL MOUNTAINEERING CONFERENCES, BUXTON

1974 Mar. 2	1985 Oct. 19	Nat. Hill-walking Conf.
1976 Mar. 27	1986 Mar. 22	
1978 Mar. 18	1988 Mar. 26	
1980 Mar. 28	1991 Mar. 23	Br. Mount. Festival
1982 Mar. 20	1993 Mar. 20	Br. Mount. Festival
1984 Mar. 24		

The Guides

The history of mountain guiding in Britain can be traced at least as far back as the end of the 18th century when 'guides to whose care strangers commit themselves' (Gwynedd Archives) were available for the ascent of Snowdon. The railway expansion of the 19th century saw the opening of more hotels in the upland areas to cater for increased tourism and many would advertise the services of a guide. The 1861 census notes one Robin Hughes, then 62 years of age and living at Capel Curig, as 'Guide to the Snowdonia Hills', hence recognising the vocation as a full-time occupation. However, while the exploits of John McKenzie leading clients on the ridges and peaks of Skye at the end of the century are well documented, national recognition of the term 'mountain guide' had to wait until after the founding of the BMC in 1944. The first certificates, were signed by Jim Cameron and Joe Williams of the Lake District and 'Scotty' Dwyer in North Wales. Another early BMC Guide practising around the turn of the decade was George Fisher, then working at Ullswater Outward Bound.

Johnnie Lees of the RAF Mountain Rescue Service, Gwen Moffat, author and Britain's first woman guide, Charlie McCormack, another outward bound instructor, and Ron James who set up Ogwen Cottage in 1959 were among the very few names added to the roll in the 50s. Certificates were issued for a renewable period of three years and identified the recipient as either a mountain or rock-climbing guide. Testing involved a day out with some notable personality of the BMC and a current guide. On one occasion when a cold drizzle set in during the afternoon it was not the calibre of the several applicants which came under test, but that of the BMC representative when the onset of early hypothermia resulted in a premature end to the programme. A very few acquired the Scottish hill-walking or mountain addenda, having passed a further test held under the auspices of the Association of Scottish Climbing Clubs (ASCC).

The popular influx to the mountains during the 60s and the accompanying outdoor educational ethos resulted in a notable increase in the number of mountain centres. A few were private concerns, but mostly they were set up by local education authorities which were following the example of the Derbyshire Whitehall Centre. As the BMC Guides certificate was the only nationally recognised mountain qualification until the Mountain Leadership Certificate became widely available towards the end of the decade, the certificate became seen as a premier requirement for employment in the mountain instructor field. A few BMC Guides had contracts with the Mountaineering Association, an organisation running climbing courses both in the UK and the Alps during the 50s and 60s. The result was an increased number of applicants to enter the assessment scheme. In 1974 eight new members completed what had by then become a very much extended series of tests including a week each of summer and winter climbing. However, even before this relatively large increase of the membership, guides were discussing ideas for future developments, particularly combination. While most of the membership worked in centres, a few practised in the freelance market. The entry of the United Kingdom into the EEC particularly focused the minds of an astute few.

In January 1972 a group of guides met with officers of the BMC at a Liverpool college to review the future organisation of British guiding. Already, the North Wales guides, then the area with the largest membership, had set up a regional organisation with Ron James as Chairman and the Secretary, K. C. Gordon, organising a rota for engagements derived from a token advertising budget. At the Liverpool meeting they were joined by Neil Allinson and Colin Firth from the Lake District, along with John Baxter the BMC Guides officer who represented the guides on the Council. On the BMC side were National Officer Dennis Gray, President Tony Moulam and Peter Ledeboer, the Honorary Secretary. This was a period when both rock and ice climbing standards were rising year on year so that the standard of testing had to follow suit. The increased administration of the tests along with the growing number of guides seeking to combine, cemented the need for a national organisation. The BMC, itself feeling the pressures of the ever expanding affairs of mountaineering, recognised this and readily agreed to relinquish responsibility for much of the affairs of the Guides, but would continue to provide administrative services. However, the certificate would still be issued in the name of the BMC. The post of Guides Officer was disbanded to be replaced by Bob Lewis as the new organisation secretary. The following three years saw a number of modifications to the qualification. The certificate no longer appertained to a single region, the distinction between rock and mountain guide was removed and a winter mountain endorsement set at a higher level replaced the ASCC addendum. Later, Lewis and what was then called the Guides Sub-Committee (of the BMC) set about composing a constitution. By February 1975 a draft was ready, put out to ballot of all guides and on 27 May the Secretary was able to report a unanimous agreement for the formation of the Association of Mountain Guides. The constitution provided for an autonomous body with BMC and MCofS representatives sitting on a committee made up of two guides from each area and the Secretary.

Bob Lewis, having done so much of the ground work, relinquished the post to Colin Firth and at the December committee meeting nominations were sought for the post of Chairman, K. C. Gordon eventually being elected. Initially both positions were to be limited to a term of three years, but a subsequent constitutional amendment extended the secretary's term. Firth was to serve for nine years when he was recognised with honorary life membership before passing the baton to Harold Edwards in 1984.

The BMC continued with its services to the new association and as events were to progress would give assistance and funding for what immediately became the next hurdle.

As new members of the EEC, the opportunities to work in the Alps became an obvious attraction to many members. While the door to Europe was now open, British Guides lacked the credentials to pass through. Several members already had a history of organising alpine courses or climbing with private clients, but the British carnet issued to each member was not recognised and difficulties were sometimes experienced at huts. International recognition and parity was required, which only the Union Internationale des Associations des Guides de Montagne (UIAGM) could provide. An immediate application to join was rejected at the General Council of the UIAGM annual meeting in October 1975 as was a second application the following year. The problem concerned the constitutional nature of ABMG. Whereas the profession of mountain guide was recognised in law in most UIAGM member countries, this was not the case in the UK where anyone could use the term to describe themselves. With the assistance of Dennis Gray, now BMC General Secretary and National Officer, Peter Boardman, (himself a Guide and due to become chairman in 1979 when Gordon's term finished) a letter from the Minister of Sport was secured which recognised the status of the Association relative to the governing body. In 1977 a third application was made which would be discussed by the UIAGM Technical Committee in June and decided upon at the November meeting of the General Council. Warm support from French and German delegates was not enough to counter Swiss and Austrian misgivings about the training of British Guides. At the November meeting held in Aosta, Boardman, Firth and John Brailsford (the latter a Francophile and very much the driving force on entry into the UIAGM) attended to hear the verdict. Opinion had softened in some quarters, enough for a proposal to admit the British to be passed by 23 votes for with 8 against, being the Austrians and a sole Canadian representative – an expatriate Austrian. However, there were two provisos, alpine and ski guiding components should be included in the assessment scheme.

As the membership increased, the following years saw the necessity for the creation of further posts. In 1979 Colin Wornham was appointed treasurer to deal with the growing financial affairs; pressure from the membership to broaden the image of the Association resulted in Roger Baxter-Jones taking on the role of publicity officer in 1981, which he held for three years before going to live in the Chamonix valley. The ever expanding training and assessment scheme was devolved to a training officer the following year, Tim Jepson agreeing to take on this most difficult and responsible of roles. All were, and remain, unpaid honorary positions, a token honorarium plus accountable expenses being the sole return. They also became members of the committee.

Seven years after joining the UIAGM the Association was proud to host the annual meeting of the General Council, held at Plas y Brenin on the weekend of 9/11 November 1984. Delegates were met at Manchester Airport on the Friday, trips arranged for wives during the council meeting on Saturday, followed by dinner at a Betws y Coed hotel when many of the visitors wore national dress. Dispersing after breakfast the next day, one notable British guest was to remark "that was the best climbing dinner I've ever been to". In effect the weekend only endorsed the pattern of camaraderie which British delegates to Council meetings had grown to expect.

By 1985 there were over sixty full guides with a further dozen at various stages of the assessment scheme. Although both National Centres encouraged new staff to become members, no longer was the certificate being used as a qualification for mountain centre work. A large number of the newer generation of members practised as freelance Guides, either full-time or part-time in conjunction with some other means of income. The social aspect of the annual general meeting weekend has developed and in recent years the following day has been used for in-service training.

In 1988 representatives of the Italian, French, German and British Guide Associations met with the objective of seeking EC recognition of the profession. During the next two years the four Associations agreed the close harmonisation of the training and assessment of Guides culminating in a platform document being signed in the autumn of 1990 under the aegis of the newly formed European Guides Commission (EGC). The subsequent application to the EC for a Directive foundered in a bureaucratic log jam, every other profession in Europe had the same object in mind. Finally the EGC agreed to accept being placed in an all-encompassing category of 'sports trainer'. At the time of writing Spain is in the process of forming a guide association while the recent entry of Austria into the European Union automatically brings EGC membership. The next round of EU entrants is likely to include a further one or two countries which will have UIAGM recognised associations or be moving in that direction. With the traditional ideals of mountaineering in decline across much of Alpine Europe, notwithstanding the signing of the Kathmandu Declaration, it will be interesting to see how the new professionals of emerging mountain countries in central and eastern Europe develop their style of ascent on both crag and mountain. While British guides are content to work within the local 'modus operandi' when in Europe, the same applies when working in the UK. If style and method are reviewed and changed to satisfy best practice, they continue to be built on a foundation of traditional British mountaineering, albeit accepting some of the new demands. it seems to be a rare client who now, on a day of wind and rain, would accept a proposal to do a long easy classic in boots and sack when better things had been planned. The standard alternative appears to be "where's the nearest climbing wall?"

The sometimes hazardous nature of guiding was recognised at an early stage so that arrangements were made for members to have personal negligence insurance (PNI) which later became a compulsory condition included in the EGC document. Given the direction in which the insurance market is moving, the Association is at the time of writing involved in becoming a company with limited liability. This will give protection to the committee and officers who would continue to act in voluntary capacities.

This year (1995) the number of full Guides has passed the hundred mark with a record eleven Aspirants receiving their diplomas from the President, Nigel Shepherd, at the November AGM. The membership continues to include a diversity of backgrounds, an ex-landscape architect, a professor, twins, a current competition wall listing, a sprinkling of climbing authors and an ex-President (as the title became on entry to the UIAGM) who is now completing a round the world sailing trip. Many have made their mark on the British climbing scene and elsewhere. Today's young mountaineer, while ticking off the routes, will see the Alcock, Crymble, Fyffe, Grindley, Littlejohn et al in the guidebook. Perhaps they will not read of Collister (President 1991/3), Hall, Hinkes and others regularly leading in the greater ranges, of Roger Mear adventuring on his own or ex treasurer David Hopkins on a joint expedition of disabled people and minor royalty succeeding on a 6000er. They certainly will read of Alan Kimber being rung at home from a mobile telephone requesting advice on how to cross the Gap on Tower Ridge. They should read about one of the great adventures of the decade in the esoteric yet purposeful Alpine traverse completed by Simon Jenkins and Martin Moran. Diverse indeed.

Joint liaison is maintained with the Association of Mountain Instructors and the British Association of European Mountain Leaders while representatives sit on the home nation training boards, the UK board and the BMC. The President and Training Officer or other delegate attends the biannual meetings of the UIAGM at a variety of venues across Europe. The quantity of work undertaken in the Alpine countries rises steadily each year with several members now living in France and Switzerland. During July and August it sometimes appears there are more members in and around the Chamonix valley than back in the UK.

The Association has honoured three of its founding members, Brailsford, Firth and Lees, a few others of that generation have opted for the retired members list while the present batch of Trainees and Aspirants will qualify before the turn of the century. We hope also that they will never exceed the number of the six members who have lost their lives: John Cunningham when going to the aid of a drowning student, Roger Baxter-Jones in an avalanche in the Alps, Peter Boardman lost high on Everest, Mick Hardwick and Dave Harries in an air crash en route for Annapurna and Trainee Greg Hall hit by stonefall in Coire an t-Sneachda.

K. C. Gordon

The First Professional Guides

1947	Sept.	D J Cameron	(Lakes Rock Climbing Guide)
		C W Hudson	(Lakes Rock Climbing Guide)
		C R Wilson	(Lakes Rock Climbing Guide)
		G Dwyer	(North Wales Climbing Guide)
		E Roberts	(North Wales Climbing Guide)
1948	Jan.	R A Ewin	(Lakes Mountain Guide)
		V Veevers	(Lakes Rock Climbing Guide)
		J S Williams	(Lakes Rock Climbing Guide)
1948	July	L Barlow	(Lakes Mountain & R C Guide)
1950	Aug.	G B Fisher	(Lakes Mountain Guide)
		T B Campion	(North Wales Mountain Guide)
1952	Mar.	W Peascod	(Lakes Rock Climbing Guide)
		S Styles	(North Wales Mountain Guide)
1956	Mar.	J R Lees	(N. Wales Mountain & RC Guide)
		G J Sutton	(North Wales Rock Climbing Guide)
		Mrs Gwen Moffat	(N. Wales Mountain & RC Guide)
		R O Downes	(North Wales Rock Climbing Guide)
1961		J A Baxter	(North Wales Rock Climbing Guide)
		W F Dowlen	(North Wales Rock Climbing Guide)
		G D Gower	(Lakes Mountain & R C Guide)
		P F Lockey	(Lakes Rock Climbing Guide)
		W F Watson	(Lakes Rock Climbing Guide)
		R James	(North Wales Rock Climbing Guide)
		J A Staley	(Gritstone Climbing Guide)
		C E MacCormack	(Lakes Mountain Guide)

The ASCC also provided certificates for Scottish Winter Mountaineering as well as Winter Hillwalking.

International Meets – a selective summary

In the early years of mountaineering, decisions to travel depended very much on individuals and personal wealth. By the 1950s however it became a matter of National prestige to succeed on the highest mountains of the world and big expeditions obtained sponsorship relatively easily. Co-operation did exist in a variety of ways and even for the first ascent of Everest there was an immediate link between Britain and New Zealand. Links with the Iron Curtain countries however were almost non-existent and therefore the start of International Meets is even more surprising.

Since the Russian Revolution only one British expedition had managed to enter their area – that by Joyce Dunsheath when she ascended Elbruz. The idea that an approach should be made to visit the Caucasus was conceived in the Alps in 1953 by John Neill who had already persuaded Ralph Jones and Mike Harris. During discussions, Chris Brasher, John Mawe and Dave Thomas also became enthusiastic. Two key factors then swung the balance. First and foremost was the fact that Sir John Hunt had lectured on the Ascent of Everest in Moscow during 1954. Second, Chris Brasher visited Moscow with the British Athletics Team in 1955 and then received valuable advice during the 1956 Olympic Games in Australia. Eventually after various political approaches the Climbers' Club party was completed with the addition of Derek Bull, George Band and Alan Blackshaw (when John Mawe withdrew), but it was not until 1958 that the party was able to go ahead. After a successful trip a 'return fixture' was organised for May-June of 1960. This Russian visit was to be the first of many International Meets which have served to promote goodwill links between Britain and the other countries world-wide.

1960 RUSSIAN VISIT

The party of six Russians was led by Mikhail Borushko (Master of Sport) who was a metallurgist from the Ukraine. At home it was his brief to arrange courses and give lectures. The other members of his party included: two climbing and skiing instructors from the Caucasus, Josef Kachiani and Mischa Khergiani; Anatoly Ovvnikov – an engineer; Yevgeni (Eugene) Tur worked at a tractor plant in Gorki; and Yevgeni (Eugene) Gippenreiter, the liaison officer, who was from the Foreign Relations Department of the Central Council of Physical Culture and Education.

Travelling by mini-bus the party spent a week in North Wales which included climbing Brant Direct Start. While on Cloggy one of the Russians fell from Chimney Route and had to visit the Bangor hospital. Things were evened up however as the British climbers notched up a broken leg and damaged hands. During several days in the Lake District one highlight was an ascent of Kipling Groove. Later after several days in Glencoe, the fine weather eventually broke and led to a wet finish in Skye.

John Hunt reported that the Russians seemed to have no special techniques or equipment but, instead of waist loops, they wore webbing harnesses to which they could attach karabiners. They found the British climbs to be slimier but with lots of character which gave great fun. Several films and lectures on Russian mountaineering were well received and the party was filmed by the BBC.

The Russians were reported as being charming, keen to have a go at anything, full of fun, and with attitudes very similar to our own. Beyond climbing they showed interest in our road system, Marble Arch oratory and aspects of the University at Oxford.

1960 STAUNING ALPS (N.E. GREENLAND) EXPEDITION
During the 1950s various organisations began to take young people on expeditions into mountainous areas abroad. Sir John Hunt, who later worked closely with Dick Alcock (National Training Officer of the National Association of Youth Clubs N.A.Y.C.) planned three successive trips. The first in July-August was a large party of 38 including three youth leaders and 21 boys aged between 17 and 20. The senior scientists and climbers were: Sir John Hunt, John Jackson, Alan Blackshaw, Ian McNaught-Davis, Dr Malcolm Slesser, George Lowe, Tom Weir, Dr Iain Smart, John Sugden, Roddy Cameron, Dr David Jones, Capt. Tony Streather, Joy Hunt and Susan Hunt. Several first ascents were made.

1962 BRITISH-SOVIET PAMIRS EXPEDITION
Following the 1960 Russian visit this SMC/AC party was a compromise between friends and the nation's best climbers: John Hunt, Malcolm Slesser, Wilfrid Noyce, Joe Brown, Ralph Jones, Robin Smith, Ian McNaught-Davis, Graeme Nicol, George Lowe, Ken Bryan, Ted Wrangham and Derek Bull. This expedition was marred by the deaths of Smith and Noyce.

1963 PINDUS MOUNTAINS (GREECE) EXPEDITION
During March and April, 22 boys and 12 seniors made a three-week traverse of the range. The seniors were: Sir John Hunt, Tony Streather, John Disley, Lady Hunt, John Jackson, George Lowe, Mrs Lowe, John Sugden, D Sugden, Dick Alcock, A Bough and D Giles.

1965 BRITISH TATRA MOUNTAINS VISIT

The third of Hunt's N.A.Y.C. visits included 13 young women and 12 young men who all held the Duke of Edinburgh's Gold Award (or equivalent), while amongst the seniors were: Hamish Nicol, John Disley, Roger Orgill, John Longland, Alf Gregory and George Lowe. Itineraries varied from a stroll up Rysy from the Czech side to Hamish Nicol climbing Zamartwa Turnia, one of the most impressive cliffs on the Polish side.

1966 POLISH VISIT

The visit organised by Sir John Hunt started in Scotland where the party was entertained by the SMC. The Poles then spent time in the Lake District with the F.R.C.C. before travelling to Wales where the C.C. acted as hosts.

1967 CZECHOSLOVAKIAN VISIT

As a result of negotiations with the Czechoslovak section of Tourism, between 7th and 22nd October a party of mountaineers visited as guests of the BMC and the National Association of Youth Clubs. Led by Dr Ludovik Koupil, the party of eight included one young woman, Maria Kasalicka. This visit was made possible through the added financial support of the Sidney Black Trust, the Central and Scottish Councils of Physical Recreation as well as by several of our climbing clubs.

After two days in London the party went up to Glenmore Lodge where, despite bad weather, they sailed and walked as well as doing several climbs with members of the SMC. Two good days were then spent in Derbyshire on gritstone (Stanage) and limestone looked after by Nat Allen and others. During appalling Welsh weather Snowdon was traversed and they made a first visit to see the ocean along a storm-swept Anglesey beach.

After leaving Plas y Brenin they visited the Crystal Palace Recreation Centre as well as Surrey Secondary schools with John Disley. During an Alpine Club dinner the visitors showed an excellent film of a Czechoslovakian expedition to the Hindu Kush.

1967 BRITISH VISIT TO THE POLISH TATRA

During the summer two Scots, Jimmy McDowell and Jimmy McCartney arrived in Zakopane, with Yorkshiremen Dennis Gray and Tom Morrell. They quickly discovered, despite early misgivings, that the people were easy-going, warm and very hospitable with much singing, vodka and cool draught beer. Nearly all the climbers had a university tradition as the working class had only just become aware of climbing. Equipment was also very basic with slippers and baseball boots in evidence for bouldering. The two Scots impressed the locals with a fast free ascent of the direct route on Mieguszowiek, plus a new direct finish, while the Yorkshiremen went for the peaks and ridges. The Poles who tended to place pitons wherever they wanted were amazed to see the use of slings and nuts for runners by the British climbers.

1968 BRITISH VISIT TO GERMANY
Paul Nunn and C.J. Woodall climbed in the Bavarian Alps. The main climb done was the Gonda Groove in the Oberreintaldom.

1969 BRITISH VISIT TO THE ARDENNES
Dennis Gray and Dave Musgrove represented Britain to join the UIAA Meet.

1972 FRENCH VISIT
During September a team of ten top climbers visited Britain. It comprised: Jean and Michel Afanassief, Simone Badier, David Belden, Patrick Cordier, Jean-Claude Droyer, Monique Fort, Luc Gimbert, Dominique Marchal and Eric Vola.

Although the weather was far from good Marchal and Gimbert set a blistering pace and amongst other hard routes they all ascended Vector at Tremadoc with apparent ease. Afanassief also astounded the observers by his nonchalant style on some of the hard routes. During a visit to Dinas Cromlech while wearing boots, Left Wall was climbed with minimal aid. Epitaph was also ticked off. On Gogarth, Big Groove and Winking Crack were among the climbs completed. Some of the party stayed on for a day's hard climbing and soloing in Derbyshire and another day was spent on Southern Sandstone where they were joined by Royal Robbins who confounded Droyer and Cordiet with the jamming, while they in turn starred by on-sight solos of several testing 5c routes.

This visit, along with the American climber Henry Barber's blitz of our hardest routes and other powerful performances by Steve Wunsch and Jim Erikson, made the British climbers sit up and take notice. Perhaps we were no longer at the forefront of world climbing.

1973 UIAA YOUTH MEETING
Dennis Gray's first problem was how to sort out 51 climbers from 18 nations — as there was a huge range of ability and very few understood English. On the first day the Russian star from Siberia, Alexander Kubanov (one of 20 in the party who could climb to Grade VI) caused a stir at Tremadog when he cruised up Vector wearing Bolshoi-type

'galoshes' – described at the time as 'sawn-off wellies'. He had neither discovered PAs nor knew anything about the intricacies of nut protection. The Swedish climbers, Olof Ohgran and Kenth Lindstrom also climbed Vector but with more conventional protection, having already had some experience of the British system.

On day two the Swedes were to climb White Slab on Cloggy while down below there was much excitement in the Pass. Hanz Kanfler from the Tyrol competently led the delicate Diagonal wearing heavy mountain boots while on Cyrn Las the young Russian and Gordon (Speedy) Smith made fast timing to tick off The Grooves and Subsidiary Groove. Sepp Steger from Vienna, however got into difficulty on Main Wall. Having got to the top of the gangway without placing runners (!) he slipped and fell 80 feet. His second, Rita Wernli from Switzerland, held his fall using a shoulder belay, but without gloves suffered badly burnt hands. Ron James with Ed and John Cross stepped into action for the rescue and combined with 22 Squadron RAF helicopters from Valley. Speedy Smith and the Russian ace raced up to rescue and lower off the Swiss girl using a rope tragsitz, friction brakes etc. After medical attention by Ieuan Jones, the climbing doctor, the patched-up Austrian was able to rejoin his two companions, Herbert Lackner and Gunter Gruber (who was part of the first ascent team on Dhaulagiri II in 1971).

After the accident Alexander Kubanov led Cenotaph Corner in 12 minutes flat with only 5 runners, but then ground to a halt on Grond until Speedy Smith showed him how to jam the crack.

By Tuesday the very fit Swiss girls raced round the Glyders and Tryfan while the others went for the Idwal Slabs. Several hard climbs were done on the East Wall while Suicide Wall climbs were led by Howard Johnston. During this time Pete Boardman and Kubanov had elected for a damp Llech Ddu where they eventually succeeded on The Groove and The Great Corner.

After a wet day of darts and arguing about the control of climbers in the mountains using the Russian system, the Russian party (which included Anatol Tschernishov and Vladamir Schataev) went for Snowdon while ten teams raced off to blitz Gogarth. In thick mist the Russian Master got lost for a while below Lliwedd while the disappearance of the Guatemalans was not even noticed until they rejoined the main group. Under sunny skies Howard Johnston and Olaf Ohgran completed four routes while the overall bag included: Mousetrap, Concrete Chimney, Gogarth, Wen Slab, Dream of White Horses and The Big Groove.

The highlight of the tour for many was Joe Brown's faultlessly sung rendering of Sergeant Major, while others said that completing the consumption of rather a large quantity of free brewery ale was a never-to-be-forgotten highlight in the annals of British mountaineering.

1974 BRITISH VISIT TO FRANCE
A party went out in May.

1974 BRITISH VISIT TO AN INTERNATIONAL MEET IN THE PAMIRS
Between July and August. The party included: Doug Scott, Gordon Smith, Paul Nunn, Paul Braithwaite, Guy Lee and Clive Rowland.

1974 BRITISH VISIT TO GERMANY
In September Dennis Gray and Tim Jepson visited the Wetterstein Alps.

1975 ITALIAN VISIT
Between 20th and 26th April eight Italian climbers stayed at Plas y Brenin on a visit organised by Pete Boardman.

1975 BRITISH VISIT TO BERCHTESGADEN
Between 17th and 21st August.

1975 BRITISH VERCORS MEET
Between 7th and 14th September. Geoff Birtles and Tom Proctor represented. Plenty of VS/HVS limestone routes were done.

1975 LUXEMBOURG UIAA YOUTH MEET
Between 29th August and 2nd September, in the Ardennes. Martin Wragg and Stewart Dale represented on this 12-nation meet. One area visited had the potential to be like Stanage. On the Mullerthalles all the pegs were cemented in and visitors were warned against climbing past pegs – as the steepness would tire them!

1975 POLISH VISIT
Between 26th September and 5th October a Polish party visited the Peak District and stayed at Plas y Brenin.

1976 BRITISH CAUCASUS VISIT
During February/March, Mick Geddes, John Porter, Alan Burgess and Adrian Burgess represented. Peter Boardman was also invited. Political problems!

1976 GERMAN (DAV) VISIT
Eight climbers including Manfred Sturm and Reinhard Karl Sturm spent ten days in Yorkshire, the Lake District and North Wales.

1977 FRENCH VISIT
In April; this was Pete Boardman's third year of organisation.

1977 AUSTRIAN VISIT
Only one person came!

1977 BRITISH CAUCASUS VISIT
Tim Jepson was the sole representative who climbed 4 peaks in the company of Austrians. The journey was only started after a midnight car race to obtain a visa. On landing the hosts did not at first accept their visitor as they had been expecting Ann Redman.

1977 BRITISH VISIT TO FRANCE
In October 6 Brits including Pete Livesey went out to the Verdon.

1978 BRITISH VISIT TO UIAA CZECHOSLOVAKIAN YOUTH MEET
Two climbers represented Britain: Willie Todd and Nicholas Donnelly.

1978 BRITISH VISIT TO UIAA AUSTRIAN YOUTH MEET
In August a party including Dennis Gray was sent out to Lizume Hut.

1978 JOINT NORWEGIAN/SWEDISH VISIT
The Lake District, Derbyshire and Yorkshire were visited.

1978 CHINESE VISIT
September. Despite Dennis Gray having delivered a picture of Doug Scott on the summit of Everest to the Chinese Embassy in London, the Chinese declined the offer to visit.

1979 FRENCH VISIT
The BMC put out the word that they wanted a top ice team and they got it! Well it was two teams really as the two Pyreneans (Dominique Julien and Renier Munsch) had had no previous contact with the four Chamonix-based guides (Jean Marc Boivin, Jean Franck Charlet, Rene Ghilini and Gilles Rotillon). Alex MacIntyre, Brian Hall and Roger Durban were among the hosts who also had to endure porridge and 5 a.m. starts.

On Meagaidh, to which they raced up in an hour two days running (but drew the line at a third day), they used the direct ice pitch starts to climb both South Post and Last Post. On the latter the French climber led the first 150-foot pitch in a mere 5 minutes while the Brit was still putting on his crampons. The Pyrenean pair knocked off Smith's Gully in 45 minutes which was even more impressive as a British team was repulsed by the thin ice.

The Ben was plastered with snow and there was poor ice, which dictated a six-man ascent of Point 5 in under two hours. On Lochnagar, Alex MacIntyre climbing with Rene Ghilini, ticked off Eagle Ridge/ Grovel Wall, Parallel Buttress Direct, Pinnacle Face, a new route on Winter Face/Grovel Wall, Shallow Gully as well as Eagle Ridge and Parallel Gully B in the same day. It can't be often that the major Grade Vs on Lochnagar get done on one day. Also on Creag an Dubh Loch there were ascents of Labyrinth and Labyrinth Edge.

The French were all highly fit, experienced in mixed climbing including close quarters gully trickery and each sported the new Simond Chacal axe. Audrey Salkeld reported: 'They probably never got the full measure of the friendly rivalry between the Scots and the English climbers in the host party. It would also be good to know what they made of the non-competitively competitive Alex MacIntyre; Brian Hall and his use of the walk up to sober up from the night before, Patey style; or the enigmatically unemployed Nick Donnelly appearing wherever there's climbing to be done.'

1979 BMC VISIT TO NORWAY FOR UIAA MEET
Nipper Harrison and Steve Bancroft represented the BMC and they did some hard new routes as well as making several first free ascents.

1979 COMBINED DUTCH/BELGIAN MEET
During the summer.

1980 BRITISH VISIT TO NORWAY
During March, 6 climbers represented – this was Alex MacIntyre's third year as organiser.

1980 POLISH VISIT
During March two weeks were spent in Scotland – one at Glenmore Lodge. Originally the Czechoslovakians were invited but sadly the political situation prevented them from leaving their own country.

1980 FRENCH WOMEN'S MEET
Although on previous meets one or two women climbers had sometimes been included amongst the visitors it was hoped that an all-women group could be encouraged to pay us a visit. In due course 6 women arrived from France on 23rd April. They were: Miriam Baltardive, Meije le

Cottier, Joelle Couturier, Catherine Destivelle, Benedicte Reynaud and Martine Rolland. Their minders were Mark Hutchinson and Roger Durban, while Alex MacIntyre went in search of British women who could lead at least HVS, finding: Christine Crawshaw, Gill Price, Jill Lawrence, Fiona Percy, Angela (Faller) Soper, Kit Stewart, and Kathy Woodhead.

To get the French climbers used to placing nuts, two days were spent in Derbyshire warming up prior to more serious stuff in North Wales. While in the Peak however Meije le Cottier discovered that 'The English are purists for climbing and purists for alcohol'. However not even the smooth tongues of Steve Bancroft and Bernard Newman could get them to exceed their limit of a half pint of lager. The French were also surprised by the British habit of climbing all day without a break and in Wales became ravenous at the end of an 11-hour day. Although most days were sunny there was a bitingly cold wind on Cloggy. Despite this, ascents were made of Great/Bow combination, Cloggy Corner, White Slab and Ghecko Groove. At Tremadog routes ticked included: Barbarian, Pincushion, Plum, Fang, Meshach and Vector. Catherine Destivelle, with Jill Lawrence, showed her considerable talent with ascents of Void and Vulcan despite needing a point of aid on each one. In the Pass, Catherine also did the Superdirect on Dinas Mot and Left Wall and Grond on Dinas Cromlech.

To escape the cold, the party headed for sunny Gogarth on two days and the tally included: Britomartis, Central Park, Gogarth, Strand, Concrete Chimney, and Big Groove. Catherine Destivelle, who climbs very fast owing to competing in speed climbing competitions in France, also led T-Rex and Citadel – a notable achievement. These were perhaps the best leads by a woman in Britain up to that time.

1980 JAPANESE VISIT

The first Japanese party to visit Britain for climbing was led by Yoshikazu Takahashi. His friends were: Yasuhiko Forukawa, Kiyoshi Hinotani, Tetsu Kimoto, Akira Nishimura, and Naoki Toda. On arriving in Manchester on September 7th the party paid a visit to Millstone Edge where it reminded the Japanese of one of their own crags – but without the pitons. The next day the visitors posed for TV on the Embankment routes. Looking too 'British' the Japanese were asked to wear head bands to distinguish them! At Stanage Edge the soft-handed Japanese found the harsh gritstone very different to the rock to which they were accustomed. As a contrast they were taken to High Tor where Toda seconded Cubby Cuthbertson on Supersonic, 6a.

Despite bad weather the visitors went to Tremadog and Gogarth then finished at Wilton Quarry in Lancashire by which time they were starting to get accustomed to British climbing. It was said that if they too could become full-time climbers (instead of working!) then they would soon reach 6b.

1980 BRITISH VISIT TO FRANCE
During September a mixed party of 6 visited the Verdon.

1981 BRITISH VISIT TO BELGIUM
Between 19th and 25th April a party climbed at Freyr.

1981 BRITISH VISIT TO LUXEMBOURG
Between May and 6th June the party which included Dick Swindon and Chris Griffiths went out Berdouf.

1981 BRITISH VISIT TO JAPAN
Between May and June a party of six represented Britain, on what was regarded as perhaps the most important overseas visit by British climbers. Our representatives were Mark Vallance, Paul Dawson, Nigel Gifford, Richard Hazko, Mike Trebble and Dennis Gray. A wide range of crags was visited and one or two hard new routes were done.

1981 BRITISH VISIT TO TYROL FOR UIAA YOUTH MEET
Between 16th and 22nd August.

1981 BRITISH UNDER 25 YOUTH VISIT TO SWITZERLAND
Between 30th August and 5th September based near the Furka.

1981 SWISS VISIT
In September a team of 10 visited the Peak District and Wales.

1982 SPANISH VISIT
In March six climbers visited Glencoe and Ben Nevis. Poor weather.

1982 FIRST INTERNATIONAL WOMEN'S MEET IN BRITAIN
In June, 13 twelve women from seven countries came together in London: Rosie Andrews (USA), Anne Aurdal (Norway), Maire ni Chiosain (Eire), Meije le Cottier (France), Katherine Freer (USA), Anne Fyhn (Norway), Paola Mazarelli (Italy), Renata Rossi (Italy), Susanne Rydfelt (Sweden), and Sally Westergard (Denmark). It wasn't long however before they split into enthusiasts and rock technicians to form the 'A' and 'B' teams.

The British party consisted of the chauffeurs and photographers in the form of Mark Hutchinson and Simon Horrox as well as: Antonia Freem, Alison Hargreaves, Bonny Masson, Grace Penny, and Geraldine Abrey-Taylor.

From the Alpine Club where an audio-visual presentation on British rock-climbing by Ken Wilson started things off, the party moved on to the Sobell Sports Centre for a Press conference. A visit to Harrison's Rocks notched up Unclimbed Wall, Bulging Wall, Birchden Wall and The Niblick – spurred on by Ian McNaught-Davis, Ken Wilson and Terry Tullis. Rosie Andrews impressed with effortless ascents and a near completion of Sosblitz. Then it was north to the Peak District to join Fiona Percy, Janet Robinson, Angela Soper and Sarah Williamson.

On Stanage, despite murderous midges which swarmed in, some classic routes were done including: Right and Left Unconquerable, Congo Corner, and Flying Buttress Overhang Direct. In the morning at Millstone it was: Regent Street, Great West Road, Embankment Route 3, Lyons Corner House, Bond Street and The Mall. On Wednesday the 'A' team went for Debauchery and Darius on High Tor. A quick Thursday morning workout on Curbar netted L'Horla, Scroach, The Peapod, and Right Eliminate for Katherine Freer (a Yosemite expert) as well as Valkyrie and Tody's Wall on Froggatt. Then it was off to Karrimor in Accrington for a visit and a banquet.

The weather cleared up in Wales for Fang, One Slip and Leg Slip which were all done in the afternoon, prior to the arrival of British reinforcements: Stella Adams, Brede Arkless, Sheila Cormack, Christine Crawshaw, Jill Lawrence, Gill Price, Kath de Mengel and Pat Taylor. Next day after looking for dry rock, a return to Tremadog netted routes such as The Plum, Grasper and Geireagle.

With sunshine and blue sky on Gogarth the 'A' team cruised Rat Race, Strand, Park Lane, Fifth Avenue, T-Rex, Quartz Icicle, If, Concrete Chimney and Dream of White Horses. The other team stayed inland for Cenotaph Corner and Cemetery Gates. More rain and the Llangefni climbing wall led to an escape to the Lake District. Katherine Freer and Alison Hargreaves made the best of the poor weather on Pavey Ark then Gimmer for Kipling Groove. On the last day at Castle Rock the 'A' team ticked North Crag Eliminate, Harlot Face, and the other two eliminates. There is no doubt that Rosie Andrews was the star performer and she made a formidable team with Jill Lawrence.

The Americans stayed on in the Peak District for Tippler, Dangler and The Rasp as well as Robert Brown on the limestone. They finished with a return to Gogarth for Super Crack and Wonderwall. Undoubtedly this was a thrilling finale to a superb and highly successful meet.

1982 AMERICAN VISIT

In early September five men and one woman from the American Alpine Club began a 2-week tour which was merely a prelude to a European tour. The American team included Maria Cranor, Randy Vogel, Dan Lepeshka and the hot-shot Alex Lowe. The strong British contingent was made up of: Choe Brooks, Chris Gore, Mark Hutchinson, Jill Lawrence, Dominic Lee, Jerry Moffatt, Ian Parsons, Andy Pollitt, and Johnny Woodward. The scene was set for the action to start in North Wales.

On the first day on the Cromlech a key point of discussion was the comparison between English and American grades. Thus of the hard routes climbed they graded: Resurrection 5.11b, True Grip 5.11c and Right Wall as 5.11c. Alex Lowe made one of four ascents of Atomic Hot Rod declaring it to be 5.12 a/b but it was generally thought to be as hard as some of the 5.13s in the States.

With good weather, two days on Gogarth yielded all the hard classics including: Strand 5.10a, Dinosaur and Big Groove 5.10c, Strike 5.11a, Citadel and Positron at 5.11c. On Citadel a fall with several snapped slings as well as stripped etrier runners landed Dan Lepeshka, who had got 'pumped out', close to his belayer Chris Gore.

The brooding steep limestone cliffs of Great Orme giving strenuous climbing impressed the visitors who quickly adapted to bag: New Dimensions 5.11a, Axel Attack 5.11c/d, Mayfair 5.11c/d, Psychic Threshold 5.11 and Rude Awakening 5.11d. Then at Craig y Forwyn (dubbed Craig y Forearm by Vogel) all the classics plus: Quickstep 5.11a/b, Great Wall 5.10d, High Plains Drifter, Moonwind Direct and Space Mountain all at 5.11c.

At Tremadog the hard routes given 5.11 were: Bananas, Void 5.11a/b, Marathon Man 5.11d, Zukator 5.11c, Hitler's Buttock and Neb Direct. Groove of Horror was thought to be 5.12, while the big lead by Johnny Woodward was Strawberries which his second, Alex Lowe, grudgingly admitted was 'Definitely hard 5.12'! (i.e. 5.12d). At that point it was decided that the visitors were sufficiently tuned up for the rigours of the Peak District, so it was off to the Downes Hut. In a relaxed atmosphere some of the harder routes done on gritstone were: 5.10s such as Tippler Direct, Fernhill, Tom Thumb, and 5-Finger Exercise, while at 5.11 there were: Downhill Racer, Reticent Mass Murderer and Coventry Street.

On a sunny High Tor it was a pleasure to climb Darius 5.10b and Delicatessen 5.10a before hitting the 5.11s such as: Supersonic, Flaky Wall, A6, Laurin and Tales of Yankee Power 5.11d – as well as Bastille 5.12a. The guests however were not too keen about Chee Tor's mud and nettles but still enjoyed the 5.11s of Golden Mile 5.11c/d and Apocalypse

— to say nothing of the farewell party thrown by Geraldine Taylor in Sheffield. The climbing (in relation to the grades of the day) was the hardest seen so far by a visiting party.

1983 JAPANESE VISIT
During February four climbers led by Naoe Sakashita (who has climbed Kangchenjunga and K2) climbed in Scotland where there were excellent conditions on Ben Nevis and in the Cairngorms. The party was hosted by Don Barr, Mark Hutchinson and the staff of Glenmore Lodge.

1983 FFM INTERNATIONAL MEET
Andy Pollitt, Ron Fawcett, Steve Bancroft and Alison Hargreaves represented Britain and met up with the likes of: Jean Pierre Bouvier (France), Patrick Edlinger (France), Scot Fry (USA), Wolfgang Guillich (Germany), Wolfgang Kraus (Germany), and Louise Shepherd (Aus). As expected there was lots of action on the French crags such as Fontainebleau and the Verdon Gorge.

1983 BRITISH VISIT TO SWITZERLAND
Chris Hamper and Bill Birkett attended this meet, accompanied by Tom Price, Bill Peascod and Ian Parsons.

1983 BRITISH VISIT TO SWEDEN
Three climbers represented Britain.

1983 VISIT OF FRENCH MINISTER OF SPORT
This was solely to study the design and construction of climbing walls.

1984 YUGOSLAVIAN VISIT
During late February six climbers arrived for some excellent winter ice climbing on the Cairngorms, Ben Nevis and in North Wales. The final team was: Biscak Bogdan, Janko Humar, Rok Kovak, Marjan Kreger, Igor Skamperle, and Zarko Trusnovec, while for the Brits it was: Chris Dale, Ian Dunn, Calum Fraser, Mark Hutchinson, Colin Jamieson, Mark Miller, Sean Smith, Ewen Todd, and Willie Todd.

The visitors were put to the test in Sheffield as soon as they arrived, but struck back with a toxic clear liquid that they had brought to eclipse the Yorkshire ale. Sobered up by Sunday the party regrouped at Glenmore Lodge. The first day they climbed The Chancer, Hells Lum Chimney, Salamander, Devils Delight and Kiwi Slabs. Creag Meagaidh was visited for Pumpkin, The Wand and North Post Direct, and North and South Pipe.

After a rest day the guests were ready to fend for themselves and the team split up for Northern, Hells Lum and Stag Rocks. Most of the routes at Coire Lochan and Coire An Sneachda were done as well as a new one up the grooves left of Savage Slit. Owing to bare rock, only Amphitheatre Gully was ascended at Stag Rocks. The party then went west for The Ben to grab another two days on deteriorating ice. Nevertheless the routes done included: Point Five, Zero, The Curtain, Green Gully, Vanishing Gully, Route 2 Direct finishing up Route 1, Tower Ridge, Orion Face, and Rubicon Wall. Most of the team was then moved to Wales.

1984 CAF INTERNATIONAL RASSEMBLEMENT
Sean Smith and Mark Miller represented.

1984 UIAA MEET AT GRIGNA
J Fotheringham and N Crouch represented.

1984 BMC/PINNACLE CLUB INTERNATIONAL WOMEN'S MEET
This visit was to be a significant breakthrough in rock-climbing terms which was to confirm quite clearly that women leaders had really made the breakthrough into the big league. But let a woman tell it as it really happened (to quote Angela Soper):
'Dinas Cromlech, May 29. Hardly room for any more on the sloping ledges. Leaders on Left Wall, Resurrection, Cenotaph Corner, and Right Wall. All women, with women waiting to climb. Madelaine had settled for a damp Cenotaph Corner and Christine for a dry Resurrection. Janet had queued for Left Wall while Alison moved round to The Thing. Jill and Rosie, who have climbed together extensively since the last Women's International, tossed a coin about Right Wall. Jill won and chose to go for it. How did it feel to be the first woman to lead Right Wall and break into the E5 grade? …
… As the sun warmed the Right Wall, she won the battle in her head, committed herself to the unprotected moves of the first crux – and made them safely. A rest, the second crux, and twenty voices shouting "Well done, Jill". Rosie then led Right Wall confidently while we others dispersed to Grond, Curfew and Crucifix … Next day both French girls (Catherine Destivelle and Christine Gambert) led Right Wall.'
The climbers for the meet were as follows: Judy Adam, Stella Adams, Rosie Andrews (USA), Brede Arkless, Sheila Cormack, Catherine Destivelle (France), Claudie Dunn, Mandy Glanville, Alison Hargreaves, Verena Jaggin (Switzerland), Christine Gambert (France), Jill Lawrence,

Pippa Manson, Nicole Niquille (Switzerland), Elaine Owen, Gill Price, Madeline Haven, Janet Robinson, Angela Soper, Kit Stewart, Geraldine Taylor, Paula Turley (Eire), Jay Turner, An Verbeeck (Belgium), Sonja Vietoris Jenny Wong. The BMC organisers were Ian Dunn and Mark Hutchinson, while Ian Smith was the photographer.

The list of achievements for this meet was extensive. In addition to routes mentioned above, the following Pass routes were climbed: Comes the Dervish, Foil, Hangover, Super Direct, Nexus, Slape Direct, First Amendment, Curfew. In the Snowdon South area: Cream, Fingerlicker, Zukator, Vulture, Void, Silly Arête, Pippikin, Technical Master, Pellagra, Vulcan, Grasper, Tensor, Vector, Nimbus, Itch, Dragon, The Snake, Leg Break, Hardd, Barbarian, Falcon, Neb, Valour, Diadic, One Step in the Crowds, Laser Crack, Integral and Sorry Sally. The Gogarth climbs were also impressive: Positron, Big Groove, Aardvark, Strand, Eternal Optimist, Zeus, North West Passage, Freebird and Fail Safe. There were also many leads and solos on Stanage, Froggatt, Millstone Edge and High Tor – as well as a visit to the Altrincham climbing wall. But to sum up let Angela Soper have the last words starting with a thought on the Right Wall success:

'Would these ascents have been made but for the meet? Probably not, yet in Rosie's words, "If it hadn't been for the others wanting to do it, I'd have waited till I was ready". Group psychology makes you think, "If she can do it, why not me?" ... When the guidebook says strenuous, you feel braver if a woman tells you that "I found I could use my feet." ... Grace and style. Women climb with imaginative footwork, balance, exact positioning of the body. They become stronger from climbing, but depend mainly on technique. During this meet well over a hundred Extreme leads were made, at least thirty E3 or harder, on all types of rock.'

The Right Wall ascents marked a major step forward for women's climbing; but Louise Shepherd's ascent of Lord of the Flies, the following year, probably marked the closest women have yet come to the top standards of the day in Britain (written in 1995).

1985 FFM INTERNATIONAL MEET
During the summer Martin Atkinson, Ben Moon and Mandy Glanville represented the BMC at Verdon and Fontainebleau.

1985 FIRST YOUTH MEET
At the beginning of May 78 boys and 2 girls met up and were based at the North Lees Camp Site at Stanage. The three-day meet, which was sponsored by The Sports Council and the Conville Trust, had poor

weather but the climbing standard was high. Routes were climbed at Stanage, Millstone, Froggatt and Stoney Middleton. For the evening lectures John Beatty, Ron Fawcett, Craig Smith and Johnny Dawes all helped to make the meet a success. Dennis Gray, Mark Hutchinson and Ian Dunn hosted for the BMC.

1985 KOREAN VISIT
Between 10th and 15th July – poor weather.

1985 FRENCH VISIT
Between August 31st and 15th September five men and three women visited. The party included Jean Claude Droyer, Alain Gherson and Isabelle Patissier. Poor weather.

1986 CZECHOSLOVAKIAN VISIT
Between 31st May and 14th June five Czechs including Thomas Czarda went to Yorkshire, the Peak District, Cornwall and Wales. Rowland Edwards, Dennis Gray and Ian Smith hosted this visit. 'The standard was a joy to behold, their committed leads, and solo climbing causing some heart-stopping moments, and the fact that one of them was climbing in his carpet slippers, impressed even the most chauvinistic of Yorkshiremen when they visited that part of the world.' On-sight solos of 6bs and an ascent of Strawberries impressed all.

1986 BRITISH VISIT TO TURKEY
Between 10th and 19th July. Oliver Knowles and Mike Quinn represented.

1986 BRITISH VISITS ABROAD
Tom Curtis and Mark Miller represented the BMC on a winter trip to Japan, while Jon Sparks went to Meteora in northern Greece to rock-climb. Alison Hargreaves and Brede Arkless attended a women's meet in Chamonix to celebrate the 200th Anniversary of climbing Mont Blanc.

1986 INDIAN VISIT
Between 6th and 23rd August three people (Lobsang Tshering, Neema Chewan and G.C. Shah) climbed on Southern Sandstone and in the Peak District, but also attended a 2-week course at Plas y Brenin.

1987 POLISH VISIT
Between 5th and 23rd February seven climbers went on Ben Nevis, Meagaidh and in the Cairngorms.

1987 USSR VISIT
From 13th to 27th June the party which included Valerie Balezin went from Cornwall to North Wales then the Peak District.

1987 BRITISH VISITS ABROAD
British climbers attended meets in Czechoslovakia, New Zealand, Austria and Yugoslavia.

1987 BRITISH VISIT TO FRANCE
Between 7th and 20th July Alison Hargreaves and Brede Arkless represented in Chamonix.

1987 2nd INTERNATIONAL YOUTH MEET
Between 21st and 26th July there were 58 British and 27 overseas climbers from 11 different countries.

1988 BRITISH TATRA VISIT
Brian Hall, Mike Woolridge and Andy Fanshawe had problems with high avalanche risk conditions.

1988 AUSTRIAN VISIT
Between 5th and 21st February – poor climbing conditions in Scotland.

1988 3rd INTERNATIONAL YOUTH MEET
On 24th July nearly 100 climbers (aged between 14 and 25) from 8 countries arrived at Eric Jones' camp site at Bwlch y Moch in North Wales. Most impressive were the Czechs who arrived with a 12-year old lorry which experienced mechanical failure! Nevertheless the young Czechs were to lead the way on the rock. During the week visits were made to the Tremadog cliffs, Gogarth, Llanberis Pass and the slate. Many classic routes were done by mixed ropes of Brits and foreign climbers, e.g. Indian/English and Czech/Scots. The exceptionally high standard was shown by successes on routes such as: The Big Sleep, Barbarossa, Bell Dance and Right Wall. 16-year old Will Nazarian (USA) led Geireagle while Adam Wainwright (also 16) led Flashdance/Belldance at E6 6b.

At the evening lectures John Beatty, Ron Fawcett, Dennis Gray, Andy Pollitt and Andy Fanshawe all spoke to the gathered assembly.

It is perhaps worth noting that until 1988 the BMC, unlike the majority of other European countries, had made a firm stand against competition climbing which had in the past been pushed by Eastern European countries (notably Russia) but by this time had been adapted into a European form by Italy and France. However by 1988 many top British climbers were going abroad to take part in European competitions and, in addition, by then sponsorship had become part of the climbing scene. Consequently subsequent exchange visits usually failed to attract the top young climbers of their day.

1989 HUNGARIAN VISIT
24th February to 12th March. Various venues in Scotland were visited but 'grim' climbing conditions were the order of the day and instead of winter climbing the party was forced south of the Border in search of rock.

1989 4th INTERNATIONAL YOUTH MEET
From July 22nd to 29th Plas y Brenin hosted this visit for about 80 people – very few of whom were women.

1990 ISRAELI VISIT
This was accepted but later cancelled owing to political implications and 'security problems'!

1991 ROMANIAN VISIT
Between 11th and 24th March four climbers arrived after a far from easy overland journey, after the 'walls' came tumbling down in Eastern Europe. In pouring rain they squelched their way up a variety of Scottish winter routes. Although very poor by western standards they charmed everyone whom they met. The culmination of the trip was the Buxton Conference where they expressed utter delight to meet so many famous climbers.

The new pattern after this visit is to invite all UIAA members to send representatives biennially – rather than to invite specific top climbers.

1992 BMC/UIAA INTERNATIONAL MEET
Between 8th and 16th May, climbers from 12 countries met in Wales, and among the participants was Jan Wolf, husband of Mrufla who died on K2 with Alan Rouse. He climbed in boots on most of the hard routes, carrying a video camera round his neck. This was somewhat unnerving for his seconds as when on a hard move they would invariably find lots of slack rope owing to the fact that Jan was busy filming. (Sadly Jan was killed two years later.) This meet was specifically to promote adventure/ traditional climbing on bolt-free crags – in an effort to influence the

INTERNATIONAL MEETS
A British party was invited to climb in the Caucasus in 1958 and a group of Soviet climbers came to Britain in 1960. This was an exchange at the height of the Cold War that attracted much media interest. Though not a BMC event it set the style for the scores of foreign visits that were to follow. The upper photo shows the party in the Lakes: (*left to right*) Anatoly Ovchenikov, Josef Kachiani, Dave Thomas, Mikhail Borushko, Sid Cross, Ralph Jones, Misha Khergiani, Yevgeny (Eugene) Tur and Ken Lombley (interpreter). In Wales (*left*) Derek Bull, Tur, Michael Hewson, Sir John Hunt and Yevgeni Eugene Gippenreier pose for the press after a Main Wall ascent (*overleaf* — Hunt climbing).

There have been regular French exchanges, with the ACG nominees to ENSA and periodic return visits where Gallic stars demonstrated their prowess. At Harrison's Rocks in 1972 Fontainebleau-trained Frenchmen made short work of local testpieces — (*above: left to right*) Dave Cook, Royal Robbins, Ian McNaught-Davis, Eric Vola, David Belden, Jean Claude Droyer and Patrick Cordier. In North Wales the party also excelled, particularly Simone Badier (*inset*) who completed several extreme leads.

Six French ice climbers made rapid ascents of some of the hardest Scottish routes in 1979 — a trip that also forged the successful Ghilini/MacIntyre Himalayan partnership (tragically broken on Annapurna in 1982). The photo shows (standing: *left to right*), Dominique Julien, Gilles Rotillon, Renier Munsch, Rene Ghilini, Alex MacIntyre, Jean Marc Boivin and Brian Hall, with Nick Donnelly and Jean Franck Charlet (kneeling).

The Japanese report of their 1980 visit to Wales and the Peak (*Mountain 77*) revealed the impact of exchanges on countries with little free-climbing tradition — every aspect of the rock-climbing they experienced being carefully studied. Naoki Toda joined Dave Cuthbertson on an ascent of Supersonic as the technical highpoint of the visit. In the photo are (standing, *left to right*) Cuthbertson, Dave Wilkinson (translator), Richard Haszko, Yoshikazu Takahashi (leader), Akira Nishimura, Tetsu Kimoto and Alex MacIntyre; (seated) Yasuhiko Furakana, Toda, Kiyashi Hintotani and Mikiko Wilkinson (translator). Also in the host party were Dave Pearce and Willie Todd.

Below: The three Women's meets in the Eighties established firm international contacts and pushed standards. The prima donnas, all of whom led major climbs, were Jill Lawrence, the Americans Rosie Andrews and Kathy Freer, and the French climbers Catherine Destivelle and Christine Gambert. They were supported by a talented chorus (Arkless, Masson, Soper, Taylor, Crawshaw, Hargreaves and others). This photo of the final meet in 1984 provides a lasting reminder of a memorable series of encounters.

Catherine Destivelle's 1980 leads (T.Rex, Left Wall, Grond etc.) and those of Jill Lawrence, Rosie Andrews and Kathy Freer in 1982 (Rat Race, T Rex, Supercrack, Rasp, Right Eliminate etc), set the scene for dynamic events in 1984. The target for all was Right Wall (E5), first climbed by Pete Livesey (belayed by Jill Lawrence) in 1974 — a climb that dominated the aspirations of top climbers for the next decade. No woman had led the climb. It was therefore particularly fitting that Lawrence should be the first to make this psychological breakthrough (*above right*). Andrews made her ascent on the same day and the following day Destivelle (tackling the upper wall — *right)* and Christine Gambert each led the climb. Other hard climbs led in 1984 were Resurrection, Vulture, Zukator, Cream (Lawrence — *above left*) and Positron (a determined ascent by Geraldine Taylor). In 1985, the Australian climber, Louise Shepherd, took the process further by leading Lord of the Flies (E6) thereby bringing women's climbing close to the top traditional standards of the day. The four who led Right Wall in 1984 are inset on the right.

Jill Lawrence

Rosie Andrews

Catherine Destivelle

Christine Gambert

The American climber, Jason Stern (17), soloing Narcissus E6,6b (Froggatt) during the 1987 International Youth Meet — Andy Fanshawe, Dennis Gray and Craig Smith plus other members of the meet look on. Fanshawe later expressed concern about the competitive soloing that developed during the event. Other youth meets were held in 1985 and 1988.

other Europeans. British hosts included: Fliss Butler, Mick Hardwick, Kev Howett, Steve Mayers, Mike Mortimer, Al Phizacklea and Angela Soper.

One Romanian failed to arrive until Thursday – along with the princely sum of 4p. After climbing on Cloggy on the Friday, Johnny Dawes organised a whip-round for him at the Saturday disco. Later the Sheffield team took him home to stay for a few days – but he didn't climb much! What did emerge however was a perplexingly large phone bill for Andy Pollitt. This was tracked down to lots of late night 08 – sex calls! – unlike the Romanian who disappeared one morning and was never seen again.

1993 BRITISH IRANIAN VISIT
A group of Lake District climbers represented Britain.

1994 BMC/UIAA INTERNATIONAL MEET
Between 8th and 14th May 28 climbers from 14 countries visited along with a large group of British hosts. Again this was held at Plas y Brenin with the aim of introducing the visitors to the delights of traditional bolt-free climbing in the hope that the message would get back to the home countries.

In addition to the many people who have represented Britain abroad through our National Body, it should also be realised that many expeditions from the affiliated clubs and universities, who go to mountainous regions throughout the world, have received substantial financial help. This has frequently been through Sports Council grants administered by the BMC in conjunction with the Mount Everest Foundation. In the last 20 years, about 500 expeditions have received grants to help them and currently about 40 expeditions are being subsidised annually to a total of £20,000.

Geoff Milburn

International Expeditions

The following expeditions applied to the Mount Everest Foundation for grant aid and successfully received Sports Council backing through the BMC:

1975
Northumbria Baffin Island; North of England Himalayan; British/ Nepalese Army Himalayan; University of East Anglia Hindu Raj; Yorkshire Karakoram; North West Karakoram (Biafo); Kishtwar Himal; Trent Polytechnic Hindu Kush; Edinburgh University Expedition; South Patagonian Ice Cap; East Greenland; British East Greenland; British Patagonian; Two-man Gharwal; Baffin Island; and Cumbria Paine; (Total £5,000).

1976
Scottish Peruvian Andes; Changabang South Face; McKinley South Face; Imperial College Hindu Kush; British Baltoro Himalaya; British Trango Tower; Hong Kong Kanjiroba; Cambridge Hindu Kush, Fortress South East Pillar; British South American; Bristol Zanskar and North Himalayan; Changabang West Wall; Peruvian and Patagonian Andes; University of Bristol Himalayan; Oxford University Baffin Island.

1977
North of England Himalaya; Reading Himalayan Kishtwar; Manchester University Hindu Kush; Northumbria Himalayan; Merseyside Himalayan; Sisne Himal; British Ogre Himalayan; Cambridge University Hindu Kush; Oxford Hindu Kush; Anglo/Polish Hindu Kush; British Nanda Devi; Cambridge Gharwal Himalayan; St Helens M.C. Andean; Kishtwar Expedition 1977; Irish Himalayan; 1977 British Kishtwar; Carlisle M.C. Kishtwar; Charlotte Mason College Himalayan; Yorkshire Karakoram; Scottish Tierra del Fuego; Edinburgh University Himalayan; Zanskar Winter; University of Southampton Himalayan.

1978
Gasherbrum IV West Face; South Wales Himalayan; Annapurna II; New Guinea Snow Mountains; British Himalchuli; British Caledonian Cerro Torre; British Chocktoi I; British Jannu; British Latok; North of England Kishtwar; Anglo/Irish/Dutch Sanctuary 1978; Sheffield North East Greenland; British Fortress 1977/78; Kishtwar 1978; Anglo/American

Women's; Nanda Devi North Wall; British Ladies Karakoram 1978; North London Hindu Kush; 1978 East Kulu; British Hindu Kush; Anglo/Polish; (Total £6,000).

1979

Nepalese/British Gaurishankar; British (Derbyshire) Nanda Devi; Biafo Himalayan; Tierra del Fuego; British Kangchenjunga; Kantega West Ridge; Cerro Torre (1980); Border Himalayan; British Annapurna II; Cumbria Himalayan; Sheffield Peruvian; Sheffield University M.C. Hindu Kush; British Everest (West Ridge); British Peruvian Andes; Tirich Mir; British Barnaj (Padar); British Kishtwar; (Total £6,000).

1980

Anglo/Polish Dhaulagiri; British Conway Ogre Karakoram; Kingston Agayasol Group; Royal Aircraft Establishment Kishtwar Himalayan; British Western Karakoram; British Padar Himalayan; British Langtang Himalayan; British Nanga Parbat; Pinnacle Club 1980; Cumbrian Himalayan; British Alaskan; British K2; 1980 British K7; 1980 Devonshire McKinley; British Makalu Baruntse; British Shivling; British Everest Winter 1980/81; (Total £6,000).

1981

Oxford University M.C. Kishtwar Himalaya; British Kunyang Kish; British West Karakoram; Anglo Indian Gangotri Sanctuary; British Trans Greenland; British Ruth Glacier; Hunza Spire; Peak District Alaskan; RAFMA A.C. of Pakistan Masherbrum; British Alaskan; British Annapurna III; British Nanda Devi; Kashmir 81; Ladakh Winter. 16 expeditions.

1982

British Tualliraju South Face; British Latok 2; Rondoy West Face; British Yaksingardon Karakoram; British Women's Kwangde; Nanda Devi Region; British Gangotri Gal; Bristol Devil's Thumb; British Garhwal; Annapurna 82; British Alpine Style Andean; British Nilgiri North. 17 expeditions.

1983

Parnassus 21st Anniversary Himalayan; Mount Deborah East Ridge; Scott Antarctic 83/84; Salford University Iceland; North London M.C. Kwangde; Mount St Elias; British Bhagirathi Parbat; Gwent Andean; British Annapurna III; British Kishtwar/Shivling; Lhotse/Cho Oyu;

British Gangotri; Pakistan-British Karum Koh; Anglo-Canadian Nepalese; British Gangotri Glacier; Hagshu-Kishtwar Himalayan; British Himalayan Winter; University of London Baffin Island.
26 expeditions (£6,784).

1984

British Trango; SE Kishtwar; British Gangotri; North Leeds Peruvian Andes; British Lhotse Shar; Kederdome East Face; Anglo/Indian East Karakoram; West Karakoram; Oundelian Tirich Mir; Pakistan/British Karum Koh; British Bojohagur; Mont Forel; Tierra Del Fuego; British Baruntse Chamlang Makalu; Bristol Cho Oyu; Manaslu Winter.
16 expeditions (£10,000).

1985

Alpine Club Joint East Karakoram; Sickle Moon; British Pamirs; I.M.C. Altai; Sheffield Singu Chuli; South Wales Karakoram; London Shivling; Siula Grande/Ninashanca/Rasac West Faces; British Gangotri Meru; Leeds Gangotri; British Peruvian Andes; Dhawmsura (White Sail) West Face; British Rakaposhi/Nanga Parbat; Cordillera Oriental; Cambridge Anglo-Chilean Patagonian.

1986

Cho Oyu in Winter; Cape Farewell; Barutse East Traverse; Sunderland East Greenland; British Gasherbrum IV; Everest NE Ridge; East Greenland; British Bhutan; Pakistan; British Mount Hunter; K2; Caucasus; Andean; Chogolisa; British Himalayan Winter; Salcantay; Hindu Kush; Nevado Cayesh; Sickle Moon; Paldor; Mid-Wales Karakoram; Janka Raju; Kishtwar; GB/Indian Police; Lobsang Spire; Anglo/Scot Andean; GB/NZ Andes; Hunza.

1987

British Latok II; Plymouth Polytechnic Khurdopin; British New Zealand Gasherbrums; Greenland Two Summits; NLMC Spantik; Markhun Karakoram; Leeds/Boulder Karakoram; Gangotri; Anglo French Garhwal; Siula Chico; Cambridge/St Andrews Karakoram; Hushe Valley; Ama Dablam South Ridge; Bublimotin Hopefuls; British West Karakoram; Yorkshire Andean; Kongde Ri; London Hospital Swachand Bamak; British Xixabangna; Indo-British Swargorohini I; British Broad Peak 87; British Amne Machin; Anglo Scottish Karakoram; Anglo American K2; British Everest NE Ridge; UK/NZ Patagonian; British Hagshu.

1988

British India IBEX; 1988 Karakoram; Bristol Nun Kun; Cho Oyu South West Ridge; British Altai; British Andes; GB Kunyang Kish; GB East Kishtwar; GB Nanga Parbat; Ganesh 3; Annapurna II; Gharesa – Karakoram; Hushe – Karakoram; Annapurna I South Face; British Caucasus. 34 expeditions (£18,000).

1989

British Unnamed Peak, 6230m; Hushe Valley; Snow Lake Peak; Ogre North Face; Bath University Peru; Manchester Karakoram; Milne Island; RYE Peru; Manaslu; British Kedar Dome; Women Gash II; Langtang Lirung; Shani; Hushe Valley; Mt Foraker; Kedarnarth East Face; Anglo Indian East Karakoram; Flight of the Condor; South Patagonia Ice Cap; Manaslu South West Face, Peak 29; UK/NZ Barnaj Hagshu; Baruntse; East Ridge of Meru; Hispar; Taboche Winter; Hushe Valley; Hagshu; Sheffield University Vilcanota; Anglo Australian Hushe; Lo'boro Andes; Anglo Irish Shimshal; Masherbrum; Polish West Ridge Everest; Nilkanta; Dibibokri; Hagshu North Face; Cerro Kishtwar; Everest North East Ridge; Karakoram; Gharesa Karakoram; Anglo Swedish Nanga Parbat.

1990

British Thalay Sagar; British Hispar; British Mt Foraker; British Pumori; Trinity Peak; British Turkestan; British Gangotri; British Cheo Himal; British K7; TWTCC Central Lahul; NW Ridge Ama Dablam; North Group East Greenland; Nilkanta; Malangutti; Bath University High Altai; Cerro Kishtwar; British/New Zealand Kishtwar; British Latok; Hagshu North Face. 18 expeditions.

1991

Anglo Kiwi Latok; Saga; British Winter Himlung Himal; British Makrong Chish; Leeds Baffin Island; Ultar – Karakoram; Masherbrum II; Chamlang; Langtang Lirung; Masherbrum; Gasherbrum 2; Chong Kumdau; Bhrigupanth; British Winter Everest; Altai; Tien Shan; Achat Valley; Pamirs; Kusum Kanguru; Chogolisa; Naltar Valley; Cerro Kishtwar; Basinthang; Karakoram Traverse; Batura; Anglo Polish Nanga Parbat; Kishtwar Nordic Ski; South East Greenland Traverse; OB Trust Himalchuli; Yorkshire Karakoram; British Winter Manaslu; British Andean Volcanoes.

1992
Sokha Brakk; Saipi; Thalay Sagar; Swargarohini; Api; Scottish Kumaon; Torres del Paine; Mongol Attai; Indo-British Panchuli; Scottish Nanga Parbat; Broad Peak Traverse; K2 North Ridge; Scottish Stauning; British Nanga Parbat; British Latok II; British Barnaj II; Scottish Nersaerskertinde; Southampton UMC Bolivia; Cambridge Gangotri; British Eastern Kishtwar; British East Greenland; British Kahiltna South; Big Wall Biafo; Anglo/Irish Coz Sar; Gemini Karakoram; Shani North West Face; North Wales Annapurna I South Face; British Khumbu Alpine; British Alaskan Multi Peak; Tien Shan Valikhanov Ridge; British Biafo Glacier; International Dorje Lhakpa; British Hagshu North Face; British Garhwal; Imperial College Pamir; Matho Kangri; Russia; British Peri Himal; British West Biafo Wall; Everest 1st British Female Attempt. 35 expeditions (£20,000).

1993
British Masagang; Sarmiento; Jordanhill College E Greenland; British Extremely Chile; British Cerro Torre; Cerro Kishtwar, ARG Svalbard (scientific); Bolivia – UK Apolobamba; Rolwaling Ski-Mountaineering; Gangchempo; British K2; NI Greenland; British Lemon Bjerg; Irish Mount Everest; British Tien Shan; British Salcantay; Greenland Sermersoq; Anglo/Irish Koz Sar; Asan Pamirs; British Gasherbrum IV; British K7; British Mount Augusta; Welsh-Scottish Tien Shan; Batura; British Mera Peak West Face; British Tokositna/Kahiltna; Nilkanta; British Greenland; Meru Shark's Fin; Tasermuit Fjord; British Kukua; Cambridge University Causasus; Karakoram Conquest; British Shani North Face; Chukatan; Nanga Parbat; Cathedral Spires; British Muchichul Glacier. 39 expeditions (£20,000).

1994
Kamchatka Volcanoes; British Ultar; Cumbrian Hindu Raj; Karabiner M.C. Greenland; British Himlung; Oxford & Cambridge Rudyard Kipling Memorial Expdn. to East India Himalaya; Cherskiy Mountains; Scottish Alaskan; British/Ukrainian Joint; British Chamar; British Women's Karakoram; Cardiff University Greenland; Imperial College Hidden Garhwal; Hagshu – North Face; British Admiral Peak; British Mount Asgard; British Ellsworth; Arabia Felix '94 – 1001 Arabian Heights; British Hispar; British Trinity Peak; Durham University M.C.

Sim Gang Glacier; 1994 British Nanda Devi East; British Latok North Ridge; Nyegi Kangsang; Indian/British Kinnaur; and British Phola Ganchen; (£16,300). Also approved were: Medical Mount Everest; RAF Menthosa; K2 North West Ridge; British South Tower of Paine; RAF M.A. Tilicho Peak; TransGreenland.

Other Officers, Officials and Professional Staff

HONORARY SECRETARY

1945-47	J E Q Barford	1960-64	T H Sinclair
1947-52	J A Stewart	1965-71	H D Greenwood
1952-55	F Shuttleworth	1971-73	J P Ledeboer
1955-60	M Holton	1973-75	D W Partridge

From 1975 duties undertaken by professional staff.

ASSISTANT HONORARY SECRETARY (GENERAL)

1945-47	E C Pyatt	1959	F E Smith
1947-50	B Donkin	1959-63	Dr E S Williams (enquiries only)
1950-55	L P Taylor	1965-73	T H Sinclair
1955-58	Dr E S Williams		

ASSISTANT HONORARY SECRETARY (Education & Training/ Schools/ Information Service

1947	G A Dummett (E&T)	1964-65	A Oakes (IS)
1959-64	G A Hutcheson (Schools)	1965-	S H G Taylor

ASSISTANT HONORARY SECRETARY (Huts and Films)

Pre-1962	C M Dixon (Films)	1964-65	G A Hutcheson (Huts & Films)
1962-64	G A Hutcheson (Films)		

ASSISTANT HONORARY SECRETARY (Guides)

1947-62	R G Folkard	1969-73	J A Baxter
1962-69	E J Hammond	1973-74	R Lewis

From 1974 duties undertaken by Association of British Mountain Guides.

HONORARY TREASURER

1945-51	H L Roberts	1969-74	J Llewellyn Jones
1951-52	A Medlycott	1974-76	I MacCallum
1952-55	T T Hardwick	1976-81	B Monk
1955-57	Lt Col J A Crawley	1981-85	J Ashcroft
1958-59	G Starkey	1985-87	M Watson
1960-66	J H Della Porter	1987-92	B Monk (second term)
1966-69	J M Kretschmer	1992-96	B Griffiths
		1996-	G Adshead

ASSISTANT HONORARY TREASURER

1947-48	A E Rideout	1969	R Lewis
1967-69	W R Neate	1972-73	J E Crewe

HONORARY LEGAL ADVISOR

1955-66	Sir E Herbert (later Lord Tangley)	1978-	M Wragg
1973-90	M Bennett	1986	P Mann
1974-92	Prof. H W R Wade	1990-	S Porteus
1975-	M Baker	1990-	H B Sales
1978-92	C R Simpson	1993-	A Rich

HONORARY MEDICAL ADVISOR

1978-	Dr C Clarke
1989-	S Bollen FRCS

HONORARY AUDITOR

1945- ?	F J Guest	1974-75	J E Crewe
1956-67	R A Tyssen-Gee	1976-90	G R Astles
1968-72	H N Fairfield		

For 1973 and 1991 on a professional firm was used.

CIRCULARS

From 1944 produced by J E Q Barford (Hon Sec of the BMC) for purely internal circulation.
1946-47 produced for general circulation
Superseded by *Mountaineering* in 1947.

EDITOR of *MOUNTAINEERING*

1945-46	R S Russell	1958-59	D Aldridge
1947-48	Wing Cdr. A J M Smyth	1960-66	P N Pirie
1948-50	W K Pearson	1966-67	R A Brown
1950-55	H Coates	1968-70	K G Fitzgerald
1955-57	R H A Staniforth	1970-71	R Lewis

(In 1968-69 K G Fitzgerald also produced BMC Newsletters. In 1970 a BMC Newsletter was produced by Mrs Audrey Salkeld.)

MOUNTAINEERING ASSISTANT EDITOR

1945-46	J M Baron	1950-51	Mrs F Solari
1947-49	R S S Wood		

MOUNTAINEERING ASSISTANT EDITOR (Printing)

1947-50	Mrs S L S Thomas

MOUNTAINEERING ASSISTANT EDITOR (Sales)

1949-53	H C Parker	1959-63	P J R Vereker
1953	A B Whiteley	1964-67	G E Green
1954-55	J M Ramsay	1967-69	W R Neate
1956-58	H Coates		

MOUNTAINEERING ASSISTANT EDITOR (Advertising)

1947-50	Dr S L S Thomas	1954-58	R H A Stainforth
1950	H McArthur	1958-59	D Aldridge
1951-52	Mrs F Solari	1960-65	Dr J H P Tynan
1952-53	R W Clark		

MOUNTAINEERING ASSISTANT MANAGER

1966-70	Dr J H P Tynan

MOUNTAINEERING TREASURER

1947-48	A E Rideout	1964-66	G E Green
1949-52	Mrs F Solari	1967-69	W R Neate
1952-55	T T Hardwick	1969-70	R Lewis
1955-59	H Coats	1971	J E Crewe
1959-63	P J R Vereker		

Mountaineering was replaced by *Mountain Life* in 1972.

EDITOR of *MOUNTAIN LIFE*
1972-73   B L Bedford (when published by West Col)
1973   A J J Moulam (when published by West Col)
1973-75   C W Brasher (when published by Mountain Life Ltd)
1973-75   J S Cleare (when published by Mountain Life Ltd)

TREASURER
1972-73   J E Crewe
Mountain Life incorporated in *Climber and Rambler* in 1976.
The BMC section in *Climber and Rambler* was replaced by a section in *High* in 1985.

PROFESSIONAL STAFF
General Secretary
1974-89   D D Gray
1989-95   D W Walker
1995-   R Payne

National Officer

1972-74	D D Gray	1981-86	M Hutchinson
1975-77	P D Boardman	1986-89	A Fanshawe
1978-80	A MacIntyre	1989-95	R Payne
		1995-	A MacNae

Administrative Officer
1973-75   Capt H V Gilpin
1975-77   F A Smith

Access & Conservation Officer
1979-80   M Hutchinson (part-time)
1981-86   M Hutchinson (in conjunction with National Officer's job)
1987-93   W Wright
1993-   J Barlow

Access Liaison Officer		Technical Assistant (later Technical Officer)	
1993-96	Kath Pyke	1983-86 I Dunn	

Training Administrator (joint BMC/MLTB)
1981-89   C Dodd
1989-94   I Peter
1995-   A Last

Development Officer
1993-95   H Harris

South-West Development Officer
1995-   I Parnell

Assistant Secretary (professional/Office Manager)
1945-62   Miss Corby
1962-63   Miss McPeake
1963-66   Miss C M Ramsay (loaned from AC part-time)
1966-68   Mrs J A Jackson (full-time)
1968-70   Miss C Robertson
1970-71   Miss S MacMillan
1971   Miss P Mathew
1971-73   Miss C Robertson
1973   Miss V Cohen
1973-74   Miss J Hall
1974-84   Mrs R Hallam
1985-89   Miss L Smithson
1989-91   Miss J Nicholson
1991-92   Miss H Berry
1992-93   Miss J Nicholson
1993-95   Mrs K Brown

Membership Services Co-ordinator
1995-   Ms E Guest

Marketing Co-ordinator
1995-   Mrs K Brown

Finance Co-ordinator
1995-   A Heron

Associate Members of the BMC

Climbing Walls
The Warehouse, Undercover Rock Company.

Local Authority
Avon Community Leisure Department, Blue Peris Mountain Centre, Cambridgeshire County Council, Cheshire Education Authority, Devon County Council, Glaisnock Outdoor Education Centre, Pencoed College, Rock-climbing Panel Selston Youth and Community Centre, Surrey Education Services, West Sussex County Council, Wiltshire County Council Education Department.

Mountain Rescue
Buxton Mountain Rescue Team, Calder Valley Search and Rescue Team, Kinder Mountain Rescue Team, Ogwen Valley Mountain Rescue Team.

Multi-Activity Groups
Alpine Action, Avon Outdoor Activities Centre, Blyth Jex Outdoor Pursuits Club, Bradford Pothole Club, Coven/Chasewater Outdoor Education Centre, GMMT Caswell Outdoor Pursuit Group, Garelochhead Outdoor Centre, Horsforth Fellandale Club, Kent County Constabulary, MacIntyre Adventure, Meet The Challenge, Milton Outward Bound, Mountain Ventures Ltd, Old Bromsgrovian Expedition Club, Portsmouth Youth Activities Committee, RAF Alconbury Services CC, SABC Clubs for Young People, SLUGS, Saltley Outdoor Pursuits Group, Sheffield University High Peak Society, Sherborne Area Youth Centre, Ski Club of Great Britain, Superchoice Adventure Ltd, Swaledale Outdoor Club, TSB Outdoor Sports Club, The Adventurers, The Old Vicarage Centre, Tyne & Wear Metropolitan Fire Brigade Sports and Social Club, University of Plymouth Students Union, Walsall Outdoor Pursuits, Walton Firs Scout Camp Site.

National Body
British Mountain Guides, Fire Service Sport and Athletic Association, Lake District National Park, Ramblers Association, Scottish National Ski Council, Scout Association Birmingham, Scout Association London, Welsh Scout Council.

Other

Barclays Bank Rambling and CC, Birmingham Teachers Mountaineering Association, Bootle Alternatives, Challenge Group Ltd, Foundry Climbing Association, Grimsby Fell Walking and CC, Highdown MC, Imperial College Exploration Board, Logica MC, Manchester University Hiking Club, University of West of England CC.

Outdoor Training/Expedition Organisers

APN Development Training, Adventure Dolphin, Allen Christer and Associates, Arcturus Expeditions Limited, Association of Heads of Outdoor Education Centres, Association of Mountaineering Instructors, Associated Training Centres Ltd, Bowles Mountaineering Outdoor Pursuits Centre, Bryntysilo Outdoor Centre, CWM Pennant Centre, Calshot Activities Centre, Calvert Trust Adventure Centre, Civilian Technical Training School Deeside, Civilian Technical Training School Barry, Consett YMCA Training Manager Ltd, Conway Centre, Cop Out, Crowden Outdoor Centre, Dartmoor Expeditions Centre, Dartmoor Training Centre, Dean Field Studies Centre, Derby Youth Service Outdoor Pursuits Centre, Derwent Hill Centre, Derwent Outdoor Pursuits, Dewsbury Adventure Camp and Camp Windermere, Fairbridge, Gay Outdoor Club, Ghyll Head Outdoor Pursuits Centre, HF Holidays Limited, Hagg Farm Field Study and Outdoor Pursuits Centre, Harlow Environment and Outdoor Education Centre, Joint Services Mountain Training Camp, Lindley Educational Trust, Longtown Centre, Low Mill Residential Young Peoples, Maes y Lade, Nant Bwlch yr Haearn, Nantmor Mountain Centre Association, Newlands Adventure Centre, Northants Association Youth Clubs and Action Club, Outward Bound Loch Eil, PGL Travel Ltd, Peak Training, Rhosygwaliou Outdoor Education Centre, Storey Arms Outdoor Education Centre, The Rock Centre, Thurrock Environmental and Outdoor Education Centre, Towerwood Education Centre, UKLF School of Adventure Training, Welsh Leisure Activities, West Malvern Outdoor Education Centre, West Pelton Activity Centre, Whickham Thorns Centre, White Hall Centre, Wirral Outdoor Pursuits, Woodlands Outdoor Pursuits Centre, Worldwide Outdoor Pursuits Centre, Worldwide Journeys and Expeditions, YMCA National Centre.

Overseas

New Zealand Mt Safety Council, Village Camps SA.

Trade

Allcord, Alpine Climbing and Ski Centre, Barn Door Shop, Bendcrete Climbing Walls, Berghaus Ltd, Climber Magazine, Crickhowell Adventure Gear, DB Mountainsport Ltd, DR Climbing Walls, Europa Sport, Field and Trek Ltd, First Ascent, Inglesport, Living Stone Climbing Walls Ltd, Lyon Equipment, Marshalls (Aberdeen) Ltd, Nick Estcourt Ski and Climb, North Cape (Scotland) Ltd, Outdoor Shop, RAB Down Equipment, Rockworks, Silva (UK) Ltd, Snow and Rock Sports Limited, Summitreks Ltd, Touchwood Sports, Trailwise, Trek Nepal Ltd, Troll Safety Equipment Ltd.

Youth/Schools/Groups

Abbotsholme School, Air Training Corps, Aston Students Guild, Atlantic College Coastguard Service, Bolton School, Boys Brigade MC, Bradfield College, Brockenhurst College, Broxbourne School, Cheltenham Bournside School, Community Links, Durham School Combined Cadet Force, Giggleswick School MC, Haberdashers Askes School, Harrow School Marmots Club, Herts Young Mariners Base, Highgate School Duke of Edinburgh Scheme, Ivanhoe Youth Centre, Kent Mountain Centre, King Henry VIII School, Kings School, Lancashire County Council, Latymer Upper School, Lowton High School Rambling Club, Marlborough College MC, Millfield School, Molineux Youth and Sports Centre, Moseley Park School, Northampton School for Boys, Oundle School MC, Portsmouth Grammar School, Queens College Taunton, South Glamorgan Scouts, St Albans School MC, St Bees School, St Davids College, St Pauls School MC, St Peters School, The College of St Mark and St John, The Guides Association, Trinity College, Westminster School, Weston Super Mare College, YHA Edale, Yorkshire Schools Exploring Society.

Clubs Affiliated to the BMC (1995)

Channel Islands
Jersey Rock CC, 25.

Lancashire and Cheshire
Acme Walkers, 23, Anabasis MC, 43, Caper Montis MC, 25, Chester MC, 235, Clitheroe MC, 69, Costain Climbers and Hill-walkers Club, 24, Craven MC, 33, Fylde MC, 174, Gwydyr Mountain Club, 58, Innominata Mountain Club, 66, Karabiner MC, 133, Lancashire Caving and CC, 220, Lancashire MC, 150, Lancaster MC, 25, Liverpool MC, 25, Liverpool University MC, 106, Liverpool University Open Air Club, 34, Manchester University MC, 43, Merseyside MC, 151, MC of Bury, 53, Oldham MC, 16, Pendle CC, 11, Powers MC, 25, Preston MC, 86, Rucksack Club, 264, Salford University Mountaineering Society, 38, Shadsworth Rambling and CC, 15, South Cheshire CC, 34, St Helens MC, 45, Summit MC, 32, University of Central Lancashire MC, 31, Vale Royal MC, 20, Vertigo CC, 22, Wayfarers, 219, Worden Ramblers, 25.

Lakes
Barrow MC, 64, Carlisle MC, 145, Eden Valley MC, 49, Exhull Mountaineering and Caving Club, 23, Over The Hill Club, 79, West Cumbria MC, 27.

London and South East
AGC MC, 27, Aldermaston MC, 32, Alton MC, 22, Anglian Fell and Rock Club, 63, Aylesbury CC, 74, Basingstoke CC, 68, Bedford MC, 70, Brampton Rock CC, 5, Cambridge Climbing and Caving Club, 30, Cambridge University MC, 129, Canterbury MC, 11, Caterpillar Walking Club, 74, Chelmsford MC, 36, Churchill College MC, 25, Clare Rats (Rock and Trek Society), 25, Cliffhangers CC, 34, Cragrats MC, 60, Cromwell MC, 25, Croydon MC, 58, Dacorum Adventure Club, 45, De Montford University (Bedford) MC, 43, East Grinstead CC, 40, Figure of Nine Club, 43, Flintstones CC, 20, Foster Wheeler Fellwalking Club, 25, Goats MC, 54, Green Lane MC, 30, Guildford MC, 76, Halton MC, 22, Hampshire Mountaineering Association, 24, Hastings Rock and Fell Club, 37, Hertfordshire MC, 68, Hillingdon MC, 36, Imperial College

MC, 25, Ipswich MC, 105, Kings College London MC, 28, Kingston University MC, 30, Kodak CC, 21, Lancing College Mountain Club, 25, Lensbury MC, 42, London Guildhall University MC, 25, London Hospital MC, 22, London MC, 225, Lord Mayor Treloar College CC, 21, Loughton MC, 26, Maidstone MC, 53, Marylebone MC, 104, Meadhurst MC, 44, Mid Sussex Crag and Peak, 22, Milton Keynes MC, 58, Mountain Activities Club – Harwell, 14, Natural History Museum MC, 31, Newbury Mountain Club, 25, Nimrod MC, 38, North Kingston Hill-walking Club, 25, North London MC, 230, Norwich Caving and CC, 22, Not the MLC MC, 15, Oxford Brookes University CC, 14, Oxford MC, 133, Oxford University MC, 25, Peterborough MC, 127, Reading MC, 73, Reading University MC, 25, Roche Rambling and Hill-walking Club, 37, Rockhoppers MC, 78, Royal Veterinary College MC, 25, Sandstone CC, 25, Selwyn College MC, 25, Slough MC, 53, Southbank University Mt and Outdoor Club, 27, South Essex CC, 23, Southampton Rats CC, 39, Southampton University MC, 131, Southern Trekking and MC, 76, St Albans City Campus Climbing and Hill-walking Club, 25, St Bartholomews and Royal London Alpine Club, 25, St Catherines Crag and Mountain Club, 15, St Marys Hospital MC, 75, Surbiton and Kingston MC, 34, Surrey Scout and Guide MC, 74, Sussex Mountaineering Federation, 130, Tuesday CC, 104, Tunbridge Wells MC, 59, University College London MC, 29, University of East Anglia Fell and Cave Club, 100, University of Essex MC, 25, University of Kent at Canterbury MC, 78, University of London MC, 25, University of Portsmouth MC, 25, University of Surrey MC, 17, University of Sussex MC, 109, Vectis Rock-climbing and Potholing Club, 27, Walkers and Novice Climbers Club (WANC), 25, Wellcome MC, 25, Wellington CC, 41, What Crisis CC, 24.

Midlands
Bewdley and District MC, 24, Birmingham University Fellwalkers, 75, Bowline CC, 102, Bromsgrove and Redditch MC, 56, Cave and Crag Club, 34, Ceunant MC, 150, Coleshill MC, 16, Congleton MC, 25, Coventry MC, 84, Coventry University Mountaineering Society, 28, Crewe and Alsager College MC, 63, De Montford University (Leics) Caving and Mountaineering Club, 25, Derbyshire Pennine Club, 55, Five Towns Mountaineers, 20, Hinckley MC, 61, John Clare MC, 28, Keele University MC, 44, Leicester University MC, 25, Leicester ML Association, 22, Lichfield MC, 22, Loughborough Students MC, 91, Mercian MC, 96, Midland Association of Mountaineers, 492, Mountain Club – Stafford, 52, Ounsdale MC, 53, Pint and Peak MC, 25, Potteries

CC, 19, Rugby MC, 35, Shrewsbury MC, 50, Skyline MC, 21, Solihull MC, 25, Staffordshire Police MC, 24, Staffordshire University CC, 25, Staffordshire University MC, 25, University of Birmingham MC, 29, University of Wolverhampton CC, 20, Walsall MC, 21, Warwick CC, 56, Warwick University MC, 10, Wellingborough MC, 112, Wolverhampton MC, 46, Worcester MC, 38, Wrekin MC, 93, Yeti Club, 29.

National
ABMSAC, 266, Achille Ratti CC, 559, Alpine Club, 1091, Army Mountaineering Association, 1105, British Airways Fellwalking and Mountaineering Section, 52, Camping and Caravanning Club – Mountaineering Section, 37, Chamois MC, 181, Christian Rock and Mountain Club, 91, Climbers' Club, 931, Eagle Ski Club, 131, Fell and Rock CC, 820, Gentian Club, 118, Ibex, 232, Junior MC of Scotland, 44, Meteorological Office MC, 27, North British Outdoor Team, 26, Open University Mountaineering Society, 82, Pinnacle Club, 142, Red Rope, 649, Royal Air Force Mountaineering Association, 162, Royal Navy and Royal Marines MC, 291, University of London Graduate MC, 251.

North East
Cleveland MC, 183, Darlington Outdoor Club, 15, Durham University MC, 25, Newcastle Outdoor Activities Club, 22, Newcastle University MC, 68, Northumbrian MC, 195, Sunderland MC, 40, Tyne Valley Climbers, 31, UEA Rock-climbing and MC, 56, University of Northumbria MC, 25, University of Teeside Rock CC, 25, Wanneys CC, 40.

Peak
Arête MC, 25, Barnsley MC, 64, Buxton MC, 43, Castle MC, 119, Derby MC, 24, Derwent MC, 36, GPT Sports & Social Club – Mountaineering Section, 31, High Peak Climbing Group, 35, Kodak Outdoor Pursuits Society, 20, Lincoln MC, 42, Lincolnshire Police Cadets Mountain Club, 25, Munro-pineapple Society Nottingham University, 117, Mynydd CC, 185, Nottingham Rock and Heather Club, 39, Nottingham Schools Climbing and Rambling Association, 40, Nottingham University Explorers Club, 79, Oread MC, 41, Peak CC, 28, Phoenix MC, 34, Polaris MC, 60, Sheffield University MC, 23, Sphinx MC, 23, Tricouni Club, 13.

South West and Southern

Avon MC, 71, Bath City MC, 22, Bath University MC, 114, Cerberus Spelaeological Society – SIG, 14, Clingons CC, 43, Dockyard Ventures, 25, Exeter University CC, 38, Exploration Group of North Somerset, 57, Forest of Dean Hill-walkers, 24, Gloucestershire MC, 79, Harper Outdoor Pursuits Club, 33, Hereford Mountain Club, 23, Lands End CC, 56, Malvern MC, 20, Royal Agricultural College CC, 18, SWEB Mountaineering and Outdoor Pursuits Section, 27, South Devon MC, 63, Stoke Damerel CC, 50, Swindon MC, 92, Thames Valley CC, 40, University of West of England Mountaineering and Hill-walking Club, 25, University of Bristol MC, 52, University of Plymouth MC, 81, Wessex MC, 235, Yeovil MC, 23.

Wales

Aberystwyth MC (University of Wales, 25, Afan MC, 20, Bangor University Mountaineering Society, 130, Clwb Mynydda Cymru, 184, Clwyd MC, 76, G S Exiles MC, 40, Gwent MC, 110, MC of North Wales, 120, Pembrokeshire CC, 21, Prestatyn High School MC, 27, South Wales MC, 71, University College of Swansea MC, 101.

Yorkshire and Humberside

Bridlington Walking and CC, 28, Calderdale MC, 26, Doncaster MC, 18, East Yorkshire Mountaineering and CC, 24, Gritstone Club, 106, Hull University MC, 20, Leeds MC, 69, Lindsey CC, 37, Mountain Sports Club – TASC, 25, Off Vertical Outdoor Pursuits, 20, Scunthorpe MC, 25, Vibram MC, 55, York Alpine Club, 49, York MC, 22, Yorkshire MC, 151, Yorkshire Ramblers Club, 186.

The Alpine Club Involvement

In the aftermath of the Great War a recuperating climber with great vision, who it must be remembered had just lost a leg, had ample time to reflect on life's priorities and the part which mountaineering had to play in the greater scheme of things. He had started rock-climbing while at Trinity College, Cambridge (1895-1898) but his thinking on mountains was closely linked to his connection with the famous Trevelyan family with whom he spent a great deal of his time at their country seat in Northumberland – and it must be remembered that the previous generation of their families had close Alpine links as well. Certainly Charles Trevelyan made two spirited attempts to get a Bill passed which would allow legal access to the British mountains.

In a letter (dated 1 March 1920) Geoffrey Winthrop Young made a sweeping proposal that there should be a national body to represent the Mountaineering, Climbing and Rambling clubs of Great Britain. This lengthy and well-reasoned letter finally surfaced in the Climbers' Club Bulletin of January 1921. Summing up Young stressed:

'Finally, I would make a very earnest appeal to all members of British Clubs to recognise that the renascence of our Associations gives to our generation a possibly unique opportunity. Some of our Clubs have local and climbing advantages, others have civic and social advantages. All have a legitimate pride in their own flourishing independence. But it is our responsibility to think now not only of our exclusive amenities or of our local interests, but of the future of mountain climbing in this country as the finest, sanest tradition which we possess, and which it is our privilege to hand on to the next, very different, generation ...

... We need no reminder that, below our Club designations and above our wholesome rivalries, we are all fellow mountaineers united by a bond that gives us an almost affectionate responsibility not only for the members of any small community to which we may belong, but for all other climbers or potential climbers, however distant from us in space or time.'

A response followed with comments such as, 'To what extent an amalgamation of some or more of the mountaineering clubs of Great Britain is either possible or desirable is a question upon which opinions may very well differ'. Reading between the lines there were fears that local clubs might lose their individuality. It was however admitted that:

> *'Again, questions from time to time arise of general interest to the whole body of climbers in Great Britain, on which any individual club can only give an individual opinion and can only bring to bear an individual influence. If it were possible, on such questions, to present the collective opinion and the collective influence of the whole body of British climbers, considerably more effective work could be performed.'*

Time passed, and the issue was not brought up again until 6 June 1922 when there was a general Meeting of the Alpine Club with Professor Norman Collie in the Chair. It appears that Winthrop Young had primed the Vice-President, Godfrey A. Solly to invite the Alpine Club to join the Advisory Council of British Mountaineering Clubs. After giving a general outline of the plan Solly moved that the invitation be accepted. The motion, seconded by Winthrop Young, was carried *nem. con.*

The scheme did get off the ground at that time, as is shown by bits of evidence. For example a note of 1924 in the SMC Journal states that Goggs and Unna were to represent the SMC at any meeting of the Advisory Council of the British Mountaineering Clubs. Another extract from 1925 from the Advisory Council asked the SMC (Goggs) and the Rucksack Club (Morley Wood) for their views on the proposed Access to Mountains Bill. It appears that although discussions did take place throughout Britain the Council drifted into non-existence.

Sadly, Winthrop Young was a man before his time and his proposals had to wait another twenty years before another World War could provoke people to consider in which direction they wished to go. Nevertheless Young did provoke controversy within the Alpine Club but this did not prevent him from becoming Vice-President in 1938 and then President in 1941. In C.A. Elliott's obituary of G.W.Y. (Vol. LXIV, A.J., May 1959) he clearly states that:

> *'As President he was confronted by two major problems. First he had to keep the Club not merely in being during the war years but actively in being, and this with the help of Donkin, the Honorary Secretary, he most successfully achieved by increasing the number of meetings, by organising Alpine Club meets in Wales and the Lakes, and by welcoming foreign mountaineers who were in England. Secondly, he had to meet the situation arising from the already rapid growth in the number of British climbers and their probable need for expert guidance, and also from the pressing demands for help and advice from Government Departments and others who were concerned with the uses of mountaineering for warfare or education. It was to deal with these developments that he took the leading part in forming and fostering, under the aegis of the Alpine Club, the British*

Mountaineering Council, representative of virtually all British clubs, and whenever need should arise, to give expert advice or to speak in the name of British climbers.'

The problem was that the Alpine Club had declined as a force to be reckoned with since Victorian times and was in no position to give expert advice which might help the war effort. It appears that Winthrop Young seized the opportunity to put forward a package which would incorporate not only his own precious ideals but also the more urgent needs of a country at war.

In his wartime Valedictory Address, read before the Alpine Club on 7 December 1943 Geoffrey Winthrop Young significantly stated that:

'The Alpine Club has a responsibility to mountaineering in general, one given to it by its origin as the first mountain organisation, by its Constitution, and by the historic position with which it has become invested by public opinion: a responsibility for our mountaineers, for their tradition and guidance, and for the home mountains which they frequent, their scenic protection and due control. They decided that it falls properly to us, to take the lead in promoting a common policy and a single and authoritative mountaineering voice, in all matters affecting our own mountain regions and the climbing in them; and that it no less belongs to our province, to improve our machinery and assemble our experience, the better to give assistance and guidance in all more distant exploration. As a first step, we have invited the leading climbing clubs in our islands to send representatives to meet ours, in February, 1944 to consider, under the chairmanship of our President, how best we may constitute a joint Standing Advisory Committee on mountaineering. We trust that this Committee when constituted will take into its purview all the problems as they arise which concern our mountain areas or the well being of our climbers while in the hills; and that they will make recommendations to our several clubs such as will enable joint and responsible action to be taken.

Secondly, with the valuable co-operation of the Climbers' Club, we are putting in hand an elementary guide to hill walking and scrambling, such as, when once our intercommunication of organisations is in being, can inform and bring some discretion into the influx of ordered and untutored scramblers at present flooding in rapidly increasing numbers over our crags, with ever attendant danger to themselves and resultant tragic nuisance to the local inhabitants.

Thirdly, we are offering our services or those of the Standing Advisory Committee when formed, as the responsible consultative mountaineering body, in the event of bringing of all our mountain districts under a National Parks scheme.

Fourthly, our widening of policy has coincided almost startlingly with an invitation from the Director of the Armed Cadet Force, Lord Bridgeman, and the Inspector of Physical Training to the War Office, Colonel Wand-Tetley, to accept the affiliation of the Army Cadet Force in all that affects its adoption of mountain climbing as a 'peak' subject for its cadets: to appoint our representatives at its H.Q., and to nominate instructors to organise the experimental camp and to design the courses.'

Winthrop Young's successor was the very able politician Leo Amery who had served in the House of Commons for 34 consecutive years, during which time he had been First Lord of the Admiralty, Secretary of State for the Colonies and finally as Secretary of State for India and Burma. Two letters which have survived give some indication of the talks which were taking place behind the scenes.

India Office Whitehall
30th December 1943

My Dear Geoffrey,

I was most interested to read Wedderburn's letter. Some time ago Lovat himself came to see me, very anxious that their mountaineering training should not be wasted, and I had some talk with the C.I.G.S. [Chief of Imperial General Staff] about it, but had never heard how things had actually developed. What I did urge was that they should be sent to Italy for use in the Abruzzi and it may be that Wedderburn is there.

I like your message and am delighted to be associated with it.

Yours ever,
Leo Amery

7 January 1944

My Dear Geoffrey,

I have just had a long talk with the C.I.G.S. who is genuinely keen on the whole subject of Mountain Warfare and is I think quite well disposed to the idea of the War Office consulting with a small advisory Committee of the A.C. on Mountain Warfare problems. He is going to consult with his people and let me know if he can before the meeting on the 10th.

Meanwhile, I should be glad of your views as to who might be suitable members of the A.C.

a) for such an Advisory Committee here,

b) for the instructional staff of a School of Mountain Warfare to be set up in the Apennines as soon as we can get another 20 miles on (After all if we can get to Pescara the whole Majella Massif ought to be in our hands together with the skiing centre of Rocca Rasa),

   c) of other members who might be roped in for actual work with troops whether for combatant purposes or for organising Italian mountain porters etc.

Yours ever,
Leo Amery

The following extracts from the Alpine Journal shed light on the next series of events which lead up to the formation of the BMC as well as indicating some of the pivotal figures who were involved at that time.

THE STANDING ADVISORY COMMITTEE ON MOUNTAINEERING

The Inaugural Conference was held at the Alpine Club, on February 5, 1944. Those present were:
I.C. Aitchison (Ski Club of Great Britain),
J.E.Q. Barford (Climbers' Club),
G.L. Bartrum (Alpine Club),
Wing Commander E.B. Beauman (Alpine Ski Club),
C. Chubb (Yorkshire Ramblers' Club),
F. Lawson Cook (F.R.C.C.),
N.R. Davis (Y.R.C.),
Miss Dolling (Ladies' Alpine Club),
Bryan Donkin (Alpine Club),
Dr. J.M. Edwards (Climbers' Club),
Dr. Wilson Hey (Rucksack Club),
John Hirst (Rucksack Club),
Robert Jeffrey (Scottish Mountaineering Club),
Mrs. Worsley Leech (Pinnacle Club),
C.T. Lehmann (Midland Association of Mountaineers),
C. Scott Lindsay (Alpine Ski Club),
Arnold Lunn (Ski Club of Great Britain),
Mrs. N.E. Morin (Ladies' Alpine Club),
Major T.U.L.S. O'Connor (Alpine Ski Club),
H.L. Roberts (Wayfarers' Club)
P.J.H. Unna (S.M.C.),
Graham Wilson (F.R.C.C.),
G. Winthrop Young (Alpine Club).

In the unavoidable absence of L.S. Amery, President of the Alpine Club, and H. McRobert, Senior Vice-President, G.L. Bartrum, Vice-President, took the chair and opened the meeting. He conveyed Mr. Amery's message of very sincere regret that he could not be present.

He asked Mr. Geoffrey Winthrop Young to address the meeting. Mr. Winthrop Young described how the necessity for such an organisation as the proposed Standing Advisory Committee had grown more urgent and more generally apparent as the war proceeded. He contrasted the limited assistance and advice to our war departments which we had been able to give to their Services.

A central organisation was needed to act as a clearing house for advice and personnel for Service Departments, and also to speak in the name of all mountaineers and climbers in this country on matters affecting the appearance and usage of mountain country, such as power schemes, deforestation, and the location of industry.

Thirdly, in view of the great increase in hill walking and climbing outside the Clubs it was essential that means should be devised for passing on our own special experience and advice to the newcomers. This could best be done through a central body.

Fourthly, during the war, hill walking and climbing had been used in military training on a very large scale and more recently it had been introduced into pre-service training. The Army Cadet Force had asked officially for assistance in this training. Further requests had been received from industry, shipping lines, and educational authorities. It was necessary to co-ordinate all this work through a central authority. He had, therefore, suggested this conference so that, if agreement could be reached, some collective organisation could be set up to deal with these matters, supported by the authority, help and advice of all British Mountaineering Clubs.

The following shall be asked to serve on the ad hoc Committee, who shall have power to co-opt:

The Rt.Hon. L.S. Amery	J.E.Q. Barford	G.L. Bartrum
Bryan Donkin	Robert Jeffrey	C.T. Lehmann
Mrs Worsley Leech	Arnold Lunn	Mrs N.E. Morin
Maj. T.U.L.S. O'Connor	A.S. Pigott	H.L. Roberts
W.M. Roberts	Graham Wilson	G. Winthrop Young

A General Meeting of the Alpine Club was held in the Hall, 74 South Audley Street, London, W.1, on Saturday March 4, 1944, at 6 p.m., The Rt. Hon. L.S. Amery, President in the Chair.

The President made a statement concerning the formation of a Standing Advisory Committee on Mountaineering, which had been affected since the Club last met. Delegates from about 10 kindred clubs had met in conference and agreed in principle on the advisability of the formation of such a Standing Advisory Committee, whose object would be to give effect to a common policy on all matters in which their respective clubs are jointly interested. This Committee had met for the first time that afternoon. The President also mentioned that the Club had been approached by the War Office in the matter of training selected members of the Army Cadet Force in rock climbing and mountaineering. The Committee had nominated what is to be known as the Pre-service Advisory Sub-committee to deal with these matters.

* * * *

The Annual General Meeting of the Alpine Club was held in the Hall, South Audley Street, London, W.1, on Tuesday, December 5, 1944, at 6 p.m., the Rt. Hon. L.S. Amery, M.P., President, in the Chair.

The President informed the meeting that the inaugural meeting of the British Mountaineering Council took place at the Alpine Club on December 2, 1944, when 32 representatives of 23 clubs, representing about 7,000 mountaineers, were present.

Concerning the British Mountaineering Council the President referred to a letter he had received from J.E.C. Eaton and eleven other members suggesting that the present scheme was launched in the name of the Alpine Club on November 10, 1943, and that this took place without the Committee having been consulted; further, that this project had not so far been brought before the members at a General Meeting for their approval. The President read his reply to Mr. Eaton and the other members, and said that copies would be available in the Secretary's office for the information and perusal of members.

It was clear that a revolt had started and one can imagine the consternation which swept through the club. On the one hand were the progressives trying to make sweeping changes. On the other hand there were those who were worried that a new body might steal the thunder and prestige of the Alpine Club. The old guard members with Strutt at the helm were ready to fight any action. Then of course there was the fiefdom of the S.M.C. north of the Border. In no way did they want their authority to be usurped. The clans were about to rise and with a hearty shout the claymore was quickly brandished. A copy of a letter to the President of the Alpine Club, dated 21 January 1945 reads as follows:

Dear Amery, As the circumstances surrounding the formation of the British Mountaineering Council give rise to considerable concern, we think it well to place them on record:

(1) A similar project was brought forward by the Climbers' Club about twenty years ago, and the Alpine Club was invited to join. The committee of the Alpine Club decided that this was a question for the general meeting and at a general meeting it was agreed that the club should join. For reasons which are immaterial now, the scheme proved abortive.

(2) The present scheme was launched in the name of the Alpine Club on 10th November, 1943; and we understand that this took place without the committee of the Alpine Club having been consulted. To this date, the general meeting of the Alpine Club has not been asked for approval.

There can be no doubt that the matter must eventually be discussed at a general meeting, for the committee is merely charged with the management, as distinct from the policy of the club. When such discussion takes place, grave objections to the scheme are certain to be brought forward; and it is therefore suggested that the various clubs which have joined the council, or have been asked to do so, ought to be informed without delay that any part presumed to be taken by the Alpine Club is, as yet, unauthorised.

Copies of the above have been signed by:
J.M. Davidson (ex-Pres., Yorkshire Ramblers' & Wayfarers'),
W. Garden (ex-Pres., SMC & Cairngorm Club),
G.T. Glover (ex-Pres., SMC),
Alexander Harrison (ex-V-P, SMC)
W.N. Ling (ex-V-P, A.C., ex-Pres., SMC),
H MacRobert (ex-V-P, A.C., ex-Pres., SMC)
J.A. Parker (ex-Pres., SMC & Cairngorm Club),
Sydney Spencer (ex-V-P. & ex-Hon. Sec. A.C.),
E.L. Strutt (ex-Pres., A.C.),
P.J.H. Unna (ex-Pres., SMC),
C.F. Meade (ex-V-P., A.C.).

Yours sincerely,
J.E.C. Eaton

No doubt Amery and Winthrop Young quickly put their heads together to head off the attack but Amery's skilful response only took a few days to be delivered.

INDIA OFFICE
2 February, 1945

My dear Eaton,

I have to acknowledge the letter sent by you on January 22nd on behalf of yourself and eleven other members of the Club with regard to the formation of the British Mountaineering Council.

In that letter it stated that the present scheme was launched in the name of the Alpine Club on November 10th, 1943, and that you understand that this took place without the Committee of the Alpine Club having been consulted, and that the General Meeting of the Club has not been asked for its approval up to this time.

I have now had time to look into the matter, and find that the question was raised by my predecessor, Winthrop Young, at a meeting of the Committee on April 6th, 1943 (at which both MacRobert and Strutt were present), in the shape of a memorandum on 'Inter-Club Relationships'.

Winthrop Young's memorandum was approved in principle by the Committee on June 8th, 1943, and it was decided to form a sub-committee to consider and report such action as might be recommended in order to achieve the objects of the memorandum. (Strutt was at the meeting.)

At the meeting of the Committee on October 2nd, 1943, the Honorary Secretary reported that the External Affairs Sub-Committee, appointed at the meeting of June 8th, recommended a Standing Advisory Committee on Mountaineering should be set up. As an initial step, they recommended consultation with a few of the larger British Mountaineering Clubs on the outlines of the scheme. This proposed action was approved by the Committee. (Colonel Strutt was present.)

At the Committee Meeting of November 30th, 1943; the Secretary reported that invitations to join a conference had been issued to certain Clubs (presumably this is the 'launching' of the scheme referred to in your letter), and that those Clubs had promised to refer the matter to their Committees. I understand that throughout the discussion of the matter at these various meetings of the Committee the proposals in question were warmly supported by the Committee.

The whole matter was brought before the General Meeting of the Club on December 7th, 1943, by Geoffrey Young in his valedictory address (A.J. 54, p.232). In this he clearly stated that the Committee had decided to take action 'to invite the leading climbing Clubs in our islands to send representatives to meet ours in February, 1944, to consider ... how best we may constitute a Joint Standing Advisory Committee on Mountaineering'. The next public announcement of the action taken by the Committee was reported by myself to the General Meeting on March

Brian Donkin

Jack Longland

Geoffrey Young

John Barford

Leo Amery

THE ALPINE CLUB DOGFIGHT A classic establishment political struggle was fought over the BMC's inception. Those in favour (*above*) were led by the distinguished politician Leo Amery (whose 'In the name of God, go!' speech had toppled the Chamberlain administration in the darkest days of the war). They were opposed by a powerful AC/SMC cabal (*below*) led by the ex-Intelligence Officer J.E.C. Eaton and the tenacious Colonel Edward Strutt. Anxiety that the BMC would usurp the status and influence of the major clubs seemed to be the underlying reason for the opposition.

Teddy Eaton

Edward Strutt

Sydney Spencer

Harry MacRobert

Joseph Davidson

Charles Meade

Willie Ling and George Glover

4th, 1944, when I reported that delegates from some ten kindred Clubs had met in conference and agreed in principle on the advisability of the formation of a Standing Advisory Committee. In A.J. 54, pp. 305-6, there is a full report of the events leading to the invitation to kindred Clubs to join the preliminary conference, and this clearly states that this was done with the full agreement of the Committee. In the same issue, pp. 318-21, it is stated that the inaugural conference unanimously agreed a number of motions which subsequently resulted in the formation of the British Mountaineering Council. The next publication to the Club of the action taken by the Committee was contained in the Club Circular dated October 28th, 1944, in a note stating that the constitution of the proposed British Mountaineering Council had been examined and approved by the Committee, and that the members interested might examine the constitution, copies of which had been deposited at the Club. Lastly, at the Annual General Meeting of December 5th, 1944, I informed the meeting that the inaugural meeting of the Council had taken place at the Club on December 2nd, when 32 representatives of 23 Clubs, representing about 7,000 mountaineers, were present. After describing briefly the business transacted, I said, " ... in conclusion it may be said that the inaugural meeting of the British Mountaineering Council showed clearly that the initiative of the Club in taking the lead in forming the BMC has been rewarded by the active and interested support and encouragement of practically all the active and progressive mountaineering Clubs in this country".

You will I think agree, in view of the above facts, that the matter was fully before the Committee for nearly two years, and before the Club as a whole, both at the Meetings, by the reports in the A.J., and in the Club Circular, for over a year before you wrote your letter, and that there were during this time abundant opportunities for those members who disagreed with the policy to ventilate their disagreement on the Committee or at Meetings or, indeed, to have called upon a special General meeting under Rules 17 and 18.

You mention in your letter that a similar project was brought forward by the Climbers' Club about twenty years ago and that the Alpine Club was invited to join, the Committee deciding that this was a question for a General Meeting which subsequently agreed that the Club should join though the scheme for reasons now immaterial, proved abortive. I understand from Winthrop Young that in appointing representatives and establishing this 'abortive' Committee to come into existence, action was taken by the Committee of the Alpine Club, and that this action was reported in the normal way to the Meeting, without any formal vote or resolution of the Club being taken.

I might add that similarly the action of the Committee in co-operating with the Royal Geographical Society in connection with the Everest Expedition was reported to the Club, and the Club kept duly informed, but that no formal resolution of approval was taken.

You draw in your letter a distinction between the duties of the Committee as charged with the management, as distinct from the policy of the Club. It seems to me, without endeavouring to lay down a definition as to where the management ends and policy begins, that the Policy of the Club is clearly outlined in its object as defined in Rule 2, namely 'the promotion of good fellowship among mountaineers; of mountain climbing and mountain exploration throughout the world, and of better knowledge of the mountains through literature, science and art'. The Club has for very good reasons confined its actual membership to those who have attained a certain definite standard of mountaineering efficiency. The natural way, therefore, for the Committee to fulfil the main object of the Club would seem to be, on the one hand, as in the case of our co-operation with the Royal Geographic Society, in close association with bodies concerned with exploration and, on the other hand, in bringing about friendly co-operation and the promotion of good fellowship with all other bodies genuinely connected with mountaineering. In thus carrying out the objects of the Club it has naturally been the duty of the Committee to keep the Club as a whole informed of any developments, and it has always been open to members of the Club to express their dissent if they thought that the Committee had in any way misconstrued their duties, or had taken action inconsistent with the objects of the Club as defined in the constitution. That opportunity was not taken at any stage during the formation of the British Mountaineering Council, nor were any of the unspecified 'grave objections' referred to in your letter raised at any time. It seems to me somewhat curious, therefore, that it should now be suggested that the various Clubs which have joined the Council, or have been asked to do so, should be informed that 'any part presumed to be taken by the A.C. is, as yet, unauthorised'.

Yours sincerely,
L.S. Amery

Amery, being a smooth politician, had marshalled his facts well and had cleverly tried to undermine the opposition in one fell swoop. However, despite Amery's less than subtle attempts to point out that Strutt certainly knew exactly what was going on, the opposition quickly regrouped and within three weeks were ready to deliver a second thrust which would formally try to find a chink in the armour of the formidable Young/Amery combination. The war in Europe might have been coming to a close, but the Scots were still thirsting for blood. Eaton then delivered the next salvo:

24 February, 1945

Dear Amery,

Thank you for your letter of 2nd February. The question of approval by the committee before 10th November, 1943, can best be settled by production of the entries in the agenda and minutes, dealing with the formal resolution.

2. You say that Young tells you that the 1922 scheme was not submitted to the general meeting. He actually seconded the formal resolution passed at the general meeting of 6th June, 1922 – see A.J., 34, p.506.

3. Although a precedent in which the committee is alleged to have acted incorrectly can scarcely be put forward as an excuse for incorrect action now, it is necessary, in fairness to former committees to point out that the second example you cite is also inaccurate. The part played by the A.C. committee in regard to Everest was all that could be desired; for not only did Norman Collie, who was President, obtain the formal approval of the general meeting at the first opportunity, but he also apologised for having to take some preliminary action as soon as the Royal Geographical Society had invited the A.C. to co-operate in the expedition, see A.J., 33, p.465.

4. You say that members had full information from Young's address, from the annual report, and from other particulars given in the A.J., but none of these announcements were submitted for the formal approval of the general meeting. Further, they indicated periodical changes in the scheme, but the most important one – change of the BMC from a purely advisory to an executive capacity. This was only disclosed by posting the BMC rules on the club notice board, at the end of last October.

5. This was the first BMC circular so posted. Copies of the earlier ones were sent to the secretaries of the other clubs, but none were even deposited at the Alpine Club for the inspection of members.

6. Thinking it peculiar that the A.C. committee had not adopted the ordinary procedure, Unna asked Bartrum, who was deputising for you at the SACOM committee meeting held in March, 1944, whether it was intended to obtain approval of the A.C. general meeting, and he said he did not know. To emphasise the point, Unna then asked the delegates of the various clubs whether they had power to act from their general meetings or committees. (One had authority from general meetings, two from committees, and the others none.) Thus the other clubs were warned,

through their delegates, that due authorisation from the A.C. general meeting had not been obtained.

7. We have acted at the proper time – when it became evident that you did not propose to ask the general meeting for the customary authorisation, and when definite information was forthcoming as to the scope of the BMC

8. The Alpine Club is recognised by the public, by Government departments, and by public bodies generally, as representatives of British mountaineering, and is expected to play its part. For instance, when it is consulted by a Government department, it is not expected to refer that department to a third party, as has been the case. And when a public body asks the club to appoint representatives, it is not expected that the power of appointment should be transferred to a third party, as has quite recently been done without the knowledge of the general meeting.

9. We may mention that it was largely on the ground that the Alpine Club should play the principal part, and that the scheme is bad because it involves the Alpine Club in an evasion of its responsibilities, that the principal Scottish clubs have refused to join the BMC; and that the Ski Club of Great Britain refused because it would not 'take any step which in effect would delegate any part of its authority to another body'. We appreciate that the Scottish clubs also took account of the fact that the rules almost completely eliminated Scottish representatives on the BMC committee, a defect which shows the impracticability of trying to set up a body of this cumbrous nature, consisting to date of no less than 23 clubs, with rules that will work satisfactorily.

10. Further, the decision to extend the scope of the BMC to the whole of the British Empire, taken at the BMC meeting held on 13th May, 1944, seems to have resulted in the Himalayan Club being admitted as a founder club, to the exclusion of the older Canadian, New Zealand, and South African ones. We quote this as another example that those responsibilities for promoting the BMC have failed to produce a rational scheme.

11. With regard to the last paragraph of your letter, there is no need to draw a hard and fast line between management and policy. So long as the committee bear in mind that in managing they are deputising for the general meeting, and that they are expected to act in accordance with the wishes of the general body of members, they will automatically bring any borderline case before the general meeting for decision.

12. As to the rule you quote, about the promotion of good fellowship among mountaineers, we think that all members will agree that the club has in the past, shown too little interest in climbing in Great Britain. If it takes steps to stimulate its own concern in that direction it will at the same time promote the good fellowship required. That might be

implemented by initiating some sort of conference of the various British clubs, under the management of the Alpine Club, and with advisory but not executive powers. By management being vested in the Alpine Club, and not in a committee such as that set up by the BMC, many of the difficulties in the latter body would be got over.

13. But our main point is that the present scheme involves the Alpine Club surrendering the position it holds in the mountaineering world, in the first place in Britain, and by corollary abroad, to the detriment of British mountaineering. It is on that ground that we say the scheme is bad.

Yours sincerely,

J.E.C. Eaton

(And approved by the other 11 members)

This letter was duly dissected clinically by the leading luminaries and to avoid further debate the President and Committee prepared a motion for the general meeting of 10 April 1945. This read as follows:

> 'This meeting confirms the action of the President and the Committee in taking the lead with other mountaineering clubs in this country in the formation of the British Mountaineering Council and approves the Committee's choice of officers and representatives on the Council, namely, President Mr. G. Winthrop Young; Hon. Secretary, Mr. J.E.Q. Barford; third representative Mr. Bryan Donkin.'

Eaton and Unna delivered a parting shot with an amendment to the motion:

> 'That whilst this meeting considers that the Alpine Club should take a more active interest in climbing in Britain than it has done in the past, it regrets that the President and Committee did not ask for prior approval of the steps they have taken in the formation of the British Mountaineering Council, and does not approve that body as at present constituted.'

The circular of 22nd March 1945 also pointed out that special recognition had been paid to the importance of the Scottish Mountaineering Club by the offer to give them the right to nominate the BMC Vice-President.

Despite the political manoeuvrings, however, the BMC continued to take its first faltering steps and began to gain momentum. After the war had finished it was interesting to look back through the eyes of L.S. Amery who had unwittingly been thrust into the hot seat, while Winthrop Young cleverly organised his troops for a new battle. He had seen his brainchild sink beneath the surface once before and this time there was to be no retreat.

It should be realised that not only was Amery a prominent figure in British politics but that at the end of the war he suffered a shattering blow. (His son was tried and hanged as a traitor for having made broadcasts as one of a team which included Lord Haw-Haw.) Amery's subsequent stoicism was breathtaking as he continued with his own life, maintaining great dignity. His Valedictory Address was eventually delivered before the Alpine Club on December 9, 1946. He began:

'*It is now three years since you did me the honour of electing me to the Presidency of the Club. I accepted, rejoicing in the thought that I had attained the summit of all mountaineering ambition, where I might repose in godlike ease aloft, in other words, take the Presidential armchair at your meetings and close your proceedings with a few well chosen words of thanks to the reader of the evening's paper. I was soon undeceived. A designing body of men, your then Committee, led by that archplotter, my predecessor, had for many months past been planning a revolution, and had fastened on me as one of the most respectable, essentially conservative and, above all, innocent-looking of your senior members, in order to see it through. I was to be set on the egg which they had laid and, in due course, by my proud maternal cluckings, to reassure all concerned that what had emerged from the shell was, indeed, a young phoenix and not an infant crocodile.*

There was no question of my figuring as a Napoleon to Geoffrey Young's Robespierre, or even as a Stalin to his Lenin. He was in no sense contemplating his own liquidation; the President of the British Mountaineering Council is, in fact, today a highly active force as well as a very tangible fact.

In any case, Geoffrey Young is a revolutionary of an essentially British type. It is characteristic of our British Constitution that all the most revolutionary stages in its development, from the Magna Carta to the Petition of Rights and the Statute of Westminster, have professed to be merely the restoration of ancient rights, or the assertion of universally accepted principles. Most of you here tonight will remember that eloquent Valedictory Address of Geoffrey's, so artlessly persuasive in its preparation of your minds for the shocks that would be coming ...

Accordingly on February 5, 1944, representatives of nearly a score of clubs met in this room to consider the formation of a Standing Advisory Committee on Mountaineering. Not only did this modest suggestion commend itself to the clubs concerned, but in the course of developing it they very soon found themselves led on to the creation of a more regularly constituted and permanent body in the shape of the British Mountaineering Council.

It was not unnatural that these developments should create apprehension in the minds of some of our members. It was feared, on the one hand, that we might be giving our endorsement to a movement which might peter out; on the other hand, that we might be creating something which would encroach upon the position and prestige of the Club itself. We enjoyed a vigorous debate on the subject in April 1944. The subsequent course of events has, I think, justified the confidence of the majority of the members present in the action of your Committee and has, I trust, allayed the anxieties expressed at the time. The British Mountaineering Council has certainly given every sign of increasing vitality and influence. It numbers over thirty clubs on its main body. There is a Scottish Committee on which a dozen Scottish clubs are represented, vigorous District Committees for the Lake Country, North Wales, and the Peak District, as well as Sub-Committees dealing with First Aid Equipment, Huts, and Publications.

In this last field its first significant effort was the sponsoring, as a Pelican Book, of Climbing in Britain, by John Barford, who is Secretary of the Council. The fact that this excellent little work will soon be in its second fifty thousand is a striking testimony to the volume of the popular interest in mountaineering which exists today. The mountaineering side of the location and organisation of National Parks was worked out by a small Sub-Committee in consultation with the clubs and District Committees and an agreed statement submitted to the Ministry of Town and Country Planning. The Council has successfully carried on in North Wales the series of meets in conjunction with the Central Council of Physical Recreation which we initiated, through G.A. Dummett's energy as organiser and instructor, in 1945, at Langdale.

It is in touch with the Boy Scouts Association, which has now included a Climber's Badge, with the Youth Hostel Association and with the County Educational Committees. It has also taken over from us the work of the Pre-Service Training Committee, providing instructors for a very successful Easter meet at Aviemore for the Scottish A.T.C. The Army, I am sorry to say, has for the time being found it impossible to continue the cadet camps which we inaugurated so successfully in 1944 and 1945. The Council has also been actively occupied in considering the problems of increasing and improving hut and bivouac accommodation, in the expansion of First Aid work, in working out a scheme for the registration and testing of professional guides, and with the study of rope and equipment. These are well worth while activities. Nor can it be said that they have in any way encroached upon the proper domain or authority of the Alpine Club, or in any way prejudiced our own specific life and character. On the other hand, as the President and Secretary of the British Mountaineering Council MUST be, and a majority of its members, somehow or other HAPPEN to be members of the Alpine Club, I am rather surprised that some suspicious Molotov has not yet discovered and denounced this flagrant instance of Alpine Club imperialism carried out by a group of fascist reactionaries emanating from South Audley Street.

We, for our part, can, I think, look forward with some confidence to a steadily increasing recruitment to our own ranks through the clubs that have thus been brought into closer and more understanding association with us. In any case, we have every reason to be grateful to Geoffrey Young, Bartrum, Barford and, indeed, to all those members of the Club who, through the British Mountaineering Council, are fulfilling the wider purposes for which this Club was first founded and are handing on to the ever growing rising generation of climbers the great tradition which our founders created and which we have been proud to maintain during the years between their pioneer age and the nation-wide movement of the new era.'

Compiled by Geoff Milburn (with help from the Alpine Club research team of Sheila Harrison (Secretary), Margaret Eccleston (Librarian), and Livia Gollancz (Archivist). Note: This was assembled before Jack Longland's *The Alpine Club Dogfight* (see page 280) was discovered.

The Alpine Club Dogfight

During May 1996 Nick Longland had a look through some of his father's efficiently filed papers and discovered a wealth of information from the 1940's. It is quite clear that, despite the war, lots of letters were being sent round the country to arrange army cadet training in the hills. Amongst Jack Longland's correspondence was a letter referring to the Standing Advisory Committee on Mountaineering, which had recently met. In it, John Barford noted rather wistfully:

9 February 1944

The SACOM seems to have got away to a pretty good start, although the Committee we have to start with has not many of the people who should be on it, Alan Hargreaves for instance.

Another literary gem which turned up related to early April 1945, prior to the forthcoming A.C. committee meeting. There was a lot happening behind the scenes as Young's supporters girded their loins for what was going to be a formidable battle of words. Young chose Jack Longland to champion the cause and one can gauge the degree of underlying feeling from the following letter, which Longland wrote to Tom Brocklebank:

6 April 1945

'Dear Tom,

Bryan Donkin has sent me a note enclosing his letter from Brigadier Bullen-Smith and almost at the same time Paul Sinker told me that you had jumped the claim and that you were running an Army Cadet Force course of your own at the end of this month.

I shall be very glad to know whether you and Peter Bicknell did, in fact, interview Bullen-Smith at the War Office and, if so, whether anything useful emerged. I don't want to occupy too many camps simultaneously, and at present I am not very clear what the party line is. I should not bother you, but have promised to speak on behalf of the committee at the A.C. meeting on the 10th April, in order to try and do down Eaton, Spencer, Strutt and the other ex-Everest rats who have crawled out of their holes.

I think, on general grounds, quite apart from the particular issue of the BMC, that these old enemies want smiting again, but it would be very embarrassing if I were to find myself in opposition to you, and I should like some reassurance on this point.

G.W.Y. has asked me to say something in my piece about the Army Cadet Force course at Llanberis, and the useful part which the Club played in bringing it about! But if this is likely to bring you to your feet with an indignant disclaimer, I shall have to leave that bit out. So will you please let me know what you think.

Yours etc.

It has always been known that there was no love lost between the two camps, and that many harsh words were spoken on the subject, but, over fifty years on, there is little concrete evidence in existence, and bland minutes are of little help. However, the carefully crafted speech, which Jack Longland delivered to the A.C. committee, has recently come to light, and can now be read in its entirety. There is no sense of pussyfooting about, as even the title clearly shows:

A C Dogfight, 10 April, 1945

'In supporting the motion of the President and Committee I find it difficult to reconcile with the amendment, the objections raised in Mr Eaton's two letters to the President. These distinguished mountaineers appear to have been in travail for an unprecedentedly long time and the result is this ridiculous mouse of an amendment. But it is a carefully contrived mechanical mouse, and worth taking to pieces for a moment. The authors of the amendment appear to have realised that they had small hope of persuading the club to agree with the serious charges made in the two letters : that the committee had been flouting the Club over a long period, that the club was giving away its birthright, and that the BMC was a wicked body which was unkind to the Scots. Turning from these extravaganzas to the amendments, we find two objections, pitched in a minor key:

1. Constitutional : already dealt with by the president. I only want to add one point :

The officers and Committee REPRESENT the club. They are not delegates with the duty of returning to a General Meeting for a mandate at every stage of a developing situation. To suggest that they should be bound hand and foot as delegates is no punctiliousness, nor even a conservative dislike of change. It is just plain anarchy. If members dislike the actions of their elected committee their remedy is plain: sack them and elect another committee. But to neglect this remedy and instead to promote a belated and calculated agitation against the serving officers and Committee is to borrow the technique made familiar by illegal strikes; of disowning your representatives, if their decisions do not happen to suit you personally. Having elected your officers and Committee you must trust them to be as jealous as you are yourself for the honour and future of the club. But I can't help thinking that the constitutional punctilios have been raised as a smoke-screen behind which the real attack is being deployed.

2. This is, bluntly, that the BMC is a bad thing, and that the CLUB OUGHT NOT TO HAVE ANYTHING TO DO WITH IT. Before trying to answer this, there is one point in the amendment to dispose of. The Club is invited to disapprove of that body "as at present constituted". Whoever expected the constitution of a new and rapidly developing organisation to be perfect and holeproof? The present constitution and rules provide a sensible and practical starting point by which urgently needed co-operation between the climbing clubs can be developed. The constitution is already under review for modification, and has already incorporated improvements suggested by the clubs. But to suggest that the club withdraws altogether because detailed points of constitution do not meet unanimous approval is to throw out this very urgently needed baby with its bath water. And it is a failure to realise that all such matters must be continually adjusted by natural compromise between the large number of interested parties.

But the main change with the amendment, and still more unhealthy, is that the BMC is a bad thing. I have had the opportunity of consulting a good many of our younger members, and I think I can in particular speak for those who are also members of the Climbers' Club, of which I have the honour to be President. These younger members are, I am convinced, not only emphatic that the BMC is a good thing, but also that its formation has been dangerously delayed and was long overdue. And here I want to say quite bluntly that the authors of the amendment, if their letters may be taken as evidence, are not living in the contemporary world of British mountaineering at all. proof of this is to be found throughout the letters but nowhere more than in the quite fantastic suggestion in para. 12 of the second letter of, 'initiating some sort of conference of the various British clubs under the management of the Alpine Club', whether this conference had only advisory powers or not (and the times call for an organisation which does not willingly consolidate [consider] itself in this way) the retort to the A.C. from the other clubs and from every single active climber in the country would be , "who made thee a Judge and a Ruler over us?"

The plain fact is that, in dissociating itself from any position of responsibility for climbing in this country (a fact which the authors of the amendment have the grace, somewhat vaguely, to deplore) the Club is virtually not regarded as an active and responsible force by the active members of the many other clubs. If the A.C. is to have a pre-eminent position, it must contrive to deserve it by associating with and taking the lead among all active and progressive forces which are working for the future of British climbing wherever it develops. Otherwise, the club will become a sadly under equipped social club for former Alpinists. I cannot overstate the importance of this. It is NOT a question of the Club maintaining its past prestige and reputation, but of taking the only possible steps to achieve a reputation, which is far more difficult to win among the multitudes of present day climbers than it was in the relatively select coterie in the days of Peaks, Passes and Glaciers, when the Club's great prestige was won by the activities of its members.

That is why the BMC is a crucial issue for the Club. The reputation and development of climbing as a sport is now in the hands of thousands and thousands of people who go regularly to the mountains to climb. On this alone the urgency of the need for some central co-ordinating and policy-making body could be based – and who else but the climbing clubs with their traditions of apprenticeship, safe climbing and consideration for others should initiate this? And what better body than the Alpine Club to take the lead, as it has done, in bringing them together. To refuse to act, or to act with the pettifogging caution bred by generations of Scottish attorneys (which is the spirit of the letter before us) is indeed to abdicate responsibility – and to leave the future of climbing, and of safeguarding our hills against the many threats that crowd on [exist in] them today, to the tender mercies of the uninitiated multitudes, and to allow those organisations whose members so much outnumber the climbing clubs but which have not had time or guidance to develop our good traditions.

In many important directions, the lead can only be given by a body such as the BMC – in preserving mountain amenities, in providing climbing literature, in co-ordinating first-aid and accident policy, in ensuring the provision of huts and hostels, and perhaps above all in guiding and training of young climbers.

In this the choice is between helping to ensure that future young generations do not miss the opportunities and the training that safe and well organised introduction to mountain climbing can uniquely give – or of shirking our responsibilities, and of allowing a great opportunity to pass. Service departments, cadet organisations, youth organisations, education authorities and the big rambling and Youth Hostel associations are all alike waiting for a lead. Already encouraging developments such as the Llanberis course have taken place, and others are under way. But the job is too big to be tackled by any one club (perhaps particularly the A.C.) and it needs the collective wisdom, leadership and resources of all the climbing clubs within the country, brought together via the BMC

The Pre-Service Training Sub-Committee of the Club has already done valuable work in starting these developments, but a much more widely representative body is needed and in this body the A.C. with its wisdom and resources can regain an honourable and leading position among all that is best in the British climbing world.

To withdraw now would

1. Forfeit the respect of the clubs and the younger climbers
2. Reduce the weight of the [reformation] of organised climbers with [mediation], service departments, LEAs and other bodies.

A last word about the letters leading to this amendment. In neither of them is there a spark of generous feeling, either of gratefulness for the fine and leading part which the Club has already played, through its officers and Committee, in bringing this urgently needed body into existence, or of awareness of the great opportunities which now lie before the BMC and this Club. Only by coming down into the arena, on level terms with the active British clubs, could the A.C. have enhanced its reputation, as it has undoubtedly done in the past two or three years.

Instead, over-generous sympathy is to be extended for Scottish nationalism – and in this context I find at best that my heart is curiously unwilling to bleed for Scottish woes. Instead I feel that the SMC (heavily opinionated in the righteousness to the letter) played a somewhat ignoble part in the negotiations leading up to the formation of the BMC – and one may be forgiven for thinking that a club which is quite unable to keep the younger and more active climbers within the club framework is scarcely the body to have any preponderant voice of shaping the future of climbing in this country.'

There seems little doubt that this carefully orchestrated broadside proved to be the final nail in the coffin for the uprising. The BMC was well and truly up and running.

Articles from *Mountaineering*

Some years ago the Editor of this publication received a parcel through the post. It contained a complete set of the BMC's magazine *Mountaineering*, from its last editor, Kevin Fitzgerald. Kevin had also included a prophetic note which said, "You may need these one day". The first two decades of *Mountaineering* contained some extremely interesting material that is not widely known. We have therefore made a selection of articles that collectively give a flavour of *Mountaineering*'s content. The preoccupation with equipment, technique and safety during the period is reflected in the article by Tarbuck.

The Editorial of September 1947 pointedly said:

'A constant question that is being asked by many climbers today is "What are we doing about Everest?" Many have read or heard about the intended exploits of Group Captain Bandit, but the plans of official circles have been wrapped in darkness. The stumbling block for all has been political permission to carry out an expedition in Tibet ... a big attempt could not be carried out secretly; in any case, the co-operation of the inhabitants is both desirable and necessary. What then is being done?'

A Charm of Routes (October 1948)

by Evelyn Worsley Leech

To define the indefinable is an ambitious aim and charm has always been an elusive quality to pin down on paper, yet since there have been sonnets to eyebrows, and since I live in a northern mill-town, I'll have a go!

The dull routes on mountains are plodded-up and forgotten as soon as may be, or remembered as a warning: the charming routes live on in fancy, bathed in a mellow sunshine often denied them in fact. To name the beads of this rosary is easy: to define their charm, more difficult. Is it the use of an unexpected line of weakness, perhaps? "Call that a line of weakness? I call that a line of strength," said my second sombrely, as I craned my neck in admiring reconnaissance.

Is it the delightful surprise of finding that God or Geology has allowed you the one rugosity without which the pitch could not go? The key to one of the Almscliff climbs is a sea-shell, and the other hidden holds discovered by desperately searching hands are too numerous to name.

There is a wall on the Engelhorn Zimilistock springing above the gloomy depths of Im Ten, reached by a Heaven-sent traversing ledge, and pitted after the first bravely optimistic stretch with neat holes for fingers and toes at the right intervals: I remember stopping half-way up to say, "It's worth coming out from England just to find this wall", and Bradley's answer: "Speaker always calls it 'the delectable wall' ".

Then there is the ingenuity of Knight's Moves, descending to ascend, the choice of the exposed step which leads to safety rather than the obvious chimney with the illusion of safety and the possibility of exhaustion. Traverses of rock faces seem always to exercise ingenuity, from the low-level Sylvan Traverse of the Milestone Buttress of Tryfan to that of Dow Crag and Scawfell Pinnacle Face. There are those routes that have a ruling characteristic, such as Rectory Chimneys on Ddysgl, each chimney entered part way up by a delicate traverse, so that the pleasure in making a continuation finish was doubled by the fact that our pitch had the characteristic approach.

Other routes charm by their variety: so varied that sometimes you feel you have sampled in one day all mountaineering in miniature. Into my mind float the North Climb on Pillar, Craig yr Ysfa's Great Gully, Longland's on Clogwyn Du'r Arddu, Direct on Glyder Fach. "It's got all it takes", we misapplied reverently.

Direct Routes also have the appeal of their directness: Mallory left his pipe on the Bowling Green on Lliwedd, so he went up the quickest way to fetch it – hence Mallory's Slab Route, short but very sweet; finding the guidebook that fell from the hip pocket during the ascent of the final pitch of Glyder Fach's Direct, lying beside the rucksacks at the foot of the climb, undamaged by the touch of a single rock; looking down from an exposed pitch high up on the Rannoch Wall at the party's discarded boots in the gully beneath.

There is the potent charm of the unexpected: the unexpected kindliness of nooks and crannies and belays. With what thankful heart I dropped down into the safe corner hidden behind the slab on the Grooved Arete of Tryfan that first time when the wind blew hard and I was young and inexperienced ... and the same heart grown older, beat as thankfully when I crept into the corner this Spring on a day when Winter's traces masked every hold on the slab and rendered even the corner less hospitable with banked snow. Those niches on Saint's Wall, willing to harbour sinners too! The rock-ring belay on the Javelin Buttress of Idwal Slabs: I appreciated its safeguard as I tiptoed up to victory, and as I abseiled down from it in defeat. The unexpected gift – for, though there is far more enjoyment in the actual climbing of the Cioch by the Direct or West, nothing will equal the memory of going up the Slab by the moderate route in shadow, and suddenly and unprepared, being greeted by that view of shining sea and fair isles. And that easiest of Dolomites that took to its wings in the dawn, because it was carpeted with sleeping ptarmigan. I have never been able to cook them since: their little white boots would rebuke me with a reminder of that day when we were all young together ... the day youngest of all.

Now the driving of a series of pitons into an otherwise unscalable wall fails to seduce me as do my leaders boots grinding into my collar bones; but the owner of the boots may redeem the situation by his wit or prowess. Besides, it may be my turn to stand on him one day, therefore I prefer giving a shoulder to hammering a piton, when such a choice is possible, and I cannot imagine ever wishing to number one of the Hammer and Nails variety in my Charm of Routes. But when one thinks of them, what a refreshing number of the routes one knows have got charm, and what charming minds therefore their pioneers must have had. Fortunate are their followers, and this one is grateful.

NOTE: I borrow their collective name from the goldfinches without apology: I feel sure that they could not care less!

Controversial (October 1948)
by Ken Tarbuck

[After the Second World War a lively debate took place. On one side were the traditionalists who advocated a shoulder belaying technique using the then normal hemp rope. The alternative was the more sophisticated Tarbuck dynamic belay which also required a waist belay sling, nylon rope and gloves to help reduce friction. The following letter gives some idea of the commitment of one of the protagonists.]

Sir, – Mr. P.R.J. Harding has written in an article, 'The New Generation', in the 1948 Rucksack Club Journal, one page of which is devoted to the faint praise, and the other, deflation of the 'Tarbuck Rope Technique'. As open discussion of his criticism may be of interest to climbers, I venture to offer you my reply for publication.

Mr. Harding has been looking through the Ashley Book of Knots (4,000 of them) and seeks to identify my knot with No. 1,734 which shows a rope wrapped several times around a wooden spar in a Rolling Hitch. If he had searched more diligently he would have found in another part of the book, a knot that came one and a half steps nearer to the Tarbuck Knot, but which still didn't make it. Mr. Harding should observe that a Clove Hitch is only one turn different from a Rolling Hitch and that a Sheet Bend is identical with a Bowline except that they are employed on different parts of the rope. The Tarbuck knot differs in three respects from the Rolling Hitch. On the evidence of Ashley alone, Mr. Harding need not be diffident with his congratulations; perhaps it is the simplicity of the idea which irks him. The important point here is that the knot should be tied correctly; I wish no one, not even Mr. Harding, to use the turns of the Rolling Hitch in error.

By contrast, Mr. Harding finds my rope-craft complicated. Anything new is apt to seem complicated, even riding a bicycle. I can assure him that in practical hands it becomes, like shorthand writing, both fluent and simple and it certainly inspires confidence. I have demonstrated many times its effectiveness in stopping severe falls of up to 50 ft., which is more than I dare invite the Shoulder Belay School to attempt. The Shoulder Belay's complications arise after the accident; climbers must make their own choice.

Mr. Harding prefers the 'accepted and well proven' English Shoulder Belay, but this form of belay is not as widely accepted as Mr. Harding may think, and certainly not by those who give thought to the matter, or who have experimented in a practical way. I quote from an American source, 'Only by close comparison of the effects of several falls held consecutively by different techniques can one realise the extreme weakness of the Shoulder Belay'. And again: 'It was soon found that different techniques varied greatly in effectiveness in checking a fall. The highly recommended Shoulder Belay was found to be the weakest of all'. Nor is it well proven; we must be careful not to confuse testimony with proof. The inability of the majority of people to correlate cause and effect is almost as widespread today as it was in the Dark Ages. The patent medicine ramp thrives on this human frailty and never lacks for testimony. The Shoulder Belay is certainly better than nothing, and there are certain limited circumstances in which it can be quite effective. In modern warfare the same argument can be applied to the bow and arrow.

Mr. Harding says that my method has two important flaws: First, that as the rope runs it may well burn through the waist loop or belay sling of the second. Mr. Harding should read my articles again more carefully and ask himself how is it that in over 50 experimental drops my waist and belay ropes are not even marked. I was probably the first to point out the susceptibility of nylon rope to frictional heat in practical use, and it took considerable persistence on my part to convince the BMC Rope Committee of the dangers, and a personal visit to the Edinburgh Ropery and a practical demonstration was needed to convince the manufacturers; this they would acknowledge freely. My suggestion that a warning should be issued with each climbing rope sold has not been acted upon. This is a pity, as this susceptibility does not lessen the value of nylon rope for mountaineering because the danger, once understood, is easy to avoid and is present to a large degree with any rope. Mr. Harding, later in his article, mentions the use of thin nylon slings for lowering the leader in emergency. He means through a karabiner. He will pardon me, I hope if I make this clearer, as direct lowering through a sling might have fatal consequences.

The other important flaw in my method, according to Mr. Harding, is that he finds it almost impossible to give a helping pull to the second, except with the arms. This is priceless, particularly in view of his subsequent advice to climbers who cannot make the grade. But Mr. Harding's is a special case. He is an outstanding climber and goes up places where I for one, would gladly accept a pull. As it happens, I have experimented quite a lot with the problem of hauling weights up awkward places, this in connection with rescue work, and I find that I can get the strongest pull by using my legs and the waist belay. However, the Shoulder Belay has much to commend it for prolonged medium haulage work, particularly with hemp rope, and the sooner it is restricted to this special use the better.

Finally, Mr. Harding cannot see any system of belaying succeeding if the snatch in the rope is greater than that which the leader or second can withstand. This is the greater fallacy, and Mr. Harding is not alone in falling into this error. Let me assure him (and some Americans) that if by snatch he means static friction, then the faster the falling leader is moving the less is the disturbing effect of static friction on the second. To obtain the best advantage from this phenomenon the restraint should be made through the centre of gravity of the second, which is what my system aims to do. I will not trespass further on your space lest I be accused of adding complexities. Mr. Harding can practise for himself with a table top, a serviette, and a cup of tea.

Mountains (June 1949)
by W.H. Murray

Only once in my life have I made an after-dinner speech in reply to the toast of 'Mountains'. The dinner occurred in the middle of the Libyan Desert, and the toast was put to me by a young German, with whom I shared the meal. In my reply I managed to say all that I have to say about mountains in three sentences. But first of all, let me explain how the situation arose.

Just one hour before I had been sitting in the bottom of a slit-trench. My battalion had been whittled down to fifty men, and we were waiting for an attack at dusk by the 15th Panzer Division. My battalion commander with the perfect frankness that such gentlemen have, had said "Murray, by tonight you'll either be dead meat or a prisoner". Thus, I sat in the bottom of my trench and went through my pockets, with the purpose of destroying anything that might be of use to an enemy. I smashed a prismatic compass, tore up an identity card, and my notes on battalion orders. Then I came upon an address book. I flicked over the pages and read the names. And suddenly I saw that every name in that book was the name of a mountaineer. Until then I had never realised how great a part mountains had played in my life. Most of the names belonged to men who are very much alive and active today. While I read over them I also realised, again for the first time, how much I had learned from these men, and had been given by them, and how little I had been able to give in return. Whatever was good in myself had been drawn out largely by them. The same had to be said of mountains. And while I sat in the slit-trench I had a clear perception of the two ways of mountaineering that mean most to me.

The first was the exploratory way, the way of adventure and battle with the elements. I could see storm winds and drift sweeping across the plateau; long hours of axe-work on ice, among sunless cliffs; the day-long suspense on rocks that have never been scratched by nails. These show the harsh aspects of reality, of which a man should know – of which he *MUST* know if he'd know mountains and know himself. Rock, snow and ice sometimes claim from a man all that he has to give. Sometimes the strain on body and nerve may be high, discomforts sharp. But the mountaineer gets all the joy of his triune craft. And his mastery of mountain-craft is, in reality, the mastery of himself. It is the foretaste of freedom.

I made no effort to think in that trench. Ideas came and went of their own accord in a matter of seconds. I saw the other aspect of mountaineering – mountaineering for the sake of mountains and not for sport. I could see a great peak among fast-moving cloud, and the icy glint where its snows caught the morning sun. There were deep corries and tall crags. All of these were charged with a beauty that did not belong to *THEM*, but poured through them as light pours through the glass of a ruby and blue window, or as grace through a sacrament. These show an ideal aspect of reality of which a man should know, of which he *MUST* know if he'd arrive at any truth at all about mountains, or about men.

At dusk the German tanks came in. When the shambles had ended a German tank commander took charge of me. It was bright moonlight.

One of the defining moments of rock-climbing exploration in the Fifties: John Streetly making the first ascent of Cloggy's Bloody Slab in June 1952— a long and very bold on-sight lead with sparse protection.

A typical post-war climbing group — Tom Ransley's photo of 'The Bradford Lads' [and lassie] in the late Fifties:
(left to right) John Ramsden, Doug Hayes, Duncan Boston, Mike Dawson, Bob Sowden, Jim Lyons and Marie Ball.

He waved a machine pistol at me and asked, in good English, if I didn't feel cold. Now, the desert at night is often exceedingly cold, and without thinking I said, "It's as cold as a mountain-top". And my German said, "Good God, do you climb?"

He was a mountaineer. We had exchanged brief notes about mountains we knew and liked. After three hours he gave me his overcoat and asked when my last meal had been. I said, "Thirty-six hours ago". So he took me to his tank and produced food. We shared a quick meal of British bully and biscuits and German chocolate. After that he fetched out a bottle of British beer and knocked off the top. "Here's to mountains", he said, "and to mountaineers – to all of them everywhere". He took a pull at the bottle and passed it to me. I drank too. I felt moved to reply. I said, "There are three good things you meet on mountains. You meet men, and you meet battle and beauty. But the men are true, and the battle's the only kind that's *WORTH* fighting, and the beauty is *LIFE*".

I smashed the bottle on the German tank.

Thoughts on Leading up Difficult Rock (February 1951)
by Arthur Birtwistle

[Birtwistle's article serves as a reminder of the realities of rock-climbing in the days before runner technique was developed and an indication of why the BMC was so keen to stress technique, caution and safety during its early years, when death or serious injury were very real possibilities in the event of a leader-fall.]

When two climbers toss a coin for the lead it is usual for them to be equally competent, and for the winner to take the honour. Some fifteen years ago two youngsters stood below Holly Tree Crack, a little-known climb on Helm Crag. The coin glinted in the sunlight, and the loser began to uncoil a brand-new rope. After one or two attempts the leader's bowline was tied, whilst the second read the guide-book. It said that the climb was Very Difficult. In due course they both arrived triumphantly at the top.

In retrospect, however, that first climb has left only two impressions: a recollection of a great determination to climb the first and hardest pitch, and a vivid image of the holds on the hardest bit of it. There is no recollection whatsoever of any misgivings about the ultimate issue, or of any fear of a fall. As neither of us had done a climb before, the danger of a fall must have been near, but I did not stop to think of it. The determination to get up as quickly as possible left no room in my mind for the plant of fear to gain a root, and in the heat of success the plant withered and disappeared completely. On that occasion I was lucky; no part of the climb was difficult enough to stop me. Some weeks later I was not so lucky.

We were in the Ogwen area and as we had no guide-book we were climbing anything which looked reasonable. We had followed the scratches up the front of the Milestone and had gone to try a wide groove on the left – the groove which is now the Soap Gut. I was in boots and naturally did not get up. I can only remember fear: not a memory remains of the determination to succeed. Somehow, between climbing and sliding, I reached the bottom, and my last recollection is one of intense relief. On that escapade there was no question of deciding that it was more prudent to retreat than to go on; it was merely that after fifty feet or so, fear – pure and unadulterated fear – got the upper hand.

I wonder how many other climbers have had similar beginnings; there must be quite a lot. It is a rough way to learn prudence, but is probably the best way – if you survive it. During this stage of a young climber's career, the enthusiastic leader does not stop to think; he acts rather like an animal, in that the desire to do something drives him on until fear gets the upper hand, and compels a retreat. This fear is of course, prompted by the insecurity of the position in which he finds himself, or the exposure of the pitch. It would be wrong to assume that this stage of a climber's career is confined to the first few routes, and then only if they are led without the benefit of any previous experience. However much a climber might have been taken up climbs as second or third man, he will still be in this stage when he starts leading. It is only by leading that a climber can get to know himself, and until he does know himself it is the instinct of fear which will dictate when a return should be made. Many climbers never get beyond this stage, but in spite of this are perfectly safe leaders. If their fear instinct and physical powers are both well developed, a long lifetime of safe climbing can be enjoyed. If on the other hand neither is particularly well developed, the time for enjoyment is likely to be seriously curtailed.

To develop beyond this stage takes some time, and certainly in my case a good number of alarming frights, too. With increasing experience and practice, and especially by continuous and regular leading, some men get to know fairly accurately their own physical and nervous strength. Eventually daylight dawns and the leader becomes a thinking climbing-machine. This graduation has been achieved when the leader has learned to master absolutely his natural fear – to eliminate it in every respect as a factor controlling his actions – and has substituted a cold judgement and deliberate reasoning.

This implies his concentration on the immediate problem on the particular piece of rock under his hands and feet whilst he bears in mind the possibility of having to descend the bit he was concentrating on a moment or two before.

"If I put this hand there, my left foot will grip better on that poor hold and I shall be able to use the hand-jam with my other hand."

Perhaps he tries it, then steps back again to wonder what is going to happen above and whether the move can be reversed once it is made. If he is a wise leader he will make the move, and if the rock ahead looks in any way difficult, he will reverse it for practice; just in case he has to descend it later when tired. I am a great believer in what I call an oscillating technique. By that I mean tackling a major difficulty by ascending to it, then retreating to the nearest resting place, then ascending again, usually a little higher, and so on until when the time comes to go for it the leader knows all the available holds and the best way of using them, and has also a good idea of what to expect when the move has been made. As an example of this I immediately think of an ascent of The Sheaf on Clogwyn Du'r Arddu. On the overhang I pulled up three or four times, until I had both sorted out the loose holds from the sound ones and had established that I could descend from the lip to the last sling without difficulty. It was then only a matter of a rather harder pull on to a ledge that I had already inspected fairly well.

Perhaps the most difficult thing to discuss is the problem of whether to turn back or go on during a lead up a hard pitch. It is a problem which has to be faced by every leader, whether his standard is Moderate or top Very Severe. Sometimes it crops up on a hard climb in rubbers, sometimes on a new route; and quite often during bad weather conditions on routes which are well known. Those leaders who are not able to rely on anything else except fear will solve it rightly or wrongly. The leader who has gone beyond this first stage will have to be prepared to do some very hard, quick and clear thinking if he wishes to climb to the safe limit of his powers. It is of paramount importance that a cool, clear head is kept, however precarious the leader's position. It should also be realised that once a leader starts relying on judgement, rather than on the unrestrained dictates of fear, he might go beyond his old turning back point. Should he then allow fear to gain control, his chances of avoiding disaster are small indeed.

Everyone has his own ideas of just when to turn back, and they vary from day to day with any individual, but not so much as one might think when expressed in terms of minimum power reserve. The chances which a leader might assess and take also vary with his larger philosophy of mountaineering, his family or other responsibilities, and the nature of the climb. My own ideas are fairly simple . When I consider that I have used up two-thirds of my reserve of physical strength, reckoning from the last sling or resting place, or half my reserve of nervous strength, then it is time to go down for a cigarette; and probably right down for a drink, if the hour is opportune.

Of course this refers to a final go at a pitch: on preliminary investigation a much greater reserve is held. Perhaps some of my readers will consider two-thirds of one's reserve of physical strength is too much to use up. I find, however, that if by using the oscillation technique one gets to know most of the knack of retreat, then to descend takes well under half the strength needed to ascend the same rock. A good example of this occurred last year when with Geoffrey Pigott I came last down an unclimbed rib of rock on Gimmer between the starts of Hiatus and the Crack. Afterwards neither of us was able to get back up the overhanging part of the rib.

Given plenty of practice, physical strength is easy to judge: nervous energy on the other hand is infinitely harder to judge, but is of at least equal importance. When a leader's nervous energy gives out, fear takes over, and there is then but little chance of avoiding a fall even though some physical strength is still left. I am not, of course, advising anyone to adopt my margins: each leader must find and decide on his own. The margin should certainly be much bigger unless the leader has had plenty of practice and is in good general form.

How rigidly a leader should obey his own self-imposed rules is also a matter for individual decision. Undoubtedly he should return when he has reached his critical point of exhaustion and no certain relief is near. Sometimes when he has reached this point he may have to make a quick decision whether to return or go on to some break which he can see ahead. It is a difficult decision, which must be taken, and it is one on which the safety of the whole party might depend. If he decides that he can continue, then his retreat is abandoned and the safety of the party is temporarily at stake. The gravity of such a decision is obvious. On climbs of a delicate nature there is often, but not always, a certain amount of time in which to reflect, since the problem here is more likely to be a nervous one. On strenuous climbs the decision has to be taken very quickly; for example it must have been so taken, with varying results, by climbers laybacking directly up the top bit of the Flake Crack on C.B. On the first pitch of Curving Crack on Clogwyn Du'r Arddu more than one climber has been unable to make up his mind and has alternated in the middle between going up and coming down, until the matter was finally settled by mother nature.

The last remarks raise another vitally important matter, that of determination, guts, singleness of purpose – the name makes no difference, every climber knows exactly what is meant. On the hardest climbs of today it is impossible to get up without applying all the physical and nervous energy available right up to the safety limit. On most of the hardest pitches the critical turning point will be reached at the top of the pitch or hard section, or, if the climber is not up to its standard, even below the top of the pitch. To climb really up to the safety limit demands a good deal of determination. What is not generally appreciated is that after the leader has climbed with determination to that safety limit, and has then decided to retreat, all the determination used in getting up has now to go into reverse and become determination to get down. At the turning point, when the quick decision to retreat has been made, it is essential that all thought of getting up should leave the leader's mind. All his determination should then become concentrated on getting back to the nearest resting place or slings as soon as possible, and as far as possible, by a reversal of the movements memorised during the ascent. This seems obvious when put on paper, but on the crag it is a very difficult thing to do, and requires a great deal of will-power. On the last-but-one Club gathering at Shining Clough I experienced a good case of this, a particularly curious case because it involved the reversal of only one move. Geoff Pigott and I had been trying to get up the first pitch of Pisa, which was then unclimbed. After some considerable time we found that a very delicate move could be made to bring a hand on to an arête on the right, but after this had been done no further progress was possible. In my case I had to use every bit of determination I had to reverse that move without falling off. It is still quite vivid, one moment I was intent on getting up, whilst the next I was intent on getting back. Had I not been able to reverse the mental driving force, I am quite sure that I should have had to jump for a grass ledge in the gully below.

A final point about determination. The kind which is of value is that based on the feeling that you can do it when you are actually at the foot of the particular pitch. Determination deriving from a bar session, or over-high ambition, is dangerous unless tempered by much common sense.

These musings and dogmas on the subject of leading on rock might be regarded by some of my friends as the ramblings of a rock-happy brain. If, however, nobody agrees with them, at least they might help someone to order his own thoughts and opinions on these matters, in which case their purpose will have been served.

(Note: This superb article originally appeared in the *Rucksack Club Journal*.)

A Chapter of Accidents (September 1951)

Easter in 1951 came unusually early, Good Friday being on March 23rd (three weeks earlier than it will be in 1952); the winter had been a very wet one and on high ground this meant heavy falls of snow: in both the Lake District and Snowdonia the depth of snow was quite unprecedented, and as multitudes of hikers and mountaineers flocked into the hostels and hotels, mishaps were perhaps only too likely. The accidents made good newspaper headlines, e.g., 'Snowdon the lethal', at a time when other news was scarce. It is to be feared that many of the hikers were ill-equipped for semi-arctic conditions, and many were actually foolhardy and paid little attention to the warnings of the more experienced mountaineers. The continued snowfall meant unusual cornices and dangerous ice-slopes, which ordinary fell-walkers were quite unable to cope with; even with ice-axes, some of the slopes, quite safe under normal conditions, had become very dangerous.

In both areas the mountain rescue teams had a very arduous time in answering the numerous calls made upon them, and no praise can be too high for the cheerful self-sacrificing spirit with which they performed their exhausting duties, the more so as many of the calls for help came towards dusk, and meant that many rescuers were often working under very difficult weather conditions in the dark.

We propose to give a detailed account of some of the accidents in the hope that discerning readers may be able to draw useful lessons from them and perhaps profit thereby.

On Easter Monday a man aged 40, wearing shorts set out from Patterdale to climb the Dodds and Helvellyn. He was advised by a farmer to go back but persisted in his intention and was later announced as missing. A party of seventeen under Conrad Sauer of the Keswick M.R. team searched for him next day between Birkett Bank and Sticks Pass; the average depth of snow was four feet, and it is not surprising that they failed to find the victim, whose dead body was found a week later near the foot of Helvellyn.

On Easter Sunday two girls from Leeds, aged 21 and 23, were walking in the neighbourhood of Fairfield; they had no ice-axe but were well equipped as regards boots, clothing and food. A severe blizzard developed that afternoon and they did not return. Their bodies were found some days later in Deepdale; they had apparently walked over the steep edge of Fairfield and it seems likely that the cornice collapsed.

On Easter Sunday, A.C. Edwards aged 23, died of exposure on Scawfell; he had been climbing with a friend and they tried to contour round the mountain in order to reach Brackenclose Hut in Wasdale; on the way Edwards collapsed and the two men spent the night, a clear but cold one, on the snow in the lee of a rock. At first light his companion set out to get help; a party from Brackenclose was not strong enough to deal with the problem and sent for additional help. At 8.50 that morning the Outward Bound School in Eskdale received news of the accident; and a party of thirteen boys and three instructors climbed the 1,600 feet and reached the spot by 11.00 a.m., only to find that the man was dead. At the inquest it was stated that if the deceased had had with him a supply of sugar or glucose, he would probably have survived.

On Good Friday a boy aged 15, when running down scree, lost control near Harrison Stickle and was killed. On this same day two climbers were rescued on Dow Crag by the Coniston M.R. team; their rope broke and they fell a considerable distance, but escaped with superficial injuries.

In the Snowdon area the accidents were even more serious than those in the Lake District, a very bad one occurring before Easter.

On Saturday, February 10th, a man and a girl aged 22, attempted to come down the pig track from the Snowdon ridge; they decided to try a controlled glissade, moving one at a time, but the man was pulled off when the girl lost control and they both slid about 500 feet and received severe head injuries. The accident was seen by three climbers from the ridge and one of these at once set out to Pen y Gwryd for help, while the other tried to reach the injured by a safe route; these two men were met on the ridge by a Mr. Turner and Dr. Anthony Woodroffe (both from Chester) who had just come up from Cwm Glas. The latter two decided that as it was getting dark, they must to save time, try and get down the ice slope; after attempting to cut steps and finding the progress very slow, they also decided to glissade one at a time, the other man holding the rope from as secure a foothold as he could get. Unfortunately this type of control again failed and they both slid down the slope. Turner was bruised and badly shaken, and Woodroffe received severe head injuries from which he died almost at once. No words can do justice to the gallantry of these two men who knowingly took such grave risks to try and save others. The P-y-G party led by P. Harding and C.B. Briggs, reached the spot by 8.50 p.m., and the stretcher party by 10.45 p.m., the injured being tended and nourished in the meantime. The party did not reach Pen y Gwryd until 3.30 a.m. and the injured girl died on the way down.

On Thursday, March 22nd, Miss Norah Batty was killed while descending the South Gully on Tryfan. She was one of a party of seven experienced climbers and they were coming down the gully unroped. There was snow in the gully and most of the party were on the edge of the snow thereby getting some help from holds on the walls of the gully, but Miss Batty decided to try the middle of the snow; she slipped and fell about 500 feet, and was dead when help reached her. It should be mentioned that conditions on that day on Tryfan were not nearly so difficult as they were later on. A severe storm set in on the Thursday evening.

At 1 p.m. on Saturday, March 24th, the police were notified of an accident to two people at the foot of Clogwyn Du'r Arddu, and C.B. Briggs from P-y-G with several members of the Climbers' Club set out with the first aid equipment. Of the two victims the man, T.J. Orrell, was dead when they arrived and the woman severely injured. On the way down the rescue party learned of an accident which had just taken place in Trinity Gully. This climb was being done by a party of three experienced climbers. The first 600 feet went without difficulty, steps being cut in good snow. Beyond the point where you leave the gully for the Snowdon 'roof', the angle became easier, but the snow had turned to ice and the wind began to blow hard across the slope. The ascending steps had been made at rather long intervals and it would not have been safe to use them for descent in a gale without putting in some intermediates; it was therefore as difficult to retreat as to ascend once the wind had risen. It was decided to proceed cautiously. cutting two steps ahead and stepping up in the lulls; the ice was very hard and it took many blows to cut a step; also the wind was strong and gusty and when stepping up it was necessary to judge the length of a lull. The leader was blown off when stepping up at a point near the top of the climb and all three climbers fell the whole of the height of the cliff. The leader and the second slid down the middle of the gully on snow and ice but the third man, Peter Koch, must have hit a rock on the way down. When the three came to rest, the leader was unconscious for a short time and Koch was dead. The two survivors were able to walk to P-y-G.

The Climbers' Club party, after helping in the Orrell tragedy went higher to take some photographs and on their return found that another man, G. Hall, had been severely injured at the same spot where Orrell had slipped; he died shortly afterwards.

Later on that same Easter Saturday night another call came to Pen y Gwryd to say that a party of twenty-one people were stranded on the summit of Snowdon, one of them being injured; this man had slipped about 50 feet on frozen snow when descending by the Watkin path and was found by a party of Dublin Rover Scouts who were staying at the rectory in Llanberis. These scouts made a rope stretcher and when attempting to carry the injured man down, found the ice at Clogwyn

Station too formidable and returned to the Summit Hotel; here they were very fortunate to find Mr. Jack Longland, of Everest fame, whose party had come up from Glaslyn and, after two vain attempts to descend, had decided to spend the night on top; a more or less silent blessing was bestowed on the benefactors who had put the hotel on the top of Snowdon. Provisions were pooled, a good fire was made, the injured Dale made comfortable, and with the storm still raging outside, the party of twenty-one waited for the dawn of Easter Sunday. At 7 a.m., on four ropes, sixteen people set off on the long walk to Llanberis, four being left with the injured man to await the help from P-y-G. At the fatal Clogwyn ice dome, they hewed big bucket steps all the way across, and slowly but safely passed over two long stretches of ice; in due time they reached Llanberis, where they found Mr. Briggs, the police, and the splendidly trained and equipped RAF Mountain Rescue Unit, all ready to resume their rescue work.

And what shall we say of it all? In spite of the Press and its thirst for sensation, we mountaineers can keep a proper sense of perspective in the matter. We must not over-stress the *fear* side of mountains; that was the feeling prevalent in the Middle Ages and we have got beyond that. Difficulties are there to be overcome, and it should be our duty to explain to the younger generation how best to overcome them, and not try to avoid them. Hundreds of children are killed on the roads every year; we do not deal with this by excluding children from the roads; we try to inculcate road sense and road tactics by careful and skilled instruction in our schools. It will not be amiss to finish by quoting from a very interesting talk broadcast by Mr. Jack Longland shortly after Easter:

'Our British hills are real mountains; an inexperienced walker may romp up them in perfect weather on paths made by better men. But good weather is not normal in our mountains, and a fine day may turn sour on you, the path be lost, and without hill-knowledge – which means a sense of the shape and moods of mountains as well as practice with map and compass – you may be lost for hours, or be caught out all night, or at the worst stray over a cliff. It is vitally necessary to have the right equipment for the time of year and the state of the mountain: plenty of warm clothing, an ice-axe each, good party discipline – no straying or hurrying on ahead – as well as a rope and plenty of spare food. And even with all this equipment, you can come to grief without training and experience.

And remember, it isn't very brave or tough to wander ignorantly on high mountains in bad weather. It is stupid and selfish: stupid for your own sake – and selfish because of your relations, and the search parties and rescue teams whose week-end you may spoil and whom you may involve in hours of exhausting and dangerous work. To love and enjoy mountains you have to learn to be humble – humble enough to go back to a hard school and learn from the beginning...

It is not very consoling to human dignity to be lost through sheer incompetence or ignorance, or to get yourself badly frightened, or to be injured, still less to end up as a blanket-wrapped package on the way to a mortuary and a coroner's inquest. Of course the mountains challenge us – but they challenge us to learn a craft with patience and humility and with consideration for all those others whom we meet among our mountains. The walker or climber, with experience and knowledge, can stretch his powers to the full on a mountain day – not by silly notions of conquering a mountain whatever conditions or your own state of fitness – but by accurately gauging all you know against the task you have set yourself to do. And though you may hoodwink a tired referee at football when you are really offside, you can't cheat twenty degrees of frost at night on a windy mountain in a pair of shorts and with too few sweaters – and on steep snow and ice and rock you can't cheat the law of gravity either.

The Threat to the Matterhorn (Sept. 1951)
The Italian company who are seeking to build a cable railway up the Matterhorn have received authority subject to the approval of the Council of State, to establish a line by way of the Furggrat to the Italian summit. They claim that this will draw 'flocks of Sunday tourists from the towns' to Breuil, and will enable a beacon for aircraft to be set up at the summit.

The Italian Alpine Club have started a press campaign against the scheme and, through the Union Internationale des Associations d'Alpinisme, have called for the support of the mountaineering organisations of other countries. A letter to *The Times*, signed by the President and surviving past-Presidents of the Alpine Club has called the attention of the British public to the scheme and set forth the objections to it, which are, we believe, shared by the vast majority of climbers in this country...

Matterhorn (Sept. 1953)
A statement having appeared in the Press that the Americans proposed to establish a radar station on the summit of the Matterhorn, the following comment was made: "Swiss and other specialists in electronics and meteorology agree that the Matterhorn should be the last place for putting such a station; the summit is only rarely without its cape of clouds charged with electricity." *Die Alpen* appealed for an expert comment on this and received the reply: "I must regretfully contradict the above statement.

Clouds do not in the slightest prevent radar from functioning. A metallic point placed above the radar antenna will protect it against lightning discharge from the clouds."

Permission has been given by the Swiss Department of Railways for the construction of a teleferic (sic) from Zermatt to the Schwarzsee, thus shortening the climb to the Hornli Hut by three hours or so. There is a reservation that the line shall not be extended.

On 21st March, 1953, under winter conditions, the Matterhorn was climbed via the Furgg ridge by two Italians, Walter Bonatti and Robert Bignani. They bivouacked at about 13,000 feet in a temperature of -13 degrees F. During the descent they took six hours to get from the summit to the Solvay Hut.

Meet the Members (March 1952)
by J.A. Stewart

[Alan Stewart's notable series of profiles on British clubs was spread over numerous issues. We have selected this chapter as typical of the whole.]

In the last two numbers of *Mountaineering* we drew Profiles of some BMC constituent clubs, alphabetically from the Alpine to the Imperial College M.C., to make them better known to other climbers. Continuing we come to:

THE KARABINER MOUNTAINEERING CLUB

One of the results of the war was the stimulation, among young men and women, of a wish to carry over into peacetime some of the spirit of good-fellowship and adventure which lightened the dark wartime days. An active climbing club is as good a place as can be for furthering such ends and for guiding those who, seeking them among hills, would otherwise lack the help and friendship of more experienced climbers. So it has come about that a number of new clubs have been formed, to serve the many new recruits to the sport, and among them the Karabiner, founded in 1945, takes a leading place. Its aims are high, its enthusiasm tremendous and its rules draconic.

The Club's aims are to foster mountaineering *by active participation* (of which more anon) and to encourage and train graduating members. Its enthusiasm shows in a fixture list of thirty or forty meets a year, including climbing on Clogwyn Du'r Arddu, Ben Nevis at Easter, and skiing in the Highlands (all these and most of the others from a H.Q. under canvas), and trifles such as Colne-Rowsley for those with insomnia. It also shows in the many constructive ideas which this small club has put forward at BMC annual meetings and in the preparation, jointly with the fellow tigers of the Rucksack and Manchester University Mountaineering Clubs, of the new Gritstone Guide. The rules, which provide for membership by anyone over sixteen, make stiff terms for the admission of full members. These include proposal by three full members who have climbed with the applicant, attendance at four meets in six months, competence in rock-climbing (of V.D. standard) and proven ability to lead a party over unknown hill country. Most, if not all, other clubs ask no more of their members, once elected, than good behaviour and an annual cheque; but it is far otherwise with the K.M.C.

Remember the bit about 'active participation' or, if you are a member, forget it at your peril, for the rules prescribe expulsion, no less, for anyone who, without good cause, fails to attend four climbing and four walking meets in a year. As most meets are in the Pennines, Wales, or the Lakes, this confines membership, in practice, to those living near Manchester, where the Club's indoor meets are also held, with speakers of a calibre unusual in a club of this size. At these meets the Club's small but growing library is displayed to encourage its use.

New members are welcome, especially those of the graduating class, of whom, naturally, no technical standard is asked, but who must first attend a few meets and become personally known to three full members.

THE LADIES' ALPINE CLUB

In the nineteenth century the high Alps were almost as exclusively a masculine preserve as are the Himalayas to this day. There were pioneers in the field, but a woman was still a rarity above the snowline, and problems of dress and accommodation, no less than inhibitions against an unwomanly pastime, must have kept many to the valleys or the better-known passes. Nowadays, inhibitions are out of fashion, the word 'unwomanly' generally rates quotation marks, and one no longer hears of skirts being worn as far as the last chalets and then surreptitiously doffed. It is hard to put a date to trends, but by the turn of the century there was a new climate of opinion towards (and among) women climbers, and mountaineering for women had even been given a royal cachet of respectability by the expeditions of the Queen of Italy. The time was ripe for a club to be founded, and in 1907, Mrs Aubrey le Blond (the first President) and several of her friends met in the Lyceum Club and established the L.A.C. Two years later Queen Margherita accepted the Honorary Presidency which she was to hold until her death in 1925.

The Club has never been large – It has currently about 135 members – but it is entirely composed of women who can show good Alpine records, or contributions to the literature, art or science of the Alps. The candidate for membership must, moreover, be personally known to the proposer and seconder. To help those who would enlarge their experience with a view to membership, the Club admits, on the strength of a single Alpine season, women not less than nineteen years of age as graduating members, who have then five years in which to qualify for full membership.

Lectures are held monthly, except in the summer, and a dinner in December, and all members have the use of a library which having grown steadily since 1907, now comprises a very good collection of Alpine literature, including the Club's own annual journal which was started in 1925 in continuation of the former Annual Reports.

THE LIVERPOOL UNIVERSITY MOUNTAINEERING CLUB

In 1931 a small and vigorous band of Liverpool undergraduates started a club under the title of the Liverpool University Rock Climbing Club. Within a couple of years, the Club did what those younger rock-climbers do who have the good salt in them – it developed a long-term interest in wider mountain matters, and in token thereof changed its name. Remaining small – it still counts only fifty or sixty members, who may be anyone of either sex, connected with the University – it has retained that close and friendly atmosphere in which the novice can best be drawn into the circle of the mountaineering community.

Second only to Manchester in its geographical good fortune, Liverpool is within easy reach of North Wales and the Lakes, and the L.U.M.C. holds frequent meets in these districts, as well as occasional expeditions to Scotland and the Alps. Within twenty miles, its members have their nursery of tigers, Helsby, and it was a former secretary, H.A. Carsten, who wrote the Helsby guide published by the Wayfarers' Club. Although the Club has no hut of its own, its members enjoy the use of other clubs' huts, an hospitable arrangement which blesseth him that gives, and him that takes, and certainly earns the gratitude of many Liverpool undergraduates who would otherwise find difficulty in arranging some of their visits to the hills.

Besides outdoor meets, the Club holds a lecture meet each term, and an annual dinner, and extends to its members a valuable service in the provision of equipment from a communal pool. Those who for various reasons do not wish to obtain complete personal gear, can borrow such items as ropes, ice-axes and guidebooks, the last being part of a general mountaineering library. The President is Dr. Graham Macphee, whose active interest has stood the Club in good stead these twenty years...

A Note from *Mountaineering* (September 1955)

On July 31st, 1855, the first ascent of Monte Rosa was made from Zermatt by Rev. J.G. Smyth, Rev. C. Smyth, Rev. C. Hudson, J. Birkbeck, and Rev. E.J.W. Stevenson; with them were the guides Johann and Peter zum Taugwald and Ulrich Lauener. The centenary of the first ascent was celebrated at Zermatt early in July, the chairman being the veteran alpinist Mr. L.S. Amery; he read to the assembly a letter he had just received from Sir Winston Churchill, who recalled that he (Sir Winston) had climbed Monte Rosa sixty-one years before, in 1894.

Rock Climbing in Britain (Autumn 1957/March 1958)

by Jack Longland

To any mountaineer who may read this, it is scarcely a paradox to say that the most important 'climbing in Britain' over the last year or two has not happened at all. Nor is this merely an excuse to dodge my task and write about climbs in the Himalayas, or the Alps, or in Arctic Norway. The truth is that it is fairly easy to define two main groups among British climbers. There are those who find all the satisfaction they need on the rock-faces of our home mountains, and who do not wish or have the opportunity to prove or enlarge their technique on bigger mountains abroad; and there are others with a longer tradition behind them, who while enjoying British climbing to the full and systematically mastering its particular disciplines, are nevertheless preparing themselves for bigger mountains.

The other night two young climbing friends turned up at my Derbyshire home for a late supper. They had been climbing, and climbing very arduous routes, on one of our little outcrops of gritstone. Nothing new about this, of course: but I found that from their base near Birmingham, they were driving up after work on every spare evening, visiting before the late sunset a different gritstone crag each time. In another fortnight they would be in the Alps, and at Chamonix they could be confident that no trick of the granite precipices there would be likely to defeat them, whether smooth slabs, or overhanging bulges, or vertical corners. On our Derbyshire miniature stage, they had practised all the tricks, and though the setting would be different with a couple of thousand feet of sheer space tugging at the leader's back and nerve instead of fifty feet or so at Black Rocks, they would be rightly sure that they knew all, or almost all the answers.

I have said that this attitude has a long tradition behind it. The pioneers who invented British climbing a century ago – dons, school-masters, clergymen and men of leisure, looked on it at first as agreeable but not very serious preparation for their summer holidays in the Alps. Flip the pages of the calendar on a hundred years and we find that the most significant mountaineering feat of 1955 is that Joe Brown, Manchester builder and house-painter, and unassailably the presiding genius of British rock-climbing today, was one of the two men first to reach the top of Kangchenjunga, the world's third highest mountain. Only as accuracy demands and everyone knows, it was five feet below the top that they stopped, because of sensitive concern for the religious susceptibilities of the people of Sikkim, perhaps the most curious recorded instance of mountaineering self-denial.

What of the others. those who never hope to go to Kangchenjunga, or even to Switzerland? Quite early on, in the days when the craft of British rock-climbing began to be elaborated, there were climbers who came to think that their companions who used British rocks as a practising ground for the Alps were missing the peculiar charm of climbing in Britain, and perhaps inhibiting the development of a strictly native sport. One reason for this belief was that on our own smaller-scale cliffs, climbing of such delicacy and technical difficulty was possible as would not normally be attempted on bigger mountains, on which the logic of time and size discouraged the slow and carefully safeguarded movement appropriate to severe climbs which were only a few hundred feet high. A better reason was the realisation that the small British hills are quite big enough for the small human animal who learns on their most inhospitable precipices to defy our ordinary pavement and staircase limitations. And better still was the discovery that to climb on British rock to the limits of your skill, week-end by week-end and year after year, afforded a varied series of tests of technique, courage and stamina quite sufficient to occupy an active climbing lifetime.

In what follows, these two strands which make up British climbing will not always be separately distinguished. There are those who have made a great name for themselves in Wales or the Lake District, and who yet discover at a later stage the challenge of the Alps. There are others with an early record on bigger mountains, whom advancing years or the ties of jobs or marriage confine later to rock-climbing in this country. But without some understanding of the way in which these two climbing groups have come into being, and how they intermingle, the contemporary pattern of climbing in Britain can not be understood.

Over the last few years there are three main changes to record. There is the change in the types of climbers most frequently to be met among the mountains; there is a marked and still developing change in technique, and there are new cliffs, not visited before, which are being forced to deliver up their secrets. There is perhaps also a fourth change, but one more difficult to define – a change in attitude towards danger.

There are more people climbing than ever before. Last Whitsun, coming down from Craig yr Ysfa towards the Ogwen valley I counted 85 tents of all sizes, colours and vintages, among the fields and hummocks bordering the London-Holyhead road. When I first began visiting North Wales, thirty years ago, I suppose one would have seen two or three at the most. Not that all the tents contained rock-climbers – there would be walkers among them, and a few who just potter around their own campsite, inventing new gadgets for their comfort and cooking elaborate and splendid meals. But the great majority were there to climb. Where do they come from, and how do they get to the mountains; what kind of climbs can they do?

When my generation began its climbing most of the other parties we met belonged to one or other of the established mountaineering clubs. Mine was for that time a very normal apprenticeship, starting with the Cambridge University Mountaineering Club, and then the Climbers' Club, with a fairly high proportion of ex-university men among its members, and its climbing hut, Helyg, under Tryfan, as our usual base. There were also the clubs based on a strong local tradition and in proximity to a particular mountain district: The Rucksack Club with headquarters in Manchester; the Wayfarers' Club at Liverpool; the Fell and Rock Climbing Club in the Lake District; the Yorkshire Ramblers' Club, whose rambling embraced the toughest caving and potholing as well as the virtual monopoly of the steep gritstone crag at Almscliff near Harrogate.

Across the Border was the Scottish Mountaineering Club, while in London, demure in the Saville Row, sat the legendary grandmother of them all, the Alpine Club, at that time officially disinterested in British rock-climbing, though many A.C. members climbed in this country fortified by the knowledge that their doings would never catch the eye of the Editor of the *Alpine Journal*. It was a small world, in which, after a year or two, the keen young climber would have got to know, or at any rate to know of, all the other groups engaged in serious rock-climbing.

The present climbing scene is utterly different, and although the historical eye can divine how the changes have been accumulating during three decades, the real revolution belongs to the last two or three years. The flood of new climbers from altogether new sources has overflowed beyond the established mountaineering clubs, and swamped the tradition and habits in which earlier climbers were brought up. Most of them come from the big northern cities or industrial towns, and with the five-day week now much more usual, they get away on Friday evenings from office stools and factory benches, from schools, laboratories and shops. There are almost, but not quite as many girls as men among them, and girls climb almost, but not quite, as well as men. As they mostly haven't much money, and as what they have must be spread over constantly repeated week-ends in the mountains, they travel there as inexpensively as they can: perhaps the majority by hitch-hiking, others on motor bikes, while some have clubbed together to share an ancient car. Arrived there, they don't stay in the mountain hotels, though they cluster of an evening in the bars of the most famous and hospitable ones, like the Pen-y-Gwryd under Snowdon or the Old Dungeon Ghyll in Langdale. Theirs are the little colonies of tents, or they sleep in barns and shacks or even in caves beneath certain famous boulders. Although not all of them climb well, the best reach a level of expert performance which only repeated week-ends, allied with keenness and courage can give them. A high proportion of the most recent and desperate new climbs have been made by the experts among them, young men whose names are now well-known to the more active members of the traditional climbing clubs.

This brings up another interesting point. Some of us hoped in the years just after the war (and after war years that introduced so many men to Commando training and the tactics of mountain warfare, when it became clear that the sport of climbing was going to attract thousands of new converts) that the older climbing clubs might somehow open their doors and enlarge their membership, and so transmit their training and their traditions to the new climbers who were beginning to crowd the mountains which they had formerly looked on as their own preserve.

These hopes were unfulfilled, and perhaps it was unreasonable to expect that they would be fulfilled. For one thing, though most clubs have increased in size during the last few years, a club ceases to be a gathering-place for like-minded friends when it becomes too large. For another, you cannot just pretend that differences in outlook and background do not exist. Nor could it be assumed that those who came to the mountains for the first time, making their own discoveries and working out their own rules and traditions, would wish to join clubs which they were apt to regard as both old-fashioned and stand-offish.

I believe now that our fears of the results of the invasion of our mountain fastness by multitudes who would pay no heed to the Ark and the Covenant and the Tables of the Mountain Law were much exaggerated, although it is true that tin cans and other litter nowadays spoil too many mountain tops, and there are still too many avoidable accidents. One very encouraging fact is that the new climbers have very largely coalesced into their own groupings. New climbing clubs have sprung up everywhere, based mostly on the places where these climbers live and work – in places as far afield as Bristol, Chester, the Potteries, Derby, and Norfolk, and in all the newer universities. There are new clubs which demand a continuing high level of performance in their members, like the Rock and Ice Club, and the Alpine Climbing Group, which is the latest of a series of attempts to prove that the younger members of the Alpine Club really can climb! There is even one very active group so determined to fly in the face of sober mountain traditions as to call themselves the Bar-room Mountaineering Club. And almost more encouraging is the way in which the best of the members of the older clubs and the most expert of the newer climbers have refused to divide into two hostile camps. Expert performance calls out a generous response from other experts, and it is noteworthy that some of the best new climbs have been pioneered by parties containing a mixture of climbers coming from both these two main sources. It was not just chance, but the wise choice of their leader Charles Evans, that ensured that the first rope up Kangchenjunga consisted of Joe Brown, founder of the new Rock and Ice Club, and George Band, Cambridge Mountaineering Club, Climbers' Club, and Alpine Club, climbing together in willing and brilliant companionship.

It is time to turn to the recent changes in technique. We owed the big technical advance that came in the ten years before the war to the emergence of a race of rock-climbing leaders, among whom the names of Colin Kirkus and Menlove Edwards shine brightest, who developed the ability and above all, the nerve, to go on making exceedingly delicate or strenuous moves even when they had reached a point a hundred or more feet above their safely-anchored second men. Their achievements opened up rock faces so smooth and with such great distances between safeguarding ledges that previous climbers had thought them an impossible test of a leader's courage. It is true that very hard stretches – 'pitches' in climbing jargon – had been safely led before, but they were mostly short, so that the leader felt protected by the physical nearness of his second, as well as by the knowledge that if he did fall, the rope would not allow him to fall far. And the leader's courage was tempered by the doctrine that a fall by a leader was a disgrace, and not a demonstration of heroism.

I remember, from a safe stance and a good belay, watching Colin Kirkus poised motionless, for ten minutes or more, composed and apparently in balance, on holds so small that I could not see them at all from where I stood 120 feet below, while he thought out the way to tackle the next equally smooth stretch ahead. When I followed him later, with the safeguarding rope ahead of me, I found the holds almost as tiny and as hard to use as they had appeared from below.

As is usual in climbing history, the technical advances made by Kirkus and a few other leaders in the 1930s, were inherited almost effortlessly by the much larger generation of post-war leaders. But it was difficult at first to see how they could improve on Kirkus' standards, though his methods were used with success on smaller cliffs, which had been neglected as much because of their steepness as because they were out of the way or so low down on the mountainside as to be overlooked by a generation that likes its rocks to lead them to the top of a mountain.

But climbing like other good sports has never ceased to develop even when the physical limit seemed to have been reached, and when all the main crags were apparently worked out – with the guide-book photographs showing a confusing criss-cross of routes, and very little virgin rock left between the dotted lines. The new advances came from a painstaking study and adaptation to British conditions of the apparatus now at the disposal of the climber, much of it new to this country, though used by Continental mountaineers for some time past. Traditionally, although some climbers have always been gadget-minded, the mountaineer has prided himself on the fact that the equipment he needed for his sport was neither expensive nor elaborate: nailed boots, a cheap pair of rubbers for specially delicate climbs, a climbing rope, and an assortment of old clothes – with a patient mother or wife to patch them when they became too outrageous. He was perhaps slow to learn the lesson of other sports, that the development and choice of equipment can make new achievements possible.

The first change came from the introduction of the nylon climbing rope: this is pleasanter to handle then hemp or even flax, does not kink badly when wet, and above all, is lighter, strength for strength, than other rope yet developed, so that the tugging and nagging weight at the leader's back on a very long run-out is considerably reduced. And strong nylon line or cord can be made in such thin diameters that a new safeguard to the leader has been developed. The leader carries round his neck as he climbs a series of loops or slings of thin nylon, and to each is attached an oval steel ring, opening on one side against a spring. This has no accepted English name, but has imported its German name, Karabiner, from the Swiss and Austrian mountains where its use was perfected. On a long and delicate lead, the leader will come upon a few tiny rock spikes or excrescences over which his rope sling can be looped, and his climbing rope down to his second man clipped into the Karabiner. This provides him perhaps as much with moral as with physical security while he makes a difficult move (or even before he reaches it since the sling may be tossed over a hold too high for him to reach with his hands), In this way the strain of a long pitch, on which all the movements may be near the limit of the leader's capacities, can be diminished, and he can use as safeguards hitches which are too small to be used as belays for his anchored second man, particularly if there is no nearby ledge on which the second could stand as he used them.

We owe the technique of slings and Karabiners in Britain largely to two fine climbers, Peter Harding and Tony Moulam, who, aided by their own abilities, achieved an astonishing record of new climbs, particularly in Wales. Nowadays, no climber is complete without his festoon of slings, the badge of his trade, whether he aspires to lead a Joe Brown 'Exceptionally Severe' or is content to potter about on the Milestone Buttress of Tryfan.

More complicated techniques have followed on logically. They start from the assumption that many otherwise delectable climbs have been barred or interrupted by a stretch of rock so smooth or so overhanging that the unaided climber could make nothing of the route at all. And if the climber can find no holds, then holds must be fashioned. Tradition still frowns on the actual hacking of a hold with chisel or wedge (though there have been certain classic exceptions), and so the modern climber carries with him not only Karabiners but also pitons, short iron spikes that can be driven into any crack in the rocks. It is unsporting to use a piton where any kind of hold exists, except possibly as safeguarding belay for the second man, but where there are no holds pitons are driven in, either as direct hold in conjunction with Karabiner clipped through the hole in the piton head, or in more complicated combined operations. The essence of these is that the leader drives in a piton as far ahead as he can reach, clips on to it one of his two following ropes, and is sustained on his holdless perch by his second man gripping that rope or even hauling on it, to raise his leader high enough for him to put in another piton. In extreme cases, the leader may advance 50 or 100 feet by these artificial means, clipping himself alternately by each rope to one piton after another, while his sweating second man has to remember which rope to slacken and which rope to haul on with all his might.

It is easy for older climbers to dismiss all this as steeplejacking, or to exclaim that a man who drives a piton into British rock is as much a scoundrel as if he were caught shooting a fox in the hunting shires. It is better to keep a sense of proportion: to remind ourselves that the earlier pioneers had most of the fun, opening up all the obvious routes on all the major crags; and that those who today wish to develop their skill and to experience the crowning adventure of leading a fine new climb, must seek new methods and new places. One may by forgiven for thinking that an entirely artificial climb, on which each move depends on mechanical aids, is hardly worth the effort. But it is clear that those who use these devices most competently are those who are our most brilliant leaders of non-artificial climbs, and that they use their technical apparatus to bring them on to rocks on which the most desperately difficult 'free climbing' then becomes possible.

It should be remembered also that the most difficult Alpine routes at Chamonix and elsewhere have depended greatly on the mastering of the new artificial techniques. Continental climbers, with so much more rock to play with, have never been obsessed by our fears that the limited acreage of British rock would be ruined if it were everywhere pin-cushioned with pitons. And it is the young climbers who have practised these new methods at home who have also restored the prestige of British climbers abroad, so much in the doldrums because of the wartime interruption of our Alpine visits, and of the consequent falling behind in technique.

The search for novelty, for new climbs, has driven the young climber to use new methods, and also to new cliffs. The last years have seen the search for and discovery of altogether new crags, such as the low rocks of Borrowdale, often half hidden by trees, or the line of cliffs above Tremadoc, or those on the Moelwyns above the scarred industrial valley of Ffestiniog. All this is natural, because a sport which does not continue to develop and to invent is already a sport which is dead. We can rejoice that so many more youngsters are turning to British mountains for recreation and adventure, that the best of them display such qualities of skill and courage, and that, despite gloomier voices, there is no sign that British mountaineering is played out. Certainly the years 1953-55, which saw Everest and Kangchenjunga climbed, as well as the terrific routes on British rocks which we owe to Joe Brown and his peers, will be regarded as vintage years by any future climbing historian.

A Note on 'Spillikin Ridge' (September 1959)
by R.J. Wathen

Since the founding of the Irish Mountaineering Club in 1948, rumours have filtered through to England of a new route of tremendous size and difficulty at Glendalough in the Wicklow Hills, thirty miles from Dublin.

It is only fair to say, before giving a short description of this interesting route, that it is not really all that hard by modern standards. By 'modern'

I mean, of course, the standards set up by Brown and Whillans and made permanent by those who have been climbing at the 'top of the pyramid' since 1953.

'Spillikin Ridge' was first ascended by Peter Kenny and Frank Winder in June 1954. This climb was a landmark in Irish Mountaineering, since it brought to a close the first period in the history of a young club. 1948-1954 were the years of intense and fanatical pioneering by climbers determined to establish the Irish cliffs as leading rock areas in the British Isles. Since 1954 the I.M.C.'s energies have been directed towards the steadier work of consolidation: the opening of new cliffs at home, work on huts and guidebooks, and forays into the Alps, Rockies, Himalaya and Andes.

Although my own knowledge of Irish Mountaineering began in 1955, in the post-Spillikin Ridge era, I have no hesitation in saying that 'Spillikin Ridge' was a very great achievement. For at that time the majority of Irish climbers could hardly be said to be in touch with the new things which were being done 'across the water' — though Peter Kenny was the exception — and furthermore there were very few Irish climbers. Half a dozen VS leaders proved to be a very small group when it came to building up that friendly spirit of competition so essential to any major advance in standards.

It is remarkable, therefore, that 'Spillikin Ridge' can be mentioned in the same breath as any post-war Welsh climbs, for Whillans and Brown had put up their new hard routes in 1953, and 'Spillikin' was climbed in June 1954. From my own experience I would rank it as follows: much harder than Barford's routes such as 'Brant' and 'Slape' and at least half a grade harder than Harding's 'Spectre' and 'Kaisergebirge'. I don't think anyone would claim more than that. Bob Downes, who led Harold Drasdo up the second ascent in October, 1956, judged it definitely XS on the crucial pitch … harder than 'Kaisergebirge'. But, as Allan Austin and Brian Evans pointed out after the third ascent in August 1957, 'Spillikin' does not rival the hardest routes in Wales or the Lakes. As I say, my own experience, after two ascents last year, is that it is in a different class from 'Spectre', and I would add that it combines the exposure of 'Kipling Groove' (without the peg!) with the fierceness of 'Spectre'. Thus by 1959 standards it is not a very formidable climb.

I think it is important to point out this contrast with 1959 standards, or Irish Mountaineering will be guilty of exaggerating its standards. Faraway hills are green, the Irish say, and Kerry cows have long horns.

Since two further ascents this summer by Paddy O'Leary and Tony Kavanagh (the first Irishmen to climb it since 1954) I should also point out that the climb has lost most of its mystery. Besides, there is a formidable 500-foot VS in Donegal called 'Nightshade' which Austin and Evans, the first perpetrators, claim has as much character as 'Spillikin'.

So much for comparisons, which are rather pointless anyway. The climb itself runs up a 300-foot arête in the centre of the left-hand buttress of Camaderry Twin Buttress, above the Upper Lake of Glendalough, the beautiful Wicklow valley near Dublin. This arête starts steep and ends vertical, with overhangs here and there to break the monotony. The first pitch (there are four) is a mild VS crack and wall followed by a ramble at Severe standard to a good ledge. The first pitch has occasioned fierce argument between Gaels and Sassenachs as to its standard. Peter Kenny – displaying an Irishman's inferiority complex, claims it as about V. Diff. But I have seen at least four good Sassenachs hesitate on it and I would say it approaches VS.

It is followed by a delightful steep wall at about Hard VS on small but perfect holds which always appear when needed. Steep, but not strenuous, it is one of the finest pitches of the cliff. Above it one ambles up the chimney behind the Spillikin, which is a needle cracked away from the face: it has been known to sway when the wind is right. The second man takes a stance on or behind it, and the leader advances up a very awkward crack of about twelve feet (very like the bit above the holly tree on 'Spectre') to an overhang. Jamming in a sort of monkey position a peg is inserted – not for direct aid but initially for resting on and later used as a running belay. It is not easy, for it once took me three hours to select the correct crack. There is, or used to be, another peg just above the overhang; laybacking up its crack for about five feet to a small finger hold allows one to look left, reach for some quartz knobs, and shuffle across vertically to a small stance on the ledge at the top of the crux of 'Scimitar Crack', which curves up from the depths below. Of course all this is child's play to a really good climber, but I found it hard enough. principally because from the overhang to the stance the standard is quite sustained.

Traversing to the right, a minute stance is reached – one foot on a knob, the other in mid-air or put away safely in one's trouser pocket, and one hangs on a peg about a foot away to the right. There is plenty of air hereabouts. The second man is invisible beneath two overhangs. He now comes up, and either takes the lower stance or, standing on the leader's shoulders uses a shoulder or stirrup to climb the last overhang which leads easily (VS) up the narrow arête to a sudden finish at the top of the cliff. I cannot describe the last pitch and have failed on it twice:

once because of a high wind and the second time because of fatigue and three stitches in my left hand collected from Cenotaph Corner the week before. I was unable to mantelshelf and had to do a sort of cock-the-leg-round-the-right-ear-move, and of course I fell off. But I didn't hurt myself, because there is only air hereabouts, and I fell free for about thirty feet. The only sufferer was my second man Peter Kenny, who cut his head open.

I have tried to give you my impressions of 'Spillikin Ridge'. Even if it is not supremely hard, it is nevertheless a first rate climb. It has tremendous character and exposure. As far as I am concerned (and subjective judgements are in the last resort the only real ones in climbing), it is the finest British or Irish rock-climb I have ever done.

Jammed Nuts (March 1964)
by Paul Hill

[At the time of the formation of the BMC, the dictum that 'the leader shall not fall' was prevalent wherever rock-climbers pursued their 'sport'. Protection methods were primitive and even after World War II when ex-WD karabiners became available protection on a long pitch would often be one sling (or at the most two) draped over convenient spikes of rock. Accidents did happen and these were even expected to happen over holiday periods. It is not therefore surprising that the early issues of *Mountaineering* dwell on accidents, the state of equipment (ropes, slings, pitons, karabiners etc.) and how to prevent accidents. The arrival of the Sixties however brought a technical revolution and just how far we have come in the last 30 years may well be seen by the following two articles on early 'nut' protection.]

Over the last three years the appearance of jammed nut running belays on the climbing scene has caused quite a deal of comment. Many talk about them in the same breath as pitons while others would not consider attempting a hard route without them.

The nut runner works on the same principle as the chock stone but it has the added refinement of having the nylon belay sling threaded through the hole in the nut. (Note: The thread of the nut should be bored out and the ends smoothed to prevent chafing.) It takes all the frustrating fiddling from the threading of a chock stone which cuts down on the loss of sweat and temper. It can often be placed on a pitch in a crack or pocket where even the most industrious chock stoner has failed. Perhaps the favourite nut runner amongst climbers who use the device is the one that is made up of about three variously sized nuts threaded on to a small nylon loop. This is clipped to the waist by a karabiner. Such a nut runner is easy to handle and to flick or push into place. Threaded piping and expanding metal wedges have also been used with great effect. But do well placed nut runners make a normally protected climb safer, and if so will their use on such a climb put down the standard?

Two of them can be successfully inserted in a crack on Belle Vue Bastion, which is famous for its comparative lack of protection. There is a super nutting crack just at the commencement of the thin traverse on Diagonal, which proves as much a comfort to a precariously belayed second as it does to a leader. The psychological effect of getting any sort of runner however dubious on a hard route when large spikes, chocks or pegs are absent is a great comfort to most rock climbers especially when difficulties are being encountered. Such a runner might be no use when fallen upon but it might be ideal to tension from if upward progress can be achieved. It might also be a haven where tired nervous muscles can be temporarily relaxed.

I was once forced to tension over an overhang using what I thought was a poorly placed nut runner. To my surprise and relief it held almost all my weight for about twenty feet. As a result of this incident I have a great deal of respect for them. Their use is becoming more and more widespread and is I think unique to this country. They are ingenious and in most cases extremely effective as well as being easy to use.

If they make rock climbing safer without downgrading routes as the placing of pitons often does, then they will have made a worthy contribution to the sport.

The Spud (March 1965)

by Ernest Bolain

What sane mountaineer uses a karabiner made from a bed bolt, or slings of knitted wool? The idea is absurd of course but doesn't using some 'uncertified nut' from the nearest scrap heap as an aid to climbing fall into the same class of absurdity?

Jammed nuts do offer some sort of psychological protection when orthodox means of attachment are lacking but they are at best a stop-gap measure and like all improvisations have certain drawbacks. One climber, an engineer I believe, once spoilt a whole climb for me by shouting from his snug belay details about stress, strain and something called 'metal fatigue', all this when I was far away from my last runner, a jammed nut. Nuts sometimes jam awkwardly and need much unnecessary labour to extract them, or again sometimes jerk out of the crack and go sliding down the rope to the sardonic jeers of the second.

What then is the answer? Shall we forego what protection jammed nuts do offer, or shall we swallow the professional pride and hammer in a peg; usually spoiling the climb if not for ourselves but for those who follow. The remedy is simple, for with the use of a small ingenious device called 'The Spud' we are able to overcome all our difficulties. 'The Spud' designed by J. Earnshaw of The Phoenix M.C. is a small piece of mild steel or duralumin (Or other high strength light alloy. Not aluminium which has very poor mechanical properties. The thickest possible sling should be used consistent with the thickness of 'The Spud'.) roughly triangular in cross-section and looks rather like a short fat wedge. Through the thickest part of 'The Spud' runs a sling, either single or double and to this is clipped the karabiner.

'The Spud' is not just another glorified nut but a tool designed specifically for jamming and when used in the same way as a nut and sling is extremely efficient. When climbing at Stoney Middleton I stood in a sling attached to a jammed spud for several minutes yet the second had no trouble in recovering it; could one do this with an ordinary nut? A sudden downward jerk such as, heaven forbid, a falling leader only serves to jam 'The Spud' tighter in the crack and it is equally resistant to an upward pull, although this may vary depending on the type of the crack. One 'Spud' does the work of a whole range of nuts, thus saving space, weight and often valuable time.

Key Dates in the Political History of British Mountaineering

1857 Formation of the Alpine Club.

1884 Bryce's Bill to gain legal access to the mountains.

1889 Formation of the Scottish Mountaineering Club. Other early clubs were Climbers' Club (1898), Yorkshire Ramblers' (1899), Rucksack Club (1907) and Fell and Rock Climbing Club (1907)

1895 Formation of the National Trust.

1908 Access to mountains legislation tabled by Sir Charles Trevelyan.

1909 G.W.Young proposed a national mountaineering organisation.

1919 Advisory Council of British Mountaineering Clubs formed.

1921 G.W.Young's proposals for a national body for mountaineering appeared in the Climbers' Club Bulletin.

1924 Legislation to gain access to mountains introduced by P.G.Thompson.

1927 Further access legislation introduced by Sir Charles Trevelyan.

1932 Kinder Mass Trespass – Benny Rothman and others gaoled.

1932 *Mountaineering Journal* suggested an amalgamation of clubs.

1930s J.H.Doughty also made suggestions for clubs to get together.

1935 Formation of the Central Council of Physical Recreation.

1937 National Physical Training and Recreation Act.

1939 Access to Mountains Act (emasculated!) passed.

1943 (Dec 7) G.W.Young proposed formation of a national representative organisation in his Valedictory Address to the Alpine Club.

1944 (Feb 5) Standing Advisory Committee on Mountaineering formed.

1944 (Dec 2) Committee formally constituted as the British Mountaineering Council.

1944 (Dec 5) The BMC announced at the AGM of the Alpine Club.

1945 (Jan 21) Letter from 11 Alpine Club members, including 8 who had held high office in the SMC, questioned the formation of the BMC.

1945 (April 10) Alpine Club General Meeting endorsed BMC.

1945 First Area Committees established: Lake District and North Wales.

1945 (Dec 15) BMC's AGM ratified name and constitution with the support of the SMC – the Scots to nominate the Vice-President.

1946 Formation of the Association of Scottish Climbing Clubs (the Scottish committee of the BMC).

1946 *Climbing in Britain* by John Barford – 50,000 sold of first edition.

1947 Peak District Area Committee formed.

1947 The BMC bulletin *Mountaineering* began publication.

1947 The Mountaineering Association formed by J.E.B.Wright – trained 15,000 people in rock and alpine skills over the next 20 years.

1949   National Park Act passed: Parks established in England and Wales.
1950   The White Hall Centre opened.
1953   First ascent of Everest had far-reaching social, sporting and
        political impact. A major benefit for the sport in Britain.
1955   Plas y Brenin established by the CCPR.
1955   The Mount Everest Foundation set up with proceeds of *The Ascent
        of Everest* – to encourage and support mountain expeditions.
1955   First ascent of Kangchenjunga further captured public attention.
1956   Duke of Edinburgh's Award Scheme inaugurated (Sir John Hunt
        as first Director) – many more people thereby introduced to the hills.
1958   Harrison's Rocks acquired – jointly administered by CCPR and BMC.
1960   Visit by USSR climbers, the first of many international meets.
1962   Gritstone Guidebook Committee formed.
1964   Mountain Training Board formed, later to become the Mountain
        Leader Training Board. Mountain Leadership Certificate launched.
1965   Mountain Instructor Certificate introduced. After debate it was
        agreed that this should also be administered by the MTB.
1965   Opening of Glenbrittle Memorial Hut.
1965   Foundation of the Sports Council, though it was not to be fully
        operational until 1972 when it received the Royal Charter.
1965   Meeting between Walter Winterbottom (Sports Council) and the
        BMC's Sir John Hunt and Hilary Sinclair to discuss future of
        mountaineering led to government funding for the BMC.
1965   Publication of *Mountaineering* by Alan Blackshaw – a successor to
        Barford's *Climbing in Britain* and comparably influencial.
1965   Formation of the North-East Area Committee.
1967   First of four BMC/CCPR Mountain Safety Conferences.
1967   'The Old Man of Hoy', the most spectacular of many live TV
        outside-broadcasts in the 1960s, further popularised climbing.
1968   The Mountaineering Association absorbed into the YHA.
1968   Following discussions with the Sports Council the BMC intro-
        duced a new Constitution. Direct power removed from the clubs
        (except the Alpine Club), and placed within a broadened Area
        Committee structure to reflect relevant Sports Council Areas.
1969   The Coruisk affair – strong opposition in Scotland and from the
        BMC. BMC Vice-President Bill Murray asked to identify the key
        wilderness areas in Scotland – forty regions thus given extra status.
1970   The Mountaineering Council of Scotland established to cover
        Scottish 'domestic' affairs. International matters conducted by
        the BMC with two Scottish reps on Management Committee.
1970   Annapurna South Face expedition.
1971   (Nov) Five teenagers and a student teacher died in the Cairngorms
        calling into question the wisdom of taking school parties into the
        mountains, particularly in winter. Subsequent Public Enquiry
        advocated tighter procedures.

1972   Dennis Gray appointed as first professional officer of BMC.

1972   BMC took over administration of MLTB scheme.

1972   Russian speed-climbing demonstration at Munich – a harbinger of competition climbing to come, though firmly opposed at the time.

1972   *Mountain Life* replaced *Mountaineering* – ran for four years until incorporated into *Climber and Rambler* in 1976.

1972   *Kinder Area* – the first guide published and financed by the BMC.

1973   New Constitution gave further powers to the Areas to elect Management reps.

1973   Formation of Access and Conservation Committee.

1973   Mountain Safety Film failure triggered resignation of President and Hon. Secretary. Future Policy Committee chaired by the new President (Alan Blackshaw) advocated move to Manchester and set up a mountain-training study group under Lord Hunt.

1974   Individual membership of the BMC introduced.

1974   The first Buxton Conference – a biennial event for twenty years.

1974   Dennis Gray appointed as first General Secretary of BMC.

1974   Peter Boardman appointed as National Officer.

1974   Yorkshire and Humberside Area Committee formed.

1975   (Jan) BMC moved its office from London to Manchester.

1975   Everest South-West Face climbed.

1975   The Guides set up the autonomous Association of Mountain Guides – incorporated into the UIAGM in 1977.

1976   Committee for Wales set up to represent the principality.

1976   Adoption of Hunt Report on Mountain Training by BMC and its rejection by the MLTB marked start of three-year dispute.

1978   BMC enacted a new Constitution for MLTB abolishing the old Board under Sir Jack Longland – reconstituted Board chaired by Dr Will Butler. The Sports Council then cut the grant to the BMC. An Alpine Club arbitration panel of J.H.Emlyn Jones, George Band, David Cox and Bill Percival asked to resolve the dispute. Hearings staged in Lands Tribunal Court in Chancery Lane.

1978   Lancashire and Cheshire Area Committee set up.

1979   Training dispute ends. Board reconstituted again as Mountain-walking Leader Training Board (chaired by Wally Keay). Logbook system replaced Mountain Leadership Certificate, BMC took control of Mountain Instructor Certificate.

1979   Craig Bwlch y Moch (Tremadog) taken into BMC ownership.

1980   First BMC Alpine Training Course held at Ailefroide.

1980   First of three international women's meets in early 1980s.

1982   BMC and MCof S joined a successful protest against development of the Northern Cairngorms (Lurcher's Gully) for skiing.

1982   New BMC Constitution enfranchised individual members.

1983   Opening of Alex MacIntyre Memorial Hut at Onich.

1985   *High* replaced *Climber and Rambler* as BMC's official Journal.

1986   Motion at AGM (heavily defeated) tabled by committee activists (Wilson and Salkeld) indicated concern about the BMC's internal communications between committees.

1987   Bill Wright appointed as full time Access & Conservation officer.

1987   Crisis in Guidebook Committee following payments made from 'its' funds by the Publications Committee to authors, thus breaching its 'voluntary service' doctrine. The Business Manager resigned and the Guidebook Committee was reconstituted as a sub-committee answerable to the Management Committee [it having previously been under the direction of the Publications Committee].

1988   Publication of the manual *Climbing Walls* by BMC and Sports Council. Influenced the development and management of walls.

1988   Attempt to stage a climbing competition at Malham thwarted.

1988   BMC decided to take control of competition climbing, while stopping short of taking any financial risk.

1988   Bogus training scheme in Brazil discovered by British Council. Sports Council asked BMC for explanation of its involvement.

1989   First UIAA competition at Leeds, won by Jerry Moffatt. Simon Nadin won 1989 series of events to become 'world champion'.

1989   Dennis Gray retired, replaced as Gen. Secretary by Derek Walker.

1989   BMC and MCofS supported the successful campaign that opposed renewed attempts to develop skiing in Lurcher's Gully.

1990   BMC installed bolt belay anchors at Pen Trwyn to maintain access.

1991   Mountain Training Reforms – establishment of UKMTB, Mountain Instructor Award scheme set up, Association of Mountaineering Instructors formed, MLTB opened branch office at Plas y Brenin.

1991   Range West Trespass led to climbing in that region.

1991   Opening of the Foundry marked a change in climbing wall development with new emphasis on top-roping and sport-climbing.

1992   Single Pitch Supervisors Award established after years of argument.

1992   BMC Bolts Policy accepted at AGM.

1992   At short notice the BMC took over organisation of Birmingham World Cup event after withdrawal of sponsor. This 'greater involvement' policy was later ratified and BMC ran world cup events in 1994 and 1995.

1993   British Upland Footpath Trust established with BMC as major partner.

1993   Opening of Don Whillans Memorial Hut

1993   Midlands Area Committee set up.

1994   (Jan) BMC became company limited by guarantee.

1995   (March) BMC moved into newly acquired headquarters in West Didsbury, which was also confirmed as the main administrative base of the MLTB.

1995   Derek Walker retired – replaced by Roger Payne as General Secretary.

1995   Ian McNaught-Davis became President of the UIAA.

1995   BMC led opposition to the threat by Council of Europe to impose bans on cliffs for environmental reasons.

SIX YEAR SUMMARY

Income

	1995	1994	1993	1992	1991	1990
Subscriptions	267k	225k·	185k	148k	130k	95k
Sports Council Grants	140k	125k	102k	80k	86k	85k
Publications	28k	36k	36k	40k	34k	25k
Insurance Scheme	92k	98k	114k	91k	86k	82k
Other Services Interest, Grants	139k	88k	63k	38k	19k	25k
Total	**666k**	**572k**	**500k**	**397k**	**354k**	**312k**

Expenditure

	1995	1994	1993	1992	1991	1990
Office Accommodation & Administration	319k	273k	261k	210k	200k	175k
Staff & Committee Expenses	34k	34k	24k	25k	21k	22k
Depreciation	49k	18k	7k	4k	9k	8k
International Activities	18k	20k	21k	3k	3k	4k
High Magazine & Distribution Costs	45k	44k	38k	31k	25k	22k
Expedition Costs	20k	20k	20k	20k	20k	20k
Competion Costs	41k	40k	32k	20k	20k	20k
Personal Accident & Civil Liability	30k	30k	12k	2k	2k	1k
Miscellaneous	52k	43k	46k	33k	13k	13k
Total	**608k**	**522k**	**461k**	**348k**	**313k**	**285k**

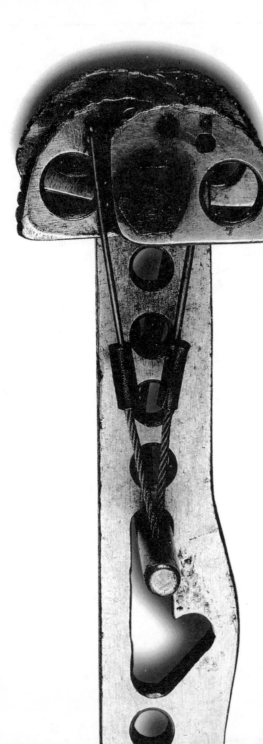

Carved into each piece
of equipment you'll find
the story of a climber.

Thanks for being a part
of Wild Country's story.

The original Friend. The first SLCD, hand-crafted in 1975.

Enjoy the complete outdoor experience with Berghaus and the BMC.

Berghaus is Europe's leading manufacturer of performance products for the outdoors and, together with the BMC's extensive knowledge, can offer you the best equipment and advice you need to enjoy the complete outdoor experience.

You can now benefit from one of the Berghaus and the BMC's joint initiatives-'The Complete Alpine Experience'. This video details the essential preparation required for mountaineers heading out to conquer Europe's highest peaks.

For further information on 'The Complete Alpine Experience' video contact the BMC on 0161 445 4747.

Berghaus is a registered trademark of Berghaus Ltd.